CAPITAL, STATE AND WHITE LABOUR IN SOUTH AFRICA 1900 - 1960
An Historical Materialist Analysis of Class Formation and Class Relations

HARVESTER STUDIES IN AFRICAN POLITICAL ECONOMY
GENERAL EDITOR Gavin Williams, St Peter's College, Oxford

This is a new series of scholarly books which seeks to present the results of recent work on Africa. It aims to publish clear and accessible writing which combines the results of original empirical research with a coherent exposition of general principle. Some titles will be written by political scientists, others by sociologists, anthropologists and historians. But all will inform other disciplines than their own and contribute to a more complete understanding of Africa's problems, its past and present development.

Books in the series will cover major problems, broad periods and wide geographical areas. Some will concentrate on particular countries, others on trends and issues common to several. The intention is to publish both theoretical and combative books.

CAPITAL, STATE AND WHITE LABOUR IN SOUTH AFRICA 1900 - 1960

An Historical Materialist Analysis of Class Formation and Class Relations

ROBERT H. DAVIES

THE HARVESTER PRESS

This edition first published in Great Britain in 1979 by
THE HARVESTER PRESS LIMITED
Publisher: John Spiers
16 Ship Street, Brighton, Sussex

British Library Cataloguing in Publication Data
Davies, Robert H
    Capital, state and white labour in South Africa,
    1900–1960. – (Harvester studies in African political
    economy).
    1. Discrimination in employment – South Africa
    2. Manpower policy – South Africa
    I. Title
    331.6'3'034068   HD4903.5.S6

ISBN 0-85527-685-1

Printed in Great Britain by
Redwood Burn Limited, Trowbridge and Esher

Contents

List of Tables

Acknowledgements

I would like to thank all those who assisted in the various stages of preparation of this work. In particular I am grateful to Martin Fransman, Dave Kaplan, Dave Lewis, Mike Morris and Dan O'Meara for numerous invaluable discussions, especially those leading to the preparation of the collective work, and to Martin Fransman, Martin Legassick, Mike Morris, Harold Wolpe and especially Dave Kaplan for valuable comments on previous drafts of the present work. The basis for this present, revised, work was my D.Phil. thesis submitted to the University of Sussex in 1977 and I benefited greatly from the help and encouragement of my supervisor, Teddy Brett, who far exceeded any formal obligations. Finally I am indebted to Marge Davies, not only for the typing of successive manuscripts but for her indispensable support, both financial and otherwise, over three sometimes difficult years.

1 Introduction

Over the course of this century the South African state has been involved in a number of interventions the effects of which have been to create a 'privileged' white stratum within the wage-earning classes. It has intervened in the process of class formation to ensure that particular places in the division of labour have been assigned to white rather than black agents. It has intervened in the class struggle to ensure that certain sectional economic concessions have been made available to white wage-earners, and it has intervened to incorporate white wage-earners into various 'industrial relations' apparatuses from which the African working class has been excluded.

The object of this study is to present an historical materialist analysis of these particular forms of intervention by the South African state during the period between 1900 and the early 1960s. For a number of reasons such an analysis is of importance for an understanding of the present South African social formation. To begin with, these state interventions have had important real effects both on the class structure and on the pattern of class relations in the social formation. In particular they have been important factors in the formation and reproduction of the well-known racist hierarchical division of labour within the wage-earning classes, and they have also significantly influenced the polarisation of certain class forces in the social formation—particularly that of the white wage-earning classes towards the bourgeoisie, but also of parts of the black petty bourgeoisie towards the working class.

In addition, a scientific Marxist analysis of these forms of state intervention is important because they have formed a major element in a particular ideological interpretation of relations in the South African social formation. In the 'conventional wisdom' of liberal historiography the state's interventions to confer particular privileges on white wage-earners are presented as being wholly against the interests of capital and, furthermore, as the major, if not the only, source of the exploitation and oppression of the black dominated classes.[1] White wage-earners, according to this interpretation, were (and are) a particular category of wage-earners unwilling for various ideological and psychological reasons to submit to 'free' competition with Africans in the capitalist labour market. This led them to demand exclusive access to certain 'privileged' places in the division of labour, and the state, in intervening to mark out certain places exclusively for whites, is thus seen to have been acting (against the interests of both capital and the African working class) either directly in response to these demands or else in response to the prejudices of a racist electorate unwilling to see any of its number 'fall below' blacks. The decisive factors underlying the state's interventions to create a 'privileged' white stratum in the wage-earning classes (seen, as we indicated above, as the major source of black exploitation and oppression) are thus held to be the prejudices of white wage-earners and the 'willingness' of the state to place demands arising from these prejudices above the demands of capital or black workers.

The critique of the 'liberal school' is by now well established[2] and I shall not labour the point here. Essentially the liberal interpretation of South African history has been identified as a form of bourgeois ideology. This is not to say that all writers within the liberal problematic were necessarily mere apologists for the existing practices of particular bourgeois interests (although a number were certainly just that). Rather it is to say that the objective role of the liberal analyses has been, quite independent of the conscious intention of any individual writers, to conceal or obscure the fundamental relations of capitalist exploitation in the social formation and the fundamental contradictions (between capital and black workers) arising therefrom. In essence, by conflating what are two separate though related secondary contradictions (that between capital and white wage-earners, and that between black and white wage-earners) and presenting these as a single principal contradiction instead, the liberal problematic seeks to present the fundamental polarisation in the society as one between white wage-earners on the one hand and capital and black workers on the other hand, thus of course providing the ideological basis for a programme of bourgeois 'reformism'. A related function has been to obscure the realities of bourgeois political domination over the social formation by confusing and exaggerating a real fact—the *relative* autonomy of the state from the dominant classes to present an image of a state in which the interests of capital have been relegated to a subordinate position.

Fortunately, thanks initially to the pioneering work of Wolpe, Legassick, Johnstone, Trapido and others, there does now exist an alternative corpus of literature which has sought to apply the tools of Marxist scientific method to an analysis of the South African social formation. Contrary to the assertions of certain critics[3] the purpose of this analysis is not to deny the existence and importance of racist ideology and racial prejudice but rather to see these as phenomena arising in the class struggle and therefore themselves requiring analysis and explanation instead of, as in the liberal problematic, the 'self evident' starting point of all 'analysis' and 'explanation'. Most particularly, existing Marxist analyses of the South African social formation have been concerned with identifying and understanding the fundamental relations of capitalist exploitation in the social formation and with questions such as the relationships between particular capitals. But there also exist within this body of literature some important contributions towards a scientific Marxist analysis of the 'white working class' in the South African social formation.

First and foremost in this connection is the excellent study by Johnstone of the struggles in the goldmining industry between 1910 and 1926.[4] The critical importance of Johnstone's work was that it showed that the demands of white wage-earners for job colour bars did not fundamentally arise from irrational racial prejudices but as a particular response to particular class problems arising from their incorporation into a limited range of job categories within which they experienced 'extreme structural insecurity' due to mining capital's economic interest in turning over as many categories as possible to 'ultra exploitable' African workers. Furthermore it showed that the formation of a racial division of labour in the industry was in accordance with the interests of mining capital, and it established that the primary source of the class oppression of the African working class lay in their incorporation into relations of capitalist exploitation (the 'exploitation colour bars'). Legassick too has taken up the theme of relating the demands of white wage-earners for job colour bars to structural class problems and has provided (albeit mainly by way of passing references in articles principally concerned with other topics) a number of important insights into the struggles of broader groups of white wage-earners over longer time periods.[5]

Another important development has been the examination of the role of white wage-earners as allied and supportive classes to different fractions of the bourgeoisie and to the bourgeoisie as a whole. This has been taken furthest in the work of Kaplan[6] who has shown how the formation of an alliance between national capital and certain fractions of 'white labour' enabled national capital to achieve hegemony in 1924.[7] But the role of white wage-earners as allied and/or supportive classes to the bourgeoisie (or particular fractions thereof) has also been referred to by Legassick,[8] Morris,[9] O'Meara,[10] and Simson[11] among others.

A further major contribution has been in the direction of introducing more analytical rigour into the identification of the structural class determination (i.e. the objective place in the relations of production) of white wage-earners. The two writers who have gone furthest here have been Simson[12] and Wolpe.[13] Both have been concerned to draw attention to the common misconception of the earlier literature[14] which equated membership of the working class with receipt of a wage income.[15] In particular both refer to the fact that large numbers of so-called white workers have in fact been involved in the task of supervising Africans and should on that account be identified as members not of the working class but of the new petty bourgeoisie. Of the two it is Wolpe's analysis which is most developed. Broadly speaking he identifies with Carchedi's position (discussed below) and is critical of Poulantzas for his reference to the role of political and ideological relations in the determination of class at the level of relations of production.[16] In making the general point about the need to distinguish between different categories of wage-earners, these contributions by Simson and Wolpe have been most valuable (though I shall express certain reservations about the position adopted by Wolpe when discussing the different positions of Carchedi, Braverman and Poulantzas below).

Despite these advances what does not yet exist in any comprehensive or systematic form is an alternative Marxist analysis of the role of the South African state in connection with the reproduction and incorporation of the white wage-earning classes. What Marxist analysis there is on the more general question of the assignment of white wage-earners to distinct places in a racial division of labour is confined almost exclusively to an examination of the goldmining industry in its early years. There is Johnstone's account to which we have already referred; Bozzoli has some interesting and important insights into the labour process in the industry in its early years[17] and an earlier paper of mine[18] has attempted to deal with the refusal by mining capital to assign whites to positions as productive non-skilled labourers. Legassick[19] has synthesised these and other works to provide the most satisfactory existing account of the labour process in the early mining industry and its effects on class formation (a topic which I shall discuss in the next chapter). But beyond these contributions there are really only the passing remarks of writers principally concerned with other topics.

Even less has been written on the emergence and particular institutional role of the 'industrial relations' apparatuses into which these classes have been incorporated. Bozzoli includes some remarks on the emergence of the 'conciliation system' in her analysis of the different ideologies of the different capitalist fractions, though I think these place insufficient weight on the rhythm of the struggle between the dominant classes and white wage-earners;[20] and an earlier work of mine,[21] which attempted to analyse some of the effects of the institutionalisation of the struggles of the white wage-earning classes on political class relations, on reflection suffers from being located within an inadequate instrumentalist view of the state.

It is then towards a particular lacuna in the analysis of the South African social formation that the present study is directed. It seeks to make some contribution towards an understanding of social relations in the South African social formation by examining in detail how and why the South African state as a *capitalist* state in a *capitalist* social formation should have become involved in intervening, during the major formative period between 1900 and the early 1960s, 1) to mark out particular places in the division of labour exclusively for whites and 2) to incorporate white wage-earners into a particular racially discriminatory 'industrial relations' system. As such it is principally a study of the emergence of a particular set of responses by the dominant classes to the struggles of the white wage-earning classes as mediated through the state. But it is also a study of the emergence of the *objective conditions* within which the prevailing practices of the white wage-earning classes came to involve, on the one hand, certain forms of institutionalised economistic struggle (which, given the specific racial character of the fundamental relations of exploitation, could not be other than racist in form) and, on the other hand, the provision of political support for the bourgeoisie and particular fractions thereof. What the study does not attempt, however, is a total explanation for the predominance of such practices within the 'white labour movement'. As Marx emphasised in opposition to Proudhon[22] it is men and not objective circumstances who make history; and it is then the white wage-earning classes themselves and not their objective circumstances who have made their own particular history of economistic struggles for sectional 'privileges' and political support for the exploiting classes. Any complete account of the emergence of particular practices among the white wage-earning classes would therefore have to include an analysis of the particular organisations of the 'white labour movement' and of the struggles within them, and this I shall not provide except briefly and in passing.[23] Having said that, however, it is necessary to be clear that, contrary to the approach adopted in those studies which have been content to take the particular practices of the white wage-earning classes as the 'self evident' starting point of any analysis, class practices do not arise in a vacuum but in specific objective circumstances which are encountered in the class struggle. The particular practices for which the white wage-earning classes are notorious could therefore have developed only as the predominant practices of these classes, because certain objective conditions existed in the social formation which made their emergence possible,[24] and it is the object of this study to examine the state's role in the creation of these objective conditions.

At this point is is necessary to be more precise about the classes and fractions with whose reproduction and incorporation we are here concerned. In particular we need to return to the important point to which Simson and Wolpe have directed attention—viz. that while all members of the working class are wage-earners all wage-earners are not necessarily members of the working class. This point is of crucial importance not for any pedantic formalistic reasons, but because *structural class determination* (the place occupied in the relations of production) is one of the critical objective elements which has to be grasped in order to understand the practices of particular class forces.[25] It is the objective place of a class in the social division of labour which establishes its objective class interests and thereby marks out the boundaries of its class practices. This is not to say that the *class positions* which any particular class takes up at particular conjunctures are determined by its class determination in any crude, uniform or unchanging fashion. In differing conjunctures certain social classes may adopt differing class positions; and indeed may even adopt class positions which do not correspond to their class interests as defined by structural class determination. In particular, non fundamental classes—that is, in a social formation dominated by the capitalist mode of production, classes other than the bourgeoisie and the proletariat—generally tend to become polarised around the two principal classes and to take up in specific conjunctures the class positions of one or other of the two principal classes. However, even where a class adopts the position of another class it does not thereby become part of that class. Class determination is not reducible to class position. This is important because when one class supports the position of another it generally does so in terms of its own experience derived from its objective place in the social division of labour, and this involves its introducing class practices into the struggle which reflect its own specific aspirations and demands. Whether any particular non-fundamental class is polarised towards the bourgeoisie or towards the proletariat, therefore, its *specific* class practices deriving from its *specific* objective interests can still have important effects on social relationships and it is for that reason that in the analysis of social class in Marxist theory priority is given to an analysis of structural class determination.

In recent years there have been a number of important contributions by Marxist theorists towards an analysis and specification of the structural class determination of different categories of wage-earners. Of these, three rather different approaches—by Poulantzas,[26] Carchedi,[27] and Braverman[28]—have perhaps been the most comprehensive and most coherent, and it will therefore be necessary for us to briefly outline and briefly review these three positions in order to produce a workable theoretical basis to begin an analysis of the particular class places occupied by white wage-earners in the South African social formation.

1) *Poulantzas* For Poulantzas social class is defined at the economic, political and ideological levels, with the economic having the determining role in the last instance. He is thus concerned to begin with an economic distinction between the working class and other categories of wage-earners, and he locates this in the distinction between productive and unproductive labour. Quite apart from the question of its relevance in the identification of social class, the

distinction between productive and unproductive labour is itself a complex and highly controversial area within Marxist theory, raising many difficult questions which cannot be discussed in any detail here.[29] Briefly, the definition as productive and unproductive has nothing whatsoever to do with any moral evaluation of the usefulness or otherwise of the labour performed or of the product produced. Rather, it is a distinction grounded in an analysis of social relations of production. Thus, in *Theories of Surplus Value* Marx defined productive labour as follows:

> Productive labour, in its significance for capitalist production, is wage labour which, exchanged against the variable part of capital, not only reproduces this part of capital . . . but in addition produces *surplus value* . . .[30]

Poulantzas explains,

> Thus what is productive in a given mode of production is labour which gives rise to the dominant relation of exploitation in that mode. . . . In the capitalist mode of production productive labour is that which directly produces surplus value, which valorizes capital and is exchanged against capital.[31]

Braverman makes the point clear in the following illustration:

> The tailor who makes a suit on order for a customer creates a useful object in the form of a commodity; he exchanges it for money and out of it pays his own expenses and means of subsistence. . . . But the capitalist who hires a roomful of tailors to make such suits brings into being a social relation. In this relation the tailors now create more than suits; they create themselves as productive workers and their employer as capitalist. Capital is thus not just money exchanged for labour; it is money exchanged for labour with the purpose of appropriating that value which it creates over and above what is paid, the surplus value.[32]

From the above it follows that several categories of wage-earners are, in terms of the social relations in which they are involved, excluded from the definition of productive labour. The first—and least problematical—group so excluded are all those employees—wage-

earners in commerce, banking, insurance, etc.—who are employed
in activities concerned with the realisation rather than the production of surplus value. Poulantzas explains,

> From the standpoint of the individual capitalist (involved in the
> circulation process—RD), these wage earners *appear* to be the
> source of his profit. But *from the standpoint of social capital
> and its reproduction*, the profit of commercial and banking
> capital does not derive from a process of value creation, but
> from a transfer of surplus value created by productive capital.
> These wage earners simply contribute towards redistributing the
> mass of surplus value among the various fractions of capital
> according to the average rate of profit. Of course, these wage
> earners are themselves exploited . . . *Surplus labour* is extorted
> from wage earners in commerce, but these are not directly ex-
> ploited in the form of the dominant relation of exploitation,
> the creation of surplus value.[33]

The second, more controversial, category of wage-earners who are
unproductive of surplus value are those who are employed to perform various services, which are consumed directly as use values and
which are exchanged not against capital, but directly against revenue
or income. This is, as previously mentioned, a particularly difficult
and controversial area within Marxist theory but the essential point
about service work can be made fairly simply. It is that capitalist
production is commodity production and that one essential characteristic of a commodity is its *materiality*; not in the sense of
'corporeal reality' but in the sense of 'social mode of existence'.[34]
The point is, that for production of *surplus value* to take place, it is
necessary that the object have an existence independent of the
labourer himself. If it does not it is not a commodity and the wage-
earner who produces it is not productive even if, as in the case of
employees in the circulation process, he has surplus labour extracted
from him. Most Marxists would probably agree that performers of
services for the bourgeoisie, including e.g. lawyers and employees in
the various state repressive and ideological apparatuses, are, in terms
of this criterion, unproductive. The controversy occurs with respect

to those wage-earners who perform services for the working class, and the question is whether or not they produce the commodity labour power.[35] This is not the place to discuss this question, but rather to identify Poulantzas' position on it. He in fact excludes those who exchange their services with the revenue of the working class. He writes,

> . . . services, from those of the laundresser to those of the lawyer, the doctor or the teacher remain unproductive labour, even if, as in the latter cases, they contribute towards the reproduction of labour power . . .[36]

Thus to sum up: for Poulantzas unproductive wage-earners, which for him includes all those employed in circulation processes or in various services, are excluded from the working class. Also excluded on this criterion are all employees in the various state apparatuses, with whom the bourgeoisie has a more complex relationship but which boils down in essence to that of 'buyer of their services'.[37]

However, while Poulantzas differentiates unproductive wage-earners from the working class by reference to differing economic relationships, in order to establish their structural class determination it is necessary to refer also to political and ideological relationships. Essentially he sees the unproductive wage-earners as part of the new petty bourgeoisie, which is

> new in the sense that it is in no way destined to follow the traditional petty bourgeoisie threatened with extinction, and that its development and expansion are conditioned by capitalism itself, and the latter's transition to the stage of monopoly capitalism.[38]

They are assigned thus on the grounds that they occupy places, defined in terms of ideological relationships, more on the mental than the manual side of the mental/manual division of labour, and/or on the grounds of their involvement in the reproduction of the political relations of domination/subordination between capital and the working class. The mental/manual division is for Poulantzas of crucial importance in the structural class determination of the petty bourgeoisie as a whole and it is therefore necessary to be reasonably clear about it. The first point to be made in this regard is that the mental/manual distinction is a distinction established through the political and ideological class practices of the bourgeoisie, and is related to the privatisation of knowledge within capitalist society. It cannot therefore be considered with reference to any purely empirical criteria such as whether or not any particular agent spends more of his time 'thinking' or 'doing'. Rather, for Poulantzas, the definition of mental labour has to be seen as encased in a series of rituals related to various ideological symbols. Various tasks, such as paper work, are set up as being more complex than 'simple manual work' and agents performing these functions are deemed to require a certain level of knowledge. Part at least of the function of the educational apparatuses in bourgeois society thus becomes to provide the obstacle course which separates those agents to be assigned to mental from those to be assigned to manual places. The second point about the mental/manual division is that it is a *tendency* which exists within capitalist social formations; it is not a rigid categorical classification. Moreover, it is a tendency which reproduces itself within each side of the mental/manual divide; a factor which is of particular importance for the formation of fractions within the petty bourgeoisie and to which we shall refer again later.

The role of political and ideological relations in the structural class determination of the petty bourgeoisie also enables Poulantzas to identify as new petty bourgeois certain categories of wage-earners which are not immediately delimited from the working class through being involved in unproductive branches. The two categories here are first, supervisory staff and second, engineers, scientists and technicians. Poulantzas' analysis of supervisory staff is based upon a recognition of the dominance, within bourgeois society, of the relations of production over the forces of production. The labour process always occurs within a definite social form and in capitalist society it occurs within a social form characterised by an antagonistic relationship at the point of production between capital and direct producers. The work of supervision is in this context two-fold: firstly to co-ordinate the labour process (a productive function necessary for the production of use values), but secondly to exercise control over productive workers necessary because of the above mentioned antagonistic social relations of production. In exercising this second function supervisors serve to reproduce within the work process itself the political relations between capital and direct producers. This is necessary to capital in order to ensure the continued extraction of surplus value. Thus, Poulantzas writes,

> The reason why these agents do not belong to the working class, is that their structural class determination and the place they occupy in the social division of labour are marked by the dominance of the political relations that they maintain over productive labour . . .[39]

However, lower level supervisory staff must be distinguished from managers, salaried staff whose function is also to reproduce the political relations of dominance over labour. Whereas the former are members of the new petty bourgeoisie, the latter are members of the bourgeoisie on the grounds that they also perform various functions associated with the ownership of capital, such as assigning the means of production to this or that use. Moreover, whereas the lower level supervisory staff may have surplus labour extracted from them (at least in so far as they are involved in productive activity) the same is not true of the managers who are on the contrary recipients of surplus value in one form or other.

The second category—engineers, scientists and technicians—are assigned by Poulantzas to the new petty bourgeoisie on the grounds of their place on the mental side of the social division of labour; and they are thus assigned despite the fact that they do in many cases perform productive labour. He bases this on an analysis of the monopolisation of knowledge and consequent role of science and technology in bourgeois society. Scientific knowledge, he argues, is never in bourgeois society appropriated in a pure or neutral form, but in forms dictated by the interests of the bourgeoisie. Bourgeois science is therefore closely interwoven with the bourgeoisie's ideological class practices; whether it be basic research (the appropriation of knowledge in bourgeois form) or the technological application of science (the materialisation of bourgeois ideology). The function of the scientist or technician is therefore directly related to the ideological class practices of the bourgeoisie and they are thus involved in the reproduction of the ideological relations of domination and subordi-- nation. Moreover engineers and technicians are in the majority of cases involved in some form of management or supervision, their relation to knowledge often serving to legitimise their place in factory despotism. Engineers and technicians do not therefore belong to the working class. They do tend to be productive because they directly valorise capital and are thus involved in the surplus value producing process. But because of the dominant place of ideological relations in their structural class determination they are not part of the working class.

Thus to summarise: for Poulantzas all unproductive wage-earners, as defined, are members of the new petty bourgeoisie, as are certain categories of productive employees—supervisors and engineers, technicians and scientists.

2) *Carchedi* Carchedi's analysis is also based upon an economic identification of social class, but it is markedly different from that of Poulantzas. It begins with a four-fold definition of the working class and the bourgeoisie under capitalist relations of production before the stage of monopoly capitalism. The working class is defined as a) the economically exploited, b) the non-owners of the means of production, c) individual labourers, d) those whose income is determined by the value of their labour power, as produced by themselves and 'paid back' to them by the bourgeoisie. The bourgeoisie is similarly defined as a) the economic exploiters, b) the owners of the means of production, c) individual non-labourers, d) those whose income is derived from surplus value.

But during the stage of monopoly capitalism various changes occur. The worker ceases to be involved in the production process as an individual direct producer, but becomes involved instead as a collective worker in an increasingly complex socialised production process. For the bourgeoisie this means that the global function of capital—the exercising of surveillance and control over labour—can no longer be carried out by an individual owner. Instead this task passes to a vast bureaucratic hierarchy. At the top of this hierarchy are salaried managers. These differ from the individual bourgeois owner in terms of elements b) and c) of the above definition. However, since in terms of function the managers represent capital personified, it is for Carchedi 'indeed necessary to classify the managers as members of the bourgeoisie'.[40] Moreover, in terms of element d) as well as element a), their definition is identical to that of the individual bourgeois non-labourer. Lower down the hierarchy, however, is another group of agents who perform the global function of capital together with some or other task of collective labour. In terms of the four-fold criterion these agents are a) non-owners of the means of production, b) performers of both collective labour and the global function of capital, c) both labourer and non-labourer, d) recipients of an income partly determined by the value of their labour power and partly by their position of privilege *vis-à-vis* the working class. They therefore occupy a place between that of the working class and that of the bourgeoisie. It is this group of wage-earners *exclusively* which Carchedi identifies as the 'new middle class'. And, as distinct from Poulantzas, they are thus defined not on account of political relations but on account of their place in economic relations—their place in the surplus value producing process. Carchedi is in principle prepared to acknowledge that political and ideological relationships may play a role in class determination, but in actual fact they play almost no part in his analysis. The only occasion when he mentions the role of political and ideological in creating divisions among wage-earners is in connection with capital's attempts to create ' "artificial" divisions' in times of 'heightened class "struggle" '. Moreover, he believes that divisions thus created in the long run 'tend to disappear'.[41] More important, he rejects any attempts to identify non-supervisory wage-earners as new petty bourgeois on the grounds of their place in unproductive or in mental labour. Thus, in reply to Poulantzas he writes,

the concept of productive labour while essential for an understanding of the capitalist production process is of less importance for an analysis of capitalist production relations, and thus, for an economic identification of classes.[42]

His position on explicitly mental non-supervisory labour is less clearly spelt out, but it emerges e.g. in the conclusion of his later article where he refers to the left in Italy overlooking the potential of employees such as technicians who are 'mistakenly' seen as 'radicalised petty bourgeoisie' whereas they are actually 'part of the proletariat'.[43]

Thus to summarise: for Carchedi the new middle class consists exclusively of those wage-earners involved in the function of surveillance and control. Other wage-earners, whether productive or unproductive—and probably whether mental or manual—are part of collective labour, part of the working class.

3) *Braverman* Like Carchedi, Braverman rejects the notion that the distinction between productive and unproductive labour has any relevance in distinguishing social classes; indeed he would probably include in his conceptualisation of productive, a range of categories which Poulantzas would exclude.[44] However, as distinct from Carchedi the political and ideological is crucial in Braverman's distinction between what he calls 'the middle layers of employment' and the remaining employees whom he describes as the working class. Braverman's central point is that the crucial distinction is between mental and manual labour. However, his use of the terms mental and manual differs considerably from that of Poulantzas. For Braverman mental labour is the labour of conception and manual labour the labour of execution. Thus the mental/manual division is equivalent to the division between conception and execution. On the basis of this definition, Braverman identifies the 'middle layer' as consisting of engineering, technical and scientific staffs, lower supervisory and managerial staff, and professional staffs in marketing, finance and related activities. They together account for about 15—20 per cent of the 'working population' of the United States, and are not therefore, he observes, as numerous as the traditional petty bourgeoisie.[45] Moreover, the thesis advanced by Braverman is that with the application of Taylorism and so-called scientific

management to clerical, service and related branches, there is a tendency towards reducing the proportion of agents who are involved in the work of conception, with the result that in these branches, too, the mass of wage-earners have increasingly become members of the manual working class.

In turning to assess the three positions it would perhaps be most useful to begin by noting the common ground between the three and then proceed to the differences. First, all agree that managers are part of the bourgeoisie and that supervisors are part of the new petty bourgeoisie or new middle class. Second, all are prepared to acknowledge at an abstract level that political and ideological as well as purely economic relationships must be taken into account in an analysis of social class. It is beyond this point that the differences arise. The first such difference is over the precise role of political and ideological relations. We have already referred to Wolpe's use of Carchedi's analysis to argue that class determination takes place on the economic level alone, and that the political and ideological enter in as an influence upon the class positions taken by particular groups and/or as an influence upon the assignment of particular agents to particular places. If, at this level of abstraction, that is indeed the position of Carchedi himself, it is not clearly spelt out in the articles under review. For example, the earlier article is specifically described as an 'economic identification' of the new middle class, and begins with the statement: 'a complete definition of classes must be worked out in terms of the economic, political and ideological . . .'[46] But, however that may be, what is clear is that the mental/manual division in particular is not regarded by Carchedi as of any relevance in producing divisions among wage-earners.

Such a position is however, as Poulantzas shows, in marked contrast to that taken in the Marxist classics. While Marx's remarks on this question contained several ambiguities, they were clear on at least two points: 1) that what gives rise to the productive collective worker under capitalism is the socialisation of the labour process; 2) that this very socialisation deepens the division between mental and manual labour. What is more, in places Marx referred to an antagonistic contradiction between mental and manual labourers. Poulantzas quotes as an example a passage from the German edition of *Capital* where Marx writes of mental and manual labour becoming 'deadly foes'.[47] The mental/manual division was thus regarded by Marx as a major division created through the development of capitalism; what its role in the determination of class is, is therefore an important question which cannot simply be avoided. As Poulantzas puts it,

> Marxist theory has long shown a certain uneasiness with respect to the question of the mental/manual division. On the one hand the Marxist classics always emphasized either the decisive role of this division for the 'historic appearance' of class division as such (Marx, Engels), or alternatively the close relationship between the abolition of the division between mental and manual labour and the suppression of class exploitation, even of class divisions in general (Lenin, Mao). On the other hand, however, this division between mental and manual labour seems to get lost whenever it comes to defining the class determination of a particular social formation, in particular the capitalist one. We are clearly dealing here with a very important problem, one that has been raised again by the Cultural Revolution in China. And if we take into account the decisive importance that the breakdown of this division has on the road to socialism we can no longer content ourselves with simple assertions or dodge the question of the precise role of this division in the actual determination of classes in a capitalist social formation.[48]

Thus, whatever the merits of Carchedi's analysis in clarifying the factors differentiating supervisors from other wage-earners, it alone cannot be sufficient for the identification of class divisions among wage-earners: it neither recognises any role for mental/manual division in the determination of class, nor does it offer any rigorous theoretical argument which would justify regarding it as irrelevant for this purpose.

For these reasons, we must proceed to the second major difference: that between Poulantzas and Braverman on the definition of mental labour. At issue here is the question whether mental labour is equivalent to the labour of conception or whether it includes as well the work of execution in some branches. The problem, I feel, with the Braverman formulation, which regards mental labour as exclusively the labour of conception is that it is unduly technicist. It is based almost entirely upon pointing to certain similarities in the labour process of the various branches. As such it does not sufficiently recognise that the distinction between mental and manual labour is produced fundamentally not by 'technical' factors but by ideological class practices; and that a definition of mental or manual produced by ideological class practices need not therefore necessarily conform rigidly to a narrower 'technical' definition.

But we cannot leave the critique of Braverman and Carchedi at this level. It is necessary for us to recognise that in the last analysis the differences between Poulantzas on the one hand and Carchedi and Braverman on the other are differences in their respective assessments of the political implications of comparatively recent changes in the labour process within the clerical, distribution and service sectors of the advanced capitalist social formations of Western Europe and North America. Poulantzas sees the application of so-called scientific management techniques to these sectors as having produced a situation in which certain 'more manual' fractions of the new petty bourgeoisie have become, in terms of objective class interests, polarised towards the working class; thus creating the historic chance for these fractions to be organised in future class struggles under the hegemony of the manual working class. Braverman and Carchedi on the other hand see these techniques as having transformed the mass of the wage-earners in these sectors into members of the manual working class, whose interests are therefore *identical* to those of the manual working class in other sectors. As such the Braverman and Carchedi positions are versions of what has been called 'the massification thesis',[49] that is, the view which sees monopoly capitalism proceeding in a purely linear fashion to eliminate all distinctions between different categories of wage-earners. Several criticisms have been offered of this position.[50] We can mention just three points here:

1) It fails to recognise that while the expanded reproduction of monopoly capitalism certainly does involve the elimination of certain forms of skill, and the debasement of particular ideological symbols, at the same time it creates new skills and ideological symbols.

2) It fails to recognise that many of the struggles in which mental wage-earners are involved may be struggles in defence of privileges associated with a mental place; and may not therefore be immediately related to the struggles of the working class whose interest lies in eliminating such distinctions.

3) It cannot offer any explanation for the continuing (though diminishing) role of these categories as allied or supportive classes to the bourgeoisies—except perhaps through reference to such historicist notions as 'false consciousness'.

But for our purposes perhaps the most important point to notice is that the position of the massification theorists is based upon a *reconceptualisation* of certain categories of wage-earners in the light of comparatively recent changes in the labour process within the circulation and service sectors of the most advanced capitalist social formations. Thus, while Braverman refers to Taylorism having been applied to the USA, to a limited range of office jobs (particularly typing), since 1917, he is principally concerned with analysing changes which have occurred in the latter half of the period between the end of the Second World War and the present day. Similarly, Carchedi's concrete examples are mainly derived from the experience of the Italian computer industry since the late 1960s. Braverman at least is prepared to acknowledge that at an earlier stage of capitalist development the situation of clerical employees was (in the main) sufficiently different for them to be identified as members of the middle class. He writes of these earlier clerical employees,

> . . . by and large, in terms of function, authority, pay, tenure of employment (a clerical position was usually a lifetime post), prospects, not to mention status and even dress, the clerks stood much closer to the employer than to factory labour.[51]

Thus, even if the merits of the massification thesis had been established for an analysis of the present conjuncture in the European and American social formations (and we have referred to various criticisms above), it would be wholly unscientific to apply their reconceptualisation of the class determination of clerical, distribution and related employees to a study of the South African social formation whose main focus is the period up until 1960, without a specific examination of the extent to which so-called scientific management had produced similar changes in South Africa. Here we are faced with the problem that there are no known studies of changes in the labour process within these sectors in South Africa. However, it seems extremely likely that to the extent that the debasement of clerical labour has been a significant tendency in South Africa it has been a recent tendency probably accompanied by the reassignment of the more manual tasks to blacks.[52] Certainly, if wage rates relative to those of a clearly identifiable new petty bourgeois group or relative to those of a clearly identifiable part of the working class can be taken as an approximate index, there is, as Table 1 shows, little evidence of a demotion of white clerical or trading employees to a point where we could begin seriously to consider them members of a 'new working class'.

For these reasons among others we shall in this study adopt as the basis for analysing class determination the position of Poulantzas on the role of political and ideological relations. We shall not however adopt the implied position that a category of wage-earners, almost indistinguishable in terms of ideological or political relations from the manual working class, is new petty bourgeois solely on account of its location in a technically unproductive sector. Such a position would seem to be contrary to the method, which Poulantzas himself has emphasised, of considering *all three* levels in analysing structural class determination. And it has been criticised sufficiently to cast considerable doubt on its validity.[53] In any case, including or excluding such marginal categories makes very little real difference to the substance of this study.

To summarise the position to be adopted:

1) Wage-earners or salaried staff employed as managers are part of the bourgeoisie;

Table 1 White clerical wages compared to average wages of new petty bourgeois white supervisors in mining industry and to average African industrial wage (Rand)

	1910	1924 (Multiple of 3)	1960 (Multiple of 3)	1974 (Multiple of 3)
1 Average white clerical wages	M R40 per month	R57 per month (9·5X)	R250 per month (8·1X)*	Clerks in banks (M & F) R375 (5·3X)
	F R17 per month	R26 per month (4·3X)	R 83 per month (2·7X)*	Clerks in building socs. (M & F) R343 (4·8X)
Average wages paid to white employees in trading (sales)	M R33 per month	R53 per month (8·8X)	R208 per month (6·7X)*	R275 (M & F) (3·9X)
	F R14 per month	R21 per month (3·5X)	R 67 per month (2·2X)*	
2 Average wage paid to white employees in the mining industry	R47 per month	R57 per month (9·5X)	R208 per month (6·7X)	R454 per month (6·4X)
3 Average wages paid to African industrial workers		R 6 per month	R 31 per month	R 71 per month

* median income

Sources: *Economic and Wages Commission* (UG 14, 1926) Table I; *Statistical Yearbook 1964*, Table I, p. 272; South African Institute of Race Relations: Annual Survey 1974. Table H.19.

2) Wage-earners employed as supervisors, in the state's repressive or ideological apparatuses, or in mental positions within the circulation process or service sectors are members of the new petty bourgeoisie, as are engineers, technicians and scientists, whether or not they are productive of surplus value.

If we now turn to Appendix 1, it will be noted that it represents an attempt to reclassify Occupational Census data in accordance with the above mentioned theoretically generated categories. Categories included under heading A—Bourgeoisie and Traditional Petty Bourgeoisie (it was not possible from the data to distinguish the two)—consist of those identified as owners of the means of production, as self-employed or as managers. Categories included under heading B consist of the various new petty bourgeois categories. Except for category B7—where the criterion adopted was 'balance of probability'—assignments to these categories have been made only on the basis of a fairly clear indication from the job description. Respondents were however not asked to clearly indicate whether or not they were involved in any supervisory function, and for that reason without doubt some supervisory new petty bourgeoisie have been included in the categories under heading C. C—a residual category—is thus described not as 'the white working class' but rather as an ensemble of the remaining supervisory new petty bourgeoisie and productive and unproductive manual workers. It has in turn been subdivided in an attempt to differentiate the skilled/craft wage-earners from the others.

What is immediately striking in the table is that throughout the period the large majority of the 'economically active' white population has occupied bourgeois and petty bourgeois class places. However, contrary to the impression which may perhaps be derived from the work of Simson or Wolpe, the largest single category of the white new petty bourgeoisie has not been those involved in supervision. If males and females are considered together, the number of wage-earners employed in the circulation process (the majority of whom were certainly not supervisors) has exceeded the number of clearly identified supervisory employees throughout. Moreover, from

1960 onwards, this is true even if we make the (untenable) assumption that all those included in C1 were supervisors as well. This indicates the crucial importance of recognising the role of the ideological in structural class determination. To have accepted the Braverman—or more especially the Carchedi—formulation would have been to create the totally misleading impression that the 'white working class' had over time been increasing in both absolute and relative terms.

If we now turn to examine changes which have occurred over time, we notice that there has been a decline in the proportion of the white population occupying bourgeois and traditional petty bourgeois places. This has mainly been due to the quite dramatic decline in the numbers of those occupying such places within the agricultural branch. In the period up until 1936, the numbers occupying places in the new petty bourgeoisie increased both in terms of absolute numbers and as a proportion of the total 'economically active' white population. However, the rate of increase over this period in these categories is noticeably less than in the case of the residual categories included under heading C. This would indicate, and we shall see that this was so later, that over this period the greater proportion of white agents leaving the traditional petty bourgeoisie, as well as those coming from elsewhere, were assigned to places in some form of manual labour. From 1946 onwards, however, there has been an important reversal with the greater proportion of agents being assigned to places in the new petty bourgeoisie. In fact, after 1946 there has been a net loss in absolute terms in the number of white agents occupying places included under heading C until according to the calculation based on the 1970 Census data, not more than 14.45% of the 'economically active' whites occupied such places in that year. What is more, there is every indication that between 1970 and the present time, the trend towards reducing the number of whites in manual, non-supervisory categories has accelerated. Here we need only refer to factors like the periodic reclassification of 'white' manual jobs in industry, construction, railways, etc.[54] and to the growing proportion of the total white population being employed in the commercial, financial and 'public' sectors in the period since 1970.[55]

It is necessary at this point to be clear that the different categories that have thus far been discussed did not necessarily constitute as such *fractions* of the classes concerned. These categories are in fact *abstract* categories which enable us to make an analysis of class determination. A fraction, on the other hand, is defined in *concrete* class struggle and is recognised, *inter alia*, by a specific presence as a fraction at the ideological and political levels. In the South African social formation as elsewhere, the new petty bourgeoisie was and is divided into fractions—the relative place in the mental/manual hierarchy being an important factor here. This study is not concerned with the whole of the white petty bourgeoisie. Rather its scope is limited to that ensemble of class fractions—the 'more manual' fractions of the new petty bourgeoisie, the craft labour aristocracy, and other manual white workers—whose common definition in terms of ideological class practices was as 'the white working class' but which we shall refer to collectively as the white wage-earning classes (meaning the white wage-earning new petty bourgeoisie and the white working class proper) or more simply as white wage-earners. In terms of Appendix 1 this would include the whole of heading C, category B6 and parts of B3, B4 and B7.

Having identified the particular classes and fractions with which we are here concerned we now need to produce the theoretical tools which will make it possible to approach a study of the role of the South African state in connection with the reproduction and incorporation of these classes.

First we need to consider the processes by which social classes are reproduced in capitalist social formations generally,[56] and to begin with we have to make the point that any given pattern of reproduction depends upon a fairly complex interaction of various forms of class struggle and cannot therefore be explained solely or even principally by reference to the 'choices' or 'aspirations' of the agents concerned. This point is of particular importance in the case of a study of the reproduction of the white wage-earning classes in South Africa in view of the various liberal interpretations which have, as we have already seen, based their explanations precisely upon such factors.

There are in fact, in the reproduction of social classes, two relatively distinct (though interdependent) stages which can be identified. The first involves the reproduction of the class places themselves, and the second the assignment of particular agents to those places. Both depend upon the outcome of class struggle: the first on the outcome of the struggle, taking place in the context of the operation of the law of value, between capital and direct producers over the labour process; and the second on a wider range of class struggles taking place at the economic, political and ideological levels. Although we are principally concerned in this study with the second aspect of the reproduction of certain classes—the assignment of white agents to particular wage-earning places—it is important for us to note that it is in fact the subordinate aspect of the reproduction process dependent upon the first stage. That is to say any given reproduction of say a particular new petty bourgeois fraction in South Africa as a white fraction is dependent upon the reproduction of the particular new petty bourgeois places in question.

The other main theoretical element which we need to make this study possible is a theory of the capitalist state and in particular of its role in respect of the struggles of dominated or subordinate classes.

Essentially the state exists in a social formation characterised by antagonistic class conflict 'to maintain the unity and cohesion of (that) social formation by concentrating and sanctioning class domination and in this way reproducing (its) social relations i.e. class relations'.[57] As such, though the capitalist state performs a number of technical and economic functions these are always overdetermined by and condensed in its principal role which is to ensure that the political class struggle between the dominant and dominated classes does not assume forms which threaten the continued existence of the essential social relations of the formation. This role imposes upon the state a twofold task—to politically organise the dominant classes and to politically disorganise and maintain in isolation the dominated classes.

The task of politically organising the dominant classes falls to the state because, unlike the working class, the bourgeoisie is characteristically incapable of raising itself to the level of political domination through its own political parties. This is principally due to the division of the bourgeoisie into fractions with contradictory interests: a division which begins at the level of relations of production. It is also due to the fact that the isolation of the different elements within the bourgeoisie arising from capitalist property relations (private property) is not compensated for, as it is in the case of the working class, by anything equivalent to collective labour.[58] Without the bourgeois state and all its apparatuses the bourgeoisie would be incapable of placing its political interests—related to the maintenance of its domination over the social formation—above the narrow fractional interests of its components, and without the state therefore the bourgeoisie would 'founder' in a mass of contradictions which would render it 'incapable of governing politically'.[59]

In fulfilling its role as political organiser of the dominant classes, the state has necessarily to assume a degree of relative autonomy from the dominant classes and all fractions thereof. The state has to realise the general political interests of the dominant classes and it has thus to be in a position to organise the unstable equilibrium of compromise between the various components of the dominant classes (as well as, as we shall see later, between these classes and certain dominated classes) which will make the realisation of these political interests possible.

However in politically organising the dominant classes the state does not eliminate all the differences between them. The contradictory interests existing among the different fractions remain and their political organisation is therefore feasible only through the formation of a particular contradictory unity which Poulantzas calls a 'power bloc'.[60] Moreover since institutionalised state power depends upon an internal coherence and cannot for that reason be parcelled out or shared out among the dominant fractions this organisation of the dominant classes into a power bloc is only possible if one class or fraction assumes leadership, 'hegemony' within it. The hegemonic fraction is that fraction which has become, through struggle within the power bloc, 1) the most dominant of all the dominant classes and fractions and 2) the fraction which has been able to set up its own particular interests as the 'general interest' of the body politic.[61] The politically hegemonic fraction, which need not necessarily be the economically dominant fraction, is thus the class which in the last analysis holds political power. But it need not necessarily be either the 'governing class' (the class whose political representatives form the régime) or the 'class in charge of the state' (the class from which the personnel who occupy the heights of the state are drawn).[62]

In respect of the dominated classes, the state's task is, as we indicated above, precisely the opposite, namely, to act to prevent these classes from organising as an autonomous political force in opposition to the power bloc. In fulfilling this task the state may of course deploy its repressive apparatus (its organised monopoly of physical repression) to repress directly any form of organisation or struggle among the dominated classes which constitutes a threat to the political domination of the power bloc. But since the bourgeoisie cannot rule by force alone the capitalist state also contains a number of juridico-political and ideological apparatuses which create or reinforce among the dominated classes what Poulantzas calls 'isolation effects'.[63] The bourgeois state, reflecting in a particular form the separation of the direct producer from the means of production under capitalist relations of production, relates to social agents not as members of classes but as individual juridicial subjects. Unlike earlier forms of state, class domination and class struggle seem to be absent from the institutions of the bourgeois state which appear instead as an ensemble of 'private' individuals.[64] The capitalist state thus sets up at its level agents of production as 'bare individuals' and this has the effect at the level of socio-economic relations of concealing from social agents the fact that their relations are class relations. Socio-economic relations become experienced by the agents

concerned as a 'specific fragmentation and atomisation'.[65] This
prevents them from realising their community of interests and their
struggles become accordingly 'fragmented', 'partial' or 'isolated'. This
isolation, produced by the effects of bourgeois juridical relations
as well as by the juridico-political ideology of the state, affects both
dominant and dominated classes. It appears,

> in a whole series of relations between wage earning worker and
> capitalist owner of private property, between wage earning
> worker and wage earning worker and between private capitalist
> and private capitalist, to relations between a worker in one
> factory branch of industry or locality and workers elsewhere,
> and between capitalists in one branch industry or subdivision
> and the others. This effect of isolation which is designated by
> the term 'competition' covers the whole ensemble of socio-
> economic relations.[66]

But whereas in the case of the dominant classes the state acts to
overcome these effects of isolation and thus to organise these classes
politically, in the case of the dominated classes it acts through its
various ideological apparatuses to reinforce their effects and thus to
maintain these classes in their isolation. It is precisely the bourgeois
state's relative autonomy from the dominant classes which enables it
to act effectively in this way. The fact that the bourgeois state 'does
not *directly* represent the dominant classes' economic interests but
their *political interests*'[67] inscribes within it (i.e. as a constituent part
of its structure) a degree of flexibility not existent in, say, the feudal
state. In particular it inscribes within it the possibility of conceding
to certain dominated classes a guarantee with respect to some of
their economic demands. Not only does this mean that certain
demands and forms of struggle by the dominated classes fail to challenge the relations of domination/subordination in the social formation (although it certainly does mean that); it also means that certain
forms of state activity and state intervention are possible in a capitalist social formation which were not possible in earlier social formations. More particularly, the capitalist state's relative autonomy gives
it the capacity to respond to certain struggles of the dominated

classes by arranging for compromise economic concessions to be made available to them, even in so doing occasionally acting against the short term economic interests of some dominant class or fraction. It also gives it the capacity to tolerate, or even, according to the conjuncture, to encourage, certain forms of (isolated partial) economistic struggle on the part of certain dominated classes. Of course in acting in this way the state 'aims precisely at the political disorganisation of the dominated classes'[68] through reinforcing isolation effects among them. By actually securing certain economic concessions for certain dominated classes the state seeks to set up itself (the unity of isolation) as the representative of the interests of those classes, thereby 'discouraging' them from seeking any alternative autonomous political organisation in opposition to the bourgeois state. And by tolerating, regulating or encouraging certain forms of struggle by the dominated classes (e.g. by making available compromise concessions) the state attempts to delimit the struggles of these classes to forms and levels which do not politically threaten the dominant classes.

This brings us to one of the critically important concepts for us in this study—the concept of a 'supportive class'.[69] The power bloc cannot in most social formations exert its dominance over the social formation on its own. It is generally in need of some degree of actual support from certain dominated classes, and to the extent that the state is actually successful in setting itself as the representative of certain dominated classes, to the extent in other words that it is successful in making these classes 'accept a whole series of compromises . . . (as) their political interest'[70] they become supportive of the form of state and hence of bourgeois rule. Supportive classes (which are usually parts of the peasantry and the petty bourgeoisie but sometimes also include certain strata of the working class) should be distinguished from 'allied classes', another important concept for us here. Allied classes are also certain dominated class fractions whose practices enable the power bloc to exert its hegemony over the social formation, but they are distinguished from supportive classes by the differences in the nature of their relationship with the dominant classes. Basically, an allied class is in a specific relationship where it receives some particular concession, usually a political concession, in its favour. A supportive class on the other hand generally receives no specific political concession in its favour. Its support is obtained because of the effect of the ideological and also sometimes because of certain, real or imaginary, fears on the part of certain dominated classes of the power of the working class. The support it gives to the dominant classes is not therefore generally manifested in immediate class relations but is more usually mediated through the state. It is thus more often a general support for the form of state than a support for any particular fraction in the power bloc, and it is for that reason critically dependent on the functioning of the ideological and thus on the state's capacity to 'feed' the ideological by organising compromise economic concessions.

However in making available economic concessions to dominated classes, whether they become supportive or not, the state remains subject to the limitations of the system within which it operates. The state is not some omnipotent entity existing above society but a particular level of the class relations in a social formation, and it cannot therefore transcend the limitations of the basic social relationships of which it is part. As Hirsch puts it, 'The bourgeois state can only maintain its form if the capital reproduction process is guaranteed and its own material basis is thus secured' and for that reason 'the basic structures and laws of development of bourgeois societies are not capable of being "regulated" politically'.[71] More specifically this means that the state's capacity to guarantee the economic interests of any dominated class or fraction is limited at the point where this guarantee endangers capitalist property relations or the process of capital accumulation. This is particularly important for us here because it means that although the bourgeois state is able to act against some of the short term economic interests of certain dominant classes it cannot fundamentally alter the capitalist social relations of which it is part. For example, although the bourgeois state is able to act in the class struggle to secure more income for certain wage-earners, it cannot alter the basic wage relationship into which these wage-earners are incorporated. And by the same token if it acts in a particular social formation at particular conjunctures to ensure the assignment of particular agents to particular places in the division of labour it does not thereby determine the fundamental class structure of the social formation. This is more particularly so in this case because of the subordination of the process of the assignment of agents to the process of the reproduction of the class places to which they are assigned.

We now possess sufficient elements to outline the propositions that will be advanced in this study. Essentially we shall argue that the South African state's interventions to ensure the assignment of white rather than black agents to particular places in the wage-earning classes (i.e. the new petty bourgeoisie and working class) and its interventions to secure certain economic concessions for white wage-earners within racially discriminatory 'industrial relations' apparatuses, far from representing the actions of a state bizarrely following the 'logic' of irrational racial prejudice, represented on the contrary the typical interventions of a *bourgeois* state acting to preserve the coherence of a *capitalist* social formation under particular conditions of class struggle. Not only then will we argue that the economic concessions made available to white wage-earners (including those related to the process of class formation) remained at all times strictly limited to those compatible with the maintenance of the conditions necessary for capital accumulation, but we shall argue further that state activity in this regard was precisely intended to eliminate various politically threatening forms of class practice/class struggle, and that its effect was to create the conditions for the white wage-earning classes to emerge as supportive classes for the form of state. In other words, we shall argue that the racist hierarchical division of labour within the wage-earning classes came into existence not as some irrational 'alien' imposition on the bourgeoisie but 1) because it accorded with the requirements of capitalist production at the various phases and stages of capitalist production during the period in question and 2) as part of a political 'solution' which served to structure political class relations in the social formation to the advantage of the bourgeoisie as organised politically under the hegemony of particular fractions at particular conjunctures.

One question which immediately arises is: why did the state respond in this way in the case of the struggles of white wage-earners but not in the case of similar struggles by African workers? This is an extremely complex question requiring an analysis of the entire field of class struggle and will thus only be partially answered in this study (which will have achieved its purpose if it indicates the way in which the particular interventions under review furthered the political interests of the bourgeoisie). Nevertheless the following points relevant to an answer to this question can be briefly mentioned at this stage.

1) White wage-earners were a small and initially militant minority of the total labour force whereas African workers were the large majority upon whose exploitation, at a high absolute rate, the accumulation of capital was critically dependent. Making economic concessions to white wage-earners was therefore a relatively small burden to capital whereas making any similar moves towards Africans would have had much more serious implications for capital accumulation, particularly under conditions where concessions were already being made to whites.

2) The highly coercive relations which the dominant classes maintained with the African dominated classes and the absence from the social formation of other potential supportive classes, obliged the power bloc to seek some degree of actual support from all white classes, a point which we shall return to in Chapter Two.

3) As Kaplan has pointed out,[72] in the 'early period' at least, isolation effects were produced among the African dominated classes at the economic level by the fact that their separation from the means of production was, under the migrant labour system, incomplete, whereas in the case of white proletarians, totally separated from the means of production, these had to be produced entirely at the level of the state.

In presenting our analysis we shall follow a periodisation based on changes in the form of state (i.e. on changes in the composition of the power bloc and changes in hegemony within it). Part I (consisting of chapters 2–4) will examine the role of the state in connection with the reproduction and incorporation of the white wage-earning classes in the period of mining capital's hegemony from 1900 to 1924. Chapter 2 will describe how certain contradictions arising from the particular imperatives of capital accumulation in the social formation gave rise to particular forms of class practice/class struggle on the part of the white wage-earning classes which had potentially damaging consequences for the power bloc at the political level. Chapter 3 will discuss how in the period between 1900 and 1919 the state became involved, in response to these particular threats, in intervening to assign whites to particular places in the division of labour; to guarantee and secure certain economic interests of white wage-earners (including interests related to job colour bars); and to create racially discriminatory 'industrial relations' apparatuses. And Chapter 4 will discuss how the crisis of 1920–1924 produced a rupture in the relationship between the white wage-earning classes on the one hand and mining capital and the state under the hegemony of mining capital on the other, which led eventually to the formation of an alliance between national capital and white wage-earners which enabled national capital to displace mining capital as hegemonic fraction.

Part II (consisting of Chapter 5, dealing with the 'Pact period' 1924–1933 and Chapter 6, dealing with the 'Fusion period' 1933–1939) will then analyse and interpret the various new forms of state activity in connection with the white wage-earning classes which emerged during the period of national capital's hegemony.

Part III (consisting of chapters 7 and 8) will examine how the crisis of the '40s led to the formation of an alliance between certain fractions of the white wage-earning classes and those class forces represented by the Gesuiwerde Nationalist Party, and how certain further concessions were made available to white wage-earners during the early Apartheid period.

Finally, Chapter 9 will draw certain conclusions about the effects of the processes analysed on class relationships at the current conjuncture.

Notes to Introduction

1 Among the major works adopting this position are G. V. Doxey, *The Industrial Colour Bar* (Oxford 1961); D. Hobart Houghton, *The South African Economy* (Cape Town 1964); R. Horwitz, *The Political Economy of South Africa* (London 1967); W. H. Hutt, *The Economics of the Colour Bar* (London 1964—probably the most extreme version) and S. T. van der Horst, *Native Labour in South Africa* (London 1971).

2 See, *inter alia*, F. A. Johnstone, *Class and Race Relations in the South African Goldmining Industry* (Oxford University D.Phil. thesis, 1972), revised version published as *Class, Race and Gold: A Study of Class Relations and Racial Discrimination in South Africa* (London 1976); M. Legassick, 'The Rise of Modern South African Liberalism: Its Assumptions and its Social Base', University of Sussex seminar paper, 1974; H. Wolpe, 'Capitalism and Cheap Labour Power in South Africa: From Segregation to Apartheid', *Economy and Society*, vol. 1 no. 4, 1972.

3 See, for example, B. S. Kantor and H. F. Kenny, 'The Poverty of Neo Marxism: the Case of South Africa', *Journal of Southern African Studies*, vol. 3 no. 1, October 1976.

4 F. A. Johnstone, *op. cit.*

5 See, *inter alia*, M. Legassick, 'Legislation Ideology and Economy in post 1948 South Africa', *Journal of Southern African Studies*, Vol. 1 no. 1, 1974: 'South Africa: Capital Accumulation and Violence', *Economy and Society*, Vol. 3 no. 3, 1974.

6 D. Kaplan, 'Capitalist Development in South Africa: Class Conflict and the State', 1974 seminar paper reprinted in T. Adler ed. *Perspectives on South Africa*, African Studies Institute, University of the Witwatersrand, 1977; 'An Analysis of the South African State during the "Fusion" Period 1932– 1939', London University, Institute of Commonwealth Studies, seminar paper, 1976; 'The Politics of Industrial Protection in South Africa', *Journal of Southern African Studies*, vol. 3 no. 1, October 1976; *Class Conflict,*

Capital Accumulation and the State: An Historical Analysis of the State in Twentieth Century South Africa, University of Sussex D.Phil. thesis, 1977 —hereafter thesis (1977).

7 The question of hegemony will be referred to later in this chapter.

8 'South Africa: Capital Accumulation and Violence' *op cit.*

9 M. Morris, 'Periodisation, Class Struggle and the State in South Africa' (mimeo, 1975).

10 D. O'Meara, ' "Christian National" Trade Unionism in South Africa 1934–1948' (paper delivered to Conference on Southern African labour history, University of the Witwatersrand, 1976).

11 H. Simson, 'Fascism in South Africa', *African Review*, vol. 3 no. 3, 1973.

12 H. Simson, 'The Myth of the White Working Class in South Africa', *African Review*, vol. 4 no. 2, 1974.

13 H. Wolpe, 'The White Working Class in South Africa: Some Theoretical Problems' (paper delivered to IDEP/UN seminar, Dar es Salaam, 1975) revised version published in *Economy and Society*, vol. 5 no. 2, 1976.

14 Including of course my *New Left Review* (no. 82, 1973) article 'The White Working Class in South Africa', Simson and Wolpe's critique of which I am now broadly in agreement with.

15 In fact this point was also made by M. Morris in his 1974 paper 'Capitalism and Apartheid: A Critique of Some Current Conceptions of Cheap Labour Power' (reprinted Adler ed., *op. cit.*). He did not however develop it.

16 *Op. cit.* p. 25 and note 6.

17 B. Bozzoli, *The Roots of Hegemony: Ideologies, Interests and the Legitimation of South African Capitalism 1890–1940* (University of Sussex D.Phil. thesis, 1975).

18 R. Davies, 'Mining Capital, the State and Unskilled White Workers in South Africa 1900–1913', *Journal of Southern African Studies*, vol. 3 no. 1, 1976.

19 M. Legassick, 'The Analysis of Racism in South Africa: The Case of the Mining Industry' (paper delivered to IDEP/UN seminar, Dar es Salaam, 1975).

20 Bozzoli, *op. cit.*

21 R. Davies, 'The Class Character of South Africa's Industrial Conciliation Legislation', *South African Labour Bulletin*, vol. 2 no. 6, 1976.

22 See Marx's critique of Proudhon's objectivist 'historical apology' for Bonaparte in the 1869 Preface to *The Eighteenth Brumaire of Louis Bonaparte* (reprinted in Marx *Surveys from Exile: Political Writings* Vol. 2 (London 1973) pp. 143–145.

23 The most comprehensive existing account (on which we shall draw heavily in the present study) is of course H. J. and R. E. Simon's seminal work *Class and Colour in South Africa 1850–1950* (Harmondsworth, 1969). The approach adopted in this work can perhaps best be described as Marxist historicist. That is to say, in contrast to the liberal approach it clearly recognises the fundamental relations of capitalist exploitation and the class struggles deriving therefrom, but it essentially sees the history of the white wage-earning classes in terms of the unfolding consciousness of a particular class subject i.e. as an historical anthropology. Very roughly, white wage-earners are seen as a particular stratum of the working class having an inherent dual consciousness—a 'class consciousness' and a 'race consciousness'. In the early period of capitalist development their 'class consciousness' is seen to have been dominant resulting in the involvement of white wage-earners in a number of militant struggles against capital and the formation by them of a number of socialist and trade union organisations. Through a series of *internal* struggles within the 'white labour movement', however, this 'class consciousness' is seen to have become subordinated to their 'race consciousness' resulting at the level of class practices in the transformation of the earlier struggles for trade union or socialist (class) objectives into a relatively successful struggle for 'privileges' within 'white society'. (On this see particularly Chapter 26; see Wolpe (1972), *op. cit.* for a critique.)

24 Of some relevance in this connection is the analysis made of the opposite case—the case of the Chinese proletariat—by Mao and developed by Bettleheim (see C. Bettleheim and P. Sweezy, *On the Transition to Socialism* (New York, 1971) pp. 119–120). The Chinese working class, though numerically small in relation to the total population is seen to have been able to play a leading role in the Chinese revolution because it was 'never seriously plagued by economism' and it is seen not to have been plagued by economism because there was no objective basis 'for economic reformism' in pre-revolutionary China.

25 On structural class determination and class position see N. Poulantzas, *Classes in Contemporary Capitalism* (London 1975) pp. 14–35.

26 N. Poulantzas, 'On Social Classes', *New Left Review*, no. 78, 1972; 1975, *op. cit.*

27 G. Carchedi, 'On the Economic Identification of the New Middle Class', *Economy and Society*, vol. 4 no. 1, 1975; 'Reproduction of Social Classes at the Level of Production Relations', *Economy and Society*, vol. 4 no. 4,

1975; 'The Economic Identification of State Employees', *Social Praxis*, vol. 3 (1–2), 1976.

28 H. Braverman, *Labor and Monopoly Capital* (New York 1974). Other Marxist or 'neo-Marxist' works on this problem include C. H. Anderson, *The Political Economy of Social Class* (Englewood Cliffs 1974); A. Giddens, *The Class Structure of Advanced Societies* (London 1973)—both versions of the 'new working class' thesis; A. Gorz, 'Technical Intelligence and the Capitalist Division of Labour', *Telos*, no. 12, 1972—an important early analysis of the class determination of engineers and technicians; M. Nicolaus, 'Proletariat and Middle Class in Marx: Hegelian Choreography and the Capitalist Dialectic', *Studies on the Left*, vol. 7, 1967—which establishes the point that in his later works Marx recognised the tendency for capitalist development to create a middle class (unproductive workers). See also P. Hirst, 'Economic Classes and Politics' (paper delivered to British Sociology Association Conference, 1977) for a critique of the theories of class determination of the new petty bourgeoisie.

29 On the productive/unproductive labour debate see, *inter alia*, I. Gough, 'Marx's Theory of Productive and Unproductive Labour', *New Left Review*, no. 76, Nov/Dec 1972; 'On Productive and Unproductive Labour: A Reply', *Bulletin of the Conference of Socialist Economists*, Winter 1973; P. Bullock, 'Defining Productive Labour for Capital', *Bulletin of the Conference of Socialist Economists*, Autumn 1974; P. Howell, 'Once Again on Productive and Unproductive Labour', *Revolutionary Communist*, no. 3–4, Nov. 1975.

30 K. Marx, *Theories of Surplus Value*—selections edited by K. Kautsky (London 1951), p. 148.

31 (1975) *op. cit.* p. 211.

32 *Op. cit.* pp. 412–3.

33 (1975) *op. cit.* p. 212 (emphasis added).

34 Marx (1951) *op. cit.* p. 168.

35 See Howell, *op. cit.* pp. 54–5 for a view that wage-earners, performing services which contribute to the reproduction of labour power, are productive.

36 (1975) *op. cit.* p. 213.

37 *Ibid.* p. 215.

38 *Ibid.* p. 211.

39 *Ibid.* p. 228.

40 No. 1, 1975, *op. cit.* p. 48.

41 No. 4, 1975, *op. cit.* p. 375.

42 *Ibid.* p. 367; original emphasised.

43 *Ibid.* pp. 403—4.

44 For example, in chapter 19 he argues that chambermaids making a bed produce a commodity and are therefore productive.

45 *Op. cit.* p. 404.

46 No. 1, 1975, *op. cit.* p. 1.

47 Quoted Poulantzas (1975), *op. cit.* pp. 232—3. Footnote 9 points out that this phrase was excluded from the French edition, but whether this was at the instance of Marx or of the translator is unclear.

48 *Ibid.* p. 230.

49 Brighton Labour Process Group, 'The Production Process of Capital and the Capitalist Labour Process' (paper delivered to Conference of Socialist Economists, July 1976) pp. 71—76.

50 See e.g. Brighton Labour Process Group, *op. cit.*; Poulantzas (1975) *op. cit.* pp. 197—199; 'On Social Classes', *New Left Review*, no. 78, 1972.

51 *Op. cit.* p. 295.

52 In the absence of any adequate study, mention can be made of a 'Special Report on the Effective Office' (*Financial Mail*, 25.6.76). The Report deplored the slowness with which so-called scientific management techniques had been introduced in South African offices. According to this report 'MDs (managing directors) of perhaps 7 out of 10 SA companies' 'still don't believe increased productivity in the office can be measured and achieved'. The report, designated 'for the bosses', however, tended to concentrate on the advantages to capital in the minority of firms where such techniques had to some extent been introduced and made no mention of the effects of dequalification of tasks, nor of any effects on the racial structure of the staff.

53 Sources: *Economic and Wages Commission* (UG 14, 1926) Table 'I' p. 272; *Statistical Yearbook* 1964 Table H19; South African Institute of Race Relations: *Annual Survey* . . . 1974.

54 Numerous examples, given for ideological purposes, can be found in the *Minutes of Evidence before the Trade and Industry subCommittee of the House of Commons into Wages and Conditions of African Workers Employed by British Firms in South Africa* (London 1973—4, 4 vols). See especially evidence by Unilever (vol. 1, pp. 159 *et seq*); British Leyland (vol. 1, pp. 138 *et seq*); Metal Box (vol. 1, pp. 196 *et seq*) and Cadbury Schweppes (Vol. II, pp. 587 *et seq*). See also South African Institute of Race Relations *Annual Surveys of Race Relations* (e.g. for 1971 pp.

232—234; for 1972 pp. 256 *et seq*; for 1973 p. 218 and p. 258; and for 1974 p. 250 *et seq*).

55 According to the figures given in the *Annual Surveys of Race Relations* for 1971 (pp. 200—43) and 1976 (pp. 294—310), the ratio of whites employed in the financial, commercial and 'public' sectors to whites employed in the manufacturing, mining and construction sectors rose from 1.57:1 in 1970—1 to 1.68:1 in 1975—6.

56 On this see Poulantzas (1975), *op. cit.* pp. 14—35 and Poulantzas, 'On Social Classes', *New Left Review*, no. 78, 1972.

57 Poulantzas (1975), *op. cit.* p. 24—5.

58 Poulantzas (1973), *op. cit.* p. 297.

59 *Ibid.* p. 298.

60 *Ibid.* pp. 234—249. The class composition of the power bloc marks out the *form of state* and it is therefore the major factor to be analysed in a periodisation of the state. The form of state must be distinguished from the *form of régime* which is a much narrower concept referring to changes which occur at the level of the *political scene* (defined by Poulantzas as the space which 'contains the struggle between social forces organised in political parties' p. 247).

61 *Ibid.* pp. 140—1.

62 *Ibid.* pp. 249—51.

63 *Ibid.* pp. 130—37.

64 Seem and appear because the state is in reality acting to organise the dominant classes *qua* classes.

65 *Loc. cit.* p. 130.

66 *Ibid.* p. 131.

67 *Ibid.* p. 190 (emphasis in original).

68 *Ibid.* p. 191.

69 *Ibid.* pp. 240—245.

70 *Ibid.* p. 285.

71 J. Hirsch, 'The State Apparatus and Social Reproduction: Elements of a Theory of the Bourgeois State' (mimeo, 1977).

72 D. Kaplan, thesis 1977, *op. cit.*

PART I

White Wage-Earners and the Hegemony of Mining Capital 1900–1924

2 Capital Accumulation 1900–1924: The Origins of the 'Poor White Problem' and the Struggles between Mining Capital and White Wage-Earners

General introduction: the composition of the power bloc and its need for supportive classes

One of the most striking features about the South African social formation during the first quarter of the twentieth century (the period with which our study begins) was that it was characterised internally by the prevalence of capitalist relations of production in all major sectors of the economy. This had come about through the effects of the relatively large investments of foreign imperialist capital which had led to the establishment of the mining industry in the latter part of the nineteenth century. Prior to that the South African social formation, though dominated from the outside by imperialist market relations, had been characterised internally by predominantly pre-capitalist relations of production. With the investments of imperialist capital in the mining industry, however, capitalist relations of production began to be established internally on an extensive scale. In the case of the mining industry itself this took place directly through the actions of the direct agents of imperialist capital. And in the case of the other productive sectors (agriculture and manufacturing)—where imperialist capital was not directly invested on any significant scale at this particular phase of the imperialist epoch[1]—this came about indirectly through various 'national' elements responding to the opportunities for capital accumulation brought about as a result of the development of the mining industry.[2] In the agricultural sector, the period between the end of the nineteenth century and the early 1920s saw the existing pre-capitalist relations of production being transformed 'from above' through a struggle between Boer junker landlords and African 'squatter peasants';[3] and the same period also saw the establishment of some capitalist manufacturing industries, generally on a small scale.

One consequence of this particular trajectory of capitalist development was that there were by the early part of the twentieth century no significant non-capitalist dominant classes and no significant land holding peasant classes in existence in the social formation. As Kaplan has argued[4] the subordination of the 'reserves' to the capitalist mode of production at the level of the reproduction of labour power rather than at the level of the production of the objects of labour severely limited the capacity for any such classes to emerge within the 'reserves'; whilst the rapid transformation of the relations of production in 'white' agriculture referred to above meant that they were absent from the white rural areas by the early 1920s at the latest.

All of these factors were of course to have critically important consequences for political class relations in the social formation. In the first place they meant that the social formation was dominated at the beginning of the twentieth century by a power bloc consisting either of already fully formed capitalist class fractions or else of class fractions undergoing a rapid transformation into capitalist class fractions. Among these was, firstly, mining capital—the economically dominant fraction of capital—identifiable in terms of the locus of the powers of economic ownership as imperialist or 'foreign' capital. Secondly, there was the small industrial capitalist fraction overwhelmingly at this time identifiable as 'national' capital. Thirdly there was the agricultural fraction, consisting at this stage both of fully formed capitalist elements and of elements in the process of transformation into capitalist elements, also identifiable in terms of the locus of the powers of economic ownership as national. And fourthly there was commercial and financial capital consisting of both 'foreign' and 'national' elements, principally the former.[5] Of these classes in the power bloc it was imperialist capital (of which mining capital was, by the beginning of the twentieth century, the leading element) which exercised political hegemony in the period up until 1924. This had been established through colonial conquest in the eighteenth and nineteenth centuries and was consolidated in the interior through the war of 1899–1902.[6]

Another important political consequence of the particular trajectory of capitalist development was that it effectively precluded the emergence of any significant potential black supportive classes. In particular it precluded, as we indicated above, the emergence of any stable (rich or middle) landholding peasantry which might potentially have acted as a supportive class for the power bloc; and, in a context where highly coercive relations of exploitation were maintained with the principal dominated classes, this must be seen as at least one of the factors which obliged the power bloc actively to seek at least some degree of actual support from all other potential supportive classes—in effect from all other white classes.

However, whilst the power bloc's need to gain the support of other white classes provides the general context within which the state's relationship to the white wage-earning classes has to be understood, it alone is not sufficient to explain the particular forms of state intervention in connection with the reproduction and incorporation of the white wage-earning classes which concern us in this study. To understand these we need to begin by analysing the effects of certain contradictions arising from the imperatives of capital accumulation in the social formation; and in particular, in this early period, it is to certain contradictions arising from the imperatives of capitalist production in the goldmining industry that we must first turn our attention.

The mining industry 1896–1922: the economic dominance of mining capital and the transition from competitive to monopoly capitalist relations of production

The first point to be made about the goldmining industry is that it was economically dominant throughout the period being discussed in this chapter. It was (as Table 2a shows) the most important source of value and surplus value throughout, and it was also (as Table 2b shows) one of the largest, and certainly the most important, employer of wage labour. Moreover, if we follow the periodisation put forward by Poulantzas (see synoptic Table 3), then the mining industry can be identified as being, in the first quarter of the twentieth century, in its phase of transition from competitive to monopoly capitalism. That is to say the first quarter of the twentieth century was a period in which there was occurring within the industry a twofold change in the relations of production: firstly a centralisation of the powers of economic ownership (the powers to assign the means of production, resources and profits to this or that use); and secondly a concentration of the powers of possession (the powers related to the direction

Table 2   Selected indices of the economic dominance of mining capital

(a) Indices of value and surplus value produced in major productive sectors (£ millions)

	Mining			Manufacturing Industry		Agriculture
	Gold-mining Industry 'Working Revenue'	Gold-mining Industry 'Working Profit'	Mining Industry (whole sector): Revenue from total output	Net Output	Net Output – Wages (i.e. 'working profit')	Gross Output
1907	24.4	10.1				
1911	38.8	11.5	47.5			29.0
1915	37.6	12.0	48.3	18.1*	9.2	33.0
1920	42.7	11.6	55.5	40.3*	18.4	76.0
1924	42.5	14.6	54.5	24.7	13.7	52.0

(b) Selected employment statistics, major sectors (all races)

	Goldmining	Manufacturing Industry	Railways	'White Agriculture' ('Economically Active' excluding bywoners, managers, farmer and family but including 'squatter' peasants)†
1911	228,815	n.a.	54,752	213,000
1916	238,054	91,335	61,080	255,000 (1918)
1924	211,026	167,748	147,261	341,000 (1925)

*prior to 1924 includes government industries, 1924 'private industry' only.
†the agricultural employment figure thus includes certain categories of non-waged labour.

Sources: Reports of the Government Mining Engineer; Statistics of Production; Union Statistics for fifty years, Tables 123–25; D. Hobart Houghton, *The South African Economy* (1966 edition) Table 13; F. Wilson, 'Farming 1866–1966' chapter in M. Wilson and L. Thompson ed., *Oxford History* Vol. II, p. 168.
(The figures in Table 2a are of course only indices. Calculated as they are from figures based on the productive capitalist's selling price they underestimate the surpluses produced in the productive sectors by excluding the surpluses accruing to capitals in the circulation process.)

and internal organisation of actual labour processes) involving, in order to gain the advantages of large scale socialised production, an enlargement of the size of the actual productive unit and a socialisation of labour processes hitherto performed under the real control of skilled artisanal workers.

Johnstone has shown[7] that the impetus for this early and comparatively rapid transition to monopoly capitalism came from the particular technical and price constraints within which capitalist production in the South African goldmining industry took place. The

Table 3 Synoptic table: periodization of the dominant/imperialist social for

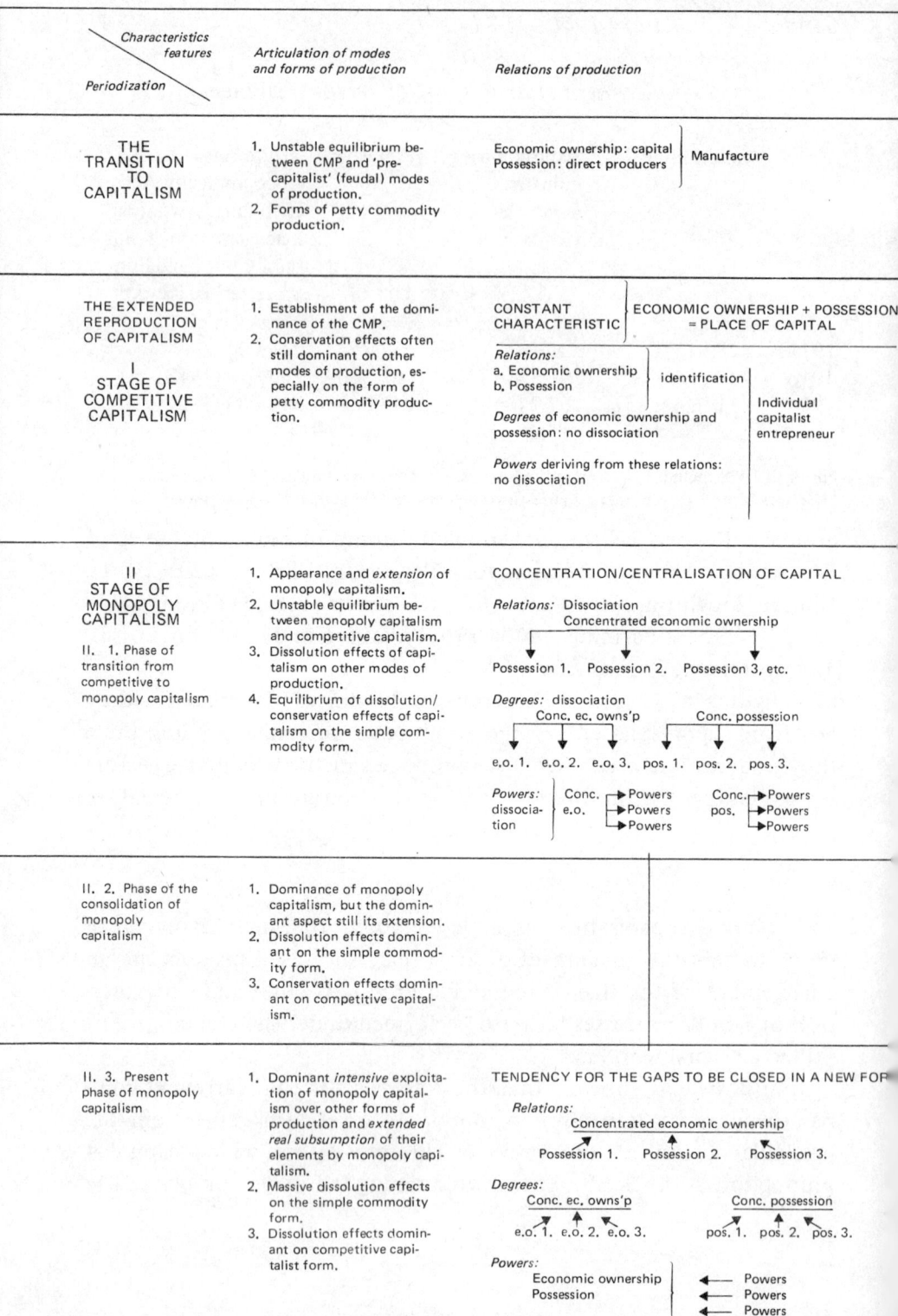

Periodization \ Characteristics features	Articulation of modes and forms of production	Relations of production
THE TRANSITION TO CAPITALISM	1. Unstable equilibrium between CMP and 'pre-capitalist' (feudal) modes of production. 2. Forms of petty commodity production.	Economic ownership: capital Possession: direct producers } Manufacture
THE EXTENDED REPRODUCTION OF CAPITALISM **I STAGE OF COMPETITIVE CAPITALISM**	1. Establishment of the dominance of the CMP. 2. Conservation effects often still dominant on other modes of production, especially on the form of petty commodity production.	CONSTANT CHARACTERISTIC } ECONOMIC OWNERSHIP + POSSESSION = PLACE OF CAPITAL *Relations:* a. Economic ownership b. Possession } identification *Degrees* of economic ownership and possession: no dissociation } Individual capitalist entrepreneur *Powers* deriving from these relations: no dissociation
II STAGE OF MONOPOLY CAPITALISM II. 1. Phase of transition from competitive to monopoly capitalism	1. Appearance and *extension* of monopoly capitalism. 2. Unstable equilibrium between monopoly capitalism and competitive capitalism. 3. Dissolution effects of capitalism on other modes of production. 4. Equilibrium of dissolution/conservation effects of capitalism on the simple commodity form.	CONCENTRATION/CENTRALISATION OF CAPITAL *Relations:* Dissociation Concentrated economic ownership Possession 1. Possession 2. Possession 3, etc. *Degrees:* dissociation Conc. ec. owns'p Conc. possession e.o. 1. e.o. 2. e.o. 3. pos. 1. pos. 2. pos. 3. *Powers:* dissociation } Conc. e.o. → Powers / → Powers / → Powers Conc. pos. → Powers / → Powers / → Powers
II. 2. Phase of the consolidation of monopoly capitalism	1. Dominance of monopoly capitalism, but the dominant aspect still its extension. 2. Dissolution effects dominant on the simple commodity form. 3. Conservation effects dominant on competitive capitalism.	
II. 3. Present phase of monopoly capitalism	1. Dominant *intensive* exploitation of monopoly capitalism over other forms of production and *extended real subsumption* of their elements by monopoly capitalism. 2. Massive dissolution effects on the simple commodity form. 3. Dissolution effects dominant on competitive capitalist form.	TENDENCY FOR THE GAPS TO BE CLOSED IN A NEW FOR *Relations:* Concentrated economic ownership Possession 1. Possession 2. Possession 3. *Degrees:* Conc. ec. owns'p Conc. possession e.o. 1. e.o. 2. e.o. 3. pos. 1. pos. 2. pos. 3. *Powers:* Economic ownership ← Powers Possession ← Powers ← Powers

s

Legal ownership, relations of production	Labour process	Type of production unit	Agents supporting relations and exercising powers	The State
Dissociations resulting from the equilibrium between modes of production (classic case being landed property).	Formal subsumption of labour to capital: manufacture.		Owners and direct producers.	Transition State: in Europe the 'Absolutist' State.
Capitalist identification of legal ownership and economic ownership: individual capitalist.	*TENDENCY* 1. *Beginnings* of the real subsumption of capital to labour. 2. *Extensive* exploitation of labour dominant. 3. Appearance of intensive exploitation of labour: first effects of co-operation and socialization (machinery and large-scale industry).	Simple and 'separate' production units.	CONSTANT CHARAC-TERISTIC: POWERS DERIVING FROM THE PLACE OF CAPITAL. Powers concentrated and exercised by the individual capitalist entrepreneur/support of the relations.	1. Determination *and* dominance of the 'economic'. 2. Liberal state.
capitalist dissociation of legal ownership and economic ownership (the joint-stock company).	*FOR THE RATE* Intensive exploitation of labour reinforced.	Concentration of simple production units, concentrated units still endowed with high degrees of economic ownership, of possession and of corresponding powers (trusts). Concentrated economic ownership SPU 1. SPU 2. SPU 3. (SPU = Single production Unit)	1. Dissociation of capitalist agents *supporting* the relations. 2. First dissociation of agents *exercising* powers. (The question of managers)	DOMINANT ROLE OF THE STATE 1. Unstable equilibrium between the dominance of the economic and the dominance of the state. 2. The interventionist state.
	OF PROFIT			Consolidation of the dominant role of the state.
	TO FALL 1. Intensive exploitation of labour becomes dominant. 2. Extended real subsumption of labour to capital. 3. Extended co-operation and socialization of the labour process. 4. Domination of 'dead labour' over 'living labour'. (Role of technological innovation.)	INTEGRATED PRODUCTION Complex production unit EPU 1. EPU 2. EPU 3. (EPU = *Elementary* Production Unit) Complex production units DPU 1. DPU 2. DPU 3. (DPU = *Dependent* Production Unit)	1. Concentration of the *supports* of the relations. 2. Reproduction of the dissociation of the agents who exercise powers. (The question of the 'centralization/ decentralization' of the 'big firm'.)	1. New role of the state in the reproduction and accentuation of its dominance. 2. New form of interventionist state.

goldbearing ore of the Witwatersrand, though plentiful, was (and still is) of a low average grade and located primarily in narrow broken seams far beneath the surface. Also the price of gold, the international money commodity, was internationally determined and set at a fixed level over long time periods. The net effect of these two constraints was that it made capital accumulation in the industry critically dependent upon 1) the ability of the mining capitalists to obtain the relatively large amounts of advanced capital necessary to bring the mines into production (a factor which made financial concentration imperative), and, 2) on their ability to bring about an extreme mini-misation of the costs of production (a factor which made large scale socialised production as well as a minimisation of wage costs impera-tive).

However for reasons which cannot be discussed here[8] the central-isation of the powers of economic ownership generally proceeds faster than the concentration of the powers of possession; and in the case of the transition to monopoly capitalist relations in the South African goldmining industry the centralisation of economic owner-ship characteristic of this phase took place between 1896 and about 1910. One observer described the juridicial form which this part of the process assumed as follows:

> Out of the 576 goldmining companies floated on the Rand during the period 1887–1932 . . . only 57 remained in exist-ence in 1932. . . . The 57 goldmining companies in existence in 1932 were, with some minor exceptions, controlled by six finance houses or groups. The process of amalgamation and financial concentration had taken form by 1897 and can be regarded as having been firmly established by the time of Union.[9]

The concentration of the powers of possession, however, the aspect of the process which generally proceeds more slowly, was not completed until 1922.

But to begin to understand the form assumed by the particular contradictions which gave rise to the particular forms of state inter-vention which concern us in this study we need first to understand how agents of particular racial groups were combined in the industry's division of labour at the start of its phase of transition in the late nineteenth and early twentieth century.

White wage-earners in the relations of production of the mining industry: the exclusion of unskilled white proletarians

Essentially the production of gold had required from the outset the co-ordination of a number of labour processes. In the mine itself the rockface had to be drilled and blasted, the ore had to be shovelled into trucks, trammed to the winches and then hoisted to the surface; the mine also had to be ventilated, pumped and provided with timber supports. Development work required, *inter alia*, shafts to be sunk, pipes to be fitted, tracks to be laid and winding engines to be installed. And above ground the ore had to be sorted and crushed and the metal extracted. However, whilst a number of these processes had been organised on the basis of socialised production under capital's real control at least since the beginnings of 'deep level' mining in 1896, at the start of the phase of transition mining capital had been compelled to rely upon artisan producers, formally subordinated to capital through the relation of property but retaining real control over the actual labour process,[10] both to organise the method of work (conceptualise) and to actually perform (execute) a number of key productive functions. These included a large number of the productive functions performed on the surface including a number of important tasks in the amalgamation and reduction process, and underground they included the operation of much of the technical equipment including (at first) machine drills.

Capitalist production in the South African goldmining industry had, therefore, required at the start of the phase of transition the assignment of agents of production to three distinct types of places in the division of labour. Firstly and most importantly it had required the assignment of agents to various places in socialised work-groups (gangs). Secondly, it had required the assignment of artisans to the various productive tasks enumerated above. And, thirdly, it had required agents to perform the dual function of supervision under capitalism i.e. the productive function of co-ordinating labour processes and the coercive function, arising from the antagonistic nature of capitalist social relations, of exercising surveillance and control over direct producers.

For the first category of agents of production (direct producers in socialised workgroups) mining capital turned to the only sizeable group at first available to it—the African indigenous classes, who had been subordinated through the colonial wars of the nineteenth century and who performed, under extreme coercive relations of production, most of the labour in the pre-existing agricultural branch. For the second category (artisans), mining capital had been obliged, since there were at first few skilled miners available in the South African social formation, to import skilled miners from the various European social formations and to pay them wage rates which were related to the value of skilled labour power in those social formations adjusted (upwards) by the higher 'cost of living' in the Transvaal and the local conditions of class struggle.[11] And for the third category (supervisors) mining capital had also turned at first to skilled white miners for two main reasons: firstly because, as we shall see later, the productive task of co-ordination was a relatively more important part of the supervisors' overall function at the beginning of the phase of transition than it became later on, and secondly because, as we shall also see later, mining capital relied upon the assumed authority which whites had under prevailing political and ideological conditions to enforce its real control over socialised groups of direct producers.

However whereas a division of labour in which whites occupied the supervisory and skilled artisan places (the latter often being part supervisory as well) and in which Africans occupied the non-artisanal productive places had emerged in the mining industry in the nineteenth century, it was only in the early twentieth century that the 'racial exclusiveness' of each section was firmly established.[12] One question in particular of critical importance to us here which had not been decided in the nineteenth century was the question of the assignment of non skilled white proletarians to places in the industry's division of labour. During the nineteenth century, with a relatively plentiful supply of African labour and a comparatively small number of unskilled white proletarians 'available' in the social formation, the question of assigning unskilled white proletarians to places in the industry's division of labour had scarcely arisen. A few Afrikaners, displaced from the agricultural sector by the rinderpest epidemic of 1896, and a few Italians had been employed as non-artisanal labourers on some mines but their numbers were so small that no definite position of the question of unskilled white employment in the industry had been formulated.[13]

It was during the early twentieth century, in the immediate aftermath of the war of 1899–1902, that mining capital first had to formulate a clear position on this question. In the first place it faced at that particular conjuncture an acute shortage of African labour partly caused by the disruption (during the war) of the coercive apparatuses necessary to produce rural Africans as wage labourers, and partly by the decision of the Chamber of Mines to retain the reduced wage rates agreed to by its members in 1897.[14] It is difficult to offer statistical indicators of the extent of this shortage with any confidence because the two sides of the subsequent debate over Chinese labour either exaggerated or minimised the position in order to make their respective cases. However, for what it is worth, the minority report of the Transvaal Labour Commission (which opposed the importation of Chinese) estimated a shortage of 34,720 in 1903, while the majority report accepted the Chamber of Mines' estimate of 129,364.[15] What seems clearer is that the shortage was a serious threat to the 'maintenance of even medium term profit levels'.[16]

At the same time, the immediate post-war period saw a considerable increase in the number of unskilled white proletarians entering the towns. Again it is difficult to be precise about the number of specifically unskilled white proletarians involved, but we can get some idea of the likely magnitude from the total population statistics, which show an increase in the white population of the Witwatersrand from 50,907 in 1896 to 123,000 in 1904.[17]

It was in these circumstances then that mining capital had to formulate its position on the question of the employment of unskilled white proletarians in the industry and immediately it had to consider whether or not to assign them to places previously filled by Africans. The reasons why it did not (and why it steadfastly refused to do so in later periods) is of considerable significance both for an understanding of the origins of the racist hierarchical division of labour in the industry and for an understanding of the 'poor white' unemployment problem, one of the particular contradictions which concern us in this study. We must therefore consider them in some detail.

The first point which has to be made in this connection is that while political and ideological factors were certainly involved in determining the eventual outcome, it was not a case of 'external' political or ideological factors producing a result contrary to that which would have been produced had the economic been free to operate 'on its own'. The 'explanations' advanced in certain of the literature,[18] to the effect that the determining factor was an ideologically derived 'abnormal' aversion on the part of whites to performing unskilled (so-called 'kaffirs' ') work, is a myth of bourgeois ideology. It is no more valid than the corresponding assertion that Africans were 'attracted' into unskilled labouring jobs in the mines.[19] It is certainly true that unskilled whites put up a resistance to their proletarianisation and that this resistance was often expressed in terms of racist ideology. But there is sufficient evidence that, in the conditions of unemployment and destitution then prevailing, there were quite large numbers of whites 'willing', to the degree that any proletarian can be described as willing, to take on such work.[20] Indeed, for a brief period some 998 whites actually performed such work, and there were during this brief period always more applicants for these places than vacancies.[21] Nor was it a case of mining capital being unable, in the prevailing political or ideological climate of 'white society' at large, to 'degrade' whites by putting them into these places. On the contrary, at that particular conjuncture mining capital would have gained enormously in terms of its relations with the other members of the power bloc, if it had contributed towards 'relieving white unemployment' or 'expanding the white population' by filling these places with whites. Indeed, numerous spokesmen for mining capital repeatedly declared both in public[22] and in private[23] that they would themselves on these grounds have favoured the employment of unskilled whites in these places.

To understand the position of mining capital on this question we have then to consider other factors and in particular we have to begin with the effects which the employment of large numbers of unskilled whites would have had on capital accumulation in the industry, particularly under conditions where profitable production was critically dependent on an extreme minimisation of working costs. There is now sufficient literature dealing with the theoretical concept of the value of labour power in the South African context not to have to develop it at any length here.[24] The basic point is that under capitalist relations of production the income of the direct producer (the wage) is not directly determined by the value which the worker creates in the process of production, but rather by the value of his or her labour power—the socially determined costs of reproducing the worker in his or her 'normal state': the difference between the value of labour power and the value created by that labour power being, of course, the surplus value which accrues to the capitalist and which he therefore seeks to maximise. In essence, the principal factor determining mining capital's position on the question of the employment of unskilled whites was that under the conditions prevailing in the social formation at the time, the value of African labour power was far less than the value of unskilled white labour power. However, the value of labour power is itself determined in the class struggle and, as Legassick has pointed out, for that reason 'cannot be invoked as a causative explanation, but only as a moment in an explanation based on class struggle and its determination'.[25] Thus, to fully understand mining capital's position on this question we have to understand why it was that at this particular moment the value of the labour power of these two strata differed. And this entails referring to the differing conditions of class struggle under which each became proletarianised.

As several writers have shown at length[26] the proletarianisation of

Africans in South Africa came about through the deliberate purposeful intervention of the exploiting classes (foremost among them mining capital). As such it had been a process accompanied by an intense and protracted struggle on the part of the dominant classes to ensure that it took forms most beneficial to the needs of capital accumulation. At the most visible level this had involved the establishment by the dominant classes of a number of coercive/repressive apparatuses which functioned both to ensure a regular supply of African labour and to create 'favourable' conditions for the value of African labour power to be driven down in the class struggle virtually to physical subsistence levels. Among these were the use of taxation to force the sale of labour power by Africans in the 'reserves', the promulgation of pass and vagrancy laws which had a similar effect on those living in the towns, and the promulgation of laws and regulations subjecting various forms of resistance by African workers (e.g. striking, desertion and even 'insubordination') to criminal as well as civil penalties. At another level it had involved the creation of particular exploitative structures and institutions which made possible an extreme minimisation of the physical subsistence costs of African workers. These have been most extensively analysed in the work of Wolpe[27] who has argued that the migrant labour system (which came into existence in the late nineteenth and early twentieth centuries) involved a particular pattern of articulation between capitalist and non capitalist modes of production. In the latest and most developed version of his basic thesis,[28] Wolpe had argued that the conservation and restructuring of the productive capacity of the pre-capitalist (African) modes of production in the South African social formation, enabled capital to avoid the costs of generational reproduction of the African working class, whilst at the same time ensuring that the workers' families continued to fulfil their essential task of producing and reproducing the recruits to replace 'worn out' members of the working class. In other words through the structures associated with the migrant labour system, capital was able to drive down the value of African labour power to the costs of reproducing the individual labourer from day to day. Moreover, as Legassick has indicated,[29] through the operation of the compound system, capital was able to minimise even the day to day costs of reproducing African migrant workers for which it remained 'responsible'. In the first place the compound system enabled capital to assume direct control over the pattern of consumption, and to regulate with some precision the quantities and qualities of the various items to the minimum levels required to rejuvenate the worker as a 'muscular machine'. It also meant that the mining capitalists became large institutional buyers and were thus able to obtain discounts, savings and other 'economies of scale'. For example a pound of meat cost mining capital 4·2*d*. in June 1904 and 3·3*d*. in June 1905, considerably less than half the 9*d*. a pound charged by the retail butchers for 'labourers' meat' in 1906.[30]

In the case of the unskilled whites, on the other hand, their proletarianisation had not been directly sought by capital at all, but had come about largely as an 'indirect consequence' of the spread of capitalist relations in the 'white' rural areas. This has been described often enough not to need any extensive elaboration here.[31] Briefly, the private appropriation of the means of production (more or less completed by the end of the nineteenth century) had resulted in the exclusion of certain whites from economic ownership. Originally many of those so excluded had become the sharecropper tenants (bywoners) of those exercising the powers of economic ownership. But, with the enhanced opportunities for capital accumulation created by the development of the mining industry, an increasing number of landowners began to transform themselves 'from above' into capitalist producers and this meant in many cases the dismissal of bywoners. With the periodic crises affecting the agricultural sector —the first being the rinderpest epidemic of 1896 and the second the war of 1899–1902—this tendency towards excluding bywoners was greatly accelerated, and from the late nineteenth and more particularly early twentieth century onwards they began in increasing numbers congregating in the towns as an urbanised proletariat, totally 'freed' from the means of production.

As the 'incidental consequence' of other social processes this particular process of proletarianisation had not been accompanied by any struggle on the part of the dominant classes to reduce the value of labour power of the resulting white proletarians. They had not been subjected to any of the particular exploitative institutions associated with the migrant labour system, and they had no base in any 'reserve' economy. The net effect, therefore, was that the unskilled white proletarians confronted capital not as potential migrant workers but as an urbanised proletariat totally separated from any means of subsistence, whose reproduction costs would thus in the long term (if not in the short term) necessarily have to be related to the subsistence requirements of an entire family unit. Moreover, as an urbanised class not incorporated into any institutions equivalent to the compounds, their necessary subsistence costs (which included a certain 'historical and moral' element) were subject to the full effects of the relatively high cost of wage goods in the urban areas at the time (the product, *inter alia*, of the high cost of transportation, and the underdeveloped nature of the local wage goods producing sectors). According to one contemporary calculation, for example, a list of wage goods which would have cost 13*s*. 6*d*. in Britain would have cost 28*s*. 2*d*. in Johannesburg,[32] and according to a Government Commission an unskilled labourer would have had to pay 30*s*. a month for the cheapest rented accommodation compared to an amount of between 12*s*. and 14*s*. in Britain.[33] What is more, their particular class origins in the rural dominant classes had also meant that the unskilled whites retained certain 'rights' in terms of political and ideological relationships, among them the right to vote and the right to form trade unions, although these particular factors were not at this specific conjuncture as decisive as some writers have suggested.[34]

The net outcome of these different patterns of proletarianisation was that whilst African labour power was for capital 'ultra cheap' unskilled white labour power was 'relatively expensive'. If we follow Marx and assume that the value of labour power was 'practically known' in the social formation at the time,[35] then Table 4 indicates that the value of African labour power was between one third and

Table 4[36] *Comparative wages and 'cost of living' estimates, unskilled whites and Africans—period approximately 1902–1908.*

1. Actual wage rates paid to single unskilled whites	2. Estimated wage rates including allowance for family subsistence	3. Estimates of the minimum levels to which the costs of family subsistence could be driven under existing conditions (rent and food only)	4. Average African wages (cash and kind) per shift
5/- a day 'all found' i.e. 9/5 to 10/2 total per shift (varying in different mines)	10/- per shift (Cresswell) 10/- per shift (Sampson) 12/- (Consulting Engineers' memorandum to Chamberlain) 16/- (Hellman)	6/2–8/4 per working day (Transvaal Indigency Commission Report) 11/2 per day (Aitken)	2/—2/8 varying in different mines

one eighth that of unskilled white labour power. What is more, if the column 3 estimates (usually based on the 'standard of living' of the British 'labouring classes') are taken as some sort of indicator of the minimum costs of reproducing white labour power within its existing structural conditions, then it also shows that the decisive factor was the 'ultra-cheapness' of African labour power rather than, as the various contemporary commissions alleged, any particularly excessive 'historical and moral element' ('extravagance' in the dominant ideology) in prevailing unskilled white subsistence levels.

Under these circumstances therefore the effects of employing unskilled white proletarians in place of African labour power would have been to increase the costs of production, and in an industry where capitalist production took place within rigid technical and price constraints this meant, other things being equal, a reduction in the rate and mass of surplus value produced. Indeed, according to the spokesmen for the interests of mining capital, the effect of substituting unskilled white for African labour power would have been to render production in a number of 'marginal' mines wholly unprofitable. In 1913, for example, the Chamber of Mines argued that the replacement of Africans by whites paid at 7s. 6d. per shift would have had the effect of closing down 16 mines, whilst the effects of substituting whites paid at 10s., 12s. 6d. or 15s. per shift would be to close 26, 35 and 41 mines respectively.[37]

There were in addition a number of other factors which reinforced mining capital's basic position on this question. In the main these were related to the various 'rights' which the unskilled whites had retained in terms of political and ideological relations. Among other things several spokesmen for the interests of mining capital expressed concern at the possibility that even if unskilled whites were not at the time extensively unionised they might become so later, thus enhancing the power of white wage-earners against capital. For example, in a widely quoted letter, a director of one mining house wrote of a feeling among several members of the group's London board, of

> . . . fear that if a large number of white men are employed on the Rand in the position of labourers, the same troubles will arise as are now prevalent in the Australian Colonies, i.e. that the combination of the labouring classes will become so strong as to be able to more or less dictate, not only on the question of wages but also on political questions . . .[38]

Another similar factor was that whites were apparently less easily dominated than Africans within the actual labour process. As one commission put it, whites were more likely than blacks to 'work in a slovenly manner or behave uncivilly to employers'.[39] It must be emphasised, however, that such factors alone were not decisive, as certain contemporaries suggested.[40] These particular objections to unskilled whites were by no means shared by all mining capitalists. On the contrary, there were several who declared themselves to be totally unaffected by any such considerations, but who nevertheless still opposed the extensive employment of unskilled whites on the grounds that it would have been 'uneconomic'.[41]

At the particular conjuncture when mining capital formulated its position on this question, however, it faced the problem of other members of the power bloc having adopted a contrary position. These included capitalist agriculture, the incipient industrial bourgeoisie and a significant minority of the commercial bourgeoisie, all of whom favoured an extension of unskilled white employment in the mines.[42] Their main reasons for adopting such a position were, that they saw an increase in white employment as enlarging the size of the local market to which they were as national capitalist fractions largely confined, and also that they saw an enlargement of the white population as a means of strengthening the position of the power bloc *vis-à-vis* the African, principal dominated, classes.[43] Moreover, during two brief phases mining capital was confronted with governing classes which were also initially sympathetic to this position. The first such phase lasted from the time of the British occupancy of the Transvaal until approximately the first quarter of 1903, when the British imperial regime took the view that the employment of more whites (in particular, English speaking whites) would serve both to promote internal political stability and also a more stable relationship between the South African social formation, and the imperialist metropolises.[44] The second such phase was in the period immediately following the 1907 'Responsible Government' elections, when the party political representatives of certain national capitalist interests (Het Volk) defeated the party political representatives of mining capital (the Progressives) to become dominant at the level of the political scene.

Under these circumstances mining capital was obliged to engage in a process of ideological struggle with the other fractions in the power bloc in order to set up its own particular interest on this question as 'the general interest'. The form which this took, was that it initiated a series of 'experiments with white labour'. The first round of these occurred during the years 1901–3 as part of its strategy to persuade the imperial régime to permit the importation of Chinese labourers, and the second during the years 1907–8 as part of its struggle to ward off the demand for state intervention to compel mining capital progressively to adopt a 'white labour policy'. In most cases these experiments involved the straightforward substitution of whites for Africans, ostensibly to discover whether or not the whites, according to racist ideology more intelligent and 'naturally' hardworking than Africans,[45] could be made to 'compensate' mining capital for their higher wage costs through an increase in productivity. Predictably the conclusion reached was that they could not. Most 'experimenters' reported that while there were in some cases increases in output per man hour using unskilled whites (ranging between 1·2 and 2·1 times the pre-war level when African labour was used), these were insufficient to cover the increased wage costs (between 3·1 and 3·6 times the African level).[46]

There was however a notable exception among the 'experimenters': F. H. P. Cresswell, later leader of the Labour Party and a cabinet minister in the Pact government, but until 1903 the manager of the Village Main Reef mine. Cresswell's contention was that although unskilled white labour was not profitable on the basis of a simple substitution white for black, it could be made equally as profitable by introducing more mechanisation into the labour process. Specifically what he proposed was that a greater proportion of the work should be transferred from the gangs of 20 to 30 African hand-drillers to groups of machine drillers, and that the machine drill process should be reorganised to replace the existing work group—consisting of five or six Africans operating two drills supervised by one white—by a group consisting of one skilled machine man assisted by one or two white helpers.[47] He also claimed (in private) that the reorganisation of the labour process along these lines would be of further advantage to capital through weakening the power of white wage-earners in struggle. As he put it,

. . . by getting the machine men on this plan into a position analogous to that of a foreman you will probably have them on your side in the event of any labour trouble. By placing them in a position of authority over the helpers you put a certain division between them and you have more chance of avoiding any combined action against you. If your machine men should strike you would be able to get along with your best helpers, and if your helpers should strike and your machine men remain loyal, you could get on somehow with kaffirs until the trouble was over.[48]

Moreover, he claimed to have proved his contention by the results obtained during the course of his 'experiment', which were, according to the figures he presented, a cost per ton milled of 6*s*. 9·549*d*. using unskilled white labour—a figure less than the 7*s*. 0·674*d*. generally obtained using African labour in 1899, and an insignificant amount above the 6*s*. 4·393*d*. per ton using (lower paid) African labour in 1903.[49]

Cresswell's results, however, reflected certain geological advantages, which when taken into account were sufficient to invalidate his conclusion, from the standpoint of capital accumulation. The Village Main was a mine with two distinct ore bearing reefs, one of which contained a much richer and more easily worked grade of ore than the other. According to the Chamber of Mines' Chief Consulting Engineer, during the course of his experiment Cresswell had greatly increased the proportion of ore taken from the more easily worked reef. When the results were adjusted to neutralise such geological advantages, he concluded that Cresswell had in fact sustained a loss —calculated at £7,840 for the nine months March–September 1902 —through the employment of unskilled whites.[50]

Various other proposals for employing unskilled whites in more mechanised labour processes likewise proved, by and large, to be less profitable than the continued use of Africans. For example, the use of unskilled whites together with the Gordon drill—a small, one-man operated drilling machine once hailed as 'the white man's chance'[51]—resulted in an increase in productivity but 'no direct economy in general use',[52] when the higher investment and wage costs were taken into consideration. Moreover, where mechanisation did, under existing social and technical conditions, prove to be profitable there were in many cases no reasons why a more mechanised process could not equally well be handled by Africans or Chinese. The view expressed by Cresswell and others to the effect that mechanised production would not be undertaken by migrant workers,[53] proved to be a myth. Indeed, he and his fellow signatories of the majority Report of the Mining Industry Commission found themselves complaining of several instances where small machine drills had been turned over to Africans or Chinese.[54]

Ultimately what these experiments proved was that there was indeed a contradiction between the accumulation of capital in the mining industry and the employment of unskilled whites outside of a narrow range of selected job categories.[55] As such, the immediate effect was that they enabled mining capital to rally sufficient support, among those capitalist fractions in the power bloc which were the most directly dependent upon the mining industry for their own extended reproduction, for it to reassert its hegemony. Fortunately for mining capital among these was the post 1907 governing class, drawn from among the 'more prosperous' agricultural capitalists of the Eastern and Western Transvaal. After a very short period of uncertainty, it soon became clear that the new Het Volk government had abandoned its 'Cresswellite' election programme and would not attempt to force a 'white labour policy' on mining capital.[56] The Majority Report of the Mining Industry Commission of 1907—8 which had recommended that a 'white labour policy' be progressively imposed upon mining capital through the state 'no longer (accepting) that there is any duty laid upon it to co-operate with employers of labour . . . in securing and controlling native labour',[57] was quietly shelved and the régime continued instead to implement, and indeed to extend, all the 'necessary' coercive and exploitative measures. Previous statements about the 'best solution to the labour difficulty' being 'a white Rand'[58] became increasingly replaced by statements about the 'impracticability' of altering 'the whole economic fabric'[59] or about the 'danger of bringing the structure down upon our heads by tampering with the foundations'.[60] At another level, the president of the Chamber of Mines began to cultivate 'friendly even intimate relations'[61] with the leaders of the new government, and within a year the Chamber of Mines was reported as being 'strongly optimistic' at the prospect of being 'no longer viewed from Pretoria with the ignorance and hostility of former years . . .'.[62] In short, mining capital had been able to reassert its hegemony without having to attempt to bring about any change in régime.

We now have one element necessary to begin an analysis of the particular contradictions giving rise to the particular forms of state intervention which concern us in this study. We have seen that it was not, given the different conditions under which unskilled white and African labour power were reproduced in the social formation and the particular cost imperatives in the mining industry, in the class interests of mining capital, the largest employer of labour power, to employ unskilled white labour power in any significant quantity. And we have also seen that mining capital had engaged in a successful struggle with the other fractions in the power bloc in order to set up its own particular fractional interest on this question as the 'general interest' of the power bloc. To understand the other contradictions in the mining industry which concern us here we need to observe certain other consequences of capital accumulation in the industry during this period. In particular we need to return to our earlier characterisation of the period from 1896–1924 as the period in the industry's phase of transition to monopoly capitalism in which the powers of possession were being concentrated under capital's real control.

The contradictions between mining capital and white wage-earners arising from the concentration of the powers of possession

We observed earlier that at the beginning of the phase of transition to monopoly capitalism, mining capital had been compelled to rely for the performance of a number of key functions upon skilled artisans, formally subordinated to capital through the relations of property but who retained control over the actual labour process. We also noted that these agents had at first been recruited from Europe (and were therefore white) and that their wage rates had been determined by the prevailing rates for skilled miners in Europe, adjusted to meet the higher price of wage goods in the Transvaal. What is more, these skilled white mine employees had at a fairly early stage (1892) formed trade unions, and they had therefore some power to defend to a certain extent those rates against attempts to erode them. As a result, the wage rates paid to these skilled mine employees were extremely high when compared to those paid to the Africans (or Chinese) who, for reasons previously discussed, performed most of the non-artisanal productive labour in the mines. For example, in the year 1903—4 the lowest paid underground white employee, leaving aside apprentices, received a wage of 13*s.* 9*d.* per shift while the highest paid received 29*s.*, amounts which were respectively about eight and sixteen times the average African wage per shift.[63]

On grounds of cost as well as on grounds of productivity, therefore, it was clearly in the interests of mining capital to minimise the degree to which it was dependent upon skilled white labour power. Indeed, in particular crisis situations a reduction in its degree of dependence on skilled whites became a *sine qua non* for continued profitability in at least parts of the industry.[64] Mining capital's struggle to concentrate the powers of possession thus took the form of a struggle to limit the role of white wage-earners in the actual production process. It did not however, even in crisis situations, ever seek to eliminate white wage-earners from the industry altogether. In the prevailing political and ideological conditions whites had an assumed authority over blacks which was considered by mining capital to be indispensable in the exercise of control over black workers. As one influential consultant put it,

> He (the black man) has to be controlled and efficiency of control demands . . . the supremacy of the white race (and) a distinct line of separation between skilled white and unskilled coloured labour.[65]

Whites were also regarded by mining capital as the only group capable of performing the tasks of conception and co-ordination. This is clearly implicit in the following typical quotation from a report signed by all the leading consulting engineers on the Witwatersrand:

The brain and industrial training are *the white's* only *superiority*. Thus . . . work among whites must be confined to . . . departments *where the brain* tells and merely muscular work apportioned to races willing (*sic*) to be considered inferior. . . .[66]

The struggle for the powers of possession in the South African mining industry was thus neither a struggle for the elimination of whites from the industry nor, as Johnstone's work has made clear,[67] a struggle in which capital sought to establish a non-racial structure of relations of production. Rather, it was a struggle in which capital took the offensive seeking to bring about a greater separation between the tasks of conception, co-ordination and control on the one hand and productive manual labour on the other, in order to restrict white employment to new petty bourgeois mental and supervisory places; principally the latter.

As Legassick has pointed out[68] this pattern of struggle is most vividly illustrated in the case of the rock drilling process. Originally large rock machines had been operated by a skilled white assisted by one or two African 'helpers'. It had however soon become apparent to mining capital that the African 'helpers' were in fact quite capable of operating the drill on their own. And thus, even before 1900, the process had, after a brief struggle, been reorganised so that the Africans became the actual operators and the white a supervisor of two drills operated by five Africans.[69] At this stage however the white supervisor combined his supervisory responsibilities with the performance of one or two productive manual tasks. He was, for instance, required to rig up the drill preparatory to its operation and to assist in the operation of the drill from time to time, as well as to handle the blasting of the ore.[70]

By 1907 it was obvious that many of these residual manual tasks could also be handled by Africans (or Chinese). Accordingly after a fairly intense struggle the process was again reorganised so that most of these tasks (except for blasting) were transferred to Africans or eliminated altogether by the introduction of smaller drills, and the white 'rockdriller', relieved of these duties, became a supervisor of three drills instead of the previous two. However, at this stage the performance of the productive task of co-ordination was still an important part of the white 'rockdriller' supervisor's duties. Thus, according to one contemporary description, he was required to 'watch' the African drillers, occasionally 'if the rockdrill went out of order' helping 'the boy to put it right'. But he was also required to exercise judgement, to know how 'to put in his holes to best advantage and to utilize his explosives in the best possible manner'; in the view of one consulting engineer 'highly skilled work'.[71]

In later periods the degree to which he performed even this remaining productive task—co-ordination of the labour process—was reduced. By 1914, for example, white 'rockdrillers' were to be found supervising up to ten drills,[72] as Africans increasingly took over the tasks of co-ordination as well. And by 1922, they had lost even their specialist identification with a particular productive task. As the Mine Workers Union put it in a submission made in 1926:

> Prior to the 1922 strike the rockbreaker did rockbreaking, the timberman timbering . . . (etc.). Today the general rule is that the rockbreaker in addition to rockdrilling has to do (read supervise—RD) one or more of the jobs enumerated above, and it is no exaggeration to say that the rockbreaker of today is doing the work which it formerly took 2 or 3 men to do.[73]

A similar pattern is also observable in the case of other departments and processes. Prior to 1913, the drivers or operators of engines, hoisting equipment, boilers and several other types of machinery had been white artisans. Indeed, the mining regulations had laid this down as law. In 1913 however capital took advantage of the weakened position of the white trade union movement, after the strike of that year, to obtain an amendment to those regulations. And from October 1913 the regulation which had previously provided that a 'competent white man' shall 'be in charge of machinery' read as follows

> The operation of or attendance of machinery shall be in charge of a competent shiftsman, and in the Transvaal and Orange Free State Provinces such shiftsman shall be a white man, but unskilled persons working under his directions may be employed

on such operation or attendance provided that the shiftsman exercises effective control.[74]

Thereafter to an increasing extent Africans took over the actual operation of the machines and the white 'engine drivers', 'machine operators' etc. became, like the white 'rockdrillers', supervisors (although in this case the completion of the transformation was delayed until mining capital's victory in 1922).[75]

In fact, with its victory in 1922 mining capital was able to impose a similar process of transformation upon almost every sphere of the production process.[76] In the reduction works the old system of stamp milling and plate amalgamation was replaced by the corduroy blanket process, with the effect that almost all the tasks previously performed by skilled whites were reorganised. In fact, according to the 'description of duties' schedule presented to the Mining Industry Board, by 1926, of the white 'reduction workers', only the mill shiftsmen (who 'replaced . . . certain broken and worn out parts such as screens, shoes and dies, stems, liners . . . etc.') were not principally engaged in 'supervising the work of the natives'. Previously, skilled tasks like plate amalgamation had 'with one or two exceptions been superseded' in the corduroy process, and the plate amalgamators had either been made redundant or else reassigned to places as concentrate shiftsmen where their duties were 'to regulate the flow of pulp over the table, and to supervise the natives employed on changing and washing the strips of corduroy . . .'.[77]

It was the same story in the case of drill-sharpening. After 1922 mining capital was able to take full advantage of the drill-sharpening machine and to replace the skilled white drill-sharpeners by Africans operating the machines under white supervision. And, in a host of other departments—ranging from boilermaking and truck repairing to compound maintenance and repair work—there were similar (if less abrupt) changes in the labour process after 1922 as well.[78]

For the white employees, as Johnstone's work has clearly shown, this process of deskilling/restricting white employment to supervision places meant 'extreme structural insecurity'.[79] The transformation of white employees into supervisors was not a process in which each individual white employee was reassigned to a supervisory place. On the contrary, by increasingly transferring the productive tasks to Africans, mining capital was able to increase the ratio of productive workers to supervisors. It was therefore, despite various claims about the white employment benefits to be derived from extending the profitable life of the low grade mines,[80] inevitably a process in which white labour was shed. This is clearly shown in Table 5 by the decline both in the absolute numbers and in the proportion of whites employed in the industry over the period.

Table 5[81] *South African goldmining industry: selected employment and production statistics showing decline in white employment*

	No. of Whites employed	No. of Africans employed	Ratio Whites: Africans employed	Ounces of gold produced per employee
1910	25,634	198,713	1 : 7·75	33·6
1911	25,882	202,933	1 : 7·84	36·1
1912	24,981	206,374	1 : 8·26	39·4
1913	24,221	196,962	1 : 8·13	39·8
1914	22,025	180,360	1 : 8·19	41·5
1915	22,901	206,354	1 : 9·01	39·7
1916	23,086	214,968	1 : 9·31	39·1
1917	23,180	193,562	1 : 8·35	41·6
1918	23,397	188,376	1 : 8·05	39·7
1919	23,803	179,807	1 : 7·55	40·9
1920	22,837	184,971	1 : 8·10	39·2
1921	21,607	181,323	1 : 8·39	40·0
1922	14,681	171,658	1 : 11·69	37·6
1923	18,613	189,889	1 : 10·20	43·9
1924	19,488	191,538	1 : 9·83	45·3

But even where redundancies were not an immediate prospect, this pattern of labour reorganisation still remained a potential threat to the position of white wage-earners. From the outset white employees in the mining industry had relied to a large extent upon capital's dependence on their skills to secure and defend their relatively high wages. They were therefore faced, through the deskilling inherent in this process with the loss of one of their most important bargaining advantages as well: a factor which mining capital was not slow to recognise.

This last point is perhaps most vividly illustrated by the events of the 1907 strike. Before 1907 capital had recruited the overwhelming majority of its white employees from among the skilled miners of Europe and had, as we have already seen, relied upon them to carry out a number of productive tasks. When these employees struck against the reorganisation of the rock drilling process, capital soon recognised that with the white 'rockdrillers'' task deskilled, the strikers were vulnerable to the effects of the (white) reserve army of labour. Unemployed whites were invited to scab on the strikers which they did in sufficiently large numbers for the strike to be defeated. They were not however taken on at the same rates of pay as the previous incumbents, with the result that mining capital was able, through this manoeuvre, to reduce the median white wage from 18*s*. 6*d*. to 17*s*. 7*d*. a shift.[82] As the government mining engineer put it

It is apparent that the mines are independent to a great extent of the skilled miner while they have in their employ natives and Chinese who have served a long apprenticeship in the mines and who are able to carry on their work under intelligent white supervision, which can be obtained in this country *at less cost than the miner from other countries.*[83]

For these reasons mining capital was resisted by its white employees at each stage of its attempt to reorganise the labour process along these lines. The form which this resistance took was that in opposition to mining capital's attempt to transfer as many of the productive tasks as possible to African workers, the white wage-earners put forward the counter demand that a range of specified tasks and functions be reserved by law exclusively for whites. The demand by the white miners for job colour bars was thus not simply an expression of some irrational racial prejudice which for some reason or other the mining capitalists did not share. Rather it was, as Johnstone has demonstrated at length, 'a response to a specific class structure from which that problem itself derived'.[84]

It was a demand which reflected both the racist hierarchical character of the industry's division of labour and the degree to which the economistic perspectives of the white wage-earners, incorporated into new petty bourgeois and craft artisanal places, failed to transcend the prevailing structures of capitalist social relations.

We have thus far through an analysis at the level of relations of production observed how the imperatives of capital accumulation in the economically dominant mining industry resulted a) in the exclusion of whites from general productive labouring places in the industry and b) in a series of offensive struggles by mining capital seeking to reorganise labour processes such that the remaining white employees were restricted to the performance of supervisory and mental functions. We now have to proceed to an examination of the effects at the level of the reproduction of the political and ideological relations of the social formation of each of these particular factors. This can perhaps be done most effectively under two headings—the first dealing with the political effects of the white unemployment or 'poor white problem' resulting in large measure from the exclusion of whites from unskilled labouring places in the mining industry, and the second dealing with the political effects of the struggles between mining capital and white wage-earners over the concentration of the powers of possession in the industry.

The effects of 'poor white' unemployment at the political level

Strictly speaking, of course, the origin of the white unemployment or 'poor white' problem should not be ascribed to capital accumulation in the mining industry alone. It was more accurately the product of the process of capital accumulation in the social formation as a whole. We have already seen that it was through the development of capitalism in agriculture that the unskilled whites were proletarianised in the first place. And of course a similar set of considerations relating to the value of unskilled white and African labour power, applied to capitalists in sectors other than mining. It was nevertheless because of the dominance of the mining industry in the capitalist mode of production in the period before extensive secondary industrialisation that the 'poor white problem' arose in the form and magnitude it did—i.e. as a relatively large scale, predominantly if not exclusively, white urban unemployment problem. We have already seen that the particular imperatives of capital accumulation in the mining industry had led to the early formulation of a definite policy to exclude unskilled whites from productive manual places in the industry, and we also saw that this had been accepted, after a brief period of struggle, by the other members of the power bloc.

In secondary industry—the other major urban productive capitalist sector—the limitations on unskilled white employment were rather less extreme. Prior to 1924 secondary industry was in the main at the stage of manufacture as distinct from machinofacture. And it was therefore dependent on a labour force consisting of artisan producers, upon whose skill the production process really depended, and unskilled labourers performing various detail and ancillary tasks in essentially handicraft processes. But whilst in most cases whites (often immigrant whites) filled the artisanal places and blacks filled the unskilled places,[85] this was not invariably the case. In the Western Cape and even to some extent in the interior,[86] there were a number of coloureds who filled artisanal places. And there were also a number of whites employed as unskilled labourers. In many cases this employment of whites in unskilled places was the employment of white women whose average wage rates (value of labour power) had been set in the class struggle at a level very much less than that of white males, on the assumption by capital that their incomes were not solely responsible for family subsistence. For example, a select committee of parliament was told in 1917 that three-quarters of the white women employees in the clothing industry received less than 17s. 6d. a week (2s. 11d. a day): many getting as little as 4s. to 5s. a week.[87] There also seem to have been cases of industrial capitalists employing unskilled whites because of ideological illusions about the greater intelligence etc. of whites,[88] or because of the marketing advantages to be derived in the prevailing ideological climate from presenting certain products—notably food products—as untouched by black hands.[89] But whatever the reasons, the net effect was that there was a rather less clear racial division of labour at the level of unskilled manual labour, and hence a less extreme minimisation of the places 'available' to unskilled white proletarians in early manufacturing industry. What is more, throughout this period, mining capital was, as we saw earlier, a very much larger employer of non skilled labour power than industrial capital. In fact, if we make the unrealistic assumption that all blacks employed in manufacturing or mining, and all white women (other than salaried staffs) employed in manufacturing were unskilled, then the following figures show that at the time of the first compulsory industrial census (taken at a time which reflected the industrial expansion which took place during World War I) there were nearly

Table 6[90] Manufacturing and mining, comparison of total numbers employed in certain categories 1915–16

	Manufacturing	Mining
Number of Africans employed (m and f)	35,065	214,968
Number of other blacks employed (m and f)	26,589	
White women (other than salaried staff and working proprietors)	3,898	
Total	65,552	214,968

Table 7[91] *Various estimates of the number of whites unemployed and/or of the number of 'poor whites'* (selected years)

Year	1. Number of registrations at Government Labour Bureaux (per month)	2. Estimated number of urban unemployed	3. Estimated number of unemployed in Witwatersrand area	4. Estimated number of 'poor whites'
1902–1910 (avg)	263			
1908			2,403	
1912	561			
1916	711			10,409 heads of families in 'dood arme' (dire poverty), 16,605 in lesser poverty, these together with families constituting 106,518 persons or 8% of white population
1922	4,450			120,000
1924	3,097	2,640 heads of families with 8,626 dependants		
1929	3,034			
1932	12,692			'conservative estimate' 300,000 (17·5% of white population)
1938	5,571			

three and a half times as many non-skilled workers employed in the mining industry as in manufacturing. It was therefore principally, though not entirely, as a result of the rigid policy pursued by mining capital, the largest employer of non-skilled labour power in the period before extensive secondary industrialisation, that the extreme minimisation of the number of places for unskilled white proletarians, and hence the white urban unemployment problem of the period, arose. Various estimates of the numbers so affected were made from time to time and some are reproduced in Table 7. None is, however, very accurate or even strictly comparable, and many of them combine the unemployed and those in various stages of the process of proletarianisation into a single category, 'the poor whites'. But what they do show is that (with cyclical variations) the overall trend was towards an increase.

In moving to assess the effects of 'poor white' unemployment at the level of the reproduction of the political and ideological relations of the social formation, we have plenty of material. Throughout the first four decades of the twentieth century, it was one of the principal issues discussed and debated within the various forums of the bourgeois state.[92] In the period between 1900 and 1924 alone, the 'poor white problem' was the specific subject referred to a Transvaal Commission which sat between 1906 and 1908;[93] to a select committee of parliament in 1913;[94] to a Transvaal Provincial Commission[95] and another select committee in 1916;[96] and to an Unemployment Commission which issued three reports during 1921 and 1922.[97] It was also discussed in the reports of a number of other commissions, such as the 1914 Economic Commission[98] as well as being the subject of numerous departmental reports, internal committee reports,[99] and of parliamentary debate each year. In addition state departments also co-operated in a number of other investigations of the 'poor white problem' undertaken by various other organisations: the most prominent being the Dutch Reformed Church which, *inter alia*, organised a conference on the subject in 1916.[100]

Underlying the 'humanitarian' ideological form of some (but by no means all) of these reports, was a recurring expression of concern at the detrimental effects which the 'poor whites' were having (or might potentially have had) on the power bloc's continuing struggle to maintain its domination over the social formation. It is this concern, which was as we shall see in later chapters to a greater or lesser extent shared by all the major fractions in the power bloc, that we need to analyse in order to understand the degree of involvement of the various apparatuses of the state in the 'solution' of 'the poor white problem'. Essentially it can be divided into two aspects: firstly there was the concern that the social mode of existence of the 'poor whites' and various forms of class practice derived therefrom threatened to undermine particular structures through which social control was exerted over the African dominated classes, and secondly there was the concern that 'poor whiteism' was a factor detracting from the capacity of the power bloc to organise the supportive and allied classes which it needed to maintain its dominance over the social formation.

In order to understand the first of these concerns we have to understand something of the social circumstances of the urban 'poor whites'. As urbanised unemployed they became in their struggle for survival dependent upon the usual means available to such marginalised strata—beggary, whatever doles or charity were available, and perhaps the occasional odd job; a mode of existence giving rise to forms of practice which the dominant ideology described in such phrases as 'idleness', 'weakness of character', or 'moral degeneration'.[101] A proportion indeed resorted to activities classified as criminal. In the abstract this would not perhaps have posed any particularly serious problem for the dominant classes, but the specific circumstances of the South African social formation had also to be taken into account. On becoming urbanised and unemployed many of these white proletarians had drifted into the large, sprawling multi-racial slums which grew up around the major cities and towns from the beginning of the century. Indeed, in some cases unemployed whites and Africans lived together in the same shanties,[102] and there were even cases of whites begging food from Africans,[103] or performing odd jobs for Africans in return for food and shelter.[104]

It was this relationship between whites existing under such conditions and Africans which most concerned the dominant classes. At the very least it was seen as a factor undermining the efficacy of the ideology of racism as a means of exerting social control over Africans. As the Chairman of the 1913 Select Committee put it,

> . . . men who reflected upon this would see that the sinking of a large proportion of the white population into vagrancy and indigency was a source of danger to the country. What would the self-respecting natives who went to Johannesburg think when they saw a large number of Europeans living on alms and doles whilst they were earning their living by honest industry? An example of this nature diminished the respect in which the European race ought to be held by the native races of the country (Hear, hear).[105]

But it was more than that. The relationship between 'poor whites' and Africans was frequently a relationship which involved the flouting of established authority and/or the contravening of specific regulations directed at the enforcement of controls over Africans in the interests of some or other member of the power bloc. By far the most prevalent 'crime' committed by 'poor whites' was the sale of liquor to Africans, who were prevented from buying it directly by a law, introduced at the behest of mining capital, for the purposes of 'improving' the social control and increasing the productivity of African workers in the mines.[106] According to a Johannesburg magistrate at least 10 per cent of the 'poor whites' living in Johannesburg in 1913 were liquor sellers.[107] And by 1915 the illicit liquor trade was considered to have become sufficiently widespread to merit an extended parliamentary debate during which it was described in such terms as 'a drain on public expenditure', 'a breeding ground of . . . habitual native criminals who are the greatest source of danger to the future of this country', and even (by Patrick Duncan) as a 'danger to the whole white race'.[108]

When factors such as these were also taken into account, the social mode of existence of the urbanised 'poor whites' became compounded into what commissions and committees of enquiry repeatedly styled 'a real social danger'. To take as an example just one (among many similar) quotations:

The magnitude of unemployment among Europeans in South Africa is possibly not greater than in other countries but the danger owing to the presence of a preponderating native population is far greater and constitutes a real social danger . . . (For among the white unemployed are) a depressing residue of incompetent and apathetic indigents whose condition forms a grave danger to society. These are people who have sunk into a demoralizing and corrupting intercourse with non-Europeans with evil effects on both sections of the population.[109]

In addition to all this there were the second set of considerations for the dominant classes: those concerning the effects of 'poor whiteism' on the capacity of the power bloc to organise the allied and supportive classes it needed to preserve its domination over the social formation. As we indicated earlier, in the absence of any potential supportive classes among the black population the power bloc was obliged to seek at least some degree of support from all white classes. And in this context 'poor whiteism' was seen as a serious detracting factor. In the first place the objective class determination of the 'poor whites' as a marginalised stratum placed severe limitations on the efficacy of the ideology of racism as a force rallying the support of the 'poor whites' themselves. There are, for example, several references in various reports to the way in which the 'widening chasm between (white) rich and poor' was leading the 'poor whites' to lose 'their pride in their race'.[110] But, secondly, the 'poor whites' were also seen as providing the supportive base which made it possible for other white classes outside of the power bloc to engage in militant and politically threatening forms of struggle. For example, although the official investigating commissions were rather vague on this point, there can be no doubt that 'poor whites' played a significant part in the rebellion of 1914.[111] And it is also clear that 'poor whites' were prominent among the rank and file participants in the so-called Rand Revolt of 1922. In fact, in the view of Smuts at least, the influence of 'the poor whites . . . people without any calling or education . . . who owing to the various disasters in this country and social conditions have gravitated to the towns' was, in 1922, decisive in 'set(ting) things going towards revolution'.[112] Finally of course in addition there was the ever-present prospect that, given their already existing relationships with Africans, they might in the future give support to some militant struggle by the black, dominated classes.

When all of these factors were taken into account, therefore, the 'poor white problem' came to be regarded as a potential threat to the continued dominance of the power bloc over the social formation. As a much quoted passage from the 1913 Select Committee Report put it,

> . . . the European minority, occupying as it does, in relation to the non-European majority, the position of a dominant aristo-cracy . . . cannot allow a considerable number of its members to sink into apathetic indigency . . . If they do and they manifest an indifference founded on the comfortable doctrine of letting things find their economical level, sooner or later, notwithstanding all our material and intellectual advantages, our race is bound to perish in South Africa.[113]

The political effects of the struggles in the mining industry

To understand the consequences at the political level of the struggles between capital and white wage-earners in the mining industry, we have to understand something of their character as a form of struggle. We have seen that white wage-earners in the in-dustry were a small minority of the total labour force whose role in the actual production process was diminishing over time. As such, they were in a position where, to an increasing extent, isola-ted strike action by individual groups was unable to seriously disrupt production. As the Secretary of Mines put it in 1913,

> The bulk of the manual work is being done by the coloured or aboriginal workman . . . His presence makes it possible for a mine like the Premier to continue work for a time at all events,

although half its white employees may go on strike, and this is merely an instance which applies very generally throughout the industry.[114]

For the white wage-earners to be in any way successful in a struggle, therefore required at least two things—first that they mobilise the support of a comparatively large proportion of their number, and second, that they successfully prevent capital from utilising the scab labour, to which they were as non-producers particularly vulnerable. There was thus a structural tendency for the strikes by white employees in the mining industry to become large scale affairs with the strikers adopting a particularly militant anti-scab stance and in the phase of mining capital's offensive there were three occasions on which this tendency became a reality—in 1907, in 1913 and in 1922. Each time the struggle in question rapidly escalated into a general strike of white mine employees, during which there were major confrontations over the use of scab labour, riots, armed clashes, and even, since the white miners had access to explosives, bombings of scabs and officials and threats to bomb the mine shafts as well.[115] Thus, although there were, as we shall see in later chapters, a number of important strikes by white wage-earners in other sectors, it was those within the mining industry which constituted the most serious political threat to the stability of the social formation.

As well as being disruptive in their own right, these struggles were, like the 'poor white problem', viewed with particular concern by the dominant classes because of their potential catalytic effects on struggles by Africans. This concern operated on a number of levels.

First there was the concern that a successful strike by whites would demonstrate to African workers that gains could be made through combination and strike action. As the 1914 Economic Commission Report put it,

> Your commissioners must call attention to the danger in South Africa under existing conditions of industrial unrest, and especially of attempts by strikes and lockouts to compel either employers or employed to grant concessions. The extracts from the evidence that follow . . . show clearly what effects such

disturbances have on the native mind. A Government Inspector
deposed thus: — 'Some natives are realizing that it is in their interests to form a combination and are engaged in bringing into existence what they call the "Native Workers Union". One said to me
"Our people are now holding a big meeting in Tembuland and are
going to form a branch of the union there so as to be able to unite
all of our people who will refuse to work except for better wages."'
In answer to the question whether he thought that the natives had
learnt lessons in combination from the events of last July (the
1913 strike—RD), the Inspector replied 'I am sure of it'.[116]
Although these 'demonstration effects' were greatly exaggerated by
the dominant ideology (which saw them as the only factor responsible for African strikes),[117] there is some evidence that on certain
occasions their effects were real. Perhaps the most notable instance
was during the 1913 strike when several groups of African workers
also came out on strike demanding a doubling of their wages (to 5s.
a day); including one group of 600 Swazis sporting red rosettes similar to those worn by the white strikers.[118]

There was also the related concern that white and black wage-
earners might come together in joint struggle. Once again, the occasion on which this most clearly manifested itself as a possibility was
in 1913, when the immediate cause of the strike had not been the
job colour bar but the issue of trade union recognition. Considerable
space was devoted in the investigating Witwatersrand Disturbances
Commission to denouncing R. B. Waterson, a trade union leader,
who made a speech encouraging African miners to strike for an increased wage of 8s. a day.[119] Perhaps surprisingly, this was also a
major concern during the 1922 strike. The main theme of the Report
of the Martial Law Judicial Commission was that the danger in the
so-called revolt lay in the fact that it was (so they alleged) led by
militants whose ultimate goal was,

> to induce the coloured as well as the European races in South
> Africa and elsewhere to adopt Communistic principles, and so
> prepare the way for the establishment of Soviet republics
> throughout the universe.[120]

But, in addition to any effects of this sort there was another factor to be taken into account. The repression of militant, often violent, struggles involving white wage-earners tied down the state's repressive apparatus and thereby weakened its capacity to exert control over Africans. This concern is particularly clearly expressed in the following extract from the Report of the Native Grievances Inquiry:

There are normally about 200,000 native mine labourers on the Reef . . . scattered over 50 miles of country in blocks of from 1,000 to 5,000 in each compound. They can mobilise themselves in a few minutes, armed with such weapons as assegais, jumpers, axes etc. A good many of them consider . . . that they have grievances against the Europeans, and most of them are savages, whose only idea of reform is violence. All of them want more pay . . . If, as is most probable, a native outbreak takes place as a result of disturbances among the Europeans . . . force(s) are almost certain to have been diverted to deal with the latter. In the case of serious riots among whites, it may easily be impossible to keep in reserve for a further contingency any part of the force available.[121]

This was a particularly serious matter for the dominant classes. Even in the least serious of the major strikes in the mining industry (that of 1907), 1,419 troops had been required to repress the 4,000–5,000 strikers;[122] a sufficient diversion of forces for the Prime Minister, Botha to call in imperial troops in case 'Chinese and natives and evilly disposed people' took advantage of the situation.[123] With the more serious disturbances in 1913 and 1922— involving 14,555 and 25,761[124] strikers respectively—fears were even expressed that the repressive apparatus was so tied up that it would have been impossible for it to have coped with any major struggle waged by Africans. For example, in 1913 the Governor General (Lord Gladstone) telegraphed the Colonial Secretary as follows:

Large bodies of strikers incessantly on roads visiting mines for purpose as they openly said of 'pulling out' the men . . . Native attitude full of peril. Had authority not been maintained no holding out mine boys could have been retained. Reduced to idleness massed in compounds, and brought to starvation by railway stoppage, only too probable, with electric light cables cut, they would have broken loose and the horror of that situation can hardly be exaggerated. Then every kraal would have heard of the white man's impotence . . . And fact remains that Union Government have not force enough to watch 6 million natives.[125]

And Prime Minister Smuts was quite clearly expressing a similar concern during the course of the 1922 strike when he told parliament that,

The fear that obsessed me above all things (during the course of the armed struggle of March 1922—RD) was that owing to the wanton provocation of the revolutionaries, there might be a wild, *uncontrollable* outbreak among the natives.[126]

We have now observed how the imperatives of capital accumulation in the South African social formation during the period of mining capital's economic dominance and political hegemony (which also corresponded to its phase of transition to monopoly capitalism) led 1) to an extreme minimisation of the number of places in the division of labour 'available' to unskilled white proletarians and 2) to a series of struggles between mining capital and its white wage-earning employees over the powers of possession in the industry. We have also observed, at a general level, how the resultant 'poor white' urban unemployment problem and the resultant militant defensive struggles waged by white employees in the mining industry came, along with other struggles by other groups of white wage-earners to constitute a potential threat to the coherence of the social formation and thus to the political class interests of the dominant classes, both on account of their potential (or in some cases actual) effects on struggles by the African, principal dominated, classes. In succeeding chapters we shall examine how the bourgeois state intervened to offset these particular threats to the political interests of the dominant classes as they presented themselves in cyclical crises.

Notes to Chapter 2

1 The investment of foreign capital in certain manufacturing activities directly associated with the mining industry (e.g. the manufacturing of explosives) being an exception.

2 Generally this has been interpreted as a response to the growth of the local market brought about by the development of the mining industry and, indeed, market forces can and do play some role in the creation of *the general conditions* which make possible *a struggle* to transform pre-capitalist into capitalist relations of production. (See Marx, *Capital Vol. III*, Chapter XX). However in the case of the transition to capitalist production relations in manufacturing and agriculture in South Africa there were a number of other ways in which the development of the mining industry facilitated the process. In particular the subordination of the pre-capitalist (African) modes of production as producers of labour power, brought about primarily to meet the demand for labour in the mining industry, also created a potential wage labour force for other sectors. (I am grateful to Dave Kaplan for drawing this point to my attention.)

3 On the development of capitalism in agriculture see *inter alia* M. Morris' seminal work, 'The Development of Capitalism in South African Agriculture: Class Struggle in the Countryside', *Economy and Society*, Vol. 5 no. 3, 1976.

4 D. Kaplan, 'Capitalist Development in South Africa: Class Conflict and the State' *op. cit.*; thesis 1977 *op. cit.* On the decline of peasantry see C. Bundy, 'The Emergence and Decline of a South African Peasantry', *African Affairs*, vol. 71 no. 258, 1972.

5 On the identification of the dominant class fractions as national or foreign/imperialist see Kaplan, *op. cit.*

6 This is not of course to say that it necessarily formed the governing class. In fact except for the brief period of 'direct rule' over the Transvaal and Orange River Colonies (1900–1906) imperial capital's hegemony was exercised in the twentieth century through a governing class drawn from certain allies within capitalist agriculture (i.e. national capital).

7 *Op. cit.* pp. 13–20.

8 See Poulantzas (1975), *op. cit.* pp. 116–138.

9 S. H. Frankel, *Capital Investment in Africa: Its Course and Effects* (Oxford 1938) p. 84.

10 On real and formal subordination (subsumption) see E. Balibar, 'On the

Basic Concepts of Historical Materialism' in L. Althusser and E. Balibar, *Reading Capital* (London 1970, reprinted 1975).

11 According to the Transvaal Chamber of Mines' *Statements Presented to the Economic Commission* (Johannesburg 1913), allowing for differences in the 'cost of living' the average wage paid to white employees in the Witwatersrand mines was 1.56 times that paid to artisans in Britain, 2.48 times that paid in Germany, 0.94 times that paid on the California goldfields, 1.23 times that paid in Australia and 1.29 times that paid in the Western Australian goldmines (p. 73).

12 This also applied to a very limited extent to blacks working in what became designated as white jobs. In the period until 1904 a small number of coloureds and an even smaller number of Africans had worked in artisanal and semi-skilled (generally subdivided artisanal) places. (See Simons and Simons, *op. cit.* p. 77 and my article 'Mining Capital, the State and Unskilled White Workers in South Africa 1901–1913': *op. cit.*; table 2 of which lists the numbers occupying such places in the years 1901–2—1903–4.) S. Greenberg in an unpublished paper (1977) of which I have seen only a short extract, points out that the numbers were limited not by any white trade union 'pressure' but by the 'maximum average' agreement between the members of the Chambers of Mines. He quotes an extract from the formal agreement which reads as follows:

> It shall be lawful for the Company to pay . . . first class, or highly trained Kafirs, such wages as the Company may think fit, provided that such first class highly trained Kafirs shall in no case exceed in number twenty percent or one-fifth part of the number of Kafirs employed in the Company.

13 See for example, *Evidence to Transvaal Labour Commission* (ed. 1897, 1904) (by F. Hellman) p. 427 who stated that although his company had 'once or twice put on Boers at low rates' before the war of 1899–1902, it had not bothered to 'keep any record' of such employment.

14 These points were all made in the 'Descriptive and Statistical Statement of the Gold Mining Industry of the Witwatersrand' presented to Colonial Secretary Chamberlain and signed by most of the leading consulting engineers on the Witwatersrand. (Summarised version reprinted in *The Times* 9.2.03). Point 'd' for example referred to 'insufficient pressure on the native to make him labour'. For a useful account see D. Denoon 'The Transvaal Labour Crisis 1901–06' *Journal of African History*, Vol. XI no. 2, 1968.

15 *Reports of the Transvaal Labour Commission . . . op. cit.* pp. 18, 57.

16 P. Richardson, 'Coolies and Randlords: the North Randfontein Chinese Miners' "strike" of 1905', *Journal of Southern African Studies*, vol. 2 no. 2, April 1976; see also A. H. Jeeves, 'The Administration and Control of Migratory Labour in the South African Goldmines: Capitalism and the State in the Era of Milner', *Journal of Southern African Studies*, vol. 2 no. 1, October 1975.

17 *Consular Report on Trade Commerce and the Goldmining Industry of the South African Republic for the Year 1897* (c. 9093, 1898) p. 44 quoting census taken in 1896; *Urban and Rural Population of South Africa 1904– 1960* (Report no. 02–02–01, 1968).

18 *Inter alia*, Doxey, Horwitz, Hutt, Hobart Houghton and van der Horst, *op. cit.* This was also the view of the various investigating commissions e.g. *The Report of the Transvaal Indigency Commission* (TG 11 1908); and the *Select Committee on European Employment and Labour Conditions* (SC 9, 1913).

19 On this point see Johnstone, *op. cit.* pp. 26–34.

20 *Evidence to Transvaal Indigency Commission* (TG 11, 1908) p. 93 (memorandum by Witwatersrand Trades and Labour Council).

21 *Ibid*; British Hansard vol. 41, February 1905, columns 495–498; see also my article, 'Mining Capital, the State and Unskilled White Workers in South Africa 1901–1913' *op. cit.*

22 See, for example, *Evidence to Transvaal Labour Commission . . . op. cit.* pp. 119–20 (by Sir Percy Fitzpatrick).

23 See, for example, *Report of a Special Committee on Unskilled White and Coloured Labour* 1902: Chamber of Mines of South Africa: Chinese Labour South African mines File 12, p. 2.

24 See, *inter alia*, H. Wolpe, 'Capitalism and Cheap Labour Power in South Africa: from Segregation to Apartheid', *Economy and Society*, vol. 1 no. 4, 1972); M. Williams, 'An Analysis of South African Capitalism: neo-Ricardianism or Marxism' *Bulletin of the Conference of Socialist Economists*, February 1975.

25 M. Legassick, 'The Analysis of "Racism" in South Africa: the Case of the Mining Economy' (IDEP/UN seminar paper, Dar es Salaam 1975) p. 21.

26 See, *inter alia*, Johnstone, *op. cit.* pp. 26–49; Bundy *op. cit.*

27 H. Wolpe, *op. cit.*; 'The Theory of Internal Colonialism—The South African Case' *Bulletin of the Conference of Socialist Economists*, Autumn 1974; 'Draft Notes on (a) Articulation of Modes of Production and the Value of Labour Power (b) Periodisation and the State' (seminar paper 1975). See also F. Molteno, 'The Historical Significance of the Bantustan Strategy'

(paper presented to Annual Congress of the Association for Sociology in Southern Africa, Swaziland, 1977).

28 1975: *op. cit.*

29 *Op. cit.* p. 35.

30 *Further Correspondence relating to Labour in the Transvaal Mines* (cd. 3025, 1906) p. 103; *Indigency Commission . . . op. cit.* Appendix 1.

31 An excellent account will be found in Johnstone, *op. cit.* pp. 51–54.

32 A. Aitken, *Cost of Living in Johannesburg* (reprinted in British and South African Association's Reports, London, 1907).

33 *Report of the Transvaal Indigency Commission . . . op. cit.* p. 209.

34 For example Johnstone, *op. cit.* As I argued in 'Mining Capital, the State and Unskilled White Workers . . .' *op. cit.*, few unskilled whites were, at the decisive conjunctures, actually members of trade unions, and the right to vote was only effective at the earliest in the 1907 'Responsible Government' elections.

35 *Capital* Vol. 1, Chapter XXII.

36 Sources: Column (1) *Evidence to Transvaal Labour Commission . . . op. cit.* Exhibit G, Statement 1; Column (2) Cresswell—memorandum to 1902 Chamber of Mines Special Committee . . . *op. cit.*, Sampson, *Minutes of Evidence: Transvaal Indigency Commission* (TG 11, 1908) p. 98, Consulting Engineers Report to Chamberlain summary in *The Times* 9.2.03, Hellman, 'Memorandum re Kaffir and Cheap White Labour' reproduced in *Evidence to Transvaal Labour Commission . . . op. cit.* p. 425; Column (3) *Transvaal Indigency Commission Report 1906–08* (TG 13, 1908) pp. 207–211. A. Aitken *Cost of Living in Johannesburg* (reprinted British and South African Association's Report (London, 1907)); column (4) *Evidence to Transvaal Labour Commission . . . op. cit.* Exhibit G, Statement 1.

37 Transvaal Chamber of Mines, *Statements Presented to the Economic Commission* (Johannesburg 1913) p. 103.

38 *Minority Report of Transvaal Labour Commission . . . op. cit.*, Appendix 3 p. 65.

39 *Report of the Transvaal Indigency Commission . . . op. cit.* p. 36, quoted Johnstone *op. cit.* p. 60.

40 *Inter alia* several of those giving *Evidence to Transvaal Labour Commission . . . op. cit.* (Cresswell, pp. 574 *et seq*; Wyburgh, pp. 611 *et seq*); and the *Minority Report of the Transvaal Labour Commission . . . op. cit.*

41 For example, Fitzpatrick (*Evidence to Labour Commission . . . op. cit.* p. 119 20); Report of the Special Committee . . . Chinese Labour file 12

. . . *op. cit.* p. 2; *Minority Report of Mining Industry Commission 1907/8* (1908) (by C. H. Spencer).

42 Identified by Cresswell in a letter to Merriman 19.5.05 (letter no. 81 *Merriman Papers*). The same letter pointed out that the 'big elements in the commercial world' were against using whites and in favour of importing Chinese. Indeed in 1906 the Johannesburg Chamber of Trade published an *Open Letter to British Workmen* to this effect (London 31.3.06). Significantly the white trade union movement was not a major force behind the demand for unskilled white labour at this time. Whilst being generally opposed to the importation of Chinese, an important element among the supervisory new petty bourgeois white miners feared that the employment of unskilled whites would be accompanied by an increase in their supervisory duties (as indeed had been the case at the Village Main Reef mine in 1902). As Cresswell put it '. . . the slave making instinct which dies hard . . . chiefly affects the miners—not the artisans—and particularly the old time miners, who like the system which enables them to sit down and smoke their pipes while niggers earn money for them'. See also: D. J. N. Denoon, ' "Capitalist Influence" and the Transvaal Government during the Crown Colony Period 1900–1906' *Historical Journal*, vol. XI no. 2, 1968 on the position of the white trade unions.

43 These were the kind of points made in the *Minority Report of the Transvaal Labour Commission . . . op. cit.* signed by J. W. Quinn, the owner of the largest baking company in Johannesburg, and by Het Volk in the campaign preceding the 1907 elections (see *Transvaal Leader* 8.1.07; 17.1.07; 25.1.07 *inter alia*).

44 See Denoon, 'Capitalist Influence . . .' *op. cit.* and also the Report of the Proceedings of a Special Meeting of the Chamber of Mines 17.7.03 (Appendix to *Minority Report of Transvaal Labour Commission . . . op. cit.*) where reference is made to Milner's tardiness in refusing to allow Chinese labour to be imported until white labour had first been tried.

45 A typical example of this form of racist arrogance is to be found on p. 34 of the *Transvaal Indigency Commission Report . . . op. cit.*, where the commissioners write: 'The white man is a more intelligent and regular worker and has more judgement than the native . . . We may treat these factors as constant. They depend in the main on racial characteristics.'

46 Transvaal Labour Commission, Minutes of Evidence . . . *op. cit.* Exhibit G Statement 1.

47 Memorandum September 1902, Chamber of Mines, Chinese Labour . . . File

12, *op. cit.* pp. 14–20; *Evidence to Transvaal Labour Commission ... op. cit.* pp. 574 ff; *Report of the Mining Industry Commission* (TG 1 1908); F. H. P. Cresswell *The Chinese Labour Question from Within* (London 1905).

48   Chamber of Mines ... File 12, *op. cit.* p. 20.

49   *Evidence to Transvaal Labour Commission op. cit.* pp. 578–9.

50   Hennen Jennings letter to Secretary of State Chamberlain, file CO 529, *Secretary of State's Tour 1902–1903* (Public Record Office, London).

51   *Transvaal Leader* 13.4.97.

52   *Further Correspondence Relating to Affairs in the Transvaal and Orange River Colony* (cd. 3528, 1907) p. 85.

53   See, for example, Memorandum to Special Committee of Chamber of Mines. Chinese Labour South African Mines file 12 ... *op. cit.*

54   See *Report of the Mining Industry Commission ... op. cit.* pp. 116–7.

55   An investigation carried out during the course of the white labour experiments by a team of consulting engineers (Price, Skinner, Spencer) decided that a few unskilled whites could 'be beneficially used' in a few departments —as 'rockdrillers' (supervisory), as operators of underground haulages, as onloaders, and as plate-layers and pipemen's assistants (see *Evidence to Transvaal Labour Commission ... op. cit.* pp. 574–5).

56   A fuller account of the change in Het Volk's position on this question is given in my article: 'Mining Capital, the State and Unskilled White Workers in South Africa 1901–1913' ... *op. cit.*

57   *Report of the Mining Industry Commission ... op. cit.* p. 116.

58   Smuts' letter to Merriman 5.5.06 included in S. van der Poel ed: *Selections from the Smuts Papers* Vol. II, pp. 302–3. Similar sentiments were expressed by Smuts in public meetings during the election campaign.

59   *Transvaal Leader* 31.7.08 reporting Smuts addressing Parliament.

60   *Transvaal Leader* 20.3.08 reporting Smuts addressing a meeting on the unemployment question.

61   L. Phillips, *Some Reminiscences* (London 1924) p. 196.

62   *The Times* 26.2.09.

63   Transvaal Mines Dept, *Report of the Government Mining Engineer* for the year ending 30.6.04 (white wages); *Correspondence Relating to Affairs in the Transvaal and Orange River Colonies* (cd. 2104, 1904) p. 45 (African wages).

64   Cf. Johnstone, *op. cit.* part II.

65   Ross E. Browne, 'Pamphlet on Working Costs of the Witwatersrand' reprinted

as Appendix to *Minutes of Evidence Mining Industry Commission . . . op. cit.* p. 1595.

66 'A Descriptive and Statistical Statement of the Gold Mining Industry of the Witwatersrand' . . . *op. cit.* (emphasis added).

67 *Op. cit.* pp. 77–86.

68 *Op. cit.* pp. 37 *et seq.*

69 E. Katz, 'White Workers and the Industrial Colour Bar 1902–1913', *South African Journal of Economics* vol. 42 1974.

70 A description of the differing process involved in the operation of large machine drills and the smaller drills used after 1907 is given in *Further Correspondence Relating to Affairs of the Transvaal and Orange River Colonies* (cd. 3528, 1907) pp. 71–2.

71 *Minutes of Evidence: Select Committee on European Employment and Labour Conditions* (SC 9, 1913) pp. 2, 14 (H. Ross Skinner, Consulting Engineer).

72 See Legassick, *op. cit.*

73 Transvaal Chamber of Mines Gold Producers Committee: *Mining Industry Arbitration Board 1926–7* (Johannesburg 1927) p. 408 (statement submitted by South African Mine Workers Union).

74 *Report of the Government Mining Engineer for the Year Ended 30.6.24* p. 54.

75 *Ibid.* p. 55; Johnstone, *op. cit.* pp. 138–9.

76 See Johnstone, *op. cit.* pp. 136–145 for a full account.

77 *Mining Industry Arbitration Board* 1926–7, *op. cit.* Annexure '1' pp. 326–329.

78 Johnstone, *op. cit.* pp. 136–145.

79 *Ibid.* pp. 57–64.

80 See for example 'Descriptive and Statistical Statement of the Goldmining Industry of the Witwatersrand' . . . *op. cit.; Evidence to Transvaal Labour Commission . . . op. cit.*

81 Sources, *Union Statistics for 50 Years; Reports of the Government Mining Engineer.*

82 *Evidence to Mining Industry Commission 1907–8 . . . op. cit.* Appendix XI, p. 1664 (calculated from tabular data).

83 *Report of the Government Mining Engineer for the year ended 30.6.07,* p. 13.

84 *Op. cit.* p. 74.

85 See, for example, evidence to *Royal Commission on the Natural Resources,*

Trade and Legislation of Certain Portions of His Majesty's Dominions (cd. 7706, 1914)—by W. J. Laite, General Secretary of South African Manufacturers Association pp. 152 *et seq.*

86 *Mines Department Reports 1911 1. Johannesburg Labour Bureau Report for the Calendar Year 1911 2. Cape Town Labour Bureau Report for the Calendar Year 1911 3. Pretoria Labour Bureau Report for the Period 1.7.11 to 31.12.1911* (UG 51, 1912) p. 3.

87 *Evidence to Select Committee on the Subject Matter of the Regulation of Wages (Specific Trades) Bill* (SC 5, 1917) (by Mrs. Cooke) pp. 64–5.

88 See, *inter alia*, the Report of the *Transvaal Indigency Commission . . . op. cit.* pp. 37–8 quoting the example of Searle's leather works in Cape Town.

89 *The Mines Dept: Reports of 1. Inspector of White Labour (Transvaal) for the Period 1.7.09 to 31.12.10 2. Government Labour Bureau (Cape) for the year ended 31.12.10* (UG 29, 1911) pp. 9–10 refers to the bakeries and abbatoirs of the Transvaal which were subjected to 'public pressure' to go all white on alleged health grounds.

90 Source: *Census of Production for the Year 1915–16* Table 8 and 10 for manufacturing, *Union Statistics for 50 Years* for mining.

91 Sources: Column 1 *Department of Mines and Industries Labour Division Reports* and *Department of Labour Reports* for the years in question; column 2 *The Official Labour Gazette* (Dept of Labour official publication) vol. 1, part 1, April 1925 quoting results of a census taken by the Advisory Council of Labour; column 3 *Indigency Commission Report . . . op. cit.* p. 119; column 4 1916: W. M. MacMillan: *The South African Agrarian Problem and its Historical Development* (Johannesburg 1919) quoting first public estimate by the Dutch Reformed Church at its Cradock Conference, 1922. *Report of the Unemployment Commission* (UG 17 1922); 1932: Carnegie Corporation Commission: *The Poor White Problem in South Africa* Part 1 Economic Report (Stellenbosch 1932) p. VII.

92 This should not be surprising, for as Poulantzas observes 'The contradictions most directly and acutely reflected within the state are those among the dominant classes and fractions and between these and the supporting classes, far more than the contradictions between the power bloc and the working class. The latter contradictions are basically expressed in the bourgeois state "at a distance" . . .' (*The Crisis of the Dictatorships*, London 1976, p. 104).

93 *Transvaal Indigency Commission 1906–8 . . . op. cit.*

94 *Select Committee on European Employment and Labour Conditions 1913 . . . op. cit.*

95 *Transvaal Relief and Grants in Aid Commission 1916* (I have unfortunately been unable to consult this particular commission, but have seen various references to and quotations from it in subsequent commission reports).

96 *Select Committee on Drought Distress Relief* (SC 3, 1916).

97 *First Interim Report of the Unemployment Commission* (UG 16 1921); *Second Interim Report of the Unemployment Commission* (UG 34 1921); *Report of the Unemployment Commission* (UG 17 1922).

98 *Report of the Economic Commission* (UG 12 1914).

99 *Inter alia*, Department of Mines Labour Division Annual Reports, *Reports in Connection with the Poor White Question* by the White Labour Superintendent South African Railways (An. 490, 1917), *Inter-Departmental Committee on Labour Resources* (Government printer, 1930).

100 Investigated through newspaper reports (especially in *Cape Times*).

101 *Indigency Commission . . . op. cit.; Select Committee on European Employment and Labour Conditions . . . op. cit.; Carnegie Commission . . . op. cit., passim.*

102 See *Select Committee on European Employment and Labour Conditions . . . op. cit.* p. 162 (evidence by T. G. Triter, Commissioner of Police); *Carnegie Commission Report . . . op. cit.* Part 1, p. V28.

103 See *Select Committee on European Employment and Labour Conditions . . . op. cit.* p. 165 (evidence by Triter).

104 See *Annual Reports of the Factories and Labour Division of Department of Mines and Industries for the year ended 31.12.19* (UG 42 1920) p. 25.

105 *House of Assembly Debates* June 4th 1913, column 3089 (John X. Merriman).

106 On the liquor laws see C. van Onselen, 'Randlords and Rotgut', *Institute of Commonwealth Studies* seminar paper, 1975.

107 *Select Committee on European Employment and Labour Conditions . . . op. cit.* p. 380 (evidence by H. O. Buckle—later president of the Chamber of Mines).

108 *House of Assembly Debates* columns 979—981 (Debate on the Police Vote).

109 *Select Committee on European Employment and Labour Conditions . . . op. cit.* p. XVI. Similar sentiments were expressed in the *Report of the Indigency Commission . . . op. cit.* pp. 117—8; the final *Report of the*

Unemployment Commission 1922 . . . *op. cit.* p. 2; also W. M. MacMillan, *The South African Agrarian Problem and its Historical Development* (Witwatersrand lectures, 1919) pp. 16—17.

110 *Carnegie Commission Report . . . op. cit.* Part 1 p. V36.

111 *The Report of the Judicial Commission of Inquiry into the Causes and Circumstances relating to the Recent Rebellion in South Africa* (UG 46, 1916) and all the witnesses giving evidence before it (UG 42, 1916) look at the causes of the revolt only at the most superficial level Hertzog leaving the cabinet, republican aspirations, latent German sympathies etc. However some indication of 'poor white' support emerges from the fact that one of the rebel Generals, Maritz, occupied and drew support from the inmates of the Karkamas Labour Colony—a 'poor relief' scheme run by the Dutch Reformed Church (see evidence by J. H. Conradie, superintendent of Karkamas pp. 275 *et seq*). And there are also several references in the *General Report in Connection with the Poor White Question submitted by the White Labour Superintendent South African Railways and Harbours* 25.2.16 (An. 490, 1917) to the 'widespread disaffection' among the 'indigent classes' at the time (see e.g. p. 8).

112 *House of Assembly Debates as Reported in the Cape Times* 21.3.22.

113 *Select Committee on European Employment and Labour Conditions op. cit.* p. iv.

114 *Dept. of Mines and Industries Annual Reports: Part 1, Labour and Industries* (UG 21, 1914) p. 10.

115 For accounts of the various strikes see, *inter alia*, E. Gitsham and J. F. Tembath, *A First Account of Labour Organization in South Africa* (Durban 1926); N. Herd, *1922 The Revolt on the Rand* (Johannesburg 1966); Simons and Simons, *op. cit.*; I. Walker and B. Weinbren, *2000 Casualties: A History of the Trade Unions and Labour Movement in the Union of South Africa* (SATUC 1961).

116 *Report of the Economic Commission, op. cit.* p. 50.

117 For example, in 1920 the President of the Chamber of Mines (Sir Evelyn Wallers) referred to the strike by African mineworkers in that year as follows: 'The professed cause of the strike was the increased cost of living. I think we may take it that the true cause was imitation of the methods of European employees. The case of the native employees of the goldmines is not nearly so strong as that of Europeans; the natives are provided, over and above their wages, with all the essentials of existence. The increased cost of food and lodging affects them only in so far as they have to provide

for dependants at a distance' (Quoted in T. Gregory, *Ernest Oppenheimer and the Economic Development of Southern Africa* (Cape Town 1962) p. 496.)

118 See *Minutes of Evidence to Judicial Commission of Inquiry into Witwatersrand Disturbances June–July 1913* (UG 56, 1913) pp. 235–237 (H. M. Taberer, General Superintendent, Native Recruiting Corporation).

119 See *Report of the Witwatersrand Disturbances Commission* (cd. 7112, 1913) p. 16 ff.; *Evidence . . . op. cit.* p. 30 ff. (by W. J. Thompson, Assistant Magistrate at Boksburg).

120 *Report of the Martial Law Judicial Commission* (UG 35, 1922) p. 26.

121 *Board of the Native Grievances Inquiry* (UG 37, 1914) pp. 64, 67.

122 *Colonial Office Confidential Print* File no. 1007—telegram from Governor General to Colonial Secretary 20.7.13.

123 *The Times* 3.6.07 reporting L. Botha.

124 *Official Yearbooks* for 1916 p. 286, for 1922, p. 333.

125 *Colonial Official Confidential Print* file no. 1007—telegram from Governor General to Colonial Secretary 13.7.13.

126 *House of Assembly Debates as Reported in the Cape Times* 21.3.22 (emphasis added).

Having outlined in the previous chapter how particular contradictions gave rise to particular forms of class practice/class struggle on
the part of the white wage-earning classes which constituted a threat
to the dominant classes at the political level, we begin to examine in
this chapter how in the course of defending the political interests of
the power bloc, a) various state departments became involved in
intervening in the process of class formation to ensure the assignment of 'poor whites' rather than Africans to particular places
in the division of labour, and, b) racially discriminatory 'industrial
relations' apparatuses came to be created to institutionalise and contain the struggles of white wage-earning employees.

We begin by noting that since both the 'poor white problem' and
the struggles of white wage-earning employees had their origins in
capitalist social relations, both were subject to the cyclical fluctuations of capitalist development. It was during periods of reduced
profitability that the struggles between mining capital and its white
wage employees were at their height. And it was during recessions—
some of which had their origins in the struggles in the mining industry
and some of which did not—that the numbers of unemployed 'poor
whites' increased most.

As the Table shows, in the period 1900—1919 (the period covered
in this chapter) there were three such phases of recession/heightened
struggle between capital and white wage-earners. The first began in
1906 and lasted until about 1909, and had several causes. One was
the contraction in the market for agricultural commodities following
the withdrawal of the British occupying forces, and another the fall

Table 8 *Selected statistics showing periods of heightened class struggle between capital and white wage-earners, and increased 'poor white' unemployment.*

	Government labour bureaux numbers of whites registered and percentage placed in employment			Numbers of whites on strike and days lost through white strikes		Goldmining industry 'working profit' per ton milled (pence)
	Cape		*Transvaal*	*Numbers*	*Days lost*	
1902	2,617	69·5%			↑	49 *d.*
1903	3,945	71·3%				52
1904	1,851	78·9%		no information		54
1905	1,912	68·0%			↓	59
1906	2,004	74·8%		49	2,646	49
1907	3,787	24·6%		6,400	288,000	102
1908	4,179	17·5%		—	—	112
1909	4,089	23·4%		—	—	101
1910	4,015	40·8%	3,039	421	10,200	
1911	7,176	38·2%	Cape and	860	16,785	117
1912	6,726	40·1%	Transvaal later	884	not available	120
1913	7,286	42·5%	including	19,771	89,887	110
1914	10,632	22·2%	Natal and	21,927	160,129	98
1915	6,972	29·6%	CFS	not obtainable		101
1916	8,532	34·0%		1,275	1,420	98
1917	9,000	34·9%		3,457	18,417	90
1918	12,240	44·7%		2,547	31,636	72
1919	15,576	35·1%		7,179	209,779	66

Sources: *Annual Reports of Department of Mines Labour Division; Official Yearbooks*

in the rate of profit on mining capital partly due to the restrictions imposed on the importation of Chinese labour after 1906. The recession in agriculture led to a marked increase in the number of 'poor whites' entering the towns—estimated to have reached 5,000 in Johannesburg alone by March 1908.[1] And the fall in the rate of profit prompted mining capital to seek the changes in the labour process which led to the 1907 general strike.

The second period of recession/crisis lasted roughly from 1912 until the outbreak of war in August 1914. It began as a recession affecting manufacturing which became intensified into a general recession by the effects of the general strike in the mining industry in 1913 and the general strike on the railways in January 1914 (the latter following an attempt by the Railways Administration to impose redundancies to match the reductions in the volume of traffic).

And the third crisis—the recession of 1916—was brought about by a severe drought, which left at least 826 former bywoner families and 4,220 individuals in a state of 'destitution'.[2]

There was also a fourth crisis during the period of mining capital's hegemony—that which began in 1920 and climaxed in the armed struggle of 1922. Its effects were however sufficiently important for us to consider it in a separate chapter.

The pattern of state activity in connection both with the 'poor white problem' and with the struggles of white wage-earning employees was correspondingly also cyclical. It was during periods of crisis or recession that the political problems associated with both loomed largest and it was thus during these periods that the major new forms of state activity tended to emerge. Moreover since with the possible exception of the recession of 1916, both tended to be heightened by the same crisis/recession, new forms of state activity in respect of each tended to coincide. However, though thus related, it would facilitate our analysis here to consider each separately, returning at the end of the chapter to draw some more general conclusions.

The state and the 'poor white problem' 1900–1919

In order to understand the particular forms of state intervention in connection with 'poor white' unemployment we have to recall something of the nature of the 'poor white problem' as a 'problem' at the level of the reproduction of the political relations of the social formation. Partly, as we saw, 'poor white' unemployment became a problem for the dominant classes at the political level because the class determination of the 'poor whites' (as unemployed lumpen proletarians) led them to become involved in various practices, such as 'illicit' liquor selling which undermined specific regulations and transgressed the bourgeoisie's legal code. But that was only part of the problem. There were a number of other ways in which the existence of large numbers of unemployed whites was potentially detrimental to the political interests of the dominant classes. In the first place the very existence of large numbers of whites reduced to conditions of 'idleness' and living in close proximity to Africans was seen as having 'corrupting' effects on Africans in particular by detracting from whatever effectiveness the ideology of 'white supremacy' had as a means of maintaining control over the African dominated classes. Secondly the objective class determination of the 'poor whites' was seen as making them prone to support militant struggles by other white classes outside of the power bloc, with the possibility also that they might, under certain circumstances, come to support struggles by the African dominated classes.

Understanding the totality of the 'poor white problem' at the level of the reproduction of the political relations of domination/subordination in the social formation is the necessary basis for understanding the state's response to it. The fact that the 'problem' extended beyond the involvement of 'poor whites' in particular 'criminal' practices, and the fact that the power bloc needed some degree of actual support from all white classes in the social formation meant that the response could not involve repression alone. A 'solution' from the standpoint of the interests of the dominant classes needed to effect some transformation in the class determination and material conditions of life of the 'poor whites' which would both eliminate the various 'detrimental' class practices at their roots and create the conditions for them to emerge as a supportive class for the form of state.

And thus although the state's repressive apparatus was an integral part of the response to the 'poor white problem' throughout ('illicit' liquor sellers were, for example, the largest single category of the white prison population throughout the period[3]), almost from the time when the 'poor white problem' first made itself felt, various state apparatuses became engaged in seeking to transform the material conditions of existence of the 'poor whites' by relocating them in various places in the division of labour.

It must be emphasised that in acting in this way the state was not principally responding to the economic demands of the 'poor whites' themselves. The 'poor whites' were, at least initially, an extremely disorganised stratum with little power on their own to enforce even limited economic demands. Fundamentally the state was acting to defend the dominant classes against the adverse political and ideological consequences of 'poor whiteism' and during this early period in particular economic concessions were granted to 'poor whites' if and only if they directly furthered these objectives. This meant, for example, refusing to provide doles or other 'welfare benefits' for the unemployed even though this was apparently the direct economic demand of a number of the 'poor whites' themselves.[4] Such measures in no way served to transform the essential material conditions of existence of the 'poor whites' and were indeed regarded, in the words of one early commission, as 'worse than useless' because they did 'nothing to stimulate or improve a recipient's outlook or strengthen his character while they accustom him to spending money without earning it'.[5] Rather, therefore, state policy became concerned, in the words of the same commission with seeking ways to 'drive him (the 'poor white') to do manual labour'.[6]

The earliest forms of state activity directed to this end consisted almost exclusively of the establishment of a number of educational/training apparatuses designed to 'train' or socialise 'poor whites' to compete for manual labouring and other places in the capitalist labour market. In the Cape where the effects of the drought of 1893[7] and the rinderpest epidemic of 1896 had been particularly severe, such measures in fact date back to the late 1890s. Consequently there was by 1900 already in existence a labour bureau in the Cape Town area whose function it was to facilitate the employment of whites (although it dealt also with coloureds). And there were also in the Cape a number of 'industrial schools', some of which were run by state departments and some of which had been established by other organisations (with or without state assistance). These were institutions, according to an official definition, specifically directed at the children of 'poor whites' and others 'likely to earn their own living by manual labour'.[8] They offered no proper apprenticeship training but existed instead to 'accustom' boys 'to the atmosphere and discipline of a workshop', and girls to 'the noble vocation of home-making'; the latter being a preparation for a future either as a domestic servant or as 'the mistress of a South African home and the mother of South African children'.[9] In addition, in 1897, the state had (by means of a grant of land, subsidies and loans) assisted the Dutch Reformed Church to establish the Karkamas Labour Colony: an institution in which 'poor whites' were 'prepared' for eventual resettlement as landowners through some training in the techniques of agricultural production and a régime of strict discipline which prohibited dancing, swearing, filthy language, immorality, laziness and untidiness among others things.[10]

In the Transvaal major state intervention in connection with the 'poor white problem' dates from the recession of 1906—09. Prior to that (apart from the state's repressive apparatus) all that had really existed for coping with the effects of 'poor whiteism' were the few unco-ordinated charitable activities which had emerged in earlier recessions, and these were completely overwhelmed by the massive influx of 'poor whites' during these years.[11]

As a result of the recession of 1906—09 a number of measures were introduced into the Transvaal similar to those already in existence in the Cape. Government labour bureaux were established in the major urban areas under the direction of an official of the Department of Mines, known as the Inspector of White Labour, who was also required to 'make known any case in which employers or trade unions hinder the use of white labour'.[12] A number of industrial and agricultural schools were established and a mine training school (whose function was to train local whites to replace immigrants in supervisory places in the mines) was established at Wolhutter.

In addition to these there was also a major new innovation in the form of 'relief works'. These were introduced in 1907 and extended during 1908 following a recommendation of the Indigency Commission. Originally they too had been seen purely as a means of training 'poor whites' to compete for places in the labour market: the idea being that instead of being given doles or charity 'uneconomical white labourers' would be temporarily employed instead of Africans in selected places in the expectation that the experience derived therefrom would enhance their competitiveness in seeking permanent employment elsewhere. So as not to offer any competition to any permanent employer of unskilled white labour whatsoever, it was made clear that 'relief' employment would take place at 'a bare living wage'.[13] Conceived as such the provision of 'relief work' had originally been undertaken by a number of private capitalist employers as well as by departments of the state. Included among these were even some members of the Chamber of Mines, who from about 1907 to 1910 took a number of unskilled whites as lashers and trammers— on the firm understanding that the employment of whites in such places was to be temporary.[14] Indeed, at first (from 1907 to 1909) even the co-ordination of 'relief work' programmes had been undertaken by a committee of 'private' capitalists (the Rand Unemployed Investigation Committee) rather than by a Department of the State.[15]

This early concentration on educational/training apparatuses as a means of placing 'poor whites' in wage-earning employment was partly a reflection of the real necessity to accept the 'dull compulsion' of the operation of the law of value. But the near exclusive reliance on such apparatuses was also partly a reflection of the way in which the origins of the 'poor white problem' were accounted for in the dominant ideology. Naturally enough this could not be an account based on any critical analysis of the structures of South African capitalism so instead the determining factors were located in various 'inadequacies' in the socialisation of the 'poor whites'; in particular in their alleged abnormal aversion to manual work ('Kaffirs' work') derived from 'the aristocratic relation between white and black races'.[16]

But since, as we argued in the last chapter, the fundamental causes of 'poor white' unemployment lay in the structures of South African capitalism and in particular in the structures associated with the migrant labour system and the minimisation of the value of African labour power, measures concerned with the socialisation/training of 'poor whites' though undoubtedly a necessary part of any solution to the 'poor white problem' could not be and were not sufficient on their own. Indeed the heavy emphasis in the early commission reports on blaming the 'poor whites' for their own plight (much modified in later reports which referred to an 'increased readiness' on the part of the 'poor whites' to perform manual labour[17]) produced its own contradiction. As several of the early Labour Reports observed, it helped to foster a prejudice among private capitalist employers against government labour bureaux and industrial schools (which became regarded as institutions for the more backward) making it more difficult for the state to place those who had passed through these institutions in 'private employment'.[18]

It was inevitable therefore that the state's struggle to defend the political interests of the dominant classes had to involve some attempt to extend the number of places in the division of labour 'available' to unskilled whites beyond the limits imposed by the 'free' operation of the capitalist labour market (though of course always within the constraints imposed by the state's prime imperative to guarantee the essential conditions necessary for capital accumulation). On the one hand this involved state departments in their capacity as employers gradually (almost imperceptibly at first) abandoning the 'logic' of the capitalist labour market and instead marking out various tasks as exclusively for whites (a process which involved dismissing previous black incumbents). This was a process which began towards the end of the recession of 1906–09 after it had become apparent that 'relief works' were to become a more or less permanent feature of the social formation. Once this was clear private capitalist employers began progressively to withdraw from the scheme and the task of providing 'relief work' increasingly passed to departments of the state. Originally they too had been considered as fulfilling this function on a purely temporary basis, but as the 'poor white problem' persisted, several tasks became effectively designated as the more or less permanent preserve of white 'relief workers'. Eventually, in some departments certain tasks came to be designated as tasks to be performed by full time white labourers. Although by 1919 this tendency was evident in departments concerned with road construction, drainage schemes, and other public works[19] it was most advanced in, and therefore most vividly illustrated by, the case of the railways.

Prior to October 1907 the 'employment policies' of the Railways Administration were more or less identical to those of most private capitalist employers, that is to say, migrant African workers were employed in most categories of unskilled labouring work. In fact during the period 1902–03 the Railways Administration had carried out an 'experiment with white labour' similar in form to those carried out in the mines from which it had, like the mining capitalists, drawn the conclusion that the employment of whites as unskilled labourers was 'economically impossible'.[20] During the recession of 1906–09 however, as part of the new Transvaal 'Responsible' Government's programme for dealing with the effects of 'poor whiteism' a number of Africans were replaced by 'poor whites' on open line maintenance and new construction work. This was begun cautiously as an 'experiment' in the Volksrust area in October 1907, but by 1908 it had spread throughout the Transvaal and Orange Free State, and was also introduced into the Cape in 1909.

As with the other measures introduced at the time this was originally conceived of as a temporary measure 'necessary' only for the duration of the immediate crisis after which it was envisaged that the railways would revert to their original employment policy. But this was not to be. With the persistence of the 'poor white problem' beyond the immediate crisis, 'the cost per mile of maintenance by whites and natives' was eventually declared to be 'an extinct comparison . . . in a white man's country'[21] and unskilled 'uneconomic' white labourers became a more or less permanent part of the railway's labour force, as the following table shows.

Table 9[22]   *Number of unskilled whites employed as labourers on maintenance and new construction*

1907	approx. 300	1912	5,316	1917	4,306
1908	1,281	1913	4,008	1918	4,441
1909	2,774	1914	5,168	1919	4,636
1910	4,022	1915	4,451		
1911	3,876	1916	4,200		

Moreover, once some sort of 'white labour policy' was recognised as more or less permanent, changes were made to provide for more permanent terms of employment. This began with the new schedule introduced on 1st April 1910. Under it unskilled whites were still taken on in the first instance as 'relief workers' (i.e. as temporary employees paid 3s. 4d. a day plus rations—a rate maintained at a level low enough so as not to entice bywoners or employees from the rural areas[23]). But the new schedule also provided for periodic increments for those who remained in the task, and those who were considered 'suitable' also became eligible after two years for reassignment to one of the newly created permanent white labouring posts or to other permanent posts such as learner shunter, learner guard, engine cleaner, learner ganger, checker or porter.[24] By 1915 3,068 white 'relief workers' had been reassigned to such places.[25] And under amendments made in 1917 and 1919 the scope for such 'promotions' was widened by a reduction in the original two year probationary period to one year and six months respectively.[26]

In addition to the changes in the employment policies of state departments, the state also became involved, from the time of the crisis of 1906–09, in pressurising private capitalist employers (other than those in the goldmining industry) to adopt a 'white labour policy' in respect of particular functions and places as well. Apart from the general propaganda activities of the Inspectorate of White Labour, which included a (not very successful) campaign to encourage the utilisation of white apprentices in place of unskilled Africans[27] these pressures also began to include more direct forms of coercion. Early examples of this included the introduction in 1910 of municipal health (*sic*) regulations which compelled the Johannesburg abbatoirs to employ whites only, and the use of officials to cajole bakeries and hospitals to do the same—again on alleged health grounds.[28] Another similar measure was the introduction, on the recommendation of the 1910–1912 Trade and Industries Commission, of a clause into the 1914 Customs Tariff Act which made the granting of the (not very extensive) tariff protection provided for in the Act dependent upon an applicant employing a 'fair amount of white labour'.[29]

With the recession beginning in 1912 however the major emphasis of state activity in connection with the 'poor white problem' began to shift somewhat. As we indicated earlier the recession of 1912–14 began as a recession affecting manufacturing industry, particularly in the interior,[30] whose effects were greatly intensified by the effects of the 1913 and 1914 strikes. Under conditions where the overall number of 'poor white' unemployed were being increased state departments concerned with the 'poor white problem' began to seek ways to supplement their existing package of measures and in particular, with the number of available places in urban employment contracting, began to seek ways of reassigning 'poor whites' to places in the rural dominant classes. This represented a partial reversal of previous policies. Hitherto, apart from providing some assistance to the Karkamas Labour Colony and administering agricultural schools, state departments had not been much involved in seeking to relocate 'poor whites' in such places, principally because the dominant classes (or at least the hegemonic fraction) saw the fact of their proletarianisation as demonstrating their inherent 'unsuitability' for such places.[31]

The first moves towards changing that position came with the passage of the Land Settlements Act in 1912. Like many Acts of parliament the Land Settlements Act was actually a measure which had a number of purposes. One of these certainly was to co-ordinate and extend the various 'closer settlement' schemes whose purpose was to enlarge the white rural population by encouraging the settlement of white immigrants with sufficient funds to purchase land at one fifth of its market price (the state paying the remaining four-fifths). But for our purposes the 1912 Act's major importance was that it was the first major piece of legislation to provide for the 'resettlement' of 'poor whites' with no access to any funds whatsoever. 'Suitable applicants' (such as the former inmates of Labour Colonies) were given the opportunity to lease land for a five year probationary period, rent free for the first year and a minimal rent thereafter with the further option of purchasing on the same terms as other settlers or of extending their lease.[32]

Complementing the 1912 Act was, of course, the 1913 Land Act which in addition to its other functions and purposes increased the area of land available for white settlement by removing large numbers of African 'squatters' from land in what became designated as the 'white' rural areas.[33]

In fact from the time of the recession of 1912–13 until the time of the drought of 1916, 'resettlement' in the 'white' rural areas became the major focus of the state's activities in connection with the 'poor white problem' (although of course all the other previously described measures were continued and extended as well). Out of twelve recommendations put forward in the 1913 'Select Committee Report on European Employment and Labour Conditions' seven (all accepted) were in some way connected with the placement of 'poor whites' on the land. Most of these were concerned with the reassignment of 'poor whites' to places as landowners (through extending the Land Settlements scheme, agricultural training schemes etc.).[34] But there was also a further recommendation: that the state initiate an intensive campaign aimed at assigning 'poor whites' to wage-earning places within agriculture.

This had, at the particular conjuncture, become feasible in a way in which it had not been earlier because of the changes which were occurring in the labour process within agriculture. Essentially the implementation of the 1913 Land Act had had the effect of accelerating the transition from the 'squatter peasant' to the 'labour tenant' form of production. And this meant, following Morris' analysis,[35] accelerating the transition from a pre-capitalist form of production, under which the landowner extracted a labour rent, to a capitalist form of production, under which the landowner began to assume a more direct control over the labour process. As a capitalist relation involving a far greater degree of control within the labour process itself, the labour tenant system required a more extensive utilisation of employees performing the functions of surveillance and control. And there was thus, during this period of accelerated transition, an increase in the demand for supervisors and overseers.[36]

Prior to the state's intervention, it was by no means the case that all or even most of these places automatically went to whites. On the contrary in several areas there were a number of coloureds and even Africans occupying these places.[37] The task of implementing the Select Committee's recommendations and ensuring that they went to an increasing extent to whites fell initially to the staff of the White Labour Superintendent of the railways. Between 1913 and 1916 they established a number of committees and labour bureaux, organised meetings and disseminated propaganda aimed at getting farmers to replace blacks in these places with 'poor whites', and indeed they seem to have had a certain amount of 'success' in this regard. At any rate in his report submitted in 1916 the Superintendent found it 'gratifying to be able to report' that partly as a result of his department's activities some 3,000 whites had been placed in wage-earning employment in agriculture in the three years since 1913.[38]

But this emphasis on reassigning 'poor whites' to places in agriculture was comparatively shortlived. With the increasing spread of capitalist relations in agriculture and the consequent reduction in the number of 'bywoners', the basic trend was towards reducing rather than increasing the number of places in agriculture available to 'poor whites', and this was dramatically highlighted by the drought of 1916 which, as we have seen, wiped out upwards of 5,000 bywoners (more than the total number of whites placed in wage-earning employment in the sector between 1913 and 1916). Certainly in the period after 1916 the number of new places being created in the agricultural division of labour 'suitable' for 'poor whites' was minimal. As the 1919 Labour Division Report put it,

. . . the number of demands from farmers for white labourers is very small, and in most cases, wages offered are so insignificant that it is impossible either to recommend or induce the men to engage.[39]

And, under these circumstances, although all the measures concerned with placing 'poor whites' in agriculture (rural labour bureaux, land settlement schemes, agricultural schools, etc.) were continued, indeed extended,[40] in the period after the 1916 drought the major focus of state activity in connection with the 'poor white problem' began to shift back towards industry and state departments.

There was also another factor determining the shift in emphasis back to industry after 1916—the measure of industrial development which took place during World War I. As is well known, the disruption of trade routes during World War I had had the effect of providing a degree of 'artificial protection' from foreign competition which enabled local South African manufacturing capitalists to expand their operations. Total manufacturing output, which had been estimated at £17 million in 1911, rose to £35,699,000 by 1915–16 and rose again to £76,849,000 in 1919–20. There had also been, corresponding with the increase in output, an increase in the numbers employed in manufacturing industry. Official statistics show a 34·6 per cent increase from the estimated 66,000 employed in 1911 to 88,844 employed in 1915–16, and an increase of 40·4 per cent to 124,702 by 1919–20.[41]

As well as providing an opportunity for the state to expand its existing range of activities directed at placing whites in unskilled places, the particular circumstances under which this development took place enabled it to extend its activities in a direction which had hitherto not been particularly successful. Despite the expansion of productive activity, there was not, during the World War I period, any particularly marked shift to mechanisation. Indeed if the money value of machinery per employee can be taken as an index of the average organic composition of capital, then official statistics show a slight decline from £94·7 in 1915–16 (the time of the first full industrial census) to £94·4 in 1919–20.[42] By and large then, South African industry had not yet reached the stage of machinofacture. Its labour processes therefore still depended upon artisan craft workers, but because of the disruption of the war, it was finding it increasingly difficult to import skilled labour power from overseas.

Under these circumstances the state became involved in creating apparatuses for the production of skilled artisan labour power from among the ranks of the 'poor whites', something at which as we have seen it had previously not been particularly successful. A Juvenile Affairs Board was established in Durban in 1914 and similar bodies became established in most centres during 1915 and 1916. According to one of their chairmen, their function was to gain 'industrial benefit from them (the poor whites)' by giving them training which would 'make men and women of them, and not the kind of industrial half breeds we have tended to produce (hitherto)'.[43] They organised and gave advice about the establishment of apprenticeship schemes, and operated Juvenile Labour Bureaux to direct white school leavers into forms of employment where they could receive such training.

Actually, as was the case with the earlier 'relief works', these Juvenile Affairs Boards were in the first instance established by 'concerned citizens', and their functions were not in fact formally appropriated by the state until the passing of an Act in 1921. Nevertheless almost from their inception state departments rendered them various forms of assistance and certainly they had by 1919 become an integral part of state policies in connection with the 'poor white problem'.

To summarise this section: we have seen how in the course of its struggle against the political threats posed by the 'poor white problem' the state had become involved in a wide range of activities concerned with ensuring the assignment of whites rather than blacks to certain places in the social division of labour (as landowners, supervisors, skilled and unskilled manual workers). It had intensified its efforts during periods of recession when the effects of 'poor whiteism' were heightened by the increased numbers, and it had taken advantage of any opportunities created by changes in the labour process in particular sectors. As a consequence, by the year 1919 there were a number of educational/training apparatuses designed to give whites an advantage over blacks in competing for skilled and unskilled places. A number of state departments had adopted a policy of reserving particular unskilled labouring places for whites only. The state had applied various forms of persuasion/ coercion to get private capitalist employers (other than those in the mining industry) to do the same. And steps had been taken to re-assign 'poor whites' to places in the rural dominant classes.

As a direct result of these measures there were by the year 1919 at least:

4,636 whites working on the railways as unskilled labourers;

3,068 plus white ex-relief workers employed on the railways in permanent places;

1,182 whites working on afforestation schemes and other 'relief works';

3,000 odd whites occupying supervisory and other wage-earning places in agriculture;

1,736 occupying places as settler landowners under the 1912 Land Settlement Act.[44]

The number occupying places in manufacturing industry as a direct result of these measures is more difficult to estimate. But by 1919 Juvenile Affairs Boards were placing 1,044 white youths in private employment.[45] And, according to one contemporary analysis, 'colour bar' measures operating in the Transvaal and Orange Free State were largely responsible for the greater proportion of whites employed in manufacturing in those provinces: an extra seven per hundred compared to the Cape, which works out in 1919 at approximately an extra 1,200.[46] The total amount expended on placing these—upwards of 13,167 whites—in such places had, as Appendix 2 shows, by 1919—20 reached £1,906,404, an amount nearly twelve times the £155,152 expended for the purpose in 1910—11.

The state and the struggles of white wage-earning employees 1900—1919

The process by which racially discriminatory 'industrial relations' apparatuses emerged in response to the struggles of white wage-earning employees was rather more complex. Until 1909 and to a lesser extent from 1909 to 1914 the basic response of all the major capitalist fractions and of the state to these struggles can, broadly speaking, be characterised as directly repressive.

This is not of course to say that it was only through repression that the state related to white wage-earners and neither is it to say that the repression directed at white wage-earners was of the same degree or intensity as that directed at blacks. On the contrary a number of factors (such as the level of economic power[47] achieved by certain fractions of the white wage-earning classes, and the power bloc's need for a white wage-earning supportive class) had obliged the state to respond to struggles by guaranteeing certain of the economic demands of white wage-earning employees from a very early period. For example, throughout the late nineteenth and early twentieth centuries laws had been passed dealing with safety,[48] workmen's compensation,[49] miners' phthisis,[50] and most importantly, job colour bars. The latter had first been introduced in respect of blasting by a law of 1893 and was added to by laws passed in 1896, 1897 and 1898 until by the war of 1899 they covered blasting, the operating of winding and other machinery and the jobs performed by banksmen and onsetters.[51] They were continued under the Crown Colony administration after the war and were indeed added to by the 1904 Transvaal Labour Importation Ordinance (repealed in 1907) which, as part of mining capital's attempt to gain the support of its white employees for the importation of Chinese labourers, reserved a wide range of artisan, supervisory and even some 'semi-skilled' jobs for whites only.[52] And they were, finally, consolidated in a schedule to the 1911 Mines and Works Act.[53] Moreover the same political considerations had obliged the state to exercise a degree of restraint in the deployment of its repressive apparatus against white wage-earners. For example, no attempt was ever made to actually proscribe trade unions; and the (technically 'colour blind') Masters and Servants Laws,[54] which were frequently used to prosecute African strikers under clauses prohibiting the breaking of employment contracts, desertion, or the 'coercion' of employers (*sic*), were seldom if ever used against white strikers.[55]

Nevertheless, despite all of the above, the basic initial response to the struggles waged by white wage-earning employees by the dominant classes and the state, acting to serve their political interests, can still broadly be described as repressive. Trade unions were not officially recognised in the mining industry, in state departments or in most of the other industries where they had succeeded in establishing themselves, and indeed every effort was made by capitalist employers to avoid negotiating with them or at least to avoid according them representative status—a policy which the dominant ideology described as 'supporting free labour'.[56] Furthermore, when strikes actually broke out in this early period the state's basic response was to seek to defend the interests of the dominant class or classes concerned by deploying its repressive apparatus to defeat the strikers as quickly as possible. Laws prohibiting meetings 'where public peace and safety are endangered' were frequently used to break up pickets and strike meetings.[57] Strike breakers were, as well as being protected from pickets by troops and police, positively encouraged by leading members of the government.[58] And strike leaders were victimised by means of, *inter alia*, blacklisting, jailing, and even, on one occasion, the chartering of a boat to transport a number of them to England.

However, despite these efforts the dominant classes did not succeed in preventing trade union combination among whites. From its beginnings with the founding of the first union in 1881, white trade union membership in the Transvaal alone increased to 2,425 in

1906 and to 14,845 in 1913.[59] Indeed, in some cases the fact that capital and the state were seen to be actively engaged in undermining trade union combination actually made unions stronger. For example, as a direct result of the Chamber of Mines virulent anti-union stance during the 1913 strike, membership of the Transvaal Miners Association increased from 2,800 on 31.12.12 to 6,700 on 31.12.13.[60] Nor did these policies prevent the outbreak of strikes. Strikes by whites occurred throughout the 1880s and 1890s; and during the period from 1900–1914, apart from the general strikes in the mines (in 1907 and 1913) and on the railways (in 1914) there were important strikes by Natal railmen in 1909, and Johannesburg tramwaymen in 1911, as well as smaller strikes by, *inter alia*, cigarette makers, stone-masons and printers.[61]

It was this failure to prevent strikes or combination by white wage-earners through repression, and the already discussed effects which strikes by whites were seen to be having on struggles by Africans, which led to the emergence of racially discriminatory 'industrial relations' apparatuses. These did not however come about through any sudden inspired move on the part of the hegemonic fraction or governing class. The apparatuses in question were created in class struggle—were indeed the condensation of particular class struggles—and their emergence therefore reflected the different phases and stages of that struggle. In particular, since, as we have already noted, it was the strikes in the mining industry which were the largest and most disruptive and therefore the most serious in terms of their political implications, it was after struggles in the mining industry that the most significant moves tended to be made.

The first real signs of a move in this direction came after the 1907 strike. In fact the first proposals emerged during the course of that strike, when strike leaders appealed to the newly installed 'Responsible Government' to act as a 'mediator' and introduce industrial relations legislation to compel mining capital to agree to a compromise.[62] Though this appeal was rejected at the time by a mining capitalist fraction determined to enforce its economic demands, the degree of disruption caused during the strike prompted a reconsideration by the dominant classes and the hegemonic fraction during the period immediately after. At the time when they were reconsidering their position on this question, there were three main types of 'industrial relations' systems already operational elsewhere in the world. The first was the Australasian system of 'voluntary conciliation and compulsory awards'; the second the French system of 'voluntary conciliation'; and the third the Canadian system of 'compulsory conciliation'.

The system favoured by the South African Labour Party and called for by the strike leaders during the 1907 strike was the Australasian system, particularly the system which had operated in New Zealand since 1894. This provided for a statutorily regulated procedure of negotiation backed up by the right of appeal to a judicial body—called an arbitration court. Under it if the two parties in an industrial dispute failed to reach an agreement about wages or conditions through a process of bargaining in a conciliation board, either party could approach the arbitration court which was empowered to make a legally binding award.[63] Although like all such apparatuses of the bourgeois state, the arbitration court system was in the last analysis a mechanism to forestall political class struggle by the working class—and indeed in New Zealand's case it reduced strikes and 'political extremism' dramatically[64]—until about 1906 it had, among trade unionists, whose sights were raised no higher than wage bargaining within capitalist society, the reputation as the example *par excellence* of 'progressive working class' legislation.[65] This was mainly due to the fact that the arbitration courts had, until the New Zealand recession of 1906, generally made their awards by splitting the difference between the claim of the trade union and the counter claim of the employer (after having ascertained that this was compatible with profitability); a process which resulted in the kind of compromise wage increases to which reformist trade unionists had become inured.[66]

Capital in South Africa, particularly but not only mining capital, was not however prepared to concede such a system for two main reasons. First, the arbitration courts were seen as making rather more concessions to the economic demands of labour than capital in South Africa was at the time prepared to concede. And secondly, the lack of any specific prohibition or suspension of the right to strike was regarded as rendering it ineffective in preventing strikes.[67] Since, as we have already seen, strikes by white wage-earners were considered a particularly serious threat to the stability of the social formation on account of their potential effects on Africans, the latter was seen as a particularly serious omission. It was in fact also the reason why the French system—which simply provided for the statutory regulation of bargaining procedures—was rejected as well.[68]

Instead the dominant classes turned to the Canadian system of 'compulsory conciliation'. This system had been introduced into Canada after a series of strikes on the railways and in the Alberta mines, through the 1907 'Lemieux Act'. Under this Act employers were obliged to give the employees 30 days' notice of any change which they proposed making in wages or working conditions and employees were obliged to give 30 days' notice of any demands which they intended to make. During this 30 day period strikes or lockouts were prohibited and either party could apply for a conciliation board to be set up. If a government minister was satisfied that a dispute existed, he could then appoint a conciliation board—a body consisting of representatives of the two sides chaired by a state official —which would attempt to reach a compromise solution. There was however no compulsion on either party to accept the findings of a conciliation board, and if these were rejected a strike could then take place.[69]

When this Act was introduced in Canada it was met by protest strikes in Western coalfields and in Western Calgary, principally because the legally enforced suspension of the right to strike was (rightly) regarded as weakening the power of wage-earners in struggle through preventing them 'taking advantage of the best moment for securing better conditions' while giving capital time to prepare its counter moves.[70] Indeed the conditions of class struggle in Canada were such that the Act could only be made to apply to a limited range of industries and occupations designated essential services, and, moreover, were seen in Britain as such that a senior civil servant was obliged to report in 1912 to the effect that whilst he much admired the principles of the Canadian Act he did not think it would be possible to introduce it into Britain—at least so long as it contained clauses prohibiting strikes.[71]

It is the fundamental principles embodied in this Act which have formed the basis of South African 'industrial conciliation' legislation (both in past and present). In fact in the first piece of 'industrial relations' legislation passed in South Africa—the Transvaal Industrial Disputes Prevention Act of 1909[72]—most of the operative clauses dealing with the establishment of conciliation boards and the prohibition of strikes were reproduced verbatim from the Canadian Act. There were however two main differences in the Transvaal version. First, in accordance with capital's general stance towards unions at the time, it did not recognise any special negotiating role for trade unions. Unions were entitled to apply for the establishment of a conciliation board, but then so was any other group of ten or more 'employees'.[73]

The second major difference in the Transvaal Act was its definition of employee which read 'Any *white* person engaged by an employer to perform . . . work.'[74]

Despite the fact that most Transvaal trade unions had racially discriminatory membership rules, this racially discriminatory definition of employee was there at the insistence of capital rather than 'white labour'. In fact the white trade unions and the Labour Party made a mild plea for the Act to be applied to employees of all races —mainly because they recognised to some extent that the more capital was able to hold down the wage levels of Africans the more vulnerable white employees were to replacement by Africans.[75] But capital, and in particular mining capital, would have none of it. Maintaining the low wage levels of African workers was the *sine qua non* for capital accumulation, particularly in the mining industry, and if therefore they were obliged by the conditions of class struggle to make concessions to white wage-earners, this would have to be through a racially discriminatory system. Furthermore it was also, as they clearly recognised, in their interests to maintain and reinforce the isolation of white from black wage-earners and not to undermine it in any way by bringing the two together in any non-discriminatory statutory system. F. D. P. Chaplin, a mining capitalist and a member of the Progressive Party, thus spoke in the second reading debate as follows:

> As regarded the extension of the scope of the Bill to coloured (i.e. African—R.D.) labour . . . such a proposal would lead to the nullification of the purposes of the bill. To think that a number of natives of the class employed in this country could hang up an industrial concern seemed highly absurd (hear, hear) . . . He was not prepared to see the provisions of the Bill extended to natives.[76]

And he was echoed by Sir George Farrar, a former president of the Chamber of Mines, who said,

> Any bill that brought contentment to the working classes was to be commended . . . (But) *I do think the maintenance of the division between the unskilled coloured labourer and the white labourer should be continued*, and I think the application of this bill to coloured labourers is absolutely unnecessary . . . They are controlled by the Native Affairs Department.[77]

The 1909 Act itself was however only of fairly limited benefit in the struggle by the dominant classes to contain the struggles of white wage-earners. It did possibly prevent a few strikes, for instance by mine mechanics over the dismissal of a colleague, printers over a demand for union recognition and a closed shop, and masons over wages; and it was used to prosecute the members of the Industrial Workers of the World (IWW) who led the 1911 Johannesburg tramways strike.[78] But it did not succeed in gaining the necessary degree of 'acceptance' among white wage-earners which such ideological apparatuses need to be really effective. This was mainly because the dominant classes were still hesitant about whether their political interests really demanded that they make the kind of economic concessions which would make the system appear 'fair'. For example, out of the seven applications for conciliation boards made between

1910 and 1912, two were refused by the minister, two resulted in sittings which led to no concession, one resulted in a sitting followed by a lost strike, and only two were followed by concessions.[79] Moreover even where concessions were agreed at a conciliation board sitting there was no compulsion on individual capitalists to implement them, and there were frequently lengthy delays between acceptance of a request for a board and its actual appointment.[80] In short the Act was administered in a fashion which seriously undermined its potential credibility among white wage-earners, and it was therefore in many cases rejected by them. For example, the Johannesburg tramwaymen who struck in 1911, made their move without ever considering any application for a conciliation board.

But the Act's real demise came with the events leading up to the 1913 strike, during which mining capital gave a particularly blatant demonstration of its determination not to be bound by the Act's provisions unless it saw fit. Under the provisions of the Act an employer was supposed to give 30 days' notice of any change in wages or conditions. In May 1913 however, the management of the New Kleinfontein Mine cancelled a half day holiday without giving the statutory notice. When the employees approached the Inspector of White Labour they were told that as no penalty applied to that section of the Act he was prepared to do nothing. At this point the South African Industrial Federation intervened and called on the Chamber of Mines to enter into negotiation, but the Chamber refused, sticking to its position that the unions 'represented only a minority of the employees on the mines and had no mandate to represent the general body of workmen'.[81] Eventually over this question of non-recognition a general strike broke out on the mines in July 1913. And, what is more, as a direct result of the effects of the 1913 strike in heightening the recession of the period, it was followed by another general strike—this time on the railways—within less than six months.

Although both these strikes were put down by the use of troops, martial law and various other repressive devices, they were, as we saw in the last chapter, viewed with particular alarm by the dominant classes because of the extensive redeployment of forces required and (in 1913 especially) their catalytic effects on struggles by African workers. Their effect on the dominant classes was therefore to emphasise both that there could indeed be a contradiction between their economic and political class interests and that it had at last become necessary to recognise the primacy of their political interests.

But as well as facing a situation of general 'unrest' in which they needed to make new initiatives to defend their political interests, the dominant classes also faced, in the wake of the 1913–14 strikes, a situation which was qualitatively different in one important respect. The state's role during these strikes had severely undermined whatever efficacy the ideology of 'free labour' had had in preventing trade union combination. During 1913 trade union membership expanded rapidly: reaching by the end of the year a total in the Transvaal alone of 14,845 compared to the 9,876 at the end of the previous year.[82] Moreover this increase in membership was matched by an increase in the level of commitment by white wage-earners to trade unions. As the Secretary of Mines put it in his 1913 Report,

> It is no exaggeration to say that to many of these men—and to those often of the strongest character—loyalty to their union has taken the place of loyalty to their Government or to their employers.[83]

What is more, the struggles of 1913 and 1914 had apparently strengthened the position within unions of syndicalists. Almost half of the same Report by the Secretary of Mines was given over to a lengthy diatribe against the 'evils' of syndicalism and other doctrines based upon 'the debatable teachings in regard to economic matters that the interests of capital and labour are always opposed'.[84] It had, in short, become no longer feasible for the dominant classes to continue trying to undermine trade union combination as such. Instead the defence of their political interests demanded that they begin to consider a strategy based on incorporating and institutionalising the white trade union movement. In the aftermath of the 1913–14 strikes therefore views began to be expressed about how recognition of unions could be made compatible with, indeed advance, the interests of capital. For example the Governor General wrote in a confidential despatch,

The mineowners attitude has hampered the development of unions. It has led the steadier and more competent men to keep aloof, and has allowed Unions to come largely under the control of irresponsible agitators. But it has also reacted unfavourably on the mineowners themselves. *In their own interests, if for no other reason, the companies should have recognized the men's organizations. For a strong organization of employees is the best safeguard of the interests of employers; it ensures them of a representative and therefore responsible body of men with whom they can negotiate, and it induces mutual confidence and understanding . . . The old order of autocratic employers and weak unrecognized unions can survive no longer . . .* a unique opportunity is offered to the Government for strong, wise action to regulate the relations between masters and men.[85]

And similar views were expressed in the Report of a Commission which recommended the recognition of white trade unions as follows:

Recognition creates responsibility . . . the organization of labour is an aid to the authority of a conciliation board because much labour can then be represented as a whole and dealt with as a whole. *Moreover the (trade union—RD) official is more likely to take the business point of view*, and examine the situation calmly, than the workman who has some personal grievance, rankling in his mind. Finally it is certain that, recognized or not, labour organization will continue among white men. All experience proves it, and experience proves also that organization in the open, *made sober by recognition*, is a very different thing from organization which has to fight against contempt or antagonism and may be compelled to keep its membership secret. It is the latter form of trade union which is so peculiarly liable to foster extreme and even revolutionary doctrines.[86]

One of the first moves taken to give effect to this new strategy was the publication of a new Bill—the Industrial Disputes Prevention Bill of 1914.[87] Like the 1909 Act this bill too was based on the

Canadian principle of 'compulsory conciliation'.[88] That is to say strikes were prohibited until (in this case 30 days after) a process of negotiation had been completed. It also, like the 1909 Act, excluded from the definition of employee any person 'whose contract of service is regulated by the Native Pass Laws and Regulations . . . etc.'[89] i.e. Africans.

But the new Bill did make procedures more flexible and it did, in accordance with the political necessities of the time, provide for a much greater degree of controlled recognition of trade unions. Two types of negotiating bodies were now provided for. The first, 'dispute boards' were like the conciliation boards in the 1909 Act, *ad hoc* bodies to be set up in the event of particular disputes on application by a registered trade union (see below), by a general meeting of employees, or by employers. However, in the event of there being no application the initiative in the establishment of such bodies could, under this Bill, also be taken by state officials. But the second type of negotiating body provided for—'standing conciliation boards'— represented a new departure. These were to be permanently existing apparatuses within which registered trade unions and employers would negotiate over a range of economic issues without there necessarily being a statutory dispute. The Bill also provided—at the insistence of mining capital[90]—for the registration of trade unions which had 'acceptable' constitutions and methods of electing officials. Registration was not to be made compulsory as such but it was the precondition for recognition within any of the above described procedures. Finally, the Bill provided that, if both parties agreed, agreements could be made legally enforceable.

However, though the 1914 Bill did pass through the House of Assembly it never became law. Technically this was because it did not reach the Senate before the end of the parliamentary session and therefore lapsed.[91] But there was more to it than that. One of the reasons why the Bill did not reach the Senate was that the Labour Party vigorously opposed it during its early stages, thus delaying its passage. As we saw previously, the 'white labour movement' emerged from the 1913–14 strikes still militant and relatively strong. It was not prepared to accept a measure which was widely recognised as a device to protect capital's interests and the Labour Party was obliged, at least to some extent, to reflect that position in parliament. In the Second Reading Debate, even Cresswell (recently returned from a month's imprisonment for addressing a meeting during the 1914 strike) denounced the Bill in the following terms:

> Reforms which sought merely to patch up the existing system were comparatively little use. The Labour Party members' view of this legislation was that they were bound to oppose it in every way in their power.[92]

But the absence of a specific statute did not deter the dominant classes from their new course of realising their class interests through attempting to incorporate the white trade unions into institutionalised bargaining procedures. However, instead of seeking this end at the level of the state, capital began, with the assistance of state departments, to seek to achieve the same ends at the industrial level. In 1915 the Chamber of Mines, whose president publicly declared that he 'regret(ed) that it (the 1914 Bill) was not placed on the Statute Book',[93] announced that from then onwards it would recognise trade unions. In 1916 it entered into an agreement with the Engine Drivers association to establish a conciliation boards system. And in 1917 it entered into an agreement with the South African Industrial Federation, representing most of the mining unions, to establish boards of reference. These were joint bodies consisting of representatives of the trades unions and of the Chamber of Mines, empowered to hear appeals and make rulings about a range of immediate grievances referred to them by white employees.[94] Between 1917 and 1919 they heard appeals dealing with such matters as victimisation by foremen against union members or former militants, 'unfair dismissals', 'bullying attitudes' of foremen, and the employment of Africans in 'white jobs'. Moreover, unlike earlier bodies, in a number of cases these boards made rulings which amounted to some concession to the appellant.[95]

In addition to the boards of reference there was also 'a standing nucleus' consisting of the Actuary and Labour Adviser to the Chamber of Mines and the Secretary of the South African Industrial

Federation whose role was to oversee the functioning of these bodies and supervise wage negotiation.[96] There were similar moves in other industries. For example, in 1918 an agreement was reached to establish a non-statutory standing conciliation board, called an industrial council, in the printing industry.[97]

Although the establishment of such apparatuses did not eliminate strikes altogether, there was certainly a noticeable reduction in the numbers and intensity of strikes by whites in the years immediately following 1914, as the statistics reproduced in Table 8 show. This ability by capital to realise at the industrial level at least some of the political objectives which it had previously sought unsuccessfully to achieve through formal state intervention can probably be accounted for by two main factors. First, although the 1909 Act technically remained in force, these moves were not accompanied by any specific new prohibition on the right to strike. And second, it was due in large measure to the effects of World War I. As in most other belligerent social formations, the imperialist war divided the 'white labour movement' in South Africa into two factions: those who opposed the war (the 'War on Warites') and those who supported 'their' bourgeoisie's position on the war. Also as in most other social formations, the effect of the intensification of the ideology of patriotism during the war was such that in the short run at least it reinforced the position of those who supported the war, and correspondingly weakened the position of those who opposed it. In South Africa, after a brief struggle, the 'war on warites' found themselves excluded from the Labour Party and considerably weakened within the trade union movement.[98] Since the militants on the war question were in many cases also the militants on industrial questions, the effect of the war was thus that it enhanced, at least temporarily, the position of 'moderates'.

That the special conditions of the war had played at least some part in reducing the number of strikes was in fact widely recognised by capital and its political representatives. Not surprisingly therefore at the end of the war further steps were taken to forestall the re-emergence of strikes. And in the period up until 1919 these involved further conciliatory moves towards white wage-earners.

Mining capital in particular began to try to distance itself from its past policies and to present itself to its white employees as having 'reformed'. This, for example, is clearly the theme in the following remarkable extract from a speech delivered by the president of the Chamber of Mines in 1919:

Undoubtedly the employer must take a considerable share of the blame for the hostile relations which in the past too often existed between him and his employees. For example the regrettable tendency to ca'canny . . . has to some extent sprung from the disposition of past generations of employers to cut rates when their employees seemed to be making what those employers thought—quite unreasonably—to be unduly large earnings. It is, therefore, I believe the duty of the employer to take the first step towards the establishment of friendly relations, and to show great patience if such approaches are met with suspicion which, I'm afraid we must accept—until we are able to remove it—as an inheritance from past conditions.[99]

Matching such changes in rhetoric were a number of more concrete changes. Further concessions were made to the economic demands of white wage-earners; the most important being the 'Status Quo Agreement' of September 1918 which provided that in jobs not already covered by the Mines and Works Act 'no billets which are held by European workmen should be given to coloured workmen'.[100] There were also a number of important additions to the 'conciliation' machinery. After a conference held in December 1918 it was agreed to widen the powers of the boards of reference.[101] And in 1919 a new tier was added with the recognition of shaft and shop stewards as participants in local 'grievance committees'.[102] By 1919 there were 46 boards and negotiating committees of various sorts in existence in the industry, and by 1920 the total had reached 88.[103] Indeed the period immediately following World War I was the period which saw the greatest proliferation of negotiating machinery in the industry's history, before or since.

But it was not only in the mining industry that moves towards extending the 'conciliation' apparatuses were being made. The steep rise in consumer prices immediately after World War I[104] led to the first reasonably widespread strikes by African workers. During the years 1918–1920 there were strikes by African miners, dockers, municipal workers and members of the police force among others.[105] And, under these circumstances it was clearly in the interests of the dominant classes to avoid as far as possible any possible reinforcement of strikes by African workers by strikes involving whites. The years after World War I thus saw the state acting to defend the political interests of the dominant classes through making a number of further interventions to incorporate other categories of white wage-earners into similar 'conciliation' apparatuses. For example in 1919 the Department of Mines and Industries Labour Division organised a 'National Conference' of all the major employers' and (white) employees' organisations at which a number of resolutions were passed and agreements made relating to the establishment of Joint Boards and the publication and enforcement of agreements.[106] Another move in the same general direction came with the passing of an Act in 1918[107] which provided for the establishment of wages boards empowered to make legally enforceable wage determinations covering women and juveniles employed in specified 'sweated trades'. This was essentially seen as a means of preventing strikes breaking out in industries which, being 'unorganised', could not be 'disciplined' through agreements with trade unions. And by 1919 eleven of these determinations had been made covering the boot and shoe, the printing and the dressmaking industries as well as shop assistants in certain areas.[108]

In short, by 1919 (the end of the period covered in this chapter) there had come into existence through the class struggle a wide range of apparatuses and institutions functioning on a racially discriminatory basis to regulate and institutionalise the struggles of white wage-earning employees. There were various boards operating in the mining industry, a number of councils and committees operating in other industries and wage boards acting to organise concessions to prevent strikes breaking out in the 'sweated trades' as well.

General conclusions

We have seen that in the period of mining capital's hegemony prior to 1920 the state had become involved in a number of activities in response to various forms of class practice/struggle by the 'poor white' unemployed and by various categories of white wage-earning employees. It had become involved in seeking to assign unemployed 'poor whites' to various places in the division of labour and in arranging for certain economic concessions to be made available to white wage-earning employees within a racially discriminatory institutionalised bargaining system. What we have tried to show is that these forms of state activity essentially emerged in response to particular forms of class practice/class struggle by the white wage-earning classes which posed a potential political threat to the dominant classes and that the fundamental role of the state in these struggles was therefore to defend the general interests of the power bloc against a potential political threat. Among the different fractions in the power bloc, mining capital, commercial capital, industrial capital and capitalist agriculture there was indeed, throughout the entire period, a remarkable degree of consensus both about the necessity for such state interventions and about the form they should take.

Mining capital, as represented either by its party political spokesmen or by the Chamber of Mines,[109] broadly speaking fully approved of the package of measures for dealing with the 'poor white' problem as it unfolded through its various stages. The 1906–08 Indigency Commission Report was hailed as 'first class',[110] and indeed, as we have already seen, members of the Chamber of Mines (including the president Lionel Phillips) participated during the immediate recession period in the 'relief work' activities of the Rand Unemployment Investigation Committee. The 1912 Land Settlements Bill was welcomed in principle by the Unionist Party and, after a few minor amendments, declared to be 'non contentious' and supported.[111] In 1913 Unionists were agreeing about the need to 'make a real effort' to solve the 'poor white problem' in order to 'provide for the dominance—on their merits—of the white people of this country',[112] and although they would have preferred a full commission rather than a Select Committee investigation, broadly agreed with the 1913 Committee's eventual proposals.[113] Indeed the Chamber of Mine's executive committee was particularly pleased with the 1913 Report because its 'main thrust' had been to seek a solution to the 'poor white problem' whilst explicitly acknowledging for the first time in an official report 'that the substitution of white unskilled for coloured labour (in the mines) was impossible on economic grounds'.[114] The year 1914 saw the Chamber advocating before the Transvaal Relief and Grants in Aid Commission schemes to resettle urban 'poor whites' on the land, more labour colonies and increased public spending on 'relief works'.[115] And finally the 1916 Select Committee report was welcomed by Unionist Party and Chamber alike.[116]

Industrial capital likewise broadly agreed about the necessity for a 'white labour policy' in respect of at least some places in industries other than mining,[117] as well as about the need for other policies in connection with state employment and land settlement.[118] And so too did capitalist agriculture.[119] Moreover, in the period prior to the crisis of 1920–1924 and the formation of the alliance with the Labour Party, there were comparatively few demands from the political representatives of these fractions to extend these measures. Industrial capital did sometimes (though less often than in the period 1920–24) put its case for effective tariff protection in terms of its ostensible concern to 'solve the white unemployment problem'.[120] And capitalist agriculture sometimes put its demands for agricultural subsidisation etc. in similar terms. Capitalist agriculture (or at least those elements represented after 1913 by the Nationalist Party) also sometimes called for a greater proportion of the funds allocated to land settlement to be allocated for the resettlement of 'displaced' Afrikaners rather than for the settlement of foreign immigrants.[121] But these demands or criticisms scarcely amounted to a call from these fractions for a generalised extension of state activity in connection with the 'poor white problem'. Indeed the only such call during this period came from the Labour Party and it received at the time scant support from the political representatives of national capital.[122]

Moreover it was more or less the same story in the case of state policy towards the struggles waged by white wage-earning employees. As Johnstone has shown at length[123] mining capital at this stage raised little objection to the implementation of job colour bars, and, as we have already seen, its position on trade unions and 'industrial conciliation' shifted in stages in accordance with conditions of class struggle. Capitalist agriculture was exempted from almost all 'industrial legislation' and therefore took little part in the struggles leading to the creation of the various 'industrial relations' apparatuses. And industrial capital, like mining capital, largely followed the stages of class struggle in its position on 'conciliation'. If, as Bozzoli suggests,[124] articles calling for 'industrial conciliation' began to appear in manufacturers' journals at an earlier stage than they did in mining journals, this was not reflected in any noticeably more rapid establishment of 'industrial relations' apparatuses in the industrial sector. For example, in the printing industry—for many years the 'model' sector so far as 'industrial relations' in South African manufacturing industry was concerned—the industrial council was formed in 1918 (about the same time as the boards of reference on the mines) and strikes over trade union recognition were still being conducted as late as 1911.[125]

In short, aside from a few comparatively minor differences, the fractions in the power bloc were in the period until 1919 relatively united on policies towards white wage-earning classes. What divided the dominant class fractions were matters related to the appropriation of surplus value and the trajectory of capitalist development, not matters such as those related to the maintenance of the general social conditions necessary for surplus value to be produced. But if there was broad agreement within the power bloc about these policies, what were their effects on the African principal dominated classes and how successful were they in achieving the required transformation in the class practices of the white wage-earning classes?

To take the first question: for the African dominated classes the implementation of a number of these measures meant an intensification of their exploitation. This was experienced directly by the minority originally in various forms of industrial and state employment, for whom a 'white labour policy' or job colour bar meant removal from (sometimes higher paid or more skilled) places. But it was also experienced, if less directly, by other black workers as well. Taking on higher paid 'poor whites' instead of blacks or granting economic concessions to white wage-earners, made capital more resistant to the economic demands of blacks. Or at least so various spokesmen for capitalist interests claimed when they gave evidence before the various economics commissions.[126] Moreover, institutionalising white trade unions on a racially discriminatory basis served to weaken any possible identification which white wage-earners might have had with even the economic class struggles of the black dominated classes thus depriving the latter of support which at this conjuncture might have proved decisive.[127] In addition to intensifying the economic exploitation of the black dominated classes these measures also intensified the national oppression. In particular they were a factor reinforcing the racist hierarchy in the social division of labour and, since supervisory places were considered particularly suitable for whites, were of especial importance in reinforcing the tendency towards the creation of an exclusively white supervisory petty bourgeoisie. Thus, while it needs to be made clear that the exploitation and oppression of the black dominated classes was fundamentally rooted in their incorporation as wage labourers into *capitalist* relations of exploitation and not, as the liberals would have it[128] in these type of measures alone, nevertheless these measures heightened and intensified that exploitation.

As to the effectiveness of state policy in bringing about the required transformation in the class practices of the white wage-earning classes, it should by now be clear that the struggle passed through a number of different phases and stages with variable results at different periods. By 1919, the year with which we end this chapter, it was by no means the case that the state had succeeded in eliminating all of the political problems posed for the dominant classes by the struggles of the white wage-earning classes. With their numbers estimated at something over 100,000,[129] the 'poor whites' remained a feature of the social formation, and many of the 'problems' associated with 'poor whiteism' thus continued to recur.[130] In fact the demobilisation at the end of World War I had led to a relative increase in the number of 'poor whites' in the years immediately preceding 1919, as Table 8 shows. Moreover, with the sharp rise in retail prices after the war, strikes involving white wage-earners continued to break out. And there were in existence, furthermore, a number of essentially 'white labour' based political organisations—such as the International Socialist League (founded in 1915)[131]—polarised towards the African working class in terms of their support for the struggles of black workers[132] and their political programmes which called for a common political struggle of white and black workers against capital.[133]

On the other hand though, by the year 1919—the peak of the postwar boom—the most serious and immediate political problems posed for the dominant classes by the struggles of the white wage-earning classes were, relatively speaking, under control. Though the signs are that the incorporation of the white trade unions into the various 'industrial relations' apparatuses had not yet had the effect of decisively subordinating rank and file union membership,[134] institutionalisation was certainly having significant effects on trade union officials. A number of union officials regarded before the war as 'extremists' had emerged by the end of the war as 'moderates' (the most notable being Archie Crawford, the president of the South African Industrial Federation[135]) and although strikes continued to break out, the official Labour Division Reports for 1919 and 1920 were referring to the way in which the 'conference spirit' was functioning to promote compromise agreements instead of strikes, especially in the mining industry.[136] Certainly when the African miners struck in 1920 they received nothing but hostility from the white mining unions as indeed from most rank and file white wage-earners.[137] Moreover, although there were within the 'white labour movement' the various left tendencies polarised towards the African working class most white wage-earners gave political support either directly to the bourgeois parties or else to the social democratic Labour Party, which was through its adherence to a racist, economistic and parliamentarily cretinist ideology essentially a political organisation supportive of the bourgeois state.[138] Indeed towards the latter part of the period the influence of the Labour Party among white wage-earners had increased as state policies gave its programme of seeking sectional economic concessions within bourgeois society enhanced credibility.[139] For example, if the relative performance in parliamentary elections can be taken as some sort of index, then by 1920 the Labour Party was at its peak receiving over 40,000 votes (13·3 per cent of the total cast[140]); this compared to the ISL which had received a maximum of 76 votes per constituency contested (described by one of its leading members as 'the irreducible minimum'[141]).

Thus if state policies had not by 1919 succeeded in effecting the required transformation in the class practices of all strata of the white wage-earning classes (which included at this time a comparatively large number of marginalised unemployed as well as—as Appendix 1 shows—50,000 odd non artisanal manual workers who still retained something of their class instinct) then they had at least succeeded in creating the objective conditions for the emergence of a sizeable and significant white wage-earning supportive class. In the next chapter we shall examine how the crisis of 1920—24 led to the partial undermining of these 'achievements' resulting in a reorganisation of the power bloc and a restructuring of some of the state policies concerned.

Notes to Chapter 3

1 *Transvaal Leader* 3.3.08 reporting a survey conducted by its own reporters.
2 *Select Committee on Drought Distress Relief* (SC 3, 1916) Appendix 1.
3 For example at the end of 1914 there were 727 whites in jail after conviction for liquor selling (see *House of Assembly Debates* 1915, column 979).

4 See *Report of the Transvaal Indigency Commission, op. cit.* p. 5.

5 *Ibid.* p. 5.

6 *Ibid.* p. 118.

7 For an account of some of the effects of the 1893 drought on white un-employment see *Cape of Good Hope Labour Commission: Minutes of Evidence and Minutes of Proceedings* (G39, 1893).

8 Official definition quoted in *Report of the Committee on Industrial Education* (UG 9, 1917) p. 1.

9 *Ibid.* pp. 15 and 8.

10 General Rules reproduced as Annexure to *Preliminary Report of the Karkamas Commission of Enquiry* (UG 55, 1919).

11 See report in *Transvaal Leader* 3.3.08.

12 Recommendation of the *Transvaal Indigency Commission, op. cit.*

13 Recommendation of *Indigency Commission . . . op. cit.* Also reiterated by the Secretary of Mines in the 1913 *Dept of Mines and Industries . . . Labour Report* (UG 21, 1914) where he wrote that relief works 'should not be made so attractive as to induce any class of men to remain permanently on it.' (p. 23).

14 *Transvaal Leader* 20.3.08 reporting L. Phillips' speech urging the mines to accept some gangs of whites; details of subsequent employment *Transvaal Mines Department: Administrative Report of the Inspector of White Labour for the year ended 30.6.09* (TG 47, 1909); *Union of South Africa: Mines Department Reports of 1. Inspector of White Labour . . . for the Period 1.7.09 to 31.12.10* (UG 29, 1911).

15 *Ibid.* and *Transvaal Leader* 12.6.09 reporting the demise of the Rand Unemployment Investigation Committee.

16 *Reports of the Indigency Commission, op. cit.* p. 22.

17 *Select Committee on European Employment and Labour Conditions* 1913 *op. cit.* p. V. See also *Department of Mines. Reports 1912 of (I) Johannesburg Labour Bureau (II) Pretoria Labour Bureau (III) Cape Town Labour Bureau (IV) Durban Labour Bureau* (UG 43, 1913) p. 8.

18 See *Union of South Africa: Mines Department Reports of 1. Inspector of White Labour . . . for the Period 1.7.09 to 31.12.10: op. cit.* p. 7; *Mines Department Reports 1911 1. Johannesburg Labour Bureaux for the Calendar Year 1911* (UG 51, 1912) p. 1.

19 *Ibid.* (1909–10) p. 9; (1911) p. 3.

20 *Evidence to Transvaal Labour Commission . . . op. cit.* pp. 307 *et seq.* (T. R. Price, General Manager of Central South African Railways). See also

Report of the Committee Appointed to Investigate the Employment of Unskilled European Workers in Railway Service (UG 29, 1947) (Chapter 1—historical chapter).

21 Chief Engineer South African Railways, *Employment of White Unskilled Labour on Maintenance and New Construction* (address to White Expansion Society 29.3.10, Duncan Papers, number 294) pp. 6–7.

22 Sources: 1907–09 *Report of the Economic and Wages Commission* (UG 14, 1926) pp. 223–4; 1910–19 *Report of the Committee Appointed to Investigate the Employment of European Workers in Railway Service . . .* 1947 *op. cit.* p. 42 (Annexure G).

23 This point was made in *The Report of the Railway Commission of Inquiry* (UG 14, 1917) p. 17.

24 *General Report in Connection with the Poor White Question* submitted by the White Labour Superintendant South African Railways and Harbours (An 490, 1917) (typed copy in Merriman Papers, item no. 72) p. 13.

25 *Ibid.*

26 *Report of the Committee Appointed to Investigate the Employment of Unskilled European Workers . . . op. cit.* pp. 2–3; *Report of the Select Committee on European Employment and Labour Conditions . . . op. cit.* Appendix E.

27 *Mines Department Labour Reports* 1911 . . . *op. cit.* p. 11, 1912 . . . *op. cit.* p. 10 (the latter reporting that the apprenticeship system was generally in 'a mess').

28 See *Mines Department Labour Reports* 1910 . . . *op. cit.* p. 9.

29 *Report of the Commission Appointed to Inquire into the Conditions of Trade and Industries* (UG 10, 1912). For an analysis of the politics of protection see Kaplan 'The politics of Industrial Protection in South Africa 1910–1939', *Journal of Southern African Studies* vol. 3 no. 1, 1976.

30 See *Mines Department Labour Report* 1912 . . . *op. cit.* p. 2.

31 See for example, *Indigency Commission . . . op. cit. passim.*

32 *House of Assembly Debates* 5.2.12 (second reading speech by Minister of Lands); also described in *Official Yearbooks* e.g. no. 7, 1910–1924 pp. 359–61.

33 This effect of the 1913 Act was discussed in the parliamentary debate on Report of the Native Lands Commission (see *House of Assembly Debates as Reported in the Cape Times* 4.5.16).

34 Four of the others related to the extension of existing measures and one 'hesitated' (on economic grounds) 'to recommend the mines as a field for

the employment of unskilled (white—RD) labour underground' (*op. cit.* pp. XIX–XXI).

35 M. Morris, 'The Development of Capitalism in South African Agriculture . . .' *op. cit.*

36 This increased demand for overseers was pointed to by J. X. Merriman, the chairman of the 1913 Select Committee in his speech presenting the Committee's Report (*House of Assembly Debates* 4.6.13 columns 3091/2), and also by J. Scott, executive member of the Natal Agricultural Union in evidence to the *Royal Commission on the Natural Resources, Trade and Legislation of Certain Portions of his Majesty's Dominions* (cd 7706, 1914), pp. 42–3.

37 See *House of Assembly Debates* 4.6.13 *ibid.*

38 *General Report in Connection with the Poor White Question, op. cit.* p. 7.

39 *Annual Reports of the Factories and Labour Division: Department of Mines and Industries Year Ended 31.12.19* (UG 42, 1920) p. 23.

40 See recommendations of the *Report of the Select Committee on Drought Distress Relief, op. cit.*

41 1911 figures taken from *Official Year Books* 1949, p. 988; 1915–16 and 1919–20 from *Union Statistics for 50 Years*, Table L3.

42 *Union Statistics, ibid.*

43 1st–3rd *Reports of the Select Committee on Subject Matter or Apprenticeship Bill and Regulation of Wages Bill (to which was also referred the Juvenile Affairs Bill)* (SC 9, 1921) p. 7 (Evidence by F. Clarke, chairman of the Cape Town Board).

44 Sources: Labour Reports, Official Yearbooks and Railway Reports, *op. cit.*

45 *Annual Report of the Factories and Labour Division: Dept. of Mines and Industries for the Year Ended 31.12.19* (UG 42, 1920).

46 'Industries and the Colour Bar' (unsigned article in *South African Journal of Industries* vol. 1 no. 13 Sept 1918—Dept. of Mines and Industries publication).

47 On the concept of economic power and its distinction from political or ideological power see Poulantzas (1973), pp. 113–14.

48 The first mining safety regulations were provided for in Laws 3 of 1893, 12 of 1896, 11 of 1897 and 12 of 1898.

49 The first Workmens' Compensation Act was a Transvaal Act of 1907.

50 The first Miners' Phthisis Allowances Act was Act 34 of 1911.

51 Colour bar regulations were included in the safety laws and were contained in the laws listed in note 48 above.

52 On this see my 'Mining Capital, the State and Unskilled White Workers in South Africa 1901–1913', *op. cit.*

53 Act 12 of 1911.

54 The first Masters and Servants Laws were Act 15 of 1856 (Cape), Ordinance 2 of 1850 (Natal), Law 13 of 1880 (Transvaal) and Ordinance 7 of 1904 (Orange Free State).

55 See, for example, E. Kahn, 'The Right to Strike in South Africa—An Historical Analysis', *South African Journal of Economics* vol. 11, 1943. However I. Walker and B. Weinbren in their *2,000 Casualties* (SATUC, 1961) pp. 2 *et seq* point out that towards the end of the nineteenth century some capitalist employers charged white strikers with desertion, for instance, after the printing strike in Cape Town in 1889.

56 The term used in parliamentary debates; see for example report on the debate on the 1914 Industrial Disputes Bill in *Cape Times* 25.4.14.

57 See Kahn, *op. cit.*

58 Particularly during the 1914 strike see, for example, *Cape Times* 8.1.14.

59 1906 figure given in *Evidence to Transvaal Indigency Commission op. cit.* (by H. W. Sampson) p. 100; 1913 *Official Yearbook* 1910–1916 p. 284.

60 *Official Yearbook, ibid.*

61 Walker and Weinbren, *op. cit.; Official Yearbook, op. cit.; Dept. of Mines and Industries Labour Division Reports, op. cit.* (strike statistics were given in table 8).

62 Meeting between deputation of strikers and Botha 2.6.07 reported *Transvaal Leader* 3.6.07.

63 *Ibid.* For a description of the New Zealand system see M. T. Rankin, *Arbitration and Conciliation in Australasia* (London 1916); V. S. Clark, *The Labour Movement in Australasia: A Study in Social Democracy* (London 1906).

64 Rankin, *op. cit.* pp. 136–60. From 1894 until the recession of 1906 there were no strikes in New Zealand and the country was hailed as the 'home of industrial peace'.

65 A view shared by Social Democrats ranging from Keir Hardie to the leaders of the South African Labour Party.

66 Rankin, *op. cit.*; Clark, *op. cit.* With the recession of 1906 however the policy began to change. The level of awards was reduced and in 1907 an amendment was introduced applying criminal sanctions to workers who struck against awards. Thereafter compulsory arbitration was dropped from the reformists' list of panaceas.

67 Transvaal Industrial Disputes Bill, second reading debate reported in the *Transvaal Leader* 8.6.1909 (the position taken in the speech by the Attorney General (Smuts) and by all the Het Volk and Progressive Party speakers).

68 *Ibid.*

69 Described in *Report to the Board of Trade on the Industrial Disputes Investigation Act of Canada, 1907 by Sir Geo. Askwith KCB, KC, Chief Industrial Commissioner* (cd 6603, 1912–13).

70 *Ibid.* p. 10.

71 *Ibid.* pp. 15–17.

72 Act 20 of 1909.

73 Chapter 3 clause 8: *Transvaal Laws* (official publication) p. 65.

74 Preamble: *Transvaal Laws* p. 59.

75 See Second reading debate reported *Transvaal Leader* 8.6.1909 (speeches by H. W. Sampson, P. Whiteside, F. Wybergh). Wybergh was reported as follows: 'The more they exempted Natives from Acts of that kind the greater was the direct incentive to the employment of natives because they were being made humble slaves.'

76 *Ibid.*

77 *Ibid.* (emphasis added).

78 See *Labour Division Reports* for 1910, 1911, 1912 *op. cit.;* and *Official Yearbooks* 1917, pp. 286–7.

79 *Ibid.*

80 Points made by W. Jackson, A. Crawford, H. Schneider and M. Murray representing the South African Industrial Federation to *Select Committee on the Industrial Conciliation Bill* (SC 5, 1923) pp. 71–77.

81. Position outlined in President of the Chamber of Mines' (J. Munro) address *Transvaal Chamber of Mines Annual Reports* 1913, p. ix.

82 *Official Yearbooks* 1910–1916, p. 284.

83 *Labour Division Report* for 1913 *op. cit.* p. 8.

84 *Ibid.* p. 4. The Secretary's view was that the 'only powers capable of touching the root of the evil (were):– Religion in the widest sense and true education.' p. 9.

85 Governor General's confidential despatch 11.8.1913 pp. 26–8, *Colonial Office Confidential Print* (CO 879/113).

86 *Report of the Economic Commission* (UG 12, 1914) pp. 47–8.

87 AB 18, 1914—Consulted in the form of a roneoed copy with handwritten amendments kept in the British Library, London.

88 As indeed, the Minister of Mines and Industries (F. S. Malan) made clear

in his second reading speech—consulted via *Cape Times* reports (*Cape Times* 25.4.14).

89 *Op. cit. Chapter V Miscellaneous.* Once again this was the subject of a mild protest by the Labour Party which put down a counter amendment at the select committee stage (see *Select Committee on the Industrial Disputes and Trade Unions Bill* (SC 10, 1914) p. xxiv). The Labour Party was however more concerned at the exclusion from the terms of the act of all employees (white as well as black) in agriculture or public sectors.

90 See Report of the Executive of the Chamber of Mines: *Transvaal Chamber of Mines Annual Reports* 1914, p. XIVII.

91 See *Cape Times* 8.7.14.

92 Second Reading Debate reported in the *Cape Times* 28.4.14.

93 President's address: *Transvaal Chamber of Mines Annual Reports*, p. IXXXI.

94 Account taken from Transvaal Chamber of Mines Department of Labour: *Reports: Boards of Reference* (Private and Confidential) Vol. I 1917–1919 (Johannesburg, 1920). Introductory chapter.

95 *Ibid.* appeals, important reports 1.11.17; 27.11.17; 7.2.18; 22.3.18; 4.4.18; 30.4.18; 25.6.18; 4.7.18; 28.8.18; 6.2.19; 11.6.19.

96 *Ibid.*

97 Walker and Weinbren, *op. cit.* p. 85; E. Gitsham and J. F. Thembath, *A First Account of Labour Organisation in South Africa* (Durban 1926) p. 135.

98 See Simons and Simons, *op. cit.* pp. 82–5.

99 Chamber of Mines: *Annual Reports* 1919 pp. 46–7.

100 Quoted in *Report of the Mining Industry Board* (UG 39, 1922). For a full account of the 'Status Quo Agreement' see Johnstone, *op. cit.* pp. 104 *et seq.*

101 Chamber of Mines: Board of Reference Reports *op. cit.* introductory chapter.

102 Chamber of Mines, *Annual Reports* 1919 p. 199.

103 *Ibid.* pp. 46–7; *Annual Reports* 1920.

104 The retail price index (weighted average for all centres) rose between 1914 and 1920 as follows 1914 1092; 1915 1126; 1916 1158; 1917 1248; 1918 1289; 1919 1376; 1920 1698 (*Official Yearbook* 1925).

105 See *Official Yearbook* 1919, pp. 316–7.

106 See *Department of Mines and Industries: Labour Report* 1919 *op. cit.* Annexure pp. 37 *et seq* for the list of resolutions.

107   Regulation of Wages (Apprentices and Improvers) Act 29, 1918.

108   *Department of Mines and Industries: Labour Report* 1919 *op. cit.* pp. 42–3.

109   As previously mentioned although mining capital was the hegemonic fraction its party political representatives did not form the governing class. This meant that the direct fractional class interests of mining capital did not necessarily find their expression, in the first instance, in the pronouncements of the governing party but rather through a) party political representatives—often themselves directors of mining companies—who sat in what was technically an opposition party (the Progressive Party until union, and the Unionist Party after 1910) and b) the representations of the Chamber of Mines. However, in accordance with the Chamber's 'non-political, technicist' ideological stance the latter tended to be confined to economic matters which affected the production process in the mining industry directly.

110   *House of Assembly Debates* 13.2.13 column 269 (comment by Sir Percy Fitzpatrick, a former president of the Chamber of Mines).

111   *House of Assembly Debates* 6.2.12; 8.1.12; 10.1.12; 13.1.12; 4.4.12; 16.4.12; quotes from Sir T. W. Smartt (Unionist) 16.4.12.

112   *House of Assembly Debates* 13.2.13 column 269 quoting Sir P. Fitzpatrick.

113   See *House of Assembly Debates* 13.2.13 columns 269 *et seq.*

114   *Transvaal Chamber of Mines: Annual Reports*, 1913, p. XIVII.

115   *Ibid.* 1914, p. XIIX.

116   *House of Assembly Debates as Reported in the Cape Times* 1915–16 Vol. 1 6.4.16.

117   On the acceptance (on 'social' grounds) of the necessity for a white labour policy in at least some trades and occupations in manufacturing industry see, for example, *Evidence to Dominions Royal Commission of 1914* by W. Erlich (a retired manufacturing capitalist representing the Bloemfontein Chamber of Commerce) and W. J. Laite (representing the South African Manufacturers Association) (*op. cit.* pp. 161 and 154); the latter stating that 'our object has always been to employ white labour as far as possible'. One additional point which should be mentioned here is that after the mines' white labour 'experiments' of 1907–8 few demands emerged from manufacturing capitalists to extend white employment in the mines. Indeed in March 1923 an editorial in *Industrial South Africa* (a journal founded by Laite in 1907) explicitly rejected any Cresswellite 'white labour' policy in the mining industry in the following terms: 'The

Mining Industry Board wisely followed the lead of all other Commissions in condemning the white labour policy usually attributed to Mr. Cresswell, which proposes to make this a white man's country by substituting natives in employment by white men at an "economic" wage' p. 134.

118   For example, an editorial in *Industrial South Africa* (Sept. 1923) on 'Unemployment' gave 'full credit' to General Smuts and his government 'for the state employment, afforestation, land settlement and other policies designed to cope with "an admitted evil" '; but it called for more tariff protection to supplement these measures.

119   On capitalist agriculture's position see the parliamentary debates cited in note 122 below.

120   For an early example see Laite's evidence to the *Dominion Royal Commission: op. cit.* p. 155. As mentioned above this demand was put much more vigorously in the early '20s. In fact it prefaced almost all comments on questions to do with white unemployment or white labour. See, for example, representation by South African Chamber of Industries to *Select Committee on Apprenticeship Bill* etc. . . . *op. cit.* (SC 9, 1921) p. 18 and editorials in *Industrial South Africa* (especially Sept. '23, Feb. '24, March '24).

121   See, for example, *House of Assembly Debates* 4.4.12 speeches by Cronje (Winburg), Grobler (Edenburg), C. L. Botha (Bloemfontein).

122   I take as an index of this the fact that organisations representing industrial or agricultural capitalist interests were conspicuously absent from those making representations to the various Commissions or Committees on the 'poor white problem' cited above; and as a further index the fact that the party political representatives of these fractions (notably the Nationalist Party or before 1913 those MPs who later joined the Nationalist Party) neither supported any of the various Labour Party motions condemning existing measures as 'palliatives' etc., nor proposed any major alternative themselves. See, for example, *House of Assembly Debates* 8.1.12; 5.2.12; 18.4.12 (Land Settlements Bill) 13.2.13; 5.3.13; 19.3.13; 4.6.13 (debate on 1913 Select Committee Report), *House of Assembly Debates as Reported in the Cape Times* 17.2.16 (debate on motion on 'poor white problem'.) See also proceedings of 1913 *Select Committee: op. cit.* pp. XXXVI–XXXIX.

123   *Op. cit.* pp. 77 *et seq.*

124   (1975): *op. cit.* pp. 202 *et seq.*

125   Walker and Weinbren, *op. cit.* p. 85; *Official Yearbooks* 1910—1916 pp. 286—7.

126   See, for example, *Economic and Wage Commission: Evidence of the Gold Producers' Committee of the Transvaal Chamber of Mines* (Johannesburg, 1925) p. 6.

127   For example, white trade unions opposed and white mine employees scabbed on the African miners' strike in 1920.

128   Perhaps one of the most extreme statements of this position is the following extract from S. T. van der Horst's *Native Labour in South Africa* (London 1971) p. 261: 'Even in the goldmining industry there is no evidence that capital secures an exceptional rate of reward which could be transferred to native labourers without diminishing the future supply of capital and consequently reducing future output, both in goldmining and auxiliary industries . . . The only significant 'margin' which might be transferred to native labourers without reducing productivity is that which accrues to those Europeans whose earnings are exceptionally high as a result of the exclusion of natives from skilled work.'

129   The Dutch Reformed Church's estimate of 106,518 was regarded by W. M. MacMillan, *The South African Agrarian Problem and its Historical Development* (C.N.A., 1919) pp. 11—12 as an underestimate.

130   There was, for example, an extended discussion of the 'poor white problem' including liquor selling in the *Labour Report* for 1919, *op. cit.* pp. 23—27.

131   The ISL—a predecessor of the Communist Party—grew out of the split within the Labour Party over the war question. Its leaders consisted of a number of prominent white trade unionists—the most notable being W. H. Andrews. For a fuller account of the ISL and other left groups of the period see Simons and Simons, *op. cit.* Chapters 9—11.

132   For example the ISL distributed leaflets calling on white wage-earners to support the African miners' strike in 1920 (Simons and Simons, p. 231).

133   See Simons and Simons. See also its paper 'The Bolshevik', e.g. of June 20th 1919, which argued that the role of white labour should be to call for 'industrial unionism for all (thus) assisting the true South African proletariat (i.e. the black proletariat—RD) on the stage in time to play his part in the great revolutionary drama.'

134   In the mining industry, for example, there was a militant shop and shaft stewards movement which often acted independently of union leadership (see, *inter alia, Report of the Mining Industry Board* (UG 39, 122) p. 21).

135 See Simons and Simons, *op. cit.* pp. 187–8.

136 *Labour Report* 1919 *op. cit.* p. 13; *Department of Mines and Industries: Labour Division Report* Calendar Year 1920 (UG 8, 1922) p. 105. The latter directly attributed the reduction in the days lost per strike to 'the conference spirit which is steadily gaining ground and which is receiving every encouragement from the Government'.

137 See Simons and Simons, *op. cit.* pp. 230–33.

138 For critiques of the Labour Party see, *inter alia*, Simons and Simons, *op. cit.*; R. K. Cope, *Comrade Bill: the Life and Times of W. H. Andrews, Workers Leader* (Cape Town, 1940?); A. Lerumo, *Fifty Fighting Years* (London, 1971).

139 This was an outcome not without its contradictions. The hegemonic fraction had no wish to see the Labour Party enhance its position at the political scene at the expense of the other bourgeois parties. Thus, when the Labour Party won 21 seats in the 1920 elections and was regarded as 'holding the balance of power', it provoked the calling of a snap election in March 1921.

140 Walker and Weinbren, *op. cit.* pp. 330–1.

141 Simons and Simons, *op. cit.* p. 246.

4   The Crisis of 1920—1924

Like a number of other crises affecting the South African social formation, the crisis of 1920—1924, whose effects on the relationships between capital, state and white wage-earners we shall be examining in this chapter, had its origins in a more generalised crisis affecting the whole of the imperialist chain. The whole capitalist world, which had been experiencing a period of steeply rising prices as a result of the massive expansion of credit during the First World War and immediate post war years, began in about 1920 to experience a sharp recession accompanied by an abrupt and rapid fall in prices.

Capital in the subordinate South African social formation was far from immune from the effects either of the recession or of the preceding period of inflationary price rises. It was dependent on the imperialist metropolises both for a wide range of imported materials and for the sake of a number of its imported materials, and as such it had during the war and post war inflationary period been obliged to pay higher prices for its imported materials. In fact, as Table 10 shows, the prices of South African imports tripled between 1913 and 1920. Furthermore, higher import prices had reflected themselves in

Table 10[1]   *South African imports: index of prices paid* (base 1910 = 1000)

1913	1017	1916	1651	1919	1515
1914	1106	1917	2091	1920	3185
1915	1325	1918	1464		

higher prices for wage goods and, under the conditions of class struggle described in the last chapter, capital in South Africa had been obliged to grant a number of money wage increases to its white wage-earning employees. During the inflationary period between 1914 and 1920 white wage-earners employed in the mining industry had received various 'war bonuses' and 'cost of living allowances'[2]— equivalent, in money terms, to increase in wages of 54 per cent— with the result that the index of real white wages in the industry had maintained its level at an index of 899 in 1920 compared to 902 in 1914.[3] Over the same period, too, the wages of white adult males employed in manufacturing industry rose by an average of 78 per cent, representing an increase in real terms from an index of 953 to 1027.[4] Even black workers, who began to organise and engage in strike action, managed to secure some money wage increases during this period—although at an average of only 14 per cent this represented, at a time when the cost of wage goods rose by some 50 per cent, a fall in living standards in real terms.[5]

Now, of course, rises in money wage rates need not necessarily be indicative of any particularly serious problem for capital, and in fact, during the war and postwar boom period, the above described increases in money wage levels had not posed any serious threat to capital accumulation in South Africa. For industrial capital and capitalist agriculture they had been more than offset by the 'artificial protection' they had enjoyed as a result of the disruption of trade routes, and the period was, overall, one of expansion for both fractions. Even mining capital, which could normally be expected to be particularly vulnerable to a 50 odd per cent increase in its white wage bill, a 12 per cent increase in its black wage bill and a 39 per cent increase in the cost of stores,[6] was, despite the closure of three 'low grade' mines in 1918,[7] cushioned from the effects of rising costs during the postwar boom period. This had occurred through Britain's temporary abandonment of the gold standard after the war, which had the effect of raising the price of gold in terms of the British and South African pounds to a 'premium price' of between 116 per cent and 144 per cent of the normal price of £4.28 per ounce.[8]

From the middle of 1920 onwards, however, the effects of the world recession began to be felt in South Africa, and it was during this recession that the previous money wage increases (particularly those granted to white wage-earners) began to create the problems for capital accumulation in South Africa, which led to the struggles we shall be examining in this chapter. The first point to be made about the recession in South Africa is that it affected all of the major fractions of capital in a similar way—by imposing particular (though rather different) restraints on the prices of their products. Capitalist agriculture experienced this most directly through a disastrous fall in the price for its products on the world market. The price of wool, for example, fell from a peak of 32·9*d*. per pound in the early part of 1920 to 10·7*d*. per pound in 1921.[9] And to make matters worse for capitalist agriculture the years 1921 and 1922 were also years of serious drought.[10] Mining capital experienced the recession through a decline in the 'premium' gold price which fell from a high of £5.59 per ounce in 1920 to £5.30 in 1921 and to £4.61 in 1922.[11] And manufacturing capital experienced it through the effects of intense price competition from abroad as trade routes were reopened and world prices slumped. This was reflected in the decline in the mass of surplus value realised in a number of the most important manufacturing industries (e.g. from £248,000 in the year 1919–20 to £123,000 in 1920–1 in the boot and shoe industry, and from £649,000 to £459,000 in the clothing industry[12]) and it was also reflected in the considerable number of factory closures which began to take place from the latter part of 1920 onwards.[13]

But although the recession hit each of the major capitalist fractions in a similar manner, it could not be resolved through any common economic policy which did not differentiate between them. As well as their common interests the different capitalist fractions had contradictory interests and, during the course of the recession, it was these contradictory interests which became emphasised. For capitalist agriculture and industrial capital, the fractions of national capital, one important part of any solution to their problems would have been the implementation of a more effective policy of tariff protection and subsidisation. But this was directly contrary to the interests of mining capital and its ally commerce, which stood to gain nothing from 'protectionist' economic policies except a further increase in costs which would exacerbate their problems still more.[14] The state's economic policies during the crisis therefore depended upon the outcome of a struggle within the power bloc and, during this phase of mining capital's hegemony, they were essentially those of mining capital. As has been shown at length elsewhere,[15] the demand by national capital for increased protection was effectively denied. The Board of Trade and Industries which operated during this period (which was in any case only set up after the strike of 1922) was a facade alternatively ignored or dictated to by government ministers committed to the 'free trade' ideology of mining capital. It produced few recommendations for effective tariff protection and even fewer duties were actually introduced as a result of its deliberations. Indeed, for some sections of national capital the 1920–24 recession period was a period in which they lost some of the protection which they had hitherto received. Among those in this position were beef. farmers, who were subjected to enhanced competition from Rhodesian beef imported duty free, and wheat farmers who faced keener competition from imports with lower freight charges.

One of the consequences of recession was thus that it divided the members of the power bloc and brought about an intense struggle between them (a point to which we shall return later). But for our more immediate purposes its importance was that it made imperative—principally for the benefit of mining capital (but in the absence of a policy of protection for the benefit of the other fractions too)—a determined struggle to reduce the costs of production in all sectors of the economy which affected white wage-earners by imposing upon them, directly or indirectly, certain economic losses including the loss of certain specific concessions granted in previous struggles. The climax of this process—the struggle in the mining industry in 1922—has been more than adequately analysed in Johnstone's work,[16] but the events leading up to that climax are also quite important for an understanding of the relationship between the dominant classes and white earners as well as for an understanding of state policies in the later Pact period.

In fact, throughout the cost cutting offensive of 1920–1922, whenever the interests of white wage-earners were at stake, the power bloc under the hegemony of mining capital proceeded, at first, with extreme caution; seeking for as long as possible to avoid the rupture inherent in the pursuit of the political interests of the power bloc *vis-à-vis* the white wage-earning classes and the economic imperatives of this crisis conjuncture. The first effects of the cost cutting policies were thus experienced by white wage-earners not as a direct offensive against their wages or conditions but through the indirect effects of the denial of the protection to agriculture and manufacturing which could at least have cushioned the effects of the recession in these sectors. From mid 1920 onwards factories began to close and white (and black) wage-earners began to be laid off. Official statistics show a decline in the number of whites employed in manufacturing industry from 46,382 in the year 1920–1 to 44,507 in 1921–2, a decrease of 1,875.[17] And, at the same time, the effects of these policies on agriculture contributed towards a considerable increase in the numbers of 'poor whites' leaving the land.[18] One of the first effects of the policy of cost restraint on white wage-earners was, in short, rising unemployment. The official registration figures, which are by no means a complete estimate although they do indicate the trend, show a rise in the total number of applications for employment from unemployed whites from 15,306 in 1919 to 20,712 in 1920 and to 33,732 in 1921.[19] Indeed, as early as December 1920 the Department of Mines and Industries Labour Division was reporting that it was 'almost impossible to provide employment for the unskilled applicant'.[20]

Moreover even when it became inevitable that the cost cutting offensive would have to involve a struggle to reduce white wage rates, the first phase of the struggle was conducted not against the well organised white wage-earners employed in the mining industry but against other groups whose wages represented an indirect cost to mining capital either through the appropriation of taxation revenue (largely provided out of surplus produced in the mining industry) or through the various fees, fares or other charges levied on mining capital for specific services. Throughout the first half of 1921, whilst white wage-earners in the mines continued to receive wage increases,[21] white (and black) wage-earners in the post office, the Transvaal education department, the defence force, the railways and other state departments[22] had their 'cost of living' allowances reduced. Of the groups so affected, the most important were the white wage-earners employed on the railways. By the end of the financial year March 1920–March 1921 the railways had been in deficit for five years and, moreover, the deficit had been rising—from £10,000 in 1916–17 to £1,049,000 in 1920–1.[23] This was due in part at least to the wage increases (granted by way of 'cost of living' allowances) to white (and also to some extent to black) employees during the wartime inflationary period. Total wage costs which stood at £6,106,000 in 1916–17 had risen to £10,277,000 by 1920–1 (an increase of 68 per cent).[24] Although not increased at the same rate (hence the deficit), increased costs had inevitably meant some increase in tariffs. In fact, in the 17 months preceding March 1921 freight rates had been increased four times.[25] With the onset of the recession therefore there were inevitably demands from mining capital and from parts of capitalist agriculture for a reduction in rates and in the size of the deficit.[26] Moreover, in addition to the generalised cost cutting demands of these fractions, there was a specific and immediate demand from the capitalist owners of the coal mines for an urgent reduction in their freight rates to enable them to retain their international competitive position in the bunkering trade.[27]

The year 1921 thus witnessed an intense effort to reduce railway costs followed by periodic reductions in freight rates. In addition to various minor economy measures (cutting down on new works etc.) this involved an offensive struggle by the state, in its capacity as employer, against railway employees, blacks and whites, but more particularly whites. In the railway budget effective from 31.3.21 the 'cost of living' allowance for all employees was reduced by 25 per cent and it was announced at the same time that the remainder would be phased out over the following nine months. Next to go was the eight hour day—introduced, interestingly enough, against the protests of the Nationalist Party in 1919. This was withdrawn in August 1921. And finally from about the same date, the railways administration embarked upon a policy of limited retrenchment of whites; by means of a stricter enforcement of the 60 year retirement rule and by not making up the losses incurred through 'natural wastage'.[28] As a consequence of these measures the total wage bill fell from its high of £10,277,000 in 1920–1 to £8,748,000 in 1921–2,[29] and the number of whites from its high of 43,801 in March 1921 to 42,578 by December of the same year[30] (and furthermore there were to be more measures of this sort later).

However, whilst these sorts of measures were of some assistance in the struggle to maintain profitability during this crisis period, they could not provide a solution on their own. To the extent that they were successful they reduced the amount paid out by mining capital for 'stores' and the amount paid in taxation. Both items were however only marginally reducible through such means. 'Stores' consisted of a large number of imported items, the major proportion of whose final price was determined outside South Africa; and taxation

Table 11[31]   *Costs and taxation: Witwatersrand goldmines*

	1914	1920	Variation
1 Wages and salaries of white employees (£ millions)	7·1	11·3	+ 58%
2 African wages (£ millions)	5·3	6·0	+ 12%
3 Stores (£ millions)	10·2	14·2	+ 40%
4 Taxation paid (£ millions)	1·2	1·8	+ 50%

(which represented in any case an appropriation out of surplus value already produced) was only slightly reducible by reductions in the wages of government employees. Given these limitations, then, there were, as Table 11 shows, only two cost items for mining capital which were potentially reducible to the required extent—white and black wages—and since black wage rates (which had in any case increased by a much smaller amount than white wages) were at an almost irreducible minimum, the only real option for mining capital in its struggle to retain its rate of profit was to reduce its white wage costs.

As Johnstone has shown,[32] there were, in principle, three possible ways in which white wage costs could be reduced: first by reducing the rate of wages; second, by reorganising and socialising labour processes still performed by white artisans or 'semi-skilled' workers (turning over the functions to 'gangs' of lower paid African workers); and, third, by amending the mining regulations such that productive tasks still performed by white new petty bourgeois supervisors along with their supervisory duties were turned over to African workers. (The latter would also have the effect of eliminating delays in the commencement of work, hence lengthening the effective African working day.) Although there had been, following a recommendation by the Low Grade Mines Commission, some abortive negotiation in the early part of 1920 over the least painful (so far as white wage-earners were concerned) of the three options—reorganisation of the labour process underground so as to increase the effective African working day—mining capital delayed in really pressing its demands for as long as possible.[33] Eventually however it could delay no longer. With the premium gold price continuing to tumble it became, by May 1921, compelled in its struggle against a falling rate of profit to begin to demand reductions in its white labour costs—through changes both in wage rates and in the racial allocation of jobs.[34]

The caution reflecting the realities of class power, which was manifested in the indirect, circuitous route by which mining capital and the state, under the hegemony of mining capital, reached the confrontation with white wage-earners employed in the mining industry was also reflected in the cautious manner in which mining capital initially approached the withdrawal of concessions from its white wage-earning employees at each phase of the struggle. Mining capital and its political representatives were well aware that these moves could result in politically and economically damaging defensive action by white wage-earners and they were concerned therefore to preserve as far as possible the efficacy of the various institutions and apparatuses previously established to contain the struggles of white wage-earners.

White unemployment, which was met by a number of demonstrations and campaigns during 1920 and 1921,[35] was thus the subject of an 'investigation' by a Commission, which included two trade union representatives and which issued three reports during 1921 and 1922.[36] Apart from the largely ineffective and palliative nature of its recommendations (which essentially amounted to an extension of relief work) this commission is notable for the direct and unabashed fashion in which it functioned as an ideological device directed at white trade union leaders. For example, the final report of the majority (issued in 1922 but written in 1921) contains a lengthy diatribe, obviously directed at white trade union leaders, arguing that unemployment had its roots not in capitalism but in 'world conditions' and unalterable 'economic laws', and urging them therefore to forsake 'fanatical fervour' and 'the doctrines of Karl Marx', to recognise instead 'the defects and evils of the business system are only the exceptions which show up against a background of efficient and honest operation', and to 'rely upon public opinion to see that (they) get a square deal . . . rather than . . . the arbitrary methods of strikes and the ruinous methods of force'.[37]

Similarly in imposing wage cuts or withdrawing other concessions from white wage-earners, the initial strategy was to 'observe the rules' and try to win acceptance for such measures through a process of persuasion and negotiation in the conciliation boards and other negotiating bodies. Even J. W. Jagger, the Minister of Railways, whose own class origins and instincts led him to view such an approach with a certain scepticism, began by 'opening the books' to

and negotiating with the National Union of Railways and Harbours
Staffs (NURAHS) and indeed when he sought to adopt too aggressive
a stance too early in the struggle he was criticised by members of his
own party.[38] Also on the railways, the Board of Reference (Grievance Board) was retained throughout the 1921 struggles despite the
fact that it was technically experimental and that it was blamed for
'a growing tendency to challenge disciplinary decisions'.[39] In the
mining industry too capital initially put its demands through the
negotiating machinery and, indeed, from August until December of
1921 through these negotiations, succeeded in obtaining a small wage
reduction and some agreement over relatively minor changes to the
Mining Regulations.[40]

Moreover, at the same time as the above described concessions
were being withdrawn, the state continued, as part of the ongoing
ideological struggle, to organise a number of other forms of concession for white wage-earners. Apart from a general extension of 'relief
works' to cope with the increase in the number of unemployed, perhaps the most important measure of this sort was the Wages Board
Bill,[41] which passed through the House of Assembly but not the
Senate in 1921 and probably would have been reintroduced in the
1922 session but for the effects of the strike. Essentially the Bill
provided for the establishment of Wages Boards consisting of employers' and white employees' representatives to negotiate *minimum*
wage rates for white employees in industries or areas not already
covered by a joint board or conference. The idea was that the rates
so negotiated would be legally enforceable in all plants in the industry
or area concerned. Frankly acknowledged as a means of 'preventing
strikes', it amounted to the state offering up as a sacrificial lamb
petty manufacturing capitalists who undercut 'fair and square'
employers by 'sweating' their employees.[42] And, interestingly
enough, given their later position during the Pact period, it was for
that reason denounced by a number of Nationalist Party MPs in such
terms as 'a serious interference with private enterprise' and 'a sur-
render to trade unions'.[43] There were also two other 'labour bills'
introduced at the same time—the Apprenticeship Bill, also objected

to by the Nationalist Party,[44] and the Juvenile Affairs Bill, designed to formally incorporate into the state apparatuses the Juvenile Affairs Boards—the latter passed into law, and the former was re-introduced in 1922.

But the contradictions were too great for mining capital in particular to be able to secure the kind of economic changes it needed to make at the expense of the white wage-earning classes and at the same time to maintain intact the ideological apparatuses which had functioned to secure the support of white wage-earners for the form of state. As the gold price continued to plummet towards the latter part of 1921 (it fell by 7s. 5d. per ounce in the last three months of 1921 alone[45]) it could no longer rely upon the inevitably lengthier process of ideological struggle. A rupture was becoming inevitable. In fact, the point of rupture was reached first in the case of the railways, which was to all intents and purposes a dress rehearsal for the later rupture in the mining industry itself. In November 1921 NURAHS, which had been involved in negotiation with the railways administration, issued a statement effectively accusing the administration of cooking the books. Their point was that the railway deficit was a 'paper deficit' caused by the reduction in freight rates and the transfer of large amounts to reserve funds and that in 'real terms' the railways accounts were in the black. What it indicated to the administration however was that the limits to what it could achieve by negotiation had been reached. Denounced in the pro-government press for its 'studious insolence' NURAHS had its official recognition withdrawn by the railways administration on the 15th November and thereafter the administration embarked on a programme of reducing costs through the partial undermining of the 'white labour policy'. White labourers employed on branch lines were replaced by Africans and though this did not mean immediate dismissals (the men were transferred to main lines) it was met by various protest actions including a number of small strikes and work-to-rules.[46]

But the rupture within the railways was small beer compared to that within the mining industry itself. By the end of 1921 mining capital had decided that the time had come 'to face' its white employees. On 8th December the Chamber of Mines informed the white unions that the negotiations had not produced a sufficient reduction in costs and it demanded further wage cuts, the elimination of the *status quo* agreement and a *carte blanche* to reorganise underground work. When the unions refused, it announced its intention to implement its demands unilaterally and eventually in January 1922 this move was met by a strike. Even after the strike had broken out there were still some attempts at negotiation but when these came to nothing the Chamber finally announced through a particularly forthright statement issued in March 1922 that it would no longer negotiate with the South African Industrial Federation. Thenceforth the struggle passed into a new phase. The leadership of the strike passed from the 'more moderate' Augmented Executive of the SAIF to the 'more militant' Action Committee, and the strike commandos— bodies of armed men consisting of 'poor white' lumpen proletarian elements as well as striking white miners[47]—began to get involved in 'pulling out scabs' and attacking African miners who tried to go to work. Eventually the state's forces intervened and an armed conflict ensued. Although the strikers' forces achieved some initial successes their commandos could not withstand the massive deployment of state forces—including 7,000 troops, artillery and bomber planes— and after the deaths of between 150 and 200 and the injury of between 500 and 600 the struggle was eventually put down.[48]

Despite the fact of armed clashes against the forces of the state and despite being popularly known as 'The Rand Revolt' there is in actual fact little evidence (except for one isolated speech by a Labour MP[49]) of any attempt by white wage-earners to seize state power. Rather the struggle of 1922 began as and remained essentially an economic class struggle which had assumed the particular form of armed conflict because of various historical and structural factors, including the fact that white wage-earners in the mines were, as a minority of the mainly supervisory petty bourgeoisie particularly vulnerable to strike breaking by capital.

Mining capital's victory over its white employees in 1922 was far from being the pyrrhic victory it is sometimes described as.[50] It secured a number of important and far reaching economic gains which were either not reversed or else only partially reversed during the later Pact period. Among these were a reduction in white wage rates of between 25 and 50 per cent and the withdrawal of two paid holidays. But, as we indicated in chapter 2, the most important gains made by mining capital in 1922 were those made in terms of its control over the labour process itself (the powers of possession). Through its defeat of its white employees, mining capital was able to remove a number of barriers to its assumption of certain powers of possession and was thereby able to bring about a number of changes in the relations of production such that it passed into its phase of monopoly capitalism proper. Indeed the gains made in this respect through the victory in 1922 were so far reaching that capital accumulation in the goldmining industry was able to proceed at least until the early 1970s without any further major restructuring of the relations of production.[51]

With the defeat of the strike, the status quo Agreement which had obliged mining capital to employ whites in certain semi-skilled manual places was annulled and in 1923 the colour bar regulations in the Mines and Works Act were declared by the courts to be *ultra vires* the Act and therefore invalid. In addition shaft and shop stewards, regarded as having 'encroached upon . . . management authority' through their activities on local grievance committees, had their recognition withdrawn—with, according to one Commission, 'most beneficial effects on efficiency'.[52] Whites previously employed as semi-skilled manual workers, performing such functions as drill-sharpener, wastepacker, engine driver, pumpman, handyman, etc., were correspondingly replaced by Africans, and the production processes in most of the departments were reorganised such that whites were restricted to the performance of (an extended range of) supervisory duties. Moreover, the mining regulations were amended so as to permit Africans to begin work without there being present a white supervisor (thereby lengthening the African working day). Through these changes mining capital was also able to introduce new, more productive technologies in the form of the jackhammer drill and the corduroy blanket production process.

Significantly, however, mining capital never made any attempt to put Africans into supervisory new petty bourgeois places, despite being technically free to do so with the legal invalidation of the job colour bar regulations in 1923. As Johnstone has shown[53] (and this will be of importance when we consider the restoration of these regulations under the Pact) the only substitutions made in places covered by the Mines and Works Act were made in respect of engine drivers and machine operators (semi-skilled manual positions). The maintenance of the racist hierarchy in the industry's division of labour was in mining capital's interests. What had been sought in 1922 was a modification to and not the elimination of the racial hierarchical division of labour in the industry: a modification in which almost all of its white employees emerged as supervisory new petty bourgeoisie.

In addition to the gains made by mining capital itself, the defeat of the best organised section of the white trade union movement also made possible gains at the expense of white wage-earners by other capitals. In manufacturing industry the average money wage paid to white adult males was reduced from £6 9s. 2d. per week in 1921 to £5 18s. 3d. in 1922, £5 16s. 3d. in 1923 and £5 15s. 3d. in 1924.[53] On the railways and in other government departments too the wages paid to white and black employees were further reduced, and on the railways there were more white retrenchments throughout 1922 as well.[54] Even on 'relief works' wage rates were cut—ostensibly to promote among 'relief workers' a recognition of the 'economic law' that 'to find work (a labourer) must be profitable—in the wider sense—to his employer', although of course by reducing wage rates state expenditure was also reduced.[56]

However, these economic gains by mining capital (and the other fractions of capital then organised under the hegemony of mining capital) had been brought about at the expense of the near total destruction of the ideological edifice which had been previously created for containing the economic class struggle of the white wage-earning classes. The negotiating system on the mines and in the railways was in tatters, and the 'poor white' unemployed had played a significant role in the armed struggle, indicating a serious weakness in the efficacy of state interventions for dealing with the 'poor white problem'. Moreover the strike of 1922 had been the most serious ever in terms of its adverse effects on the power bloc's political interests. Not only had it been a particularly destructive indication that at least a significant proportion of the white new petty bourgeoisie and lumpen proletariat had withdrawn their support for the form of state, but it had come very close to provoking a militant struggle by Africans. For, on the one hand attacks by strike commandos on Africans had brought them almost to the point of retaliation, and on the other hand there was the very serious concern expressed by the Martial Law Judicial Commission, that some of the strike leadership had considered some sort of approach to Africans calling on them to enter into joint political struggle.[57] Indeed, as we saw in Chapter 2 what most obsessed Smuts throughout the martial law phase was that in one way or another there might have been a 'wild outbreak' by Africans. Thus, although the white wage-earners and the white unemployed were, in the immediate aftermath of their defeat, quiescent, the dominant classes remained, after one of their most serious challenges ever, without a viable structure for protecting themselves against the adverse political effects of the struggles of these classes in the long run.

Since continual repression was regarded as not being possible, it became under these circumstances incumbent upon the state as the custodian of the political interests of the dominant classes to make some sort of intervention to effect a restructuring of the apparatuses and institutions concerned. Indeed, though they disagreed about the extent and precise form which this intervention should take, the party political representatives of all the major fractions were agreed about the need for state interventions of this sort right from the moment of the strikers' defeat. Thus, in the Indemnity Debate which followed the declaration of martial law, Tielman Roos spoke for the Nationalist Party as follows:

This country would always be on the edge of a volcano so long

as they had large numbers of unemployed . . . If they did not
help to absorb the unemployed they would have recurrences of
the troubles on the Rand on a bigger scale than they had yet
had . . . Unless we are going to remove some of the troubles that
affected the (white—R.D.) working classes in South Africa we
are going to get further troubles in the future.[58]
And on this point at least he was echoed by a number of cabinet
and South African Party speakers. For example, Patrick Duncan (the
Minister of the Interior) spoke of the 'danger' to 'white civilisation',
and the 'security of property or life', which would persist unless the
'trade unions could be restored to something like their former condition, and had leaders who were not afraid to tell their men the
truth'.[59] And Smuts (the Prime Minister) spoke of the need to 'take
account of the voice of (white) labour' whilst not allowing it to
'tyrranise everything'.[60]

The years 1922–4 were thus years in which the power bloc, still
organised under the hegemony of mining capital, attempted to bring
about a major restructuring of the apparatuses and institutions concerned with containing and isolating the struggle of the white wage-
earning classes. In fact, as Appendix 2 shows, state expenditure for
this purpose was greater during the financial year 1922–3 than it was
in any of the years of the Pact Government except the year 1932–3.
However, whilst the state's basic approach was still, as before, to contain the struggles of white wage-earners through creating ideological
structures and granting certain economic concessions, the restructuring of 1922–4 did not simply involve the restoration of the structures
in the form which they had assumed before the strike. The hegemonic
fraction, mining capital, had a number of specific demands related to
the new phase of the economic class struggle and these were, as we
shall see later, reflected in the specific form which the restructuring
assumed.

In the immediate aftermath of the strike it was in fact the 'poor
white problem' which loomed largest. The combination of continued
recession, drought and the retrenchments in the mining industry
swelled the ranks of the 'poor whites' considerably. State labour

bureaux received applications from some 53,396 unemployed whites in 1922 (a number not exceeded until the depression year of 1931)[61] while the Unemployment Commission estimated the number of 'poor whites' at 120,000.[62] With an estimated 3,000 families on the Witwatersrand alone at the point of starvation and many more facing eviction from their homes,[63] all the 'problems' related to the 'social intercourse' between 'poor whites' and Africans were beginning to recur at a time when the rapid expansion of the urban African proletariat was making it more difficult for the state to maintain control in the towns. What is more, as we saw previously, a sizeable proportion of the 'poor whites' at least, had given support to the armed struggle.

In addition to various coercive measures directed at the African proletariat—especially the Natives (Urban Areas) Act of 1923 which provided for residential segregation and for the removal of 'redundant natives' from the towns[64]—the struggle by the state to maintain social cohesion in the urban areas also led to the renewal of its efforts to reassign 'poor whites' to particular wage-earning places. In part this involved an extension of 'relief works' with a new emphasis being placed on those which would assist in 'transferring the surplus white population which had accumulated on the Witwatersrand to other areas'.[65] Afforestation and railway construction work (both forms of state employment usually carried out outside the major urban areas) were regarded as particularly suitable and the numbers of places turned over to white 'relief workers' in these departments was increased. Also brought in to provide 'relief work' were the irrigation department and the municipalities of the smaller Transvaal towns, while the Provincial Councils were encouraged to extend their own activities particularly on roadworks.[66] By August 1922 the number of whites employed on relief works of all sorts had risen to 7,919 compared to the 2,460 at the beginning of the year,[67] and although the numbers declined thereafter, as the immediate recession began to ease, by June 1924 (when the Pact Government assumed office) there were still some 4,102 whites occupying places in state departments as unskilled 'relief workers'.[68]

In addition to the extensions of the 'relief works' there were also further state interventions directed at placing unemployed whites in permanent employment as skilled and semi-skilled workers. The Board of Trade and Industries established in 1922 was mainly a limited concession to the demands for tariff protection by national capital but it was also a response to growing white unemployment (in fact it was established following a recommendation by the Unemployment Commission[69]). Although as previously mentioned, its deliberations resulted in the imposition of comparatively few protective tariffs, where tariffs were introduced they were (in theory at least) conditional upon an industry or factory employing a sufficient number of white workers. More important at this stage was the re-introduction and the passing into law of the Apprenticeship Act in 1922.[70] Although the Act did not explicitly prohibit Africans from becoming apprentices, the requirement that an apprentice should have passed standard 6 acted in practice as a barrier against Africans and the Bill was widely acknowledged as a means of placing local whites into places as skilled manual workers.[71] It was also a concession to the demands by the trade unions for protection against encroachment upon the 'skilled trades' through the use of semi-skilled or unskilled (Africans or white youths) in certain processes, although significantly in the 1922 Bill the final executive authority was, apparently after demands by the Chamber of Mines and the Johannesburg Engineering Employers Association, placed in the hands of the minister instead of as under the 1921 Bill in the hands of the Apprenticeship Committee (consisting of employers' and trade union representatives).[72] Although barely operational by the time the Pact government assumed office (the first committee was only formed in 1923) nevertheless by the end of 1924 there were some 266 white youths serving apprenticeships under 15 committees operating in terms of the Act.[73]

The years 1922–1924 were also years in which the power bloc still under the hegemony of imperialist capital made a major attempt to restructure the 'industrial relations' system. The Mining Industry Board—the Commission appointed to investigate the economic issues at stake in the 1922 struggle and which unanimously endorsed practically every one of mining capital's gains—was also given the task of working out a new 'industrial relations' system for the mining industry. Although the resulting system (which functioned from 1922 until 1933) was presented ideologically as 'the Brace plan', thus trading on the reputation as a 'labour expert' of the class collaborating ex-British trade unionist who agreed to serve on the commission principally for the financial gain involved,[74] it was actually a system, which in the fact of its existence reflected the overall conditions of class struggle in the social formation as a whole (the need to contain the struggle of white wage-earners) and in its modifications reflected the improved position of the mining capitalist class fraction in the economic class struggle. It was thus still a system through which economic concessions would be granted to white employees after negotiation with trade unions, but there were a number of limitations (advantageous to mining capital) compared to the previous (Boards of Reference) system. Shaft and shop stewards and Grievance Committees were no longer to be recognised and instead individuals and small groups were limited to an appeal to managers against any grievances, with the provision that groups of ten or more could appeal to the company's board of directors if not satisfied with the response of the managers. Wages, hours and conditions were to be negotiated between individual unions and the Gold Producers' Committee of the Chamber of Mines and if no agreement was reached the matter was to be referred to a standing conciliation board consisting of six representatives of the Chamber and six elected by various categories of employees (not necessarily trade union officers).[75] Before being granted recognition a union had to agree *inter alia* to suspend any strike action until the negotiating procedure had been exhausted, to include in its constitution a clause providing for a secret ballot before any strike action could be taken, and to agree to its members working with non-union employees.[76]

This system also formed the basis of the first draft of the Industrial Conciliation Bill[77] introduced in 1923. The 1923 Bill was, as was previous legislation of this sort, based upon the principle of

'compulsory conciliation' i.e. it suspended the right to strike until
the conciliation procedure had been employed, and it also, again like
previous legislation, included (against the mild protests of the Labour
Party and white trade unions[78]) a definition of 'employee' which
excluded 'pass bearing' Africans. Like the system established in the
mining industry, it provided for a 'standing conciliation board' consisting of equal numbers of employers' and 'employees'' representatives, to meet in the event of a dispute or, in the event of there being
no standing board, for the establishment of an *ad hoc* conciliation
board on application from either party (with the proviso that there
could be no applications in respect of matters affecting only an individual). Finally it provided for the registration of trade unions,
which although not compulsory *per se* was a precondition for recognition under the system. Registration was to be denied to any union
which did not meet certain requirements in terms of its membership
and constitution (although, as distinct from the system in the mining
industry, a registered union was not obliged to have a clause
providing for compulsory strike ballots).[79]

But the system presented in this bill could not gain the necessary
degree of acceptance among the white wage-earning classes to have
functioned effectively as an ideological state apparatus. Its origins,
in the recommendations of a commission which had seen one of its
major tasks as the elimination of shop stewards, were well known
and even those Labour MPs and trade unionists who described themselves as being in favour of 'conciliation' legislation in principle,
rejected it as too 'one sided'.[80] They called instead for something
along the lines of the Whiteley Council 'voluntary conciliation' system operational in some industries in Britain since 1917. Like their
previous 'panacea' (the Australasian 'compulsory arbitration' system
then out of favour) the Whiteley system was essentially an ideological structure set up by a capitalist state to contain the economic class
struggle of wage-earners in the political interests of capital, but it was
one which was potentially more advantageous in terms of economic
gains than the system contained in the 1923 Bill. Unlike the system
of 'compulsory conciliation' it did not seek to suspend the right to

strike by law, but instead sought to minimise strikes in practice through 'enlisting the active and continuous co-operation' of trade union officials 'in the promotion of industry'.[81] This was to be achieved through the establishment of a hierarchy of negotiating and consultative councils which would meet regularly to discuss and negotiate over a range of economic issues, without there necessarily being a formal 'dispute'.

Capital, particularly mining capital, was not however prepared to accede to the demand for such a system. The closest it had come to being established in South Africa was the Boards of Reference system operational on the mines and this was regarded by mining capital as having resulted in a series of concessions without any *quid pro quo* in terms of a reduction in the number of strikes. Nevertheless, in a situation in which even reformists within the white labour movement rejected the alternative proposed system, reflecting the widespread withdrawal of support for the form of state by the white wage-earning classes (and also, concomitantly, the growth in the relative importance of those factions which argued in principle for 'direct action' instead of 'negotiation'[82]), it became necessary for the state, in its struggle to establish a structure to contain and isolate the economic struggles of white wage-earners, to assert its relative autonomy and make some concessions to the reformists' demands. These were incorporated in the revised bill presented by the Select Committee. Under it, the fundamental demands of capital—a suspension of the right to strike and a racially discriminatory definition of 'employee'—were retained, but provision was now made for the voluntary establishment in any industry or area of a permanent negotiating body, consisting of trade union and employers' representatives, called an industrial council. There was also provision for the referral of all matters (including those relating to an individual) to a conciliation board.[83] In other words, though the Whiteley system proper was not conceded and the principle of 'compulsory conciliation' was retained, there were certain concessions made in the revised bill—in fact sufficient for reformists to present it within the 'white labour movement' as 'substantially improved' and thus a major gain.[84]

In this form it was however unacceptable to mining capital particularly because the revised clauses relating to the setting up of
conciliation boards were seen as opening up the way to a possible re-
emergence of the 'grievance committees'.[85] Eventually this demand
by mining capital was met and the clause in question was amended
(against the protests of the Labour Party) to provide that 'no conciliation board shall be appointed . . . if the dispute is in regard to an
individual'.[86] And thus 'shorn of its most objectionable features',[87]
so far as mining capital was concerned, the bill passed into law to
become the basis for the structure which has regulated and contained
the economic class struggles of white (and also to some extent
Coloured and Asian) wage-earners to this day. However although, as
we shall show later, the structures set up under this Act contributed
significantly to advancing not only the political but also some of the
economic interests of capital, it was, significantly, at the time of its
passage into law, viewed with some hostility both by the Federated
Chambers of Industry and the Chamber of Mines. For example an
editorial in *Industrial South Africa* (a journal edited by the founder
of the Federated Chamber of Industries) regretted that the only
'industrial legislation' passed in the first session of parliament in
1924 was 'what is euphemistically termed a Conciliation Bill . . .
(thus) continuing to *burden* the industrial community with legislation of a social character, whilst refraining from action in regard to
tariff revision'.[88] And the president of the Chamber of Mines commented on the Bill in its final draft form as follows:

> I think I may say that, in its present form, it will do little active
> harm. That is the most that can be said in favour of this type of
> one-sided legislation, which appears to be chiefly designed to
> catch votes by harassing employers.[89]

However, despite these interventions by the state and despite the fact
that some at least had had some success in winning support among
white wage-earners for at least some of the institutions and structures
of the capitalist state (i.e. those established under the Industrial

Conciliation Act), the state under the hegemony of mining capital could not fully restore the white mining petty bourgeoisie and other sections of the white wage-earning classes to their position as supportive classes (to the extent that they had been in 1919 at least). The state's role in the 1922 strike had plainly revealed its partisan class character thereby seriously undermining its capacity to pose as the neutral representative of the (white) nation—people as a whole. Moreover, in the period following the strike the state had been required to fulfil too many economic functions related to mining capital's transition into its phase of monopoly capitalism proper, and its demands in the continuing recession, for it to assert a sufficient degree of relative autonomy thereafter. For example, the Mining Industry Board had been required to endorse mining capital's economic gains, the railways continued to 'cut costs' at the expense of white wage-earners, and on top of that there was the uncertainty about the future strategy of mining capital with the legal invalidation of the job colour bar.[90]

In addition to mining capital's problems (as hegemonic fraction) in reorganising the white wage-earning classes as supportive classes, it was also faced during the period immediately following the strike with an intensified struggle against its hegemony by the fractions of national capital. The strike itself had had the effect of disrupting production thus deepening the effects of recession on the fractions of national capital,[91] and they continued to be denied the effective tariff protection which they demanded, indeed needed, for their extended reproduction.

With mining capital thus weakened by its inability to restore white wage-earners to their position as supportive class, and facing a renewed challenge from national capital, the conditions existed in the immediate aftermath of 1922 for a reorganisation of the power bloc. National capital, which, as we have seen, had not previously adopted a particularly different stance from that of mining capital on a number of key questions related to the demands of the white wage-earning classes, and which had indeed benefited at the expense of white wage-earners through the general wage reductions after 1922, was now able to identify some of its demands as demands which would further the economic interests of white wage-earners. In particular it was able to put forward its demands for tariff protection and a programme of development for capitalist agriculture and manufacturing as a solution to white unemployment[92] and its was thus able to present its struggles against mining capital as the struggle of 'progressive' against 'reactionary' capitalism.

As is well known, the immediate aftermath of the strike saw the formation of an alliance between national capital and those elements within the 'white labour movement' which had previously formed the core of the white wage-earning supportive class—an alliance manifested at the party political level in the formation of the electoral pact in 1922 between the Nationalist Party and the Labour Party.[93] For the reformist tendencies within the 'white labour movement' this alliance offered a new basis for them to reassert themselves after their somewhat weakened position during the course of the strike. They could now offer an alternative within capitalist society (an alliance with national capital in its struggle for a 'progressive' capitalist society) to the programmes being put forward by 'radicals' and communists (calling for militant struggle either in alliance with African workers or 'independently' against capitalism itself).[94] And this in turn enabled the party of national capital to enhance its own position both within the power bloc and among non-allligned supportive fractions (such as the white traditional and 'mental' petty bourgeoisie), by presenting itself as the 'party of order'; the bastion against 'bolshevism'. Thus, for example, in an election brochure the Nationalist Party declared that one role of the alliance was,

> to convince the working man and the poor man . . . that there is no good to be had for them out of socialism and communism and bolshevism and revolutionary excesses, but only in the maintenance of the conception of obedience and civic duty and fidelity to the State . . . It is the business of the National Party to educate the poor man so that he may realise that it is his friend . . . herein lies the explanation and the justification of

the actions of the National Party in connection with the recent happenings in Johannesburg.[95]

Eventually the struggle by national capital, in association with its white wage-earning allies, succeeded in its immediate objectives. The shock defeat in the Wakkerstroom by-elections of F. S. Malan—the Minister of Mines and Industries who had been responsible for, among other things, introducing the Industrial Conciliation Act— provided a particularly dramatic index of the degree to which the party of mining capital had failed to restore the support of white railway workers[96] at least for a state under the hegemony of mining capital. In response to the Wakkerstroom result, Prime Minister Smuts decided to call a snap election to 'test' his support in 'the country at large'. When the results came in on the 18th June 1924 they indicated that his party had lost and the Pact parties had won. It was an event which had more than mere party political significance. It created the conditions for the national capitalist fractions to begin an eventually successful struggle to assert the primacy of their own particular interests (i.e. to assert hegemony), and to introduce a number of measures, like effective tariff protection, agricultural subsidisation, etc., which altered the trajectory of capitalist development in the social formation in favour of industrial and agricultural development.

Notes to Chapter 4

1 Reproduced from *Report of the Economic and Wages Commission* (UG 14, 1926) Table XIV, p. 79.
2 For a full list of the concessions granted see Johnstone, *op. cit.* Table 5, pp. 98–9.
3 *Economic and Wage Commission op. cit.* Table F, p. 269.
4 *Ibid.*
5 Calculation for mining and manufacturing together taken from *Union Statistics for 50 years* tables G4, G6, G20. Price index from table H23.
6 Johnstone, *op. cit.* p. 100.
7 See *Interim Report of Low Grade Mines Commission* (UG 45, 1919) p. 3.

8 Johnstone, *op. cit.* p. 95.
9 *Union Statistics for 50 Years* Table I26.
10 According to an article in the *Rand Daily Mail* 6.2.24, 70,000 whites left the land between 1911 and 1921 (about $\frac{1}{5}$ of the white rural population of the Cape and $\frac{1}{4}$ of that in the OFS). During the drought of 1921–2 whites lost 308,883 cattle and 2,379,556 sheep and goats.
11 *Union Statistics for 50 Years* Table K4.
12 Calculated from statistics given in *Official Yearbook 1910–1924* pp. 552–55. The method adopted was to subtract wages and the cost of materials and fuel from the money value of total output. (Only therefore an approximation.)
13 Reported in *Interim Report of Unemployment Commission* March 1921 (UG16, 1921).
14 For a full and able analysis of the position of the fractions on protection see Kaplan, D., 'The Politics of Protection in South Africa', *Journal of Southern African Studies*, October 1976.
15 See the work of Kaplan, *op. cit.* and also Davies, Kaplan, Morris and O'Meara, 'Class Struggle and a Periodisation of the Southern African State', *op. cit.*
16 *Op. cit.* Chapter 3.
17 *Union Statistics for 50 Years* Table L3.
18 See *Dept. of Mines and Industries: Labour Division Reports* 1920 *op. cit.*
19 *Dept. of Mines and Industries Labour Division Reports* 1920 *op. cit.*, 1922 (UG9, 1924).
20 Report 1920, *op. cit.* p. 109.
21 Johnstone, *op. cit.* p. 100.
22 J. Bisset, *John William Jagger and the South African Railways 1921–1924* (University of Cape Town dissertation, September 1973).
23 *Report of the Controller and Auditor General on Railway Accounts* (UG 56, 1919, UG 46, 1921).
24 *Reports of the General Manager of South African Railways and Harbours* (UG 43, 1918, UG 42, 1921).
25 Bisset, *op. cit.* p. 3.
26 Demands for rate reductions referred to by Sir Thomas Watt in Railway Budget Debate (*House of Assembly Debates as Reported in the Cape Times* 19.5.20).
27 Bisset, *op. cit.* pp. 3–4.
28 *Ibid, House of Assembly Debates* 18.3.1925 column 1072 (J. W. Jagger speaking on Railways Additional Appropriation Bill).

29 *Reports of the General Manager of South African Railways and Harbours* for 1920 (UG 42, 1921) and 1921 (UG 37, 1922).

30 *House of Assembly Debates* 18.3.25 column 1072 (March figure, a special estimate produced by Railways administration, quoted by Jagger); *Report of the General Manager of South African Railways and Harbours* for 1921: *op. cit.*

31 Compiled from Johnstone *op. cit.* Table 6 p. 100; *Union Statistics for 50 Years* Table Q6.

32 *Ibid.* pp. 119–25.

33 *Ibid.* pp. 128–9.

34 *Ibid.* pp. 129–30.

35 *Ibid.* pp. 126–7.

36 *Interim Report of the Unemployment Commission* (UG16, 1921); *Second Interim Report of the Unemployment Commission* (UG34, 1921); *Final Report of the Unemployment Commission* (UG17, 1922).

37 *Unemployment Commission* 1922: *op. cit.* p. 6 and p. 9.

38 Bisset, *op. cit.* p. 9 quoting Sir Abe Bailey's criticism of Jagger's insufficiently 'broad view'.

39 *Report of the General Manager of Railways and Harbours* for 1920, *op. cit.* p. lxxviii.

40 Johnstone, *op. cit.* pp. 128–9.

41 AB 49, 1921.

42 *House of Assembly Debates as Reported in the Cape Times* 12.7.1921 quotations from second reading speech by F. S. Malan, Minister of Mines.

43 *Ibid.* speeches by P. S. Cilliers, C. A. van Nekerk, J. van der Merwe, P. C. Jordaan and J. W. van Eeden.

44 *Ibid.* (the 2nd readings of the two bills were on the same day).

45 Johnstone, *op. cit.* p. 130.

46 This account derived from Bisset, *op. cit.*, Walker and Weinbren *op. cit.* and *House of Assembly* Debates 12.8.24 (railway budget debate).

47 In the view of the Governor General (Despatch 21.3.22 file CO 551/151 Public Record Office, London) and Smuts (*House of Assembly Debates as Reported in the Cape Times* 21.3.22) unemployed 'poor whites' made up the bulk of the rank and file members of commandos especially in areas like Fordsburg.

48 This account derived from N. Herd, *The Revolution on the Rand* (Johannesburg 1966); Johnstone, *op. cit.*; Simons and Simons, *op. cit.*; Walker and Weinbren, *op. cit.*; *Martial Law Judicial Commission* (UG35, 1922);

Report of the Mining Industry Board (UG39, 1922); particularly Johnstone and the Mining Industry Board.

49 R. B. Waterson, who at a meeting during the strike called upon an assembly of Nationalist and Labour party MPs to 'proclaim a South African Republic, and immediately to form a provisional government for this country'. Quoted Herd, *op. cit.* p. 34.

50 See e.g. Francis Wilson, *Labour in the South African Goldmines* (Cambridge 1969) p. 11.

51 From 1973–4 onwards, however, there have been a number of important changes in the relations of production in the mining industry. Arising in response to a number of complex struggles both within the industry itself and in the labour supplying peripheral states, and occurring in the context of a sharp rise in the price of gold (e.g. from $45 per ounce in 1972 to an average of $140 in 1974), these have mainly involved: an increased reliance on South African rather than 'foreign' labour; somewhat higher wages for African workers, and an increased mechanisation of production processes. The effects on the racial division of labour have however thus far been rather slight: some functions have been 'fragmented' and transferred to Africans but the essential racist hierarchical character of the division of labour has remained intact. (On this see D. G. Clarke, 'Foreign Migrant Labour in Southern Africa: Studies on Accumulation in the Labour Reserves, Demand Determinants and Supply Relationships' (World Employment Programme Working Paper, International Labour Organization, Geneva, 1977)).

52 *Report of the Mining Industry Board op. cit.* pp. 20–1.

53 *Op. cit.* p. 145.

54 *Report of the Economics and Wages Commission op. cit.* Table F, p. 269.

55 Bisset, *op. cit.* p. 42.

56 Both points made in *Labour Division Report for 1922 op. cit.* p. 157.

57 *Report of the Martial Law Judicial Commission* (UG35, 1922). The gist of the Commission's report was to try to show that the leadership of the strike passed to the Action Committee consisting of militants committed to '(including) the coloured as well as the European races in South Africa and elsewhere to adopt Communist principles' p. 26.

58 *House of Assembly Debates as Reported in the Cape Times* 13.4.22.

59 *Ibid.* 22.4.22.

60 *Ibid.* 22.4.22.

61 *Labour Division Report for 1922, op. cit.*

62 *Unemployment Commission Final Report 1922 op. cit.*

63 Report in *Rand Daily Mail* 3.5.22.

64 D. Welsh, 'The Growth of Towns' chapter in M. Wilson and L. Thompson ed. *Oxford History of South Africa* Vol. II p. 187 quoting *Report of the Native Affairs Commission* 1921, pp. 25–7.

65 Governor General confidential despatch 26.5.22 file CO551/151 Public Record Office, London.

66 Measures described in *Labour Division Report for 1922 op. cit.; The Social and Industrial Review* vol. II no. 6 June 1926 ('Employment and Unemployment—Departmental Survey of Relief Measures').

67 *Labour Division Report for 1922 op. cit.* p. 157.

68 Statistics given in *Social and Industrial Review*, January 1927 p. 89.

69 *Op. cit.* recommendation V. On the Board of Trade and Industries and the demands of the fractions in the power bloc see Kaplan (1976) *op. cit.*

70 Act 26 of 1922.

71 *House of Assembly Debates as Reported in the Cape Times* 12.2.21, 12.5.22, 7.7.22.

72 The amendment was introduced in the senate where it was made clear that a reversal by the Assembly would result in a 'conflict' between the two houses. One SAP Senator (Schofield) in fact accused the minister of 'toadying to those bodies (trade unions)' in the first draft. F. S. Malan the Minister for Mines however indicated that he would in practice not intervene in respect of activities of apprenticeship committees.

73 *Social and Industrial Review*, April 1927, p. 411.

74 William Brace (1865–1947) was a former Welsh trade unionist and Lib-Lab MP who joined the Ministry of Mines as 'labour adviser' in 1920 after he and his group of 'moderates' were deposed from the executive of the South Wales Miners Federation. According to the Correspondence in the Colonial Office Files (file CO551/151 minutes dated 21.3.22, 27.3.22, 31.3.22), Brace was appointed to the Mining Industry Board after an approach by Smuts to the Colonial Office for someone to serve in lieu of a representative of the white trade union movement, which had decided on a policy of boycott. Brace's initial reaction on being approached was to agree 'provided that the financial terms are satisfactory' and to enquire 'what the terms proposed are'. After one or two visits to the Colonial Office to enquire further into these matters, he eventually accepted a fee of 100 guineas a month on top of his normal salary. Smuts was not however entirely successful in his efforts to sell Brace e.g. '(there is) not a better man in the British

Empire . . . to help in solving the difficulties' (*House of Assembly Debates as Reported in the Cape Times* 24.4.22). Even Boydell described him as a 'conservative trade unionist . . . who had left the labour movement and joined the capitalist class' (*Debates*. 6.9.22). (Biographical information from J. M. Bellamy and J. Saville, *Dictionary of Labour Biography* (London 1972).)

75　*Report of the Mining Industry Board op. cit.* pp. 52–55 (Schedule C 'Basis of Conciliation Machinery for the European Employees of the Goldmines . . .').

76　*Transvaal Chamber of Mines Annual Reports* 1922, p. 67.

77　AB 1, 1923.

78　See e.g. Evidence to *Select Committee on the Industrial Conciliation Bill* (SCS 1923) p. 10 (by J. Wallace, G. Brown, D. Pringle, G. Jackson and E. Cresswell for Associated Trades Unions).

79　Bill described in *House of Assembly Debates as Reported in the Cape Times* 6.2.23 (Second reading speech by F. S. Malan, Minister of Mines and Industries).

80　*Ibid.* speech by H. W. Sampson and J. Stewart, *Evidence to Select Committee op. cit.* (Evidence by Wallace *et al.* and W. Jackson, A. Crawford, H. Schneider and M. Murray for the SAIF).

81　*Interim Report on Joint Standing Industrial Councils* (cd. 8606, 1917) p. 417.

82　Mentioned in Evidence to *Select Committee op. cit.* p. 34 (by Wallace *et al.*).

83　Described by H. W. Sampson *House of Assembly Debates* 30.1.24, p. 18.

84　*Ibid.*

85　*Transvaal Chamber of Mines Annual Reports* 1923, p. 183 (report of quarterly meeting).

86　*The Industrial Conciliation Act no. 11 of 1924* clause 4(1).

87　*Transvaal Chamber of Mines Annual Reports 1923* p. 62 (president's annual address).

88　*Industrial South Africa* February 1924, p. 73.

89　*Chamber of Mines Reports* 1923 *op. cit.* p. 62.

90　As indicated earlier mining capital made no attempt in practice to replace white new petty bourgeois supervisory employees with Africans and its spokesmen repeatedly denied that they ever had any intention of doing so. Nevertheless various proposals were made for utilising the situation in which the colour bar regulations were withdrawn to the advantage of capital e.g. Prof. R. A. Lehfeldt put forward the suggestion that by stimulating 'free competition' (from Africans) the white wage rate could be lowered to about 10s. a day. (*Rand Daily Mail* 22.5.22).

91 For example, C. R. Swart, among other speakers, referred in the Debate on the Wages Bill (*House of Assembly Debates* 1.4.25 column 1777) to the farmers whose products remained unsold and unsaleable during the strike period.

92 This was done both by industrial organisations and at the party political level. See e.g. *Industrial South Africa* September 1923, March 1924 and *Rand Daily Mail* 5.5.24 reporting the Nationalist Party's election programme.

93 For an account of the mechanics of the formation of the Pact (including quotations from relevant correspondence) see M. Cresswell, *An Epoch of the Political History of South Africa in the Life of Frederick Hugh Page Cresswell* (Cape Town, 1956) (an apologist biography by Cresswell's widow under a foreword by D. F. Malan and dedicated to Albert Hertzog).

94 For an account of the position of the left, including the ambiguities within the Communist Party about whether to turn decisively to the African working class or to attempt to try to maintain a position of influence within the white labour movement see Simons and Simons, *op. cit.* Chapters 13 and 14, especially pp. 309–13.

95 Federal Council for the National Party of South Africa 'What has the National Party to do with the Labourites? . . .' (Cape Town 1922). I am grateful to Dave Kaplan for drawing this reference to my attention.

96 See for example Bissett, *op. cit.* Chapter III on the significance of the 'railway vote' in the Wakkerstroom by-election.

PART 2

White Wage-Earners and the Hegemony of National Capital 1924–1939

5   The Pact Period 1924—1932

General propositions

In the last chapter we saw how the recession of 1920—1922 had led to a crisis in the relationship of the white wage-earning classes to the state, and how this crisis had created the conditions which enabled national capital to form an alliance with certain elements within the white wage-earning classes and displace imperial capital as politically hegemonic fraction in 1924. In this section we shall examine how the relationships between the dominant classes and the white wage-earning classes were restructured during the period of national capital's hegemony: dealing in this chapter with the first period of that hegemony (the period of the Nationalist Labour Pact régime) and in the next chapter with the second period (the period of 'fusion' government).

We shall see in this chapter that the party political alliance between the Nationalist and Labour parties, and the extension (within limits) of the range of economic concessions made available to white wage-earners, facilitated the rapid and effective incorporation of the white trade union movement into the 'industrial relations' apparatuses established during the latter part of the period of mining capital's hegemony. And we shall see how the new trajectory of capitalist development, in which the emphasis was placed on developments favouring the hegemonic national capitalist fractions, created new possibilities for the state to make more effective interventions in connection with the 'poor white problem'. We shall also see how both these factors had the effect of further disorganising the white wage-earning classes as an independent 'militant' social force, and of further reinforcing the isolation of white from black wage-earners, to the ultimate political advantage not only of the hegemonic fraction but of the power bloc as a whole.

This characterisation of the effects of the state's 'white labour' policies during the Pact period needs some explanation especially in view of the fact that liberal writers (and indeed some others who have explicitly located themselves outside of the liberal problematic[1]) have described the Pact as inaugurating, if not a 'white workers' state', then a state in which white wage-earners dominated in some way over capital, or at least over mining capital. To begin with we need to be clear about the nature of the relationship between national capital and white wage-earners. Essentially the struggles climaxing in the events of 1922 had led to the formation of a *political alliance* between national capital and certain categories of white new petty bourgeois and artisan working class employees. That is to say, following Poulantzas,[2] the class forces in question had entered into a relationship operating at a determinate level of the class struggle, in this case the political, involving the granting and receipt of concessions at that level. In particular, in return for their political support in the struggle for hegemony, national capital's white wage-earning allies had received certain political concessions in the form of the advantages of an electoral pact with the Nationalist Party and the admission of a small number of their representatives to certain subordinate places in the governing class. It was also, to be sure, a relationship which placed white wage-earners in a better position to advance certain of their economic demands than they had been hitherto. National capital needed for some time to maintain its alliance with white wage-earners, and the power bloc as a whole needed to restore white wage-earners to their place as a supportive class for the form of state, and both these factors enabled white wage-earners to extract (within limits) a number of further economic concessions (including concessions related to job colour bars).

But the white wage-earning classes were not, through their relationship with national capital, placed in a position where they were able to dominate politically either over capital in general or indeed over any fraction thereof. A political alliance—particularly one between a class in the power bloc and a class outside—is not a relationship in which each comes to have equal political power. National capital remained capital and its hegemony was therefore the hegemony of a capitalist fraction in a capitalist state. The state did not become the exclusive instrument even of the hegemonic fraction, let alone of its white wage-earning ally. Rather, in assuming hegemony, national capital had to 'undertake to defend the *overall* political interests of the classes and fractions that constitute the power bloc and thus its own long term political interests'.[3] The principal overdetermining role of the state during the Pact period thus remained to politically organise the dominant classes and to politically disorganise the dominated and subordinate classes and, in so far as they constituted a potential political threat to the dominant classes, this included intervening in the class struggle to politically disorganise and subordinate the white wage-earning classes. Indeed, as we mentioned earlier and as we shall see again later, the alliance between national capital and white wage-earners created the ideological conditions which made it possible for the first time for the capitalist state effectively to integrate the white trade unions and thus eliminate them as a potential political threat to the dominant classes.

Moreover, if the political interests of capital remained dominant over those of all other classes during the Pact period so too did the essential economic interests of all major fractions thereof. The Pact régime did not bring into existence a form of state in which, in order to advance the political interests of one fraction of capital (hegemonic national capital) the economic demands of a non-capitalist allied class were placed above those of another fraction of capital (mining capital). Apart from the fact that mining capital remained, even after its removal from the position of hegemonic fraction, a powerful political force within the power bloc, there were a number of quite fundamental material reasons why such an outcome could not and did not come about. In the first place, of course, the mining industry remained throughout the period the major source of surplus

value in the social formation, and, in guaranteeing the general conditions for the reproduction of social capital, the state was therefore
obliged to guarantee the essential conditions for the production of
surplus value in the mining industry. But, more than that, the politically hegemonic national capitalist fractions' own development
depended critically on their appropriation (through taxation, protection etc.) of surplus value produced in the mining industry, and they
had therefore themselves a direct economic interest in ensuring that
the demands of other classes—including their white wage-earning
allies—did not seriously interfere with the surplus value producing
process in the industry.

Thus we shall argue that although the Pact period saw the state
organising a number of further economic concessions for white wage-
earners, these remained firmly within the limits dictated by the
state's prime imperative to create and guarantee the essential conditions for capitalist production and continued, furthermore, to be
overdetermined by the state's role as the factor of social cohesion;
being aimed precisely at the political disorganisation and subordination of the white wage-earning classes in the political class interests
of the power bloc as a whole.

In view of the mystification which has surrounded so many analyses
of the Pact régime, we should perhaps begin our attempt to substantiate the above propositions by examining the outcome of, and the
role of the state in, certain economic class struggles involving white
wage-earners; particularly those involving white wage-earners
employed in the mining industry.

The state and the economic class struggles of white wage-earning employees 1924—1932

As we saw in the last chapter, mining capital had, after 1922, made a
number of important economic gains at the expense of its white

wage-earning employees. It had reduced their wage rates by amounts varying between 25 and 50 per cent. It had removed whites from a number of specific places in the industry's division of labour. It had reorganised a large number of other labour processes such that whites were confined to the performance of essentially supervisory functions (within which the scope of their duties had been extended). And with the legal invalidation of the job colour bar regulations it was technically free to make further changes as it saw fit. When the new regime came to office, therefore, it was seen by the white mine employees as creating the prospects for them to restore the situation as it had been. Indeed it was seen by some as a means of advancing their demands even further. After all Cresswell, the arch-proponent of a 'white labour policy' in the mining industry was in the cabinet (though significantly not as Minister of Mines). The early years of the Pact period were thus years of struggle in which the white miners launched a counter offensive in an attempt to recoup their losses and advance from the level of their still 'sometimes tolerable petty bourgeois existence' (Engels) to the level of their rather more tolerable petty bourgeois existence pre 1922.

One of the first of the struggles waged was that (lasting roughly from 1924 to 1927) over wages in which the white mine employees attempted to restore their wage rates to their pre 1922 levels in terms of real purchasing power if not in monetary terms. All of the details of the fairly complex process of wage bargaining which occurred during these years need not concern us here, but the net outcome was that whilst the white mine employees did make certain economic gains, these remained nevertheless firmly within limits which were tolerable to mining capital.

Very briefly, following demands backed by several small strikes,[4] white wages in the mining industry became the subject of two 'investigations' by state officials operating under certain provisions of the Industrial Conciliation Act. The first, which took place during the latter part of 1924 and the earlier part of 1925, was conducted by a Supreme Court judge named de Villiers acting as a 'mediator', and whose report was, therefore, in terms of the Act, 'advisory' rather than binding on the two parties. The de Villiers report essentially endorsed the claim of the Mineworkers Union (MWU) for a restoration of minimum wage rates to their 1918 levels adjusted to meet the rise in the cost of living, but it was totally unacceptable to mining capital, both because the sum involved was comparatively large and because acceptance would have amounted to an acceptance of the principle that white employees, at least, had the right to be compensated for rises in the 'cost of living'.[5] Not surprisingly therefore mining capital both refused to implement the award and also put up a strong and eventually successful resistance to an attempt to enforce it through a Mineworkers Minimum Rates of Pay Bill, published by Cresswell in 1925.[6]

The second investigation, which followed a threatened general strike by the MWU over the deadlock over the de Villiers award,[7] was by the members of the Wage Board (chaired by F. A. W. Lucas), sitting significantly as an 'arbitration board' operating under the terms of the Industrial Conciliation Act rather than under the terms of the Wage Act. Their report (legally binding on both parties in terms of the Act) essentially rejected the claims of the MWU and the Reduction Workers Association for a restoration of wage rates to something approaching pre 1922 levels and, instead, awarded an increase (which governed the basic rates throughout the Pact and indeed 'fusion' periods) very little above a 'temporary arbitrary increase' which mining capital had itself unilaterally conceded and between one tenth and one twentieth that originally claimed by the MWU and endorsed by de Villiers.[8] When the 'Lucas award' was published early in 1927, the *Rand Daily Mail* commented on it as follows:

> The arbitrators have substantially upheld the position taken by the Gold Producers' Committee of the Chamber of Mines on behalf of the industry. Except to a very small extent the latter's contentions have been supported while the men's demands have been rejected. Broadly speaking the three members of the Board have endorsed the conclusions of various commissions which have dealt more or less thoroughly with the question in the past.[9]

And the President of the Chamber of Mines commented,
> The Award very definitely supports the contention which the
> Mining industry has averred before one Commission after
> another—that its rates of pay are high . . .[10]

It was as such met with widespread anger by white wage-earners and
there were even a few protest strikes.[11] Indeed if it were not for the
tactics of the MWU leadership, it may well have been followed by a
full scale general strike throughout the industry.[12] As it was, the
Lucas award was, as we shall see later, a major factor underlying the
split in the Labour Party over the question of maintaining the party
political alliance with the Nationalists.

One of the principal factors determining the state's role in ensuring that the eventual outcome remained well within the bounds
acceptable to mining capital was the intense struggle conducted by
mining capital to persuade the other fractions of the power bloc that
they all had a common interest in resisting any major increase in
white wages on the mines: not only because all had a common
interest in ensuring the continued production of surplus value in the
industry but also because any such increase might provoke a generalised rise in wage rates affecting capitalists in all sectors of the
economy. Throughout the course of the struggle, the Chamber issued
a number of booklets, pamphlets and statements to this effect. In
one of them, for example, it argued that since all wage rates in South
Africa
> must be looked upon as a coherent whole, the wage of each
> class of European workman having, in effect, an agreed relation
> to the wages of other classes; any increase in the rates of pay of
> one class of employee (would be) followed by demands for in-
> creases from the other classes including the natives . . .

Thus, the pamphlet continued,
> high wages in the industrial centres increase the cost of produc-
> tion in the rural industries, directly, by bringing about increases
> in wages in those industries, and, indirectly, by increasing the
> cost of supplies purchased in the industrial centres by the
> agriculturalists.[13]

That this, in fact correct, assessment by mining capital of the effects on national capital of a possible generalised rise in white wage levels, played a decisive role in determining actual state policy towards the wages in the mining industry cannot be doubted. Indeed the members of the Arbitration Board made this abundantly clear in the following extract from their Report:

> . . . Mr. Kentridge (for the MWU) contended that we were not concerned with the effect of our award upon wages and conditions of other employees whether on the mines or in other industries. We cannot accept his argument . . . One of the essential matters which must be considered by a wage fixing authority is the inter-relation of wages in different occupations and in different parts of the Union. As the first report of the Economic and Wage Commission said in paragraph 104: 'No wage is an isolated thing, for every worker has other workers with whom to compare himself. Every change in a wage rate, therefore, excites hopes or fears in the minds of workers outside its scope, whose own rates bear a customary relation to the rate changed.'[14]

Moreover, despite appearances to the contrary, it was essentially the same story in the case of the demands by white wage-earners concerning job colour bars and the extension of white employment in the industry: that is to say whilst they received certain concessions these were strictly within limits which were tolerable to mining capital and did not amount to a restoration of the previous situation. As in the case of their wage demands the demands of the white wage-earners on these questions were put shortly after the new régime came to office, in this case at a conference between the new Minister of Labour and representatives of the white trade unions in August 1924. One set of resolutions adopted at this conference was summed up by one newspaper as a demand for: 'the government to pass legislation to eliminate competition from African labour which came to towns at wages below white subsistence levels'.[15] More particularly, resolutions concerning the mining industry called for a Wage Board investigation to apply statutory minimum wage rates (at white

subsistence levels) to a range of places and functions; for the imposition of a fixed statutory ratio of white to black employees; for the
repeal of all laws which imposed taxes, or otherwise 'assisted in' the
recruitment of indentured African workers for the mines; and for the
restoration of the job colour bar regulations in the Mines and Works
Act.[16] These demands were seen as the means of regaining their
losses of 1922, and also of eventually moving some way towards a
'white labour policy' in the industry. If they had been even partially
implemented they would have amounted to a major restructuring of
the relations of production in the industry with major effects on
productivity and profitability, for as the chairman of one of the
leading mining houses put it in 1925,

> It must not be overlooked that without the reorganisation of
> underground work dating from the 1922 strikes . . . the industry
> could not have obtained the results of which they are now
> justly proud.[17]

But of course many of these demands were not implemented. The
Wage Board never made any determinations affecting the mining
industry and indeed an attempt to get it to do so in the course of the
struggles leading up to the appointment of Lucas 'Arbitration Board'
was successfully resisted by mining capital. The Pact régime continued to administer the taxes and laws necessary to produce indentured migrant African labour power, and it even, against the protests
of white trade unionists,[18] renegotiated the agreement with the
Portuguese colonial régime to obtain indentured African labourers
from Mozambique (though perhaps not in the numbers which mining
capital would itself have wished for[19]). In short the white wage-
earning employees in the mining industry remained restricted during
the Pact period to the petty bourgeois places to which they had been
restricted after the 1922 strike, and the ratio of white to black
accordingly remained throughout more akin to that between 1922
and 1924 than that prior to 1922, as Table 12 shows.

What the white mine employees did receive however was statutory protection against displacement from *their existing places* in the
industry's division of labour. This came in the Mines and Works

Table 12[20]   *Witwatersrand goldmines: numbers employed and ratio white : black employees 1919–1932*

	Whites	Blacks	Ratio
1919	23,803	179,807	1: 7·5
1920	22,837	184,971	1: 8·1
1921	21,607	181,323	1: 8·4
1922	14,681	171,658	1:11·7
1923	18,613	189,889	1:10·2
1924	19,488	191,538	1: 9·8
1925	20,264	187,972	1: 9·3
1926	20,685	195,062	1: 9·7
1927	21,694	199,774	1: 9·2
1928	22,532	208,658	1: 9·3
1929	22,805	205,042	1: 9·0
1930	22,895	213,410	1: 9·3
1931	23,476	221,511	1: 9·4
1932	24,335	228,939	1: 9·4

Amendment Act of 1926 which restored the validity of the job colour bar regulations invalidated by the Hildick-Smith judgement in 1923. As we saw in the last chapter, the invalidation of these regulations in 1923 had not resulted in any major attempt by mining capital to place Africans in places previously covered by these regulations. In fact mining capital had at the time disavowed any intention of replacing white supervisors by Africans and had concentrated almost exclusively on making certain limited changes affecting engine and machine drivers. Nevertheless when the bill was introduced, following the recommendation of the Mining Regulations Commission,[21] it provoked a hostile response from mining capital, and its party political representatives and allies. Indeed in the 1925 and 1926 parliamentary sessions, the bill was rejected by the Senate (which still had a South African Party majority) and it was only finally passed after invoking the clauses in the Act of Union providing for a joint sitting of both houses of parliament in the event of an irreconcilable dispute between them. To understand this opposition we need to understand that it operated at the political and ideological as well as the economic level. At the economic level, naturally enough, mining capital preferred not to be restricted either in its future or present conduct. But much of the parliamentary and extra-parliamentary opposition expressed concern at the potential political effects such a measure might have on struggles by Africans. The gist of the parliamentary debates has been well summarised by Johnstone[22] and need not therefore be repeated here at any length. Essentially the South African Party leadership declared itself to be in favour of preserving 'white supremacy' in the industry's racist hierarchical division of labour, but against the government's chosen means of achieving this end viz. a colour bar bill, on the grounds that such an 'outward and visible sign of the intention . . . to keep the native down' would provoke 'a most serious disturbance in the native mind'.[23] There was also opposition from a number of leading churchmen who signed a 'memorial' declaring that 'it was a transgression of moral and religious principles that any man should be debarred by law from doing any kind of work for which he was qualified'.[24] This opposition to the bill on political and ideological grounds was in many respects a reflection of and a response to the growth of African trade union and other organisations. The ICU was at the height of its influence and it and a number of other black organisations had naturally enough set their faces against job colour bars—one of the most crudely visible indices of African exploitation in South Africa.[25] What was reflected in this form of opposition from white classes whose own interests of course depended upon other forms of African exploitation and oppression not then currently under debate was the fear that the passage of this bill would add another grievance which would make more difficult the accommodation or control of these African organisations.

Eventually however the bill did pass into law. Its main effect in practice was to provide statutory protection for the *existing position* of the white supervisory petty bourgeoisie in the industry's division of labour, but it also had the effect of placing some limits on the trend towards 'despecialising' the white supervisors' duties by effectively reintroducing the regulations which required a white supervisor to be personally present when certain tasks were performed.[26] It thus represented a real victory for the white wage-earning petty bourgeoisie, a concession won. But it was not a victory over capital which enabled the white new petty bourgeoisie to in any way fundamentally restructure the industry's relations of production to their advantage. It was not even a victory which enabled them to restore their position to that which had prevailed before the 1922 strike and it did not therefore, represent any real loss by mining capital of the powers of possession which it had won in 1922.

What was true of the struggles between white wage-earning employees and capital in the mining industry was also true of the struggles between white wage-earning employees and capital in other sectors. White wage-earning employees in these sectors managed to secure certain economic concessions but here, too, any such concessions were strictly limited to those compatible with the requirements of capital accumulation, and a host of other demands were either refused or only partially acceded to. Among the latter were demands for an eight hour day on the railways, compulsory unemployment insurance and state old age pensions.[27] But we can illustrate this point more effectively in the case of one sector—the industrial sector—by reproducing statistics showing the movement of white wage rates during the Pact period. Table 13 shows that whilst the wages of white employees in the industrial sector increased (in real terms) over the period, there were no dramatic gains for white wage-earners at capital's expense. Indeed, the wages as a proportion of the 'value added' figure suggests the likelihood that the rate of surplus value in manufacturing industry remained constant, or perhaps even increased slightly, over the period, thus indicating that the gains made by the white wage-earners were no more than the gains 'available' to wage-earners under conditions where capital accumulation takes place through the extraction of relative surplus

Table 13[28]   *Selected   wage   statistics—industrial   sector—selected*
         years

	Average white industrial money wages (male and female) per annum	Index of real wages of white adult males employed in 'engineering and metal' and in 'general manufacturing' industries (1938 = 1000)		Total wages and salaries (white and black) as percentage of 'value added'
		Engineering	General manufacturing	
1919/20	£ 231			49 %
1923/4	£ 228			50
1924/5	£ 220			46
1925/6	£ 219	900	888	49
1926/7	£ 219	917	888	49
1927/8	£ 218	923	894	46
1928/9	£ 215	934	894	46
1929/30	£ 221	958	895	49
1930/1	£ –			–
1931/2	£ –	no census		
1932/3	£ 184	1,049	989	44

value. In short, therefore, in industry, in mining (and indeed in commerce and agriculture as well) the demands of capital accumulation continued, during the Pact period as before, to dominate over the demands of all other classes.

But the real significance of the state's intervention in respect of the struggles of white wage-earners during the Pact period lay beyond the fact that it continued, despite the alliance between white wage-earners and the hegemonic fraction, to act in defence of the essential requirements of capitalist production against the demands of the white wage-earning classes. Its fundamental role in the economic class struggle remained to defend the power bloc against the potential political threats posed by the struggles of other classes, including those of the white wage-earning allies of the hegemonic fraction. As previously indicated the means by which the state attempted to defend the power bloc against the political threats posed by the struggles of white wage-earners did not alter substantially during the Pact period. It continued to seek to isolate and contain their struggles within racially discriminatory 'industrial relations' apparatuses through that combination of enticement and coercion known as 'compulsory conciliation'. In fact as we indicated earlier even the legislative means remained essentially unchanged. The Industrial Conciliation Act, offering on the one hand legal recognition for trade unions and the prospect of securing certain economic concessions through institutionalised bargaining procedures, and on the other hand placing barriers in the ways of alternative forms of struggle, was taken over and administered practically unchanged by the Pact régime. Indeed various demands coming from the white trade union movement for 'drastic amendment' were resisted by the Pact régime, including a demand to remove the clause preventing individuals from applying for a conciliation board sitting (which was retained in modified form).[29]

But what had changed by the time the Pact came to administer the Act was that there was, in the wake of the strike of 1922, a much greater degree of political commitment on the part of the dominant classes to making a 'conciliation' system function effectively. This was true of all fractions and was indeed already evident at the drafting stage of the bill when, within limits, a number of concessions had been made in order to make the bill 'acceptable' to reformist trade unionists. But such commitment was perhaps rather firmer in the case of national capital which, as we saw earlier had put itself forward and achieved hegemony at least partly on the basis of its particular relationship with white wage-earners and its unique ability to restore order and social stability. The Pact period thus saw a considerable effort by the state directed at 'making the conciliation system work'. This involved, on the one hand, a series of state interventions to ensure that sufficient of the 'available' concessions were actually granted through the institutionalised bargaining process to entice white wage-earners to accept it. Many of the concessions granted in the mining industry, for example the 'temporary arbitrary increase',[30] were thus only granted after considerable pressure by the state. Making the conciliation system 'work', however, also involved the state in placing obstacles in the way of other forms of struggle, notably strikes. The Act itself, as we saw, effectively prohibited strikes not by formally proscribing them, but by creating so many preconditions that, in the words of one experienced participant, 'a successful legal strike' became 'almost an impossibility'.[31] The Pact régime in administering the Act thus also enforced these clauses. In part this involved state officials in a good deal of (at least sometimes effective) 'moral suasion'. When strikes were threatened state officials would intervene to persuade, cajole or threaten trade union officers or strikers that their action was 'illegal' and that they should instead rely upon 'proper channels'. One example of this was the intervention by Minister of Labour, Boydell, to persuade members of the MWU to abandon their 'guerrilla strikes' against the Lucas award.[32] In certain cases too, there were prosecutions for involvement in 'illegal strikes' under the Act. For example in 1932 there were 109 such cases.[33] In addition to the greater level of actual state activity (the securing of concessions on the one hand and the impeding of strikes on the other) there was also the fact of the party political relationship with the Labour Party which enabled the régime to put itself forward as a government 'sympathetic to the (white) working man' etc. and thereby to gain support for an acceptance of state institutions even in the absence of any real concessions or coercion. This factor should not be underestimated. There are numerous references in the contemporary 'labour press' (both reformist and left wing) to the ways in which either 'loyalty to the Labour cause' or 'hatred of Smuts' led, during the first two years of the Pact at least, to passivity and acceptance of state institutions.[34] For all these reasons, plus the fact that a large section of the 'white labour movement' consisted of organisations of petty bourgeois rather than working class elements with, potentially, a much greater degree of commitment to reformist solutions generally (see p. 195 later), the

Pact period was the period in which for the first time a really effective, comprehensive institutionalisation of the struggles of white wage-earning employees occurred. As the following table shows, during the Pact period, strikes by whites decreased both in terms of numbers involved and average duration, whilst the numbers of white wage-earners subject to institutionalised bargaining procedures increased.

But the institutionalisation of these struggles had a significance beyond the fact that it succeeded in reducing the number of strikes

Table 14[35]   *Selected strike statistics and statistics relating to the institutions set up in terms of the Industrial Conciliation Act*

	strikes		industrial conciliation act machinery		
	number of whites involved in strikes	average number of man days lost per striker*	number of industrial councils in existence at year ended 30th June	number of conciliation board agreements & awards	number of 'employees' covered
1910–1921 (average)	14,762*	14·3*	—	—	—
1925	—	—	2	7	
1926	768	1·1*	14	5	
1927	740	1·8*	22	3	
1928	710	1·9*	29	5	43,000
1929	na	na	31	8	47,790
1930	387	5·8	38	7	45,049
1931	3,811	11·1	43	7	45,462
1932	2,387	8·6	41	9	46,252
1933	1,255	11·7	35	6	40,240

*white and black.

at a particular conjuncture. Institutionalisation within the apparatuses set up by the Industrial Conciliation Act had the effect of bureau-cratising the white trade unions (or at least of increasing the level of bureaucratisation already present). To appreciate the effects of this, we have to understand something of the essential meaning of the phenomenon of bureaucratisation. It is not, as Poulantzas has argued, simply a 'technical' characteristic of organisations which reach a certain size. But rather

> in the only possible rigorous sense of the term bureaucratiza-tion is the effect in the social division of labour at the institu-tional level, of a combination of bourgeois ideology and the petty bourgeois ideological sub-ensemble, and of an embellished and deformed reproduction of the bourgeois political relations of domination/subordination. Its characteristics, which have been studied by Max Weber as well as by Marx, Engels and Lenin, consist in an axiomatized system of rules and norms which distribute spheres of activity and competence; the im-personal character of its various functions; the payment of offi-cials by fixed salaries; recruitment by appointment from above . . . ; specific forms of obscuring knowledge within the organi-zation by bureaucratic secrecy; specific forms in which the 'hierarchy' operates by way of successive stages of 'authority' . . . centralism, in so far as each level communicates with others by way of the higher level, which gives rise to a specific form of isolation of agents, etc.[36]

The bureaucratisation of the white trade unions essentially meant therefore the 'embellished and deformed' reproduction within them of the bourgeois political relations of domination/subordination, through the creation and sustenance of hierarchical structures and the concomitant disorganisation and isolation of the lower echelons. In the specific case of the white trade unions in South Africa this took the form of the creation and sustenance of a distinct hierarchy of salaried trade union officials—numbering between 400 and 500 by the latter part of the Pact period[37]—'professionally engaged' in the dual functions of negotiating compromises through the complex procedures laid down in the Act and disciplining memberships to accept compromise concessions.

Although there were no doubt a considerable number of reformists and class collaborators within the white trade union movement who welcomed the opportunity to restructure unions along these lines, this tendency towards bureaucratisation was fundamentally the product of the institutional structures (and the conditions of class struggle which enabled this institutionalisation to proceed) rather than of the volition of particular agents. The negotiating procedures laid down in the Act were complex, esoteric and centralised, in a word bureaucratised, and participation within them therefore of itself imposed bureaucratisation on the unions quite independently of the wishes of individual trade union officials. As one somewhat reluctant contemporary trade unionist explained,

> Trade union officials have an enormous amount of their time
> taken up in attending to the business of Conciliation Boards and
> Industrial Councils, with the result that the work of organiza-
> tion, which is the rock foundation of the trade union movement,
> is sadly neglected, thus rendering the various organizations in-
> capable of fighting.[38]

The inevitable result of institutionalisation was thus bureaucratisation and isolation of the rank and file membership. For a short time this disorganisation manifested itself in an actual decrease in union memberships. The official statistics show a fall in the membership of registered trade unions from 67,200 in 1926 to 58,400 in 1927, rising only slightly to 64,800 in 1928.[39] Such extreme disorganisation was however short lived (the statistics show a rise in membership to 69,900 in 1929), for capitalist employers began to see advantages in their white employees being members of bureaucratised trade unions, and they began to assist in the task of recruitment, in the main by collecting dues and entering into closed shop agreements. A Government Commission explained why:

> In these days when the employees in a single workshop often
> number many hundreds, the arrangement of individual contracts
> of service would present many administrative difficulties and

for this reason alone many employers have adopted the policy of encouraging their employees to link up with unions . . . The better type of employer also appreciates the fact that well organized and disciplined trade unions can do much to reduce evasion of industrial legislation by . . . less reputable (competitors).[40]

Except for the short initial period therefore disorganisation and isolation manifested itself not in reduced union membership but in a widely recognised apathy and acquiescence on the part of rank and file memberships.[41]

Institutionalisation in itself was of course not universally welcomed by all fractions within the 'white labour movement'. The left wing represented mainly by the Communist Party and its supporters continued to oppose the 'conciliation shackles',[42] throughout the Pact period and beyond, and in fact during the earlier years they had a fair degree of support among the unions of white manual industrial workers which were generally far more resistant to the process of institutionalisation than were the unions of mental or supervisory new petty bourgeois wage-earners or the unions of artisan workers. Thus when Cresswell attempted early in 1925 to reorganise the trade union federation as a bureaucratised wing of the Department of Labour, he was (despite the support of the unions of various artisan and new petty bourgeois wage-earners such as miners, printers, bank officials and municipal employees[43]) at least partially thwarted by the support which existed among the unions of non-skilled industrial workers for radical organisations and 'left' motions. He was for example unable to gain acceptance for his Emergency Powers Bill[44] (although the MWU delegate supported it in principle), or to prevent the election to key positions of a number of Communist Party members and sympathisers opposed to his plans.[45] Moreover, several of those actually elected to the first executive of the reconstituted South African Association of Employees Organisation (later SA Trades Union Congress) were opposed to the Industrial Conciliation Act, preferring instead 'complete liberty of action'.[46] Nevertheless, as indicated earlier, the institutionalisation of white trade unions and thus their bureaucratisation proceeded. By the time of the report of the first Government Commission to review the functioning of the Act (1935) the process was, if not completed, at least very far advanced indeed. The Commissioners and many of the witnesses giving evidence before them eulogised at length about the ways in which the Act 'made unions less militant'[47] or resulted in 'the creation of settled conditions of employment'.[48] The report noted however that there was still some opposition to bureaucratisation among white trade unionists but reported that among trade union 'leaderships' such opponents were an isolated minority e.g. of the trade union 'leaders' who appeared before the commission 'few desired (the Act's) repeal'.[49] Not surprisingly therefore it also found that among 'employers generally' there was widespread support for the Act, and not only that but in view of the various disciplinary and administrative functions unions had come to perform, several expressed the view that the 'trade union movement' had become *an almost indispensable part* of our social structure'.[50]

This was the real achievement of the Pact in so far as its policies towards the white wage-earning classes were concerned. At the cost of certain economic concessions (all well within capital's 'capacity to pay'), and greatly assisted by the party political relationship with the Labour Party as well as by the fact that a large proportion of the organised 'white labour movement' consisted of petty bourgeois rather than working class elements, the Pact régime had succeeded in bringing about the almost complete political capitulation of the 'white labour movement' to capital. By institutionalising and bureaucratising the white trade unions it had ensured that these organisations would never again pose the kinds of political threats to capital which they had previously. Moreover this had been achieved at a critically significant conjuncture. The '20s were decisive years for the African working class, with the rise of the ICU and the use by Africans of the strike weapon for the first time on a significant scale. What the Pact régime had achieved through its largely successful institutionalisation of the 'white labour movement' was thus also the elimination of any possible reinforcement (whether intentional or unintentional) of the struggles of the African dominated classes by those of white wage-earners. As it was, repeated appeals for solidarity from the ICU remained largely unheeded by the 'white labour movement'[51])—parts of which were in addition to all other considerations, hostile to the ICU on the grounds that as a general union it was potentially 'extremist' or 'syndicalist'.[52] The Pact period became in fact the first extended period in the history of South Africa during which the number of blacks on strike exceeded the number of whites.[53]

The state and the 'poor white problem' 1924–1932

Having now indicated something of the general character of the state's interventions in respect of the white wage-earning classes during the Pact period, and having examined its role in effecting an institutionalisation of the white trade unions within the 'industrial relations' structures established during the latter part of the period of mining capital's hegemony, we can now proceed to analyse state activity in connection with the 'poor white problem' during the Pact period. As we indicated earlier the new trajectory of capitalist development made possible a number of new forms of state intervention to ensure the assignment of 'poor whites' to various places in the division of labour. In fact, during the Pact period the various forms of state activity in connection with the 'poor white problem' became co-ordinated under the auspices of a newly established state department, the Department of Labour, and acquired a new name in the dominant ideology—the 'civilised labour policy' ('civilised' being the euphemism for white, apparently selected with South Africa's image at the International Labour Organisation in mind[54]).

Of course the new forms of state activity in this connection cannot be explained by reference to the new trajectory of capitalist development alone. Part of the reason for this increased activity must be located in political factors: firstly in the overall heightening at particular conjunctures of the common political problems faced by the dominant classes as a result of 'poor white' unemployment. The Pact régime assumed office in a period immediately following an acute crisis involving in part the question of the relationship of the marginalised 'poor whites' to the state. We saw in the last chapter that 'poor white' elements had played a prominent part in the armed struggle of 1922, and we also saw, furthermore, that, with the beginnings of the formation of a permanently urbanised African proletariat, there was increasing concern among the political representatives of all the dominant classes and fractions about the potential effects of 'poor whiteism' on social stability in the urban areas. Indeed with the numbers of 'poor whites' estimated to have reached between 150,000 and 200,000 by 1924,[55] there were a number of 'dire warnings' emerging from academic and other circles. For example, in an influential article written in 1924 the well known liberal academic, Edgar Brookes, warned the dominant classes that if they lost the political support of the increasing number of 'poor whites' through their failure to find a more effective solution to the 'poor white problem', the African would be placed 'in a position to bargain for himself and to entrench and improve his (political) position' at their expense.[56]

Partly therefore the increased level of state activity in connection with the 'poor white problem' at this time has to be understood as a response to the heightening of a common political problem faced by the dominant classes. In part too it has to be understood in terms of the particular political interests of the hegemonic fraction. As we have already seen national capital had achieved hegemony at least partly because it had been able to set itself up within the power bloc as uniquely placed to organise a solution to the political problems posed for the power bloc by the white wage-earning classes, and its position of hegemony therefore depended in part at least on its ability to actually implement some more effective 'solution' to these 'problems', as well as, of course, on its ability to retain some degree of direct support among the white wage-earning classes.

But if such political factors explain the 'desirability' or the necessity from the bourgeois point of view, of new state interventions in connection with the 'poor white problem', it is the new trajectory of capitalist development inaugurated by the state under the hegemony of national capital which explains how such new 'solutions' were made possible within the constraints of the capitalist mode of production. During the period of mining capital's hegemony industrial and agricultural development had been curtailed (by the denial of tariff protection etc.) for the benefit of mining capital in its struggle to minimise its costs. And one effect of this was that within the resulting pattern of capitalist development there was only a fairly limited scope for the *profitable* employment of white labour power (given the different structural conditions under which white and African labour power were reproduced in the social formation) regardless of the degree of 'political will' involved. In the goldmining industry itself profitability was critically dependent on limiting white employment to supervisory places, whilst the restrictions on the development of national capital limited the number of places available in industry both by limiting the overall development of the forces of production in that sector, and (as we shall see of crucial importance in this context) by delaying its transition from manufacture to machinofacture. By inaugurating a new phase of capitalist development in which, *to serve the interests of the politically hegemonic national capitalist fractions*, industrial and agricultural development was given priority, the state thus also simultaneously created a number of new opportunities for more effective interventions to defend the political interests of the power bloc against the effects of the 'poor white problem'.[57]

So far as the previously hegemonic mining capitalist fraction and its allies were concerned, this placed them in a somewhat ambivalent position. On the one hand they were opposed to protection and the other measures which promoted industrial and agricultural development by appropriating surplus value produced in the mining industry. But on the other hand their interests too were potentially threatened by the 'poor white problem' and they were not therefore opposed to the state's making interventions to assign white rather than black agents to the places actually created through industrialisation particularly if this could be made compatible with profitability. In practice therefore their political representatives raised a highly selective opposition to some of the measures introduced under the 'civilised labour policy' complaining about such things as the precise incidence of the cost involved or about certain specific measures (usually as proposed by the Labour Party rather than as actually implemented), but combining this with a very great deal of general political support both for the overall goals behind the policy and for a large number of specific measures. The overall degree of consensus within the dominant classes was perhaps best summed up by Smuts, when he told parliament in 1927, 'There are not many members in the House who object to a sane moderate civilised labour policy.'[58]

In turning now to examine in more detail the interventions made by the state in terms of the 'civilised labour policy' we can begin by conveniently dividing them into two categories: the first dealing with those interventions to promote the 'civilised labour policy' in the 'private sector' and the second with the 'civilised labour policy' and state departments.

1. *The 'civilised labour policy' and 'private' capital*

The main legislative and administrative measures concerned with promoting the employment of 'civilised labour' by 'private' capital consisted, during the Pact period, of the following:

1) The Apprenticeship Act, which provided for the training of white youths to fill places as artisans,

2) The Customs Tariff Act of 1925 which, like its predecessors, included a clause making tariff protection conditional upon the employment of a 'fair amount' of white labour,

3) The 'fair labour' clauses in government contracts which laid down similar conditions for capitalists tendering for government contracts, and

4) The Wage Act which provided for the application of statutory

minimum wage determinations at or above the 'civilised' minimum subsistence level.

To these should also be added the frequent propaganda campaigns conducted by the newly formed Department of Labour.

Of the above some were of little real significance in practice, some were of significance only in so far as they promoted industrial development, and some represented a real intervention by the state with determinate effects on the productive process and the relations of production. But in order to begin to analyse and interpret them more fully we need first to examine in more detail some of the changes which occurred within the industrial sector during these years.

1.1 The transition from manufacture to machinofacture

As we have seen in previous chapters, prior to the Pact period South African industry remained with few exceptions, at the stage of capitalist *manufacture* as distinct from capitalist *machinofacture*. That is to say its labour processes depended upon either the simple combination by capital of pre-existing handicraft processes or the simple division of handicraft processes into detail operations which still retained their essential character as handicraft processes. However, through the measures introduced by the Pact for the benefit of industrial capital (protection etc.) the conditions were created not only for an extension of existing productive activities but also for *the beginnings of* a transition to capitalist machinofacture in South African industry; indeed in some cases for a transition to automation along the lines of the assembly line *à la* Ford. Some indication of this trend is given in the macro statistics which show a rise in the depreciated capital stock per employee from £167 in 1924 to £200 in 1930.[59] But the picture given by such averages is limited and in some respects misleading. The Pact period represented an early phase in the transition to machinofacture, during which (and this will be of crucial importance later) only a minority of the individual capitals in any particular industry or sector actually reached the stage of machinofacture. Other indices of the transition to machinofacture are therefore perhaps more significant. Among these we can quote the numerous articles in industrial journals about the new machinery being introduced, both by locally based capitals and by new foreign investors (like General Motors which set up a plant in 1926[60]); the growing concern in such journals and in speeches by industrial capitalists with Fordism and so-called 'scientific management'; and such things as the fact that as early as 1928 a conference on 'mass production methods' urged the government to make certain changes beneficial to capitalists employing such processes.[61]

Now a transition from capitalist manufacture to capitalist machinofacture does not simply represent the addition of an external thing (a machine) to a given quantity of labour power. Fundamentally, such a transition represents a change, indeed a profound change, in the relations of production. Under conditions of capitalist manufacture, where the labour process depends upon the combination of handicraft processes, there exists only what Balibar has called, following Marx, *the formal subsumption* of the worker to capital.[62] That is to say whilst the worker has surplus value extracted from him through the relations of property, his manual labour remains 'the regulating principle of production' and control over the labour process (the powers of possession) is therefore not yet firmly in the hands of capital. Capitalist machinofacture on the other hand involves the *real subsumption* of the worker to capital. That is to say, under machinofacture, the worker is subordinated to capital not only through the extraction of surplus value under the property relationship but also in the labour process itself through the subordination of his labour to the performance of the machine. As Balibar puts it, 'The previous relationship is inverted: rather than the instruments having to be adapted to the human organism, that organism must be adapted to the instrument.'[63] In the most advanced forms of capitalist machinofacture—mass production on lines of continuous flow—that subordination is most complete. For under conditions of capitalist mass production, as well as determining the method and form of work, the machine also dictates the pace at which the worker works.[64]

The occurrence of such changes in the relations of production also have their repercussions on the characteristics which capital seeks in its labour force. As mechanisation proceeds, so capital requires less and less of the skilled (artisan) labour power supported by unskilled 'helpers' which it required during the phase of manufacture. Increasingly it requires instead operative or semi-skilled labour power which being labour power adapted to the needs of a machine is not only labour power of a different grade but labour power of a fundamentally different kind. Broadly following Gramsci,[65] the subordination of a worker to an inanimate machine cannot be achieved on the basis of simple direct coercion alone. Rather 'coercion . . . has to be ingenuously combined with persuasion and consent'.[66] It is necessary therefore that the 'automatic and mechanical attitudes' appropriate to a mechanised capitalist labour process—and distinct from the 'psycho-physical' requirements which capital demands in either skilled or unskilled workers—be to some extent internalised in the operative worker. In other words it is necessary for the operative worker to undergo some form of appropriate socialisation both inside and outside of his work. Gramsci thus saw the prohibition and puritanism which characterised the United States in the mid '20s as part of an unprecedented conscious drive by capital to create 'the new type of worker and of man' required for machinofacture. Furthermore, though the time needed to train an operative worker is much less than the time needed to train a skilled (artisan) worker, operative labour is specialised and a high 'labour turnover' can therefore reduce total productivity. Capital thus requires a degree of stability in its operative labour force: certainly a greater degree of stability than is necessary in an unskilled labour force. In short therefore it requires in an operative labour force a stable 'pool' of workers who while not skilled are disciplined, that is to say are socialised to subordinate themselves to an inanimate machine and to *internalise* various appropriate capitalist virtues: punctuality, hard work, loyalty, etc.

For those capitalists utilising machine and mass production processes in South Africa during this early transitional period, non-

skilled white proletarians were an eminently suitable source of operative labour power. In the first place they were a relatively stable
population. It was true that they were not unique in that respect but
in the mid '20s and early '30s a settled African proletariat was still
very much in the process of formation.[67] But more than that there
were several other ways in which 'poor whites' were thus suited. For
at least two decades the state had attempted, as part of the struggle
to solve the 'poor white problem', to socialise 'poor whites' in particular kinds of ways. For example as an acknowledged means of
preserving social stability 'poor white' children had received compulsory primary education.[68] A proportion indeed, as we have already
seen, had been 'familiarised' with the 'atmosphere and discipline of
the workshop' in industrial schools. The church too had played an
important part here. According to the 1932 Carnegie Commission
Report at least,

> Many of the finest qualities to be found among the (white)
> poorer classes of South African society—obedience to law,
> reverence for religion, respectable family life, good nature and
> attachment to ancestry . . . (could) in a large measure be attri-
> buted to the influence which the Church has exercised over
> them in the past.[69]

Though obviously not entirely successful in transforming the characteristics of all 'poor whites' such measures had at least produced a
stratum among them with the basic skills and general attitudes, such
as those listed in the quotation from the Carnegie Commission,
which capitalists require in operative workers. Moreover under the
particular conditions of transition to machinofacture the fact that
the socially determined costs of reproducing this white labour power
exceeded that of migrant (or indeed settled) African labour power
ceased to be an insurmountable obstacle to their employment. In the
first place machinofacture, allowing productivity to be increased
beyond the barriers imposed by traditional crafts and skills, brings
about the transition from extraction of absolute to extraction of
relative surplus value, and this means therefore that the rate of
surplus value can be maintained or even increased with an operative

workforce paid wages higher than those paid to unskilled workers under conditions of manufacture. And secondly, in a phase of transition before a particular more productive process becomes generalised it is in the interests of those capitals deploying that process to seek surplus profits by 'select(ing) and maintain(ing) in stability' the most highly productive labour force possible even at the cost of above average wages.[70] For these reasons the phase of transition to machinofacture is a phase of capital accumulation involving the payment by certain capitals of the much flaunted 'high wages'— that is to say high by comparison with the wages paid to unskilled workers under conditions of manufacture.

A word of caution—it is not being suggested that whites were the only possible source of operative labour power during this period, nor that it would have been totally impossible for capital to have obtained 'suitable' operatives from the ranks of the proletarians of other races. On the contrary even in the very early days there were some coloureds and Asians and a very few Africans employed in operative places.[71] The point being made here is, to put it no stronger, that it was, under the circumstances of the transition to capitalist machinofacture in South Africa, in the *economic interests* of capitalists utilising mechanised production processes to employ non-skilled whites, despite the fact that their socially determined wage costs were higher than those of African proletarians.

This is clearly indicated both by the large number of statements made by such capitalists at the time and by their actual employment practices. Several of the witnesses giving evidence before the Economic and Wages Commission, for example, spoke of their preference for whites in work which from their descriptions is identifiable as operative work.[72] And a number of industrialists also referred to a similar preference in journal articles. For example, one wrote that he always used whites where the work required 'steady efficiency'.[73] Furthermore what was expressed verbally also seems to have been put into effect in concrete practice. For example, the Chief Inspector of Factories reported in 1927 that there was a tendency for new more mechanised factories to employ a greater proportion of whites.

'In several factories, commencing operations,' he wrote, 'Europeans only will be employed.'[74]

But we can perhaps make the point more effectively by examining the case of General Motors. General Motors set up its plant in 1926 and although the work involved was mainly assembly work, it was perhaps the most mechanised single plant in South Africa during the Pact period. It was in fact an 'all white' establishment[75] and its managers were among the most prominent of the advocates of a 'high wage' white labour policy. On one occasion, for example, the production manager made the following clearly implicit identification of settled, stable operative labour with white,

> The highest wage an industry can pay is always the most economical in the long run, if only the question of labour turnover is considered . . . Time lost in seeking new labourers to replace transient or temporary workers . . . added to damages and waste of material handled by them is a factor not sufficiently considered by employers of cheap labour . . .
>
> To come to the local conditions in South Africa, where the cost of living for Europeans is relatively high, low wages would make it almost impossible to operate any industry aside from those of pastoral origin, requiring only the services of semi-barbarians, while a fair wage would encourage the only kind of individual that is worthwhile.[76]

It is only by understanding this tendency for more mechanised industrial capitals to employ more whites during this early transitional period that we can understand the actual effects of the state's interventions under the 'civilised labour policy' at this time. Apart from the Apprenticeship Act, under which by the end of the period some 6,898 white youths were being trained for eventual assignment to skilled (artisan) places,[77] most of the measures represented interventions to assign white proletarians to places as semi-skilled operatives. Of these the Customs Tariff Act functioned to achieve this end simply through promoting industrial expansion, for despite the various estimates that there were more whites employed in industries subject to tariff protection,[78] this was mainly due to the fact that protection of itself promoted expansion and created the conditions for mechanisation rather than to any specific effect of the 'civilised labour' provisions in the Act. There is actually very little evidence that this clause had much effect on its own. There was considerable difficulty in defining precisely what a 'fair amount' of 'civilised labour' should mean in practice[79] and there was no actual withdrawal of tariff protection on these grounds during this period. Indeed when the Minister of Justice Pirow threatened such a withdrawal in 1931 he was forced to retract by declaring that he had been speaking of his 'personal policy'.[80] As such, therefore, the continued opposition by mining capital and its allies to the Customs Tariff Act although sometimes couched in terms of the 'civilised labour policy' actually represented the continued opposition of mining capital to the appropriation of 'its' surplus value to subsidise local industrial development and not opposition to the assignment of whites to particular places in the social division of labour.

Of the other measures the propaganda activities of the Department of Labour mainly had effect in conjunction with other measures and there is little evidence that they had much significant impact on their own except perhaps in reinforcing the identification of operative with white. One possible exception however was in the case of the food industries where the ideology of racism was used with some 'success' to persuade a number of food manufacturers to 'go all white' on alleged health grounds.[81] In fact at one stage the régime even considered the subsidisation of the food industry as a means to this end (though it eventually decided against).[82] But the two remaining measures—the 'fair labour' clauses in government contracts and Wage Board determinations—did represent state interventions which of themselves did have determinate effects on the relations of production in industry. Since the former only applied to firms tendering for government contracts for the duration of the contract period and were thus, as even the Minister of Labour acknowledged, only 'temporary' in their effects,[83] the more important of the two were the Wage Board determinations whose functioning we must now proceed to examine in more detail.

1.2 The wage board and the promotion of the 'civilised labour
     policy' in industry

Wage Board determinations were made under the provisions of the
Wages Act (number 27) of 1925. The Act provided for the establishment of a Wages Board consisting of three state officials. On the
activation of a defined procedure this Board was required to investigate the wages and conditions in any industry, trade or undertaking
except agriculture, domestic service and some parts of the state
sector and to make recommendations to the Minister of Labour. If
the Minister approved the recommendation he could then issue a
'determination' declaring the wage level recommended to be the
minimum legal wage which could be paid to any employee in that
industry. The basic structure was derived from the Wages Board system operating in Australia, but there was a significant difference in
the South African Act. The South African Wage Board was (under
the 1925 Act) directed to recommend wage rates at which 'employees may be able to support themselves in accordance with
civilised habits of life'. 'Civilised habits' were defined as 'habits of
life as ordinarily understood by Europeans in the Union'.[84] But employee was defined as 'any person whatsoever employed by or
working for any employer',[85] thus in contrast to the equivalent definition in the Industrial Conciliation Act, not excluding 'pass bearing'
Africans. There was however a let-out clause. If after taking into
account *inter alia* 'the ability of employers in that trade or section to
carry on the same successfully' the Board felt it could not recommend a 'civilised wage' for all employees, it was enjoined to make no
recommendation but instead to 'report to the Minister on the conditions in such trade and the reasons for its decision'. The minister
could then, at his discretion, 'direct the board to make such recommendation as it may deem fit'.[86]

   When the Bill was introduced into the House of Assembly by
Minister of Labour Cresswell early in 1925, although it received the
support of capitalist agriculture represented through the Nationalist
Party—apparently because agriculture itself was exempt and because

a 'white labour policy' was seen as a means of preventing African labour being drawn off the farms into industry, in addition to political considerations[87]—it was greeted by the spokesmen for mining and industrial capital as the example *par excellence*, of 'drastic' anti-capitalist legislation.[88] At its second reading the bill was taken through four days of debate by the South African Party parliamentary opposition, including one 18 hour (all night) sitting during which every SAP member spoke. At the select committee stage both the Chamber of Mines and the Chamber of Industries called for massive exemptions.[89] And even when the bill finally passed into law there were several challenges to its provisions in the courts. Indeed on two occasions court judgements had the effect of declaring all of the Board's previous work null and void: the latter occasion necessitating the passing of a Validation Act in 1930.[90]

The united opposition to this bill coming from mining and manufacturing capital (the opposition to the Act coming in the form of coutroom challenges will be dealt with later) has to be understood in the context of the stated policies of the Labour Party. For years the Labour Party had recognised, quite correctly, that the fundamental causes of white unemployment lay in the fact that capital had through the state created a system under which the value of African labour power was kept at a level far below that at which white proletarians could exist. As a white labour based 'reformist' party however, its 'solution' lay not in posing any fundamental challenges to the system of capitalist exploitation as such, nor even in making any serious effort to support African workers in the economic class struggle, but rather in seeking to 'reform' capitalism by removing particular 'incentives' to the employment of African workers. In particular it sought to establish a 'free labour market' at 'civilised minimum' wage levels throughout the economy by means of a combination of measures including minimum wage regulation.[91] Pledges to 'develop the reserves'[92] notwithstanding, it was in fact a programme for the mass marginalisation of the African dominated classes with all that entails (mass starvation etc.). But it was also a programme which presented a major challenge to the basis on which capital accumulation had proceeded hithertofore. It was a bill of this sort coming from the representative of a party 'committed' to such a programme which provoked the hostility to this bill. What alarmed the spokesmen for the interests of manufacturing and mining capital was not so much the prospect that the bill would be used to raise some white wages and promote some white employment as such,[93] but the prospect that the Wage Board would (despite disclaimers from Cresswell[94]) be used to make determinations affecting a large number of places in the division of labour then occupied by Africans as a means of establishing the Labour Party's envisioned 'free labour market'. Thus, for example, when Smuts opposed the bill at the second reading debate he did so on the grounds that,

> We in this country know that all employment in South Africa has been built up on a different basis . . . It is not only in industry but in employment of all kinds that the essential racial and social difference is recognised. This Bill is going to make *a vast change* and introduce equality where there has so far been difference . . . I say that this bill will only have this effect, that it will close many industries, because you cannot, as our industries are today in South Africa, pay the black man a wage which will be a subsistence wage for a white man.[95]

Some of the more hysterical of the bill's opponents even considered that it would, through the clause allowing any 'sufficiently representative' group of employees to initiate a Wage Board investigation, be used as a means of promoting African trade unionism. J. S. Marwick, brandishing a copy of the famous Hertzog-Kadalie letter,[96] thus declared,

> I think that the minister, in introducing this bill, was at fault in not illustrating to us what the effect would be of applying it in the manner indicated in the views which he has proclaimed . . . over a long course of years . . . It seems to me that the whole policy of the legislation which has been introduced and the policy of the party led by the Minister of Labour is in the direction of forcing natives to become members of trade unions . . .

This bill will be a direct encouragement to coloured trade unionism because it will constitute for the first time an avenue whereby the native by combination can command an increase in wages, entirely apart from the rights of the situation, or entirely apart from any view which may be held about the natives' position in the land . . .[97]

If this is an instrument for laying down wage conditions generally,

he went on,

the Bill will mean a revolution of the whole of the conditions in South Africa with a consequent dislocation of every industry in the country.[98]

But of course the Wage Board did not become a general instrument for the establishment of the Labour Party's 'free labour market'. Mining capital successfully prevented it ever making any investigation affecting the mining industry (the Lucas investigation of 1927–7 took place under the terms of the Industrial Conciliation Act) and outside of the mining industry the Board confined itself to making 'civilised minimum wage' determinations covering a limited range of places. Moreover where such determinations were made, the notions of the 'civilised minimum' level and the occupations to which it should be applied were not derived from any 'perverse' ideology. Like the other concessions granted to white wage-earners those granted as part of the state's attempt to find a solution to the 'poor white problem' were restricted to those compatible with capital accumulation. What the Wage Board did in practice was therefore to base its 'civilised minimum' wage determinations upon the *actual existing* wages structures of those capitals in the particular industry concerned which paid relatively higher wages and employed more whites, and in this particular phase of the transition to machinofacture this meant the minority of more mechanised capitals. In other words in its attempt to promote white employment through the medium of the Wage Board the state was in effect harmonising itself with and promoting the trend towards mechanisation in South African industry which approximated to that of the more mechanised

capitals in the industry the Wage Board in effect gave a further competitive advantage to those capitals employing mechanised labour
processes and/or compelled other capitals to begin mechanisation.
This *modus operandi* was in fact made clear at the Board's inaugura-
tion ceremony when its first chairman explained,

> It seems to us that where one employer can pay good wages and
> give good conditions there is no reason why those who are pay-
> ing sweated wages should not be compelled eventually to rise to
> the same standard as the good employer. In trying to achieve
> that result the good employer will have no additional burden
> placed upon him that he does not carry today, but will be able
> to compete with his rival who is conducting his operations
> under sweated conditions . . . (because he will) be protected
> from undercutting on the part of the less scrupulous employer.[99]

The selection of the wage structures of the more mechanised
capitals as the norm was in fact also the basis on which the state
promoted the (more temporary) employment of whites through the
'fair labour' clauses in government contracts. The standard clause
read,

> The contractor shall pay rates of wages and observe hours of
> labour not less favourable than those commonly recognized by
> employers and trade societies (or, in the absence of such recog-
> nized wages and hours, those *which in practice prevail amongst
> good employers*).[100]

And this in effect meant in practice giving preference to more
mechanised capitals in government contracts: a factor reflected in an
early complaint by some manufacturers that the operation of 'fair
labour' clauses was giving 'unfair' advantages to the subsidiaries of
foreign firms.[101]

In the case of Wage Board determinations however, which after all
affected the whole of an industry or area, the state in fact proceeded
with a fair degree of caution. It was clearly not in the interests of the
politically hegemonic fraction to bring about even a short term disruption to the expansion of industrial capital, and the Act thus
required the Board to proceed in an orderly fashion, taking into

account the capacity of an industry to 'carry on successfully' after a Wage Determination. In practice therefore the Board in general set 'civilised wage' norms which were rather lower and covered fewer places than those in the individually most mechanised capitals in an industry. It also often allowed a fairly long period of adjustment so that other capitals could begin mechanisation, by making determinations under which minimum wages rose by stages to the 'civilised' norm.[102]

In so far as state interventions through the Wage Board essentially involved harmonising with the interests of the most productive capitals in an industry, and in so far as they were made in as 'orderly' a manner as possible, there is considerable validity in the Board's claims that (from the standpoint of capital accumulation in an industry as a whole) there were 'no dire effects from wage regulation'.[103] The Board itself gave various indications (increased output levels, constant prices, etc.) in its reports[104] but we can perhaps best illustrate this by considering statistics which might provide an index of the mass of surplus value produced. As the following table shows,

Table 15[105] *Index of mass of surplus value produced comparing industry as a whole and major industries in which wage determinations were made 1926–1933*

	All industries		Major industries subject to wage determinations	
1924/5	18,431	(£000)	2,127	(£000)
1925/6	19,563	average	2,368	average
1926/7	20,837	percentage	2,777	percentage
1927/8	23,199	increase:	3,022	increase:
1928/9	24,492	3·68% per	3,049	5·66% per
1929/30	24,526	year	3,144	year
1930–32	no census		no census	
1932/3	22,656		2,909	

in fact the figures for the money value of total production minus the money value of wages and materials consumed (an index of the mass of surplus value produced) actually increased during the Pact period faster in industries subject to wage determinations than it did in the industrial sector as a whole. In some cases indeed spokesmen for the interests of individual larger capitals argued that the Board's activities had been positively beneficial by creating the conditions necessary for mechanisation to be introduced into an industry. For example the Board reported that 'at a meeting which (it) . . . had with clothing manufacturers at the Cape during September 1931, a prominent manufacturer stated that the clothing determination had put the shirt industry on its feet' and similar comments were made by some spokesmen in the tea, coffee and chicory processing and other industries.[106]

But of course, in a class divided society no social process can be without contradiction. Gains for some class or social group are inevitably accompanied by losses for some others. And indeed there were two main class fractions which suffered, though in very different ways, as a result of Wage Board determinations. These were, among the dominant exploiting classes, small manufacturing capitalists (or petty commodity producers), and among the dominated exploited classes, unskilled (especially African) workers.

Small manufacturing capitalists were affected by being prohibited from driving down to previously prevailing levels the wages paid to workers performing certain key functions, thus having their capacity to extract surplus value from non-mechanised labour processes reduced. Although, as we have seen, the more 'progressive' of these small capitalists were often given time to begin mechanisation, and although after objections the Board in some cases made concessions to their interests, this inevitably meant that some lost their capacity to continue to extract surplus value altogether. Not surprisingly therefore wage determinations were frequently opposed by small capitalists. It was this contradiction between the state and small industrial capitalists which produced the court rulings to which we referred earlier. Barone Bros. whose case resulted in the first of the legal invalidations of the wage determinations was one of the smaller Pretoria bakery firms,[107] and Lewins whose case necessitated the passing of the Validation Act in 1930 was also almost certainly a small capitalist.[108] This contradiction furthermore, also explains the early opposition (until about 1929) on the part of the Federated Chamber of Industries to this measure which it is being argued was in no way antagonistic to the long term interests of capital accumulation in the industrial sector. At a time when only a minority of capitals in any industry were mechanised it is reasonable to suppose that the majority of the FCI's members were small capitalists and that it was speaking for their interests rather than for the interests of industrial capital as a whole. Certainly as we shall see more clearly later the FCI was speaking exclusively for the interests of small capital when it opposed a wage determination in at least one industry.

Black unskilled workers, the other group affected, suffered from the Wage determinations by being made to bear the whole of the burden implicit in any transition to machinofacture viz. 'the pitiless (elimination) from the world of labour . . . of part of the old working class'.[109] Wage Board activities had the effect of driving out of employment a considerable number of unskilled Africans as the Board candidly and unashamedly acknowledged. For example in one of its reports it wrote of how as a result of wage determinations

> there appears to have been a considerable reduction in some areas in the number of natives employed on unskilled work. The inference from this would seem to be that there had been a great waste in the employment of natives on such work, but now . . . only those necessary for carrying it on under efficient management are employed . . . It cannot be seriously maintained that any purpose is served that is useful to anyone, by conducting an industry inefficiently or by employing unnecessary persons.[110]

Moreover although the Board argued that it was from time to time involved in increasing the wages of certain categories of African workers remaining in employment,[111] in so doing it was actually fulfilling the function of containing the heightened class struggle by

African workers. This role of the Wage Board is really beyond the scope of the present study. But it should perhaps just be mentioned that it basically involved the Board setting wage rates at the *minimum* level compatible with containing the struggles and ensuring the reproduction in some condition of the settled urbanised African proletariat then in the process of formation. This emerged most clearly in a determination, covering unskilled (i.e. African) workers in Bloemfontein, made following a riot in 1925 and considerable agitation from the ICU. The determination eventually made was based on a poverty datum line type budget, compiled by a local organisation as the average of 69 budgets submitted by 'interested parties', which the Board then reduced by deducting certain items and on the now familiar assumption of more than one wage-earner per family.[112] In some of the other determinations the Board took the opportunity of adjusting 'non civilised' wages on a similar basis. However it was noticeably more flexible towards the demands of small capital on this question, and on some occasions when it would not budge on their complaints that 'civilised' wage rates were too high it made some concession to them by reducing the 'non civilised' wage levels in a proposed determination.[113]

But we can perhaps illustrate more clearly the modus operandi of the state's intervention to promote the employment of 'civilised labour' through the medium of the Wage Board (and substantiate the points made above) by examining in more detail the way in which the Board operated in one representative industry—that of sweetmaking.

1.2.1 The wage board and the 'civilised labour policy': illustrative study of the sweetmaking industry

The Wage Board began to investigate the sweetmaking industry in 1926 on a directive from the MInister of Labour. As a result of its investigations the Board found that there were 57 'establishments' in the industry ranging from one fairly mechanised factory employing

388 workers to a number of workshops in which the proprietor em-- ployed only one 'assistant'. In the most mechanised plant——that of Messrs. Wilson and Co.——the Board reported that the majority of the non-skilled employees were white women who were paid wages higher than the minimum rates provided for in terms of a determination made under the 1918 Regulation of Wages (Apprentices and Improvers) Act. Apart from Wilson's however it reported that very few of the other firms employed whites on what may be called a permanent basis; that is to say employed adults at wages which corresponded to the socially determined value of white labour power. In most cases if non-skilled whites were employed at all they were fairly low paid juveniles, who were often dismissed when they reached 18 years and became entitled to adult rates under the 1918 Act. In many cases, particularly in the smaller plants, the Board found that all the non-skilled functions were performed by Africans, and in the case of the small petty commodity producers, the proprietor's 'assistant' was without exception an African.[114]

At the end of its first report to the minister the Board concluded, as it did in the case of every other industry investigated, that

for a large number of employees in (the sweetmaking) industry (the Board) cannot for some time recommend a wage upon which the employees can support themselves in accordance with civilized habits of life.[115]

On receipt of a further directive under Section 3(3) of the Act to make such recommendations as it saw fit, the Board then recommended that the following wage rates be incorporated into a determination (which after slight adjustment they were):

1. Skilled Sweetmaker £5 10s.–£6 10s. per week varying with area[116]

2. Non-Skilled Grade I Males £2 10s.–£3 per week varying with area

Non-Skilled Grade I Females £1 17s. 6d.–£2 2s. 6d. per week varying with area

Non-Skilled Grade II £1–£1 4s. per week varying with area.

The pattern underlying these wage determinations can now be seen more clearly. The grade II rates were below the 'civilised minimum' and approximated to the rates then being paid to African workers. Grade I rates on the other hand approximated to the socially determined necessary subsistence levels for non-skilled whites—then about £3 a week for males and £2 for females. The grades in question were however defined not by race but by function. Grade II employees, in a definition frequently utilised in the case of other industries as well, were defined as those employed in 'carrying materials or utensils; cleaning workshops; washing or cleaning machines; carrying fuel to furnaces',[117] while Grade I employees were defined as all others. The intention therefore was to reduce the capacity of those capitals employing production processes in which lower paid Africans worked outside the Grade II definition to compete effectively against those employing production processes in which by and large they did not.

The extent to which the statutory enforcement of such rates represented an attempt by the Board to harmonise with the larger more mechanised capitals in the industry revealed itself on a number of levels. First of all in the fact that the larger capitals made no attempt to oppose the proposed determinations in spite of being given, in terms of statutorily defined procedures, every opportunity of doing so. As the Board reported with respect to Messrs. Wilson and Co., 'No objection was raised by that firm against the scale of wages proposed', which was indeed not surprising since it was already paying wages at rates similar to those laid down in the scale.[118] Nor was any objection made by the Transvaal Industrial Council, which consisted of three of the next largest firms, which instead voluntarily incorporated the rates into an Industrial Council agreement before the determination became effective: a move which led one of the firms in question to announce its intention to 'introduce up to date machinery'.[119] It also revealed itself, as the table below shows, in the fact that whereas the *accounting* gross profit[120] in the industry as a whole decreased as a rate on 'turnover', the accounting gross profit of seven firms 'including all the large firms' actually increased as a rate on 'turnover' during the first years of the determination (unfortunately the only years for which the Board extracted such a comparison).

Table 16[121] *Selected financial statistics, sweetmaking industry*

	seven firms including all the large firms		industry as a whole	
	1924/5	1926/7	1924/5	1926/7
Accounting Gross Profit	£185,439	£194,125	£322,295	£346,931
Percent on Turnover	37·2	37·7	35·4	35·2

On the other hand the degree to which the determination was antagonistic to the interests of smaller capitals was also clearly revealed in the Board's reports. Numerous individual small capitalists objected that the rates were 'too high' and several of these attempted to identify their own interests as the general interests of capital in the industry, arguing that the new rates would 'cripple the industry' or that they were 'beyond the ability of the industry to pay'.[122] Significantly the Federated Chamber of Industries originally supported the position of the objectors and claimed to be 'speaking for 80 per cent of the industry' in doing so.[123] However as the Board pointed out, the FCI was definitely not speaking for Wilson's or the Transvaal Industrial Council which together accounted for 34 per cent of total production.[124] This would seem to indicate that the FCI spoke in this conflict exclusively for small capital and that its stance was probably determined by the interests of the majority of the individual capitals affiliated to it, rather than by the relative economic strength of capitals in an industry.

On the claims of small capital the Board remained rigid, refusing to make any significant concession except allowing more time. For example, to a small firm who objected on the grounds that its wages bill would as a result of the determination be increased by some 68·9 per cent or £20,953 per annum it replied,

> Though the increase will be considerable in the wage bill of this firm, no case has been made out for departing from the wages set out in the proposed determination. Several *large* competitors of this firm have ... been paying those rates without complaint and there is no reason why this firm should be allowed to continue to have unfair advantage over its competitors.[125]

Moreover, since the Board was harmonising with the interests of the most productive capitals in the industry, it was able to refute the claims that the determination was damaging to the interests of capitalist production in general. The Board itself pointed out that output in the industry rose whilst average prices fell or remained constant and to this could be added the fact that the total 'value added' minus wages (a figure which we suggested might provide an index of the mass of surplus value produced) increased over the period from £346,000 in 1926 to £403,000 in 1930.[126]

The net outcome partly of the general tendency in capitalist production for more productive capitals to eliminate less productive capitals, and partly of the Wage Board's intervention to accelerate the process was that by 1933 the Board was able to report that the industry was as a whole considerably more mechanised than it had been in 1926. Accordingly the 'wide discrepancies' in the wage levels and employment structures had 'largely disappeared'.[127] And the

Table 17[128] *Sweetmaking industry: numbers employed*

	Feb. '26	Feb. '28	Feb. '30	Feb. '32
Whites	623 (30·6%)	736 (41·6%)	957 (44·0%)	961 (48·6%)
Africans	418 (20·5%)	317 (17·9%)	389 (17·9%)	336 (17·0%)
Coloureds and Asians	997 (48·9%)	718 (40·5%)	827 (38·1%)	681 (34·0%)
Total	2,038	1,771	2,173	1,978

overall intention to promote the employment of more whites and eliminate 'unnecessary' blacks had to a considerable extent been fulfilled as the comparative figures in Table 17 show. The industry had, in short, from the Board's point of view, undergone 'great improvement' since 1926.[129]

The fact that the state's *actual* interventions through the Wage Board (as distinct from the rhetoric surrounding the original Wage Bill) represented an attempt to solve a political problem common to all fractions of capital through harmonising with the most productive capitals in an industry, reflected itself in the distinct change in the stance towards the Wage Board of the Bill's original opponents within the power bloc. Mining capital, *de facto* if not *de jure* exempt, made few if any comments on the Wage Act after the compromise leading to the appointment of the Lucas Arbitration Board in 1927, and, in fact, when the revised Wage Bill was being discussed in 1937 the Chamber of Mines did not even bother to make representation before the select committee.[130] The Chamber of Industries which had in effect opposed the Bill in 1925 and raised considerable opposition to the Board during the first two years of its operations (e.g. in 1928 the FCI's outgoing chairman expressed 'alarm at the policy of the Board in some of its determinations' and declared that 'certain industries were being endangered'[131]) was already by 1929 showing signs of 'mellowing'. For example, although there was still some opposition to the Board from industrial capital,[132] an editorial in the journal, *Industrial and Commercial South Africa* commented on the Board's first three year report as follows:

> . . . while grounds for criticism do undoubtedly exist, there is much truth in the Board's contention that the industries which have come within the scope of their operations, so far from expiring are really flourishing and the pressure of higher wages which have been paid as a result of the Board's determinations, have unquestionably resulted in increased efficiency.[133]

Certainly, by the mid '30s, as mechanisation proceeded apace, opposition from organised industrial capital had all but melted away. By 1932 the Board was reporting that its work was being 'accepted in a better spirit'[134] by industrial capitalists generally. And by the time of the revised 1937 bill the FCI's boot was firmly on the other foot, as it demanded protection, not for small capital against wage determinations, but for larger capital against 'unscrupulous' competitors.[135]

This 'mellowing' by the Bill's original opponents was also reflected at the party political level. The South African Party which had in 1925 vigorously opposed the bill at second reading (indicating disapproval of the bill's principles) was by 1929 giving the Wage Board qualified support. For example, Smuts was declaring that he was 'not opposed to the Wage Board in principle'[136] and the SAP's election programme promised that under an SAP government 'The Wage Act will be maintained but will be restricted to the unorganised trades for which it was originally passed.'[137]

In short therefore the Wage Act as it eventually functioned in practice, represented part of a distinctly capitalist solution to a political problem facing all of the fractions of capital and as such, like many of the other measures concerned with assigning white rather than black agents to places in the division of labour, it too came to receive some degree of political support from all the major fractions in the power bloc.

2. *The 'civilised labour' policy in state departments*

In respect of the assignment of whites to places in state departments, the Pact period was essentially one of extension, expansion and co-ordination rather than of major qualitative change. In fact there was scarcely a programme introduced as part of the Pact's 'civilised labour' policy for state departments which did not have some precedent in state policy in earlier periods and as such the major measures implemented during the Pact period can be discussed here much more briefly.

Essentially 'relief works' were continued, and a new 'relief work' programme—the Hartebeespoort irrigation scheme—was introduced, but under the Pact the major emphasis was shifted towards expanding the number of permanent places for whites in state departments. Under a directive issued on 31st October 1924 government departments were instructed to seek ways of replacing African employees by whites, partly within their own (slightly increased) budgets and partly with the aid of subsidies made available through the Department of Labour. During the first 17 months (until the end of March 1926) some 1,361 African employees were replaced by 'civilised labourers' at an extra cost of £73,508[138] and by the end of March 1928 the total extra cost had risen to £121,111.[139] Thereafter, for ideological reasons, such calculations were discontinued,[140] but, according to Prime Minister Hertzog, by 1931 there were some 14,000 extra white employees in government departments'(including some 6,000 or so on 'relief work'),[141] indicating that by the end of the Pact period up to 8,000 places previously occupied by Africans had been turned over to whites. Some indication of the kinds of places turned over to whites under this policy can be gained from a set of guidelines produced in 1926 which recommended to 'all public bodies' that

> *where their financial position permits* the following occupations be reserved for Europeans 1. abbatoirs 2. drivers of vehicles 3. parks (labourers) 4. cemeteries (labourers) 5. forestry (labourers) 6. cleaning of water furrows 7. street cleaning 8. street repairing 9. artisan's labourers 10. market labourers 11. tram and car cleaners 12. school and office cleaners 13. messengers 14. doorkeepers.[142]

There were also similar moves in the railways. Between 1924 and 1932 the number of unskilled white labourers increased from 6,363 to 12,042 while the number of Africans employed fell from 35,532 to 17,467.[143] In addition there was an increase in the number of 'promotions' to graded posts particularly after 1927 when a new probationer scheme was introduced. Once again the estimate of the extra cost was discontinued in 1927 for ideological reasons, but between July 1924 and September 1927 the amount involved was £685,000[144] mostly met out of the railway's own budget.

Yet again while these measures certainly represented concessions to the 'poor whites' they were concessions made to defend capitalist interests within the institutions of the capitalist state and did not represent any dominance of 'poor white' interests in the state. The employment provided was by and large labouring employment in manual places and the wages, though higher than those paid to the Africans they replaced, remained at (or even below) the socially determined subsistence levels for unskilled whites. For example, in 1929 there were some white labourers in the Agriculture Department getting as little as 1s. 9d. per day,[145] and in 1930 there were 7,019 whites employed on the railways getting 5s. a day or less[146] (compared to a widely quoted 'civilised minimum' of about 8s. a day). Moreover, as between the fractions in the power bloc, most of these measures were entirely noncontroversial. Indeed, in many cases in so far as Government ministers and opposition were engaged in debates about these programmes at all, they were little more than debates about who thought up the measure first: the SAP or the Nationalists.[147] There was one exception to this however, the extension of white employment on the railways which did provoke a number of debates and conflicts. But even these were not debates about whether or not African workers should be dismissed and replaced by whites (on the contrary on that question SAP members frequently declared that it was their duty 'to co-operate with the government in a sympathetic manner to make that policy a success'.[148]) Rather they were debates about how the extra cost involved should be borne. Under the Pact régime's policies these costs were met out of the railway's own revenue funds which, under the discriminatory rating policy, meant that a disproportionate part of the cost was met by the railway's high rated customers, among them importers of machinery (notably mining capital). In several cases therefore, spokesmen for the interests of mining capital, whilst being careful to declare their support for the employment of 'civilised' rather than 'uncivilised' labourers, called for this to be met out of general government revenue. Thus, for example, in the railway budget debate in 1929 Sir Robert Kotze, SAP MP, director of the Anglo-American Corporation and former Government Mining Engineer, declared, 'I have no quarrel with the policy of employing civilised white labourers on railways, but the additional expenditure should fall on general revenue.'[149]

3. The 'civilised labour policies' and their effects on class formation

Having now examined the major interventions made by the state under the 'civilised labour policy' and having indicated something of the class interests such interventions were fundamentally intended to serve, we have now to briefly examine their overall effects on class formation. The first point to be made in this regard is that they did not at this stage totally eliminate the 'poor white problem'. The latter part of the Pact period was a period of recession affecting in particular capitalist agriculture and this coupled with the growing capitalisation of agriculture meant that the period was one in which large numbers of whites continued to be driven off the land. In fact by 1932 the numbers of 'poor whites' had reached record levels (300,000 according to one estimate).[150] Nevertheless the interventions made by the state during the Pact period were of crucial significance. In addition to the 11,000 or so assigned to places as landowners (under the Land Settlements Act) or petty bourgeois diamond diggers (under a new scheme introduced by the Pact),[151] industrialisation and the various interventions by the state had created the conditions for the first major transformation of a sizeable number of 'poor white' lumpen proletarians into members of a non-skilled manual working class. Official statistics show that the numbers of whites employed in private industry increased from 53,450 in 1924–5 to 68,981 in 1932–3 (an increase of 29 per cent)[152] and to this should be added the 16,000 or so whites who had been placed in non-skilled mostly manual employment in state departments.[153] Reference to Appendix 1 thus shows a sizeable increase between the census years 1926 and 1936 both in the absolute numbers and the proportion of the total white population occupying places in working class categories, particularly non-skilled and labouring categories.

However in bringing about this transformation of white lumpen proletarians into members of the white manual working class, the state had simultaneously placed a significant proportion of white manual workers in direct economic competition with African workers. For a sizeable proportion of the white manual working class their employment in such places depended directly upon the state's intervention to exclude African competitors, and this could be and was exaggerated by the dominant ideology to create an illusion of similar dependence among strata not actually dependent to the same degree. In transforming parts of the white lumpen proletariat into a stratum of the working class the state had thus simultaneously produced within the manual working class a 'terrifying real isolation effect' (Poulantzas) functioning along racial lines. African workers, for whom the 'civilised labour policy' meant exclusion from better paid jobs, or not infrequently actual dismissals, naturally enough opposed and resisted such interventions,[154] and this enabled African workers rather than capital to be presented as the white workers' 'enemy' while the state presented itself as the defender of their interests. Through guaranteeing certain of the economic interests of one stratum of the working class in order to protect the political interests of capital against the effects of the 'poor white problem', the state had thus also produced a division within the manual working class which must go a long way towards explaining why even among white non-skilled manual workers there was from the Pact period onwards a predisposition to adopt a supportive role for the form of state and a hesitancy about uniting in struggle with the African working class.[155]

Conclusion: the class positions of white wage-earners 1924–1932

Having now examined the relevant interventions by the state during the Pact period, we need to conclude with a few brief remarks about how they were reflected in the changing class positions taken up by the white wage-earning classes during the Pact period. In fact the contradictory character of state policy with respect to the economic demands of white wage-earners—the fact that it continued, on the one hand, to defend capital against demands incompatible with the essential requirements of capital accumulation, whilst, on the other hand, securing for white wage-earners more economic concessions than hitherto—reflected itself in fairly profound changes in the positions adopted by the white wage-earning classes during the period. On the one hand the fact that certain basic demands of some white wage-earners were denied placed a severe strain on the alliance with national capital and eventually led to its being broken. But on the other hand, the extension of the range of concessions in the context of a series of state interventions created the material conditions for a reinforcement of the tendency (deriving from their specific class determination, relationship to the state, etc.) for white wage-earners to take up class positions supportive of the form of state.

In the early years of the Pact period it was in fact the first of these two tendencies which was uppermost: the failure of the Pact régime to deliver on a number of specific demands, and in particular its role over the de Villiers and Lucas awards, shattered a number of illusions among rank and file white wage-earners (mainly but not only those in the mining industry). The years 1925–1927 were thus years which saw an increasingly bitter criticism of the Pact being expressed by rank and file white wage-earners at strike meetings,[156] trade union meetings,[157] May Day rallies,[158] and the like. For a short period in fact there were even some signs that this white discontent was spreading over into increased support for the Communist Party. This was most clearly evident in the way in which Communist Party members and supporters had been able to secure election to the executive of the South African Association of Employees' Organisations, but there was also a widely recognised general support and sympathy for the Communist Party among a number of ordinary branch members of the Labour Party. At one stage in 1925 this was in fact causing sufficient concern to the leadership of the Party for an editorial in the Party paper, *Forward*, to be devoted, under the heading 'Swat the Communists', to criticising the widespread tendency amongst party members to 'give credit to the Communists for their good intentions'.[159]

Any such moves towards the Communist Party were however short lived. As state interventions to secure economic concessions for white wage-earners became increasingly effective there was an increasing shift towards reformist politics, and this may have been accelerated slightly when the Communist Party itself shifted its stance away from the white labour movement with the adoption of its 'Black Republic' programme in 1928.[160] With the exception of a very brief initial movement to the left therefore the struggle within the white labour movement over the relationship with national capital remained within the ambit of reformist politics. In fact it was a struggle which resided very largely within the Labour Party itself.

The first signs of such a struggle within the party came at its 1926 conference when a rather complicated alliance of rank and file branch members, dissatisfied at the scale of the economic concessions being granted, and party officials, dissatisfied that the party political alliance had not meant more places for Labour members in the cabinet, united in revolt against the parliamentary leadership.[161] Although they did not succeed in their revolt at the time, they did manage to gain a majority on the party's National Council at the 1927 conference thus inaugurating the famous split between the party's branch members and its parliamentary leadership, known as the Councillite/Cresswellite split. The initial goal of the Councillites was not in fact to end the Pact. What they wanted rather was to place the parliamentary party more firmly under 'rank and file' control in order to press more vigorously for their demands within the Pact.[162] But it was not to be. Cresswell, with the support of most of the parliamentary party and a relatively small number of branches mostly in the Transvaal, split the party and organised a separate conference rather than submit to Councillite control.[163] And Madeley, the Councillites' effective leader, was prevented from fulfilling any such role through being removed from the Cabinet in the same year, ostensibly for meeting with Kadalie against Cabinet instruction,[164] though he claimed in reality for pressing for a higher minimum wage for 'civilised labourers' in his department.[165] From 1928 onwards therefore the Councillites moved to a position of opposition to the Pact itself, though within the framework of an essentially racist, reformist politics[166] which remained thus essentially supportive of the form of state if not specifically for national capital's hegemony.

In the struggle for the political support of the 'white labour movement' which ensued, it was eventually the Councillites who were to prevail. The fact that the Cresswellites secured five seats in the 1929 election as against the Councillites' three[167] was illusory. They continued to benefit from the electoral Pact with the Nationalists whereas the Councillites did not and in cases where there were straight fights between the two factions (e.g. Waterson vs Madely in Benoni) it tended to be the Councillites who came out on top.[168] Moreover, as time went on what remaining support the Cresswellites had within the 'white labour movement' tended to become further and further eroded, until finally in June 1931 the bulk of their remaining supporters agreed to a 'reunification' of the party under effective Councillite hegemony[169] and to a formal dissolution of the Pact in September 1931.[170] When the two Cresswellite cabinet ministers, Cresswell and Sampson, still refused to resign despite an appeal from the 'reunited' Labour Party they were formally expelled and although they continued in their posts until the coalition of 1933 they were, after 1931, effectively without any real base within the 'white labour movement'.

Thus by the end of the Pact period the alliance between national capital and white wage-earners was effectively at an end. It was perhaps too close and too contradictory a relationship to have survived indefinitely, but while it lasted it had created the conditions both for the restoration of the support of the overwhelming majority of white wage-earners for the bourgeois state, and for the state to complete a major restructuring of the organisations of the 'white labour movement'. The trade unions had been institutionalised within the state structures and major steps had been taken towards providing a 'solution' to the 'poor white problem' which simultaneously produced real isolation effects between white and black members of the working class. By the end of the Pact period, accordingly, the political practices of the overwhelming majority of white wage-earners were supportive of the form of state. True, for a significant proportion this was expressed through an 'independent' social democratic party, which since its lower echelons consisted of some strata of the working class and inferior strata of the new petty bourgeoisie was not available to 'the bourgeoisie as a mere "tool" for universal use'.[171] But given the requisite degree of relative autonomy from the other bourgeois parties and other institutions of the state, it was, like the trade unions, functioning fairly effectively as an institution of the capitalist state, organising support for the form of state among its white wage-earning constituency.

Notes to Chapter 5

1 Notably Johnstone. He conludes his account of the passing of the Mines and Works Amendment Act as follows: 'The pendulum had thus come full circle. The state which in 1922 had served as the instrument for the repression of the white workers, *was now in the hands of their representatives*, and implementing a protectionist policy for them . . .' (p. 167 emphasis added).

2 Poulantzas (1973), *op. cit.* p. 241.

3 Poulantzas (1975), *op. cit.* p. 98.

4 Strikes occurred during 1925 over the non-implementation of the de Villiers award and in 1927 over the magnitude of the Lucas award. For reports see *Rand Daily Mail* 15.6.25; 27.4.27; 29.4.27; 30.4.27; 2.5.27; 5.5.27; *Forward* 9.10.25; *The South African Worker* 29.4.27; 20.5.27.

5 See *Rand Daily Mail* 28.4.25 for a summary of a statement presented to all MPs in connection with the Mineworkers Minimum Rates of Pay Bill in which these points were made and also the statement by Gemmil for the Chamber of Mines to the *Mining Industry Arbitration Board 1926–1927. op. cit.* pp. 18 *et seq.*

6 AB 49, 1925.

7 A strike ballot was taken by the MWU and although the exact result was

kept confidential, it was reported that 'over 75% of the votes cast' were in favour of striking in support of the demand for the implementation of the de Villiers award (*Rand Daily Mail* 4.6.25, 15.6.25).

8 The MWU's estimate was that the original claim put to de Villiers would have cost an extra £1·4 million per annum and that put to the Arbitration Board an extra £1 million per annum. The 'temporary arbitrary increase' granted in 1925 added £50,000 to annual costs and the Lucas award an extra £24,000 on top of that; making a total increase of £74,000. (See *Mining Industry Arbitration Board op. cit.* p. 409, p. 550; *Rand Daily Mail* 28.4.25; 2.4.27).

9 *Rand Daily Mail* 2.4.27.

10 *Chamber of Mines Annual Reports* 1927 p. 11.

11 See *Rand Daily Mail* 29.4.27, 30.4.27, 30.5.27; *South African Worker* 29.4.27, 20.5.27 for reports of a number of small 'illegal strikes'. *Rand Daily Mail* 2.5.27 for report of strike meetings during which '. . . the government was severely criticised by men who declared themselves as being loyal to the labour cause'.

12 The *Rand Daily Mail* 5.5.27 reported that the leadership of the MWU supported some of the strikes but was reluctant to spread the strike as a large number of members were demanding, rationalising this as fighting the struggle on 'scientific lines'.

13 Chamber of Mines *The Wage Problem on the Witwatersrand Goldmines* (Johannesburg 1926) p. 4, paragraphs 48–51.

14 *Mining Industry Arbitration Board op. cit.* p. 545.

15 *Rand Daily Mail* 27.8.24.

16 *Ibid.*; see also Johnstone, *op. cit.* p. 156.

17 E. Oppenheimer, chairman of Anglo American Corporation's address to shareholders 16.5.25 quoted in T. Gregory, *Ernest Oppenheimer and the Economic Development of Southern Africa* (Cape Town 1962) p. 499.

18 See *Forward* 13.11.25, 14.12.25; *South African Worker* 25.5.28 for reports of the position of the white trade unions and the eventual agreement with the Portuguese régime.

19 Thus, the *Star* 13.9.28 expressed some concern that the quotas would not enable the mines to run at 'full production'.

20 Compiled from *Union Statistics for 50 Years*, Table G 5.

21 *Report of the Mining Regulations Commission* (UG 36, 1925).

22 *Op. cit.* pp. 157–67.

23 *Ibid.* p. 164 quoting Sir Drummond Chaplin and Sir Thomas Smartt speaking in the parliamentary debate.
24 M. Cresswell, *The Life of Frederick Hugh Page Cresswell, op. cit.* p. 111.
25 See for example C. Kadalie, *My Life and the ICU, op. cit.* p. 87 and *Rand Daily Mail* 2.3.25 for report of mass meeting against Bill; Simons and Simons, *op. cit.* pp. 341–2, point out that as distinct from the position in the original 1912 Act, coloureds were made eligible for these positions, as Hertzog put it, to avoid driving 'the coloured people to the enemies of the Europeans'.
26 See Johnstone, *op. cit.* pp. 157–67.
27 Report of a reply by Hertzog to demands from the National Council of the Labour Party, the *Star* 14.1.28. The members of the National Council were reported as 'disappointed' at the reply.
28 Sources: *Report of the Industrial Legislation Commission of Enquiry* (UG 62, 1951) Tables 36 and 37; *Union Statistics for 50 Years* Table G 20; Office of Census and Statistics: *Statistics of Production* for the years 1919–20; 1923–4—1929–30; 1932–3.
29 The Act was amended twice during the Pact period, in 1928 and 1930. In 1928 the main changes were, firstly, an amendment to the clause prohibiting strikes designed to close a 'loophole' in the original Act (by tightening up the definitions to make it clearer that participating in a strike as well as declaring a strike was illegal), and, secondly, a proposal in the first draft of the amending bill to allow individuals to call a sitting of a conciliation board. The latter was however dropped after representation by the Chamber of Mines, but was reintroduced, after negotiations, in 1930 in a slightly modified form. See *House of Assembly Debates* 19.3.28, 13.2.30 and *South African Worker* 16.3.28 for a critical comment.
30 This was made clear in the Evidence of Gemmill to the *Mining Industry Arbitration Board, op. cit.* p. 191.
31 W. H. Andrews, *Class Struggles in South Africa* (Cape Town 1941) p. 37.
32 For reports see *Rand Daily Mail* 2.5.27, 5.5.27.
33 *Department of Labour Report . . . for the Year Ended 1933* (UG 43, 1934) p. 36.
34 See, for example, *Forward* 15.1.25 expressing the view that the 'unanimous sentiment in trade union circles' is in favour of giving the Pact 'a legitimate chance to make good', and the *South African Worker* 10.12.26 commenting 'the white mineworkers have remained passive in expectation of great results.'

35 Sources: *Union Statistics for 50 Years* Table G 18; *Social and Industrial Review* (hereafter S and IR) December 1927 pp. 558–60, December 1929 pp. 1168–71; *Department of Labour Reports* for 1933 and 1934.

36 Poulantzas (1975), *op. cit.* p. 274. See also Poulantzas (1973), *op. cit.* Part V.

37 Simons and Simons, *op. cit.* p. 333.

38 *Forward* 26.2.26 quoting C. F. Glass of the Witwatersrand Tailors Association.

39 Statistics from Department of Labour Reports reproduced from G. Clack, *The Changing Structure of Industrial Relations in South Africa with special reference to Racial Factors and Social Movements* (London University Ph.D. thesis, 1962) Appendix C (Table 1).

40 *Report of the Industrial Legislation Commission* (UG 37, 1935) p. 90.

41 Even the 1935 *Industrial Legislation Commission, op. cit.* p. 89, referred euphemistically to the way in which 'many workers fail to appreciate the importance of continued organisation', whilst the industrial registrar referred to a 'regrettable apathy' (the latter quoted Simons and Simons, *op. cit.* p. 333).

42 See for example *South African Worker* 15.7.27, 16.3.28. *Umsebenzi The South African Worker* 11.12.31.

43 Simons and Simons, *op. cit.* p. 330. See also the *Star* 27.3.25 for a report of the conference and the role of the MWU delegate, Wilson.

44 AB 12, 1925. The Bill was seen as an alternative to proclamations of martial law during major strikes. It would have given the minister power to prevent activities of pickets, compel negotiation and prevent the engagement of scabs during strikes.

45 See the *Star* 27.3.25 report headed 'Communists Capture Trade Union Congress'.

46 C. F. Glass, executive member of South African Association of Employees Organisations and CP member, reported *Forward* 26.2.26.

47 *Industrial Legislation Commission 1935, op. cit.* p. 88.

48 *Ibid.* p. 89.

49 *Ibid.* p. 82.

50 *Ibid.* p. 90.

51 See Kadalie, *op. cit.* pp. 148–150 on the approach by the ICU for affiliation to the SATUC which was turned down. See also Andrews, *op. cit.* pp. 60–62 for TUC's statement in full.

52 For example H. W. Sampson commented on the ICU as follows: 'It is a

curious thing that the natives, many of them just emerging from barbar-ism should have adopted as their model in forming a union one of the most extreme and revolutionary types of union that exists in the world. I refer to the syndicalist union. It is open to all irrespective of any occupation, is of the IWW type, a general union . . . It is more political than industrial and on its present basis the white trade unions may never find contact.' *House of Assembly Debates* 2.4.28 columns 2773 and 2775.

53   Statistics show the number of wage-earners going on strike as follows:

	White	Black		White	Black
1925	1·2	0·7	1929	n a	n a
1926	n a	n a	1930	0·4	4·7
1927	0·8	4·4	1931	3·8	2·5
1928	0·7	5·1	1932	2·4	1·6

(Source: *Union Statistics for 50 Years* Table G 18).

54   Simons and Simons, *op. cit.* p. 339.

55   Estimate quoted by Dr. Stals (Nationalist) *House of Assembly Debates* 12.8.24 column 430.

56   'Black and White Labour' article by E. Brookes in *Industrial South Africa* June 1924. The following edition (July 1924) contained a number of com-ments from industrialists most of whom supported it. One described it as 'the utterance not of a politician but a statesman'.

57   This is of course a very different thing from saying that industrialisation came about to solve the 'poor white problem'—the position adopted by many liberal economic historians. For a critique see Kaplan (1976), 'The Politics of Industrial Protection . . .' *op. cit.*

58   *House of Assembly Debates* 7.4.27 column 2335.

59   Depreciated capital stock figure from D. G. Franzen and J. J. D. Williers, 'Capital Accumulation and Economic Growth in South Africa' chapter in R. Goldsmith and C. Saunders ed. *The Measurement of National Wealth* (International Association for Research in Income and Wealth Series VIII, London, 1959) p. 313. Employment figure from *Industrial Legislation Commission* (UG 62, 1951) *op. cit.* table 23a.

60   See *Industrial and Commercial South Africa* November 1926 for an article on General Motors. See also other articles in October 1928, July 1929 editions etc. on mechanisation generally.

61   For report see *S and IR* vol. V no. 32, June 1928.

62   E. Balibar, 'The Basic Concepts of Historical Materialism Elements for a Theory of Transition' in L. Althusser and E. Balibar, *Reading Capital*

(London 1971). In general I have found Balibar's the most useful account of the relations of real and formal subsumption although of course *Capital* Vol. 1 Chaps. XIV–XV was indispensible while Brighton Labour Process Group (1976) *op. cit.* proved useful as well. However I broadly agree with the criticism of Balibar made by B. Hindness and P. Hirst, *Precapitalist Modes of Production* (London 1975) to the effect that the stage of manufacture represents a capitalist form of production rather than a transitional mode of production.

63 *Ibid.*

64 See *inter alia* A. Sohn Rethal, 'The Dual Economics of Transition' (*Bulletin of the Conference of Socialist Economists*, Autumn 1972) and Brighton Labour Process Group, *op. cit.*

65 A Gramsci, *Selections from the Prison Notebooks* (London 1971) pp. 302–11 ('Americanism and Fordism').

66 *Ibid.* p. 310.

67 See, for example, Wilson and Thompson ed., *Oxford History of South Africa* Vol. II *op. cit.* p. 188 (chapter on 'The Growth of Towns' by D. Welsh).

68 *The Report of the Committee on Industrial Education* (UG 9, 1917) put it as follows 'the wholly uneducated (white) person is regarded as a potential danger in that he is likely eventually to become a public nuisance, and further will not be equipped to carry out the public duties as a citizen. To avoid this the state lays down a certain standard which must be reached before school attendance ceases to be compulsory'. (p. 5)

69 *Carnegie Commission* . . . , *op. cit.* Part V p. 66.

70 Phrase from Gramsci, *op. cit.* p. 303.

71 For example Wage Board chairman F. A. W. Lucas mentions in 'The Native in Industry' (*S and IR* Vol. V 1927) that some 'natives were found to be doing semi-skilled work' although most did only unskilled work.

72 See *The (Minority) Report of the Economic and Wages Commission op. cit.* pp. 338–346 quoting *inter alia* Karl Gundelfinger and J. S. Hancock representing Transvaal Chamber of Industries.

73 *Industrial South Africa* July 1924 quoting S. Craig-Bairn manager of a Port Elizabeth canning and packaging factory.

74 *Report of the Chief Inspector of Factories for 1927* (UG 38, 1928) p. 7.

75 See *Industrial and Commercial South Africa* November 1926 for an article on General Motors. See also *Rand Daily Mail* 24.4.29 for a report of Hertzog's reference to General Motors' employment policies during the 1929 election campaign.

76 *S and IR* Vol. IV no. 23 December 1927 'Condemnation of Cheap Labour Policy'.

77 *Department of Labour Report for the Year Ended 1932* (UG 37, 1933), p. 44.

78 See, for example, the *Commercial and Industrial Gazette*, June 1926 (a Board of Trade and Industries publication) which estimated a rise of 3·4% in white employment among 241 firms receiving tariff protection.

79 See Kaplan, 'The Politics of Industrial Protection . . .' (1976) *op. cit.*

80 *House of Assembly Debates* 3.2.31 column 39 (incident referred to by Smuts in debate on unemployment).

81 Thus, in a feature on industries in the *Star* 28.10.30 an advertisement for Rondis read 'All Rondis products—chocolates, sweets, bread, confectionery—are manufactured exclusively by white labour'.

82 Reported in *The Times* 6.8.30.

83 *House of Assembly Debates* 9.2.32 column 801.

84 *The Wage Act no 27 of 1925 as amended by Act no 23 of 1930 together with the regulations and the Wage Determination Validation Act 1930 and Wage Determination Validation Act 1935* compiled by M. Schaeffer (Cape Town 1935) section 3(3).

85 *Ibid.* section 18.

86 *Ibid.* section 3(3).

87 See *House of Assembly Debates* 1925, column 1602 and columns 4442 *et seq.* for references to the position of capitalist agriculture.

88 See, for example, *Industrial South Africa* February 1925, *Chamber of Mines Annual Reports* 1925 p. 57. This is also, broadly speaking, the interpretation in all the standard secondary sources (Horwitz, Hobart-Houghton, Hutt, Doxey, van der Horst, etc.), as well as of two fairly recent specific studies of Wage Board policy—D. E. Pursell, 'Bantu Wages and Employment Opportunities', *South African Journal of Economics* June 1968; 'The Impact of South African Wage Board Policy on Skilled/Unskilled Wage Differentials' (*Eastern African Economic Review* June 1969); 'South African Labour Policy: "New Deal" for non Whites?', *Industrial Relations* 1971, A. Spandau, 'South African Wage Board Policy: An Alternative Interpretation', *SAJE* 1972.

89 See *Report of the Select Committee on the Wage Board* (SC 14, 1925) evidence by Col. J. F. Duncan and H. J. Laite representing the Federated Chamber of Industries (pp. 47 *et seq.*), and P. M. Anderson representing Chamber of Mines (pp. 66 *et seq.*).

90 Act 21 1930.
91 See for example *Cape Times* 4.1.24 report of Labour Party election programme.
92 *Ibid.*
93 See for example *House of Assembly Debates* 23.3.25 column 1597 (speech by Smuts), 1.4.25 (speech by Sir Drummond Chaplin), 1673 (speech by R. Stuttaford).
94 See for example *House of Assembly Debates* 15.6.25 column 4448.
95 *House of Assembly Debates* 23.3.25 columns 1600/1601.
96 A letter from Hertzog written before the election enclosing a donation of one guinea and referring to 'our common endeavours to make this country that we love so much, great and good'.
97 *House of Assembly Debates* 2.4.25 columns 1719–1720.
98 *House of Assembly Debates* 2.4.25 column 1721.
99 *S and IR* vol. II no. 4, April 1926.
100 *The Official Labour Gazette* (predecessor of *S and IR*) vol. 1 no. 3 June 1925.
101 See Report of Transvaal Chamber of Industries protest *Industrial and Commercial South Africa* October 1928.
102 *Report to the Hon. the Minister of Labour by the Wage Board upon the Work of the Board for the Three Years 28.2.29* (Government Printer 1929) pp. 59, 20.
103 *Ibid.* p. 8.
104 See for example *Report 28.2.29 op. cit.* pp. 8–12; *Report to the Hon. the Minister of Labour by the Wage Board upon the Work of the Wage Board for the Period 1.3.29 to 31.12.31* (duplicated copy ex Dept. of Labour, Pretoria in British Library of Political and Economic Sciences, London).
105 Source: *Statistics of Production* 1924–5—1932–3. The industries effected by wage determinations were baking, tailoring, clothing, sweetmaking, furniture making, tanning, boots and shoes. Excluded from the column are tobacco, general industries (including glass bevelling and silvering) and tea, coffee and chicory processing where the determination covered too small a part of the total industry to be significant. Of course such statistics can only be *an index* of the mass of surplus value and not a precise estimate. For example, they provide no basis for calculating the amount of surplus value transferred in the process of transforming values into prices.
106 *Report ended 31.12.31 op. cit.* The Board also referred in its reports more generally to its investigations being 'welcomed . . . by good employers . . .

because wage regulation would remove (a) very unsocial form of competition'. (Example from *Report ended 28.2.29 op. cit.* p. 11).

107   See *Social and Industrial Review (special edition on Wage Board reports and Recommendations)* hereafter called *S and IR (special)* Sept. 1927.

108   I have been unable to discover any specific reference to Lewins as a firm. From this as much as anything, as well as the fact that the case arose from a prosecution for not paying wages according to one or other of the determinations, I surmise that Lewin was probably a small capitalist.

109   Gramsci, *op. cit.* p. 303.

110   *Report ended 28.2.29 op. cit.* pp. 10–11.

111   See, for example, F. A. W. Lucas, 'Natives and the Wage Act' speech reported *S and IR* vol. VI no. 39 March 1929.

112   *S and IR (special)* June 1928, Determination no. 25 (Unskilled Employment in Certain Undertakings and Trades in Bloemfontein).

113   For example, in the baking and confectionery proposed determination the Grade II minimum was lowered from £1 4s. to £1 per week following objections, in the glass bevelling and silvering industry from £1 4s. to £1 2s. 6d. and some of the lower paid clothing industry grades likewise. Grade 1 rates in each of these cases remained unaltered. (*S and IR (special)* Sept. 1926, Dec. 1926, June 1927, Sept. 1927, Oct. 1927, Nov. 1927, Dec. 1927 *et seq.*; Determinations 2, 4, 6, 13, 15, 16, *et seq.*).

114   *S and IR (special)* Sept. 1926, pp. 4–17.

115   *Ibid.* p. 25.

116   *Ibid.* p. 32.

117   *Idem.*

118   *S and IR (special)* May 1927 p. 3.

119   *Idem, S. and IR (special)* July 1928, p. 24.

120   The accounting gross profit, which is turnover minus wages and costs of materials used, is selected rather than the accounting net profit as the illustrative figure, because some of the items deducted to reach the latter figure (e.g. management expenses, interest charges) reflect the distribution of surplus value produced. Moreover, the Board in its presentation cast considerable doubt on the validity of those figures even in conventional accounting terms by e.g. presenting an 'adjusted net profit' as well as a 'stated net profit' figure. But for what it is worth the adjusted net profit on turnover for the industry as a whole fell from 6·54% in 1924–5 to 6·52% in 1926–7, whereas that in the seven firms including the largest, rose from 4·4% to 5·1% on turnover.

121 *Report ended 28.2.29 op. cit.* p. 26.
122 *S and IR (special)* May 1927, Sept. 1927, May 1929.
123 *S and IR (special)* May 1927 p. 3.
124 *Idem.*
125 *S and IR (special)* May 1929, p. 469.
126 Calculated from *Statistics of Production* 1925–6 to 1929–30.
127 Wage Board Report in *Dept. of Labour Reports for the Year ended 1933* (UG 43, 1934) p. 70.
128 *Idem.*
129 *Idem.*
130 See *Report of the Select Committee on the Subject of the Wage Bill (and of the Industrial Conciliation Bill)* (SC 5, 1937).
131 Speech reported *S and IR* vol. VI no. 33 September 1928.
132 On this see Bozzoli, *op. cit.* p. 367.
133 July 1929.
134 Wage Board Report in *Dept. of Labour Reports . . . Year ended December 1932 op. cit.*
135 See *Select Committee on . . . Wage Bill 1937. op. cit.* p. 14.
136 *House of Assembly Debates* 29.1.29 column 52.
137 *Rand Daily Mail* 1.5.29.
138 *S and IR* April 1927 p. 326.
139 *Report of the Controller and Auditor General on Union Government Finances* for the year ended 31.3.28 (UG 41, 1928).
140 On the grounds that such policies were no longer 'experimental' but 'permanent'. See *House of Assembly Debates* 1927, column 219.
141 *House of Assembly Debates* 9.2.31 column 184/5.
142 *S and IR* vol. II no. 10 October 1926.
143 White employment figure from *Report of the Committee Appointed to Investigate the Employment of Unskilled European Workers in the Railway Service* 1947, *op. cit.*, Annexure G; African figure from *Union Statistics for 50 Years* Table G15.
144 *Report of the Controller and Auditor General—Statement of Accounts South African Railways and Harbours* 1926/7 (UG 40, 1927) p. 85.
145 *House of Assembly Debates* 29.1.29 column 75 (statistics quoted by Madeley).
146 *House of Assembly Debates* 1930 column 256 (ministerial answer to question).
147 See, *inter alia, House of Assembly Debates* 1925 columns 5071 *et seq.*

(debate about which party first proposed afforestation, tenant farmer and railway employment); 12.3.25 columns 875 *et seq.* and columns 1061 *et seq.* (Jagger claiming SAP began white labour policy on railways), 7.4.27 columns 2335 *et seq.* (debate on railway's white labour policy) etc.

148   *House of Assembly Debates* 31.7.29 column 278 (Major G. R. Richards).

149   *House of Assembly Debates* 25.7.29 column 89.

150   By the *Carnegie Commission, op. cit.*

151   From figures given by Hertzog, *House of Assembly Debates* columns 184/5, 1931.

152   *Statistics of Production* 1924—5——1932—3.

153   Figures given by Potgieter, *House of Assembly Debates* 1932, column 784.

154   See Simons and Simons, *op. cit.* pp. 339 *et seq.* for an account of the opposition of African organisations to the effects of the 'civilised labour policy'.

155   Thus while a poll taken by the TUC in 1928 found some unions 'representing generally the manufacturing industries are in favour of admitting all workers in the industry to membership' a large number of others favoured African organisation only within a 'parallel union' (the *Star* 18.10.28).

156   See *Forward* 2.10.25; *Rand Daily Mail* 2.5.27.

157   See, for example, *Rand Daily Mail* 18.4.27, 19.4.27.

158   See *Forward* 30.4.26.

159   *Forward* 2.10.25.

160   For the full text of the Commintern resolution underlying the Party's 1928 programme see *The African Communist* no. 45, 1971. I have not taken up the question whether or not, with the adoption of this programme, the party prematurely abandoned potential allies within the white labour movement as certain contemporaries claimed (see Simons and Simons, *op. cit.* Chapter 17). Clearly to begin to analyse this question, one would have to consider the broader question viz. to what extent did the programme provide an adequate basis for a political organisation of the masses—i.e. the African, principal dominated, classes (the question of organising possible allies within the white working class and white petty bourgeoisie at this conjuncture being subordinate to this broader question). Such an analysis is clearly beyond the scope of the present study and in any case it is a very, very minor part of any explanation of the reasons for the dominance of reformist politics within the 'white labour movement'.

161   See *Forward* 8.1.26; M. Cresswell, *op. cit.* Chapter XIX; Simons and Simons, *op. cit.* pp. 347—49.

162 See *Forward* 8.1.26 and M. Cresswell, *op. cit.* Chapter XIX for accounts of the position taken by the challengers.
163 M. Cresswell, *ibid.*
164 *Rand Daily Mail* 3.11.28, 5.11.28, 6.11.28, 7.11.28.
165 According to interview given to *Rand Daily Mail* 17.5.29.
166 For a general description of Councillite policies see Simons and Simons, *op. cit.* pp. 347–49.
167 *Rand Daily Mail* 10.6.29.
168 See M. Cresswell, *op. cit.* Chapter XXIII.
169 Thus the *Star* 29.6.31 reported 'The new personnel of the new council points to the fact that the rank and file have definitely taken charge of the rehabilitation of the Labour Party.' For other reports see: the *Star* 18.10.30 (resolution of discontent by Cresswellite sections at Pact policies); *The Times* 29.6.31.
170 See *The Times* 3.8.31, 1.9.31, 2.9.31.
171 Poulantzas (1974), *op. cit.* p. 152.

The power bloc and white wage-earners during the 'fusion' period —general introduction

The coalition of the two major parties (the Nationalist Party and the South African Party) in 1933 and their subsequent 'fusion' to form the United National South African Party (United Party) did not, despite the rhetoric to the contrary, represent a *change in the form of state* in which hegemony reverted to mining or imperialist capital. In fact, as Kaplan has argued at length,[1] the coalition/fusion of the two parties did not fundamentally represent a change in the form of state at all. Rather it was a much narrower change: a change operating principally at the level of the political scene (the 'privileged place in which the open actions of social forces . . . take place by means of their representation by political parties'[2]), in other words a *change in the form of régime*. The coalition, he argues, was formed in response to the crisis of political representation brought about through the failure of the Hertzog government to abandon the gold standard at a time when all the major fractions of capital (national and imperial alike) were advocating such a policy. The coalition/fusion thus represented an *entente* (a term often reserved to denote co-operation at the party political level) rather than an *alliance* (the term used to denote co-operation at the broader level of political practices[3]), and as such could not and did not dissolve all the contradictions which existed between the capitalist fractions. On the contrary, the differences over such questions as protection, subsidisation etc. continued to exist, and in fact although the change in régime did alter the precise terms on which hegemony was exercised, hegemony itself continued throughout the 'fusion' period to reside with national capital.

As such the coalition/fusion of 1933 *of itself* brought about very little change in the relationships of the white wage-earning classes to the state. In fact the only real change directly arising from the change in régime, itself operated principally at the level of the political scene. Under the terms of the coalition, a demand originating with the SAP that the two Cresswellite-Labour ministers (Cresswell and Sampson) be removed from their positions in the cabinet was duly implemented, although the two continued for a time as back-bench 'coalition-Labour' MPs.[4] Since, as we indicated in the last chapter, the two Cresswellite ministers had been practically devoid of any real base in the 'white labour movement' since 1931 at the latest, their demotion, whilst representing the final formal ending of the alliance between national capital and white labour, had little real meaning in terms of class practices outside of the narrow confines of the political scene. Indeed of much more significance was the fact that under the terms of the coalition, where differences between the members of the power bloc continued to exist over the question of actual state policies with respect to white wage-earners (and we indicated in the last chapter that by the end of the Pact period these were *so far as the major fractions* were concerned essentially confined to certain differences over the administration and financing of the 'civilised labour policy' on the railways) it was the position of national capital which prevailed—thus providing a further index of national capital's continued hegemony. Patrick Duncan made this clear (as well as expressing the general ambivalence of imperial capital on this question) when he told the Council of the South African Party in 1933 that,

> . . . so-called 'civilised' labour had been a costly thing but there was no doubt that it had offered a means to many of getting established in industrial life. The new government would not lend themselves to throwing these men out onto the street and replacing them by native labour.[5]

But to say that the coalition/fusion *of itself* brought about few changes in the relationship of the white wage-earning classes to the state, is not to say that there were no significant changes and developments in state policies during the 'fusion' period. The crisis of political representation which had brought about the change in the form of régime had arisen in the context of a major economic crisis (the Great Depression) which, while not as intense in South Africa as elsewhere and while not affecting all fractions of capital in South Africa equally,[6] had, through its devastating effects on capitalist agriculture in particular brought about a massive increase in the numbers of 'poor white' unemployed. The official statistics, which of course cover only a proportion of the total, show the numbers of whites officially registering unemployed rising rapidly throughout 1932 and 1933 to a peak of 39,309 (adult males only) in October 1933, and, though the numbers declined thereafter, the averages during 1934, 1935 and 1936 nevertheless remained above the levels which had prevailed in the period between 1924 and 1930.[7]

With continuing inter-racial crime (one Commission reported that in 1932 41 per cent of all whites convicted in the courts were 'illicit' liquor sellers[8]) and some tentative signs of joint struggle by the white and black unemployed,[9] the early '30s were, not surprisingly, years which saw a plethora of further warnings emerging from various bourgeois intellectuals, politicians and organisations about the 'dangers' which would be faced by their class if some new 'solution' were not found to the 'poor white' problem. Several of the most important of these came in the reports of the American sponsored Carnegie Commission and in speeches delivered to the Dutch Reformed Church's 'National Conference on the Poor White Problem' (widely supported by industry, commerce and in the press 'loyal to' and owned by mining capital[10]). At the latter, for example, the Minister of Labour (A. P. J. Fourie) spoke of the increasingly urgent necessity to solve the 'poor white problem' in order to 'save white civilisation from going under completely (totale ondergang)'.[11] And similar sentiments were also expressed in the report of an official commission[12] as well as in resolutions coming from such bodies as the Agricultural Union, various Chambers of Commerce and the Rotary Club.[13]

On the other hand, however, the early '30s were also the years which witnessed the first real debates within the bourgeoisie about the political 'merits' of certain forms of state intervention in connection with the 'poor white problem'. This debate (to be distinguished from the earlier debates arising from conflicts between the pursuit of a perceived common political interest and particular economic interests) was initiated, in the context of a heightening of the class struggle by the African dominated classes, by the small liberal tendency within the bourgeoisie.

Like the 'republican bourgeoisie' of nineteenth-century France analysed by Marx in the *Eighteenth Brumaire*, the liberal bourgeoisie of twentieth-century South Africa 'was not a fraction of the bourgeoisie bound together by great common interests and demarcated from the rest by conditions of production peculiar to it'.[14] Rather, it consisted in the '30s at least of a relatively small number of agents identified with certain ideological apparatuses and institutions (notably the churches and the universities). Their essential defining characteristic was that they saw the creation of a small African petty bourgeois supportive class as an essential part of the defence of the bourgeoisie's political class interests.[15]

As Legassick has shown[16] until the latter part of the Pact period the liberal tendency had located itself firmly within the problematic of segregation. They had considered that the implementation of a 'fair' policy of so-called lateral segregation would provide sufficient opportunities for 'ambitious members of the (African) proletariat' to 'escape' into a petty bourgeois existence.[17] Moreover, whilst they were generally staunchly opposed to the demands of organised white wage-earners (particularly over job colour bars, but also often over wages and other questions) they none the less regarded it as necessary for the bourgeoisie to retain the political support of the 'poor whites' and had thus often been in the forefront of those urging that further steps be taken to find a solution to the 'poor white problem'. Indeed in the last chapter we referred to an article written in 1924 by one of the most prominent liberals, Edgar Brookes, in which he had urged that top priority should be given to economic developments which took place on a 'white labour basis', and argued that the consequences of not solving the 'poor white problem' would be that Africans would come to hold the 'balance of power' politically.[18]

During the Pact period however the liberal position began to shift. In the context of the emergence of a sizeable urban African proletariat expressing its demands through an increasingly assertive African nationalism, they began to 'lose faith' in segregation as a political solution. And they also began to see a contradiction between some of the measures for dealing with the 'poor white problem' which they had previously supported, and the measures which they regarded as necessary to produce a black supportive class outside of the framework of segregation. During the pact period itself the liberal position on these questions was still very much in the process of formation. But after 1929 (a year which saw two important events —the founding of the South African Institute of Race Relations and Brookes' renunciation of segregation) and more particularly during the 'fusion' period the liberal bourgeoisie began to present a distinct and coherent position.

What the liberals had come to question by the '30s was not any fundamental aspect of the class structure of the South African social formation, nor even the 'necessity' of state interventions to ensure that white wage-earners occupied, by and large, distinct and 'superior' class places to those occupied by Africans. Rather what they were questioning was the precise methods by which the state intervened to assign certain white agents to such places and the precise limits of state activity in this regard. Measures which discriminated against Africans in a blatant and overt manner (and they now saw a number of the measures introduced under the 'civilised labour policy' falling into this category) were seen as subjecting 'ambitious' Africans in particular to 'economic pressures' which drove them to adopt 'nationalist' positions.[19] And they therefore argued instead for a more concealed covert approach which would also allow more flexibility at the lower margins to grant concessions to a small number of 'ambitious' Africans. As Brookes put it in 1933, where barriers are inevitable . . . they ought to be temporary in character, and accompanied by a policy of such a nature as to make it unnecessary to retain them. Whenever possible the barrier should be based on some principle other than colour—the fixing of minimum wage rates for unskilled labour, etc. . . . we want to spare our 'poor whites', already a depressed class . . . the degradation of working under a black man. But we cannot indefinitely hold the vanguard of the Black behind the rearguard of the White, and it is not in White interests that we should do so.[20]

Although the liberal strategy with its inevitable concessions to an African petty bourgeoisie was never adopted *in toto* by any of the major fractions of the bourgeoisie (all of which, on the contrary, gave broad support to the 1936 Segregation Bills), in so far as the changes in the liberal position were a reflection of changes in conditions of class struggle which posed new political problems for the bourgeoisie—the problem of how to ensure the continued support of the white wage-earning classes whilst at the same time responding to the rise of an increasingly militant African trade union and nationalist movement—it did come to have an influence on *the form* which some of the later state interventions took. As we shall see later, towards the end of the 'fusion' period in the context of the beginnings of a period of heightened struggle by the African, dominated classes, the state did come to adopt a more concealed, less overtly racially discriminatory approach in respect of some of its interventions to assign white agents to wage-earning places.

Having now characterised the position of the bourgeoisie on this question during the 'fusion' period—as one of broad general agreement about the political necessity to continue assigning white proletarians to particular distinct places in a racist hierarchical division of labour, with some dissent about the precise methods and limits coming from the small liberal faction—we can now proceed to examine the actual state interventions of the period in more detail.

The 'civilised labour policy' 1932–1939

During the depression itself and during the immediate post-depression years considerations about dealing with a sudden resurgence of 'poor white' unemployment were dominant over any consideration about the effects which any particular form of intervention would have on struggles by Africans. During the depression itself, the state's most immediate response consisted of a series of 'emergency measures' designed to absorb the extra white unemployed in its own departments or to isolate them in various forms of subsidised employment in the rural areas. Most of the work of the Department of Labour in 1932 was thus taken up arranging for provincial administrations, divisional councils, municipalities, other government departments and the railways to take on extra white employees (in a number of cases by the provision of further subsidies and loans).[21] Similarly in 1933, mainly as a means of absorbing 'poor white' unemployed central government spent £6·7 millions on various subsidies and 'national works'.[22] In the same year too, the Dutch Reformed Church's local Armesorg Committees were brought under the tutelage of the Department of Labour and given responsibility for trying to place whites in employment in the rural areas. And in 1934, following a recommendation from the 'National Poor White Congress' a number of additional 'special schemes' were introduced to promote white employment in the rural areas[23]—including a scheme to provide subsidies and loans for bywoner housing and a scheme to provide subsidies for small dam construction, noxious weed iradication, and anti-soil-erosion projects which employed white labour.[24]

In a number of these cases of course the subsidies and loans made available went to pay for the replacement of previous African incumbents by whites. To that extent therefore, they represented the mere shifting of the unemployment burden from whites to blacks rather than any real relief of unemployment as such. To what extent blacks directly suffered from these measures is difficult to gauge as there was no official record kept of the numbers laid off in this way, nor even of the total number of Africans unemployed during the period.

One unofficial estimate by the Chief Native Commissioner put the total number of African unemployed in the Johannesburg area at 10,000 in 1934[25] (after the peak of the recession) but that probably erred on the low side. Needless to say on becoming unemployed Africans received almost nothing by way of 'social security' benefit. All that was available in fact was a dole of mealie meal from the pass offices, and even this was only given out if 'asked for', which as the paper *Umsebenzi* reported, meant in practice 'emphatically and often'.[26]

But, although white agents continued, through these and other previously introduced measures, to be placed in various forms of state and subsidised rural employment throughout the '30s it was, after the immediate depression period, principally towards industry that the major focus of state activity in this connection began to shift. This is hardly surprising. South Africa's abandonment of the gold standard in December 1932 had the immediate effect of raising the price of gold by some 50 per cent, with the result that the conditions were created for profitable production in a number of previously marginal mines. Largely financed by a massive inflow of capital from the imperialist metropolises (according to one estimate some £63 millions flowed into the South African goldmining industry between 1933 and 1939[27]) the industry underwent a major expansion with new fields being opened up in the far East Rand and massive increases in profits being recorded in existing mines. Although the amounts of foreign capital flowing into the still often internationally cost-inefficient secondary industries were very much less (one estimate put the amount of foreign capital invested in commerce, industry and agriculture combined at less than one-seventh that in mining[28]), as Kaplan has shown[29] through their position of hegemony in the state the national capitalist fractions were able to appropriate a large proportion of the new surplus value produced in the mining industry and thus to take advantage of the expansion in the goldmining industry to promote developments beneficial to them. The years 1933–1939 were thus also years of major expansion for industry and agriculture. So far as industry in particular is concerned the following statistics show substantial increases in the money value of net output, in the numbers of establishments and in the numbers of employees employed in the sector over the period.

Table 18[30] *Selected industrial statistics 1932/3 and 1938/9*

	1932/3	*1938/9*	*%age increase*
Money value of net output	R61 million	R128 million	+ 110%
No. of establish- ments	6,543	8,614	+ 32%
No. of employees (all races)	133,000	236,000	+ 77%

But although the period was one of overall expansion and increased demand for labour by industrial capital, there were a number of factors, particularly in the early part of the period, which complicated attempts by the state to ensure that a 'sufficient' proportion of the newly created wage earning places in industry were assigned to whites. In the first place in contrast to the Pact period, the 'fusion' period would seem to have been a period during which the *average* organic composition of capital in industry (the index of the rate of mechanisation and hence of the rate at which semi-skilled operative places were created relative to the development of the forces of production) decreased slightly, albeit from a higher initial base. This is clearly indicated, for example, by the figures in the following table, which show that, leaving aside the figure for the year 1933 (which reflects the laying off of workers during the depression), the overall trend during the 'fusion' period was towards a slight fall in the 'capital/labour' ratio. It would be wrong, however, to conclude from these figures that there were no further moves towards mechanisation in the industrial sector during this period. On the contrary,

Table 19[31]   *South African industry depreciated capital stock per employee* (excluding lands and buildings; at constant 1938 prices)

1924	£167	1930	£200	1935	£231
1925	£164	1931	na	1936	£230
1926	£179	1932	na	1937	£226
1927	£182	1933	£260	1938	£228
1928	£194	1934	£231	1939	£233
1929	£195				

the available descriptive evidence clearly points to further mechanisation by a number of capitals in a number of industries. For example, the Wage Board's report on the engineering industry in 1934 referred to 'the tendency . . . in engineering . . . towards . . . requiring an increased number of machine minders, who may require a certain amount of training and adeptness to warrant their being called semi-skilled',[32] while the 1935 Industrial Legislation Commission listed the printing, engineering, furniture, leather making, sweetmaking, clothing and textile industries as industries within which there were large numbers of workers employed as semi-skilled operatives. 'In some of these industries, indeed' the report continued, 'the semi-skilled class predominates.'[33] Rather, what seems to have happened during the 'fusion' period is that the overall conditions of expansion created the conditions for the emergence and survival of a number of smaller capitals employing less mechanised labour processes alongside other capitals continuing to make the transition towards more mechanised production processes. And the net result of this was that a large and perhaps even increasing proportion of the new places created in industry during the period were for skilled and unskilled rather than for semi-skilled operative workers. This at least was the conclusion drawn by the Board of Trade and Industries' Report no. 282 which noted that although the years between 1933 and 1939 had seen significant moves towards mechanisation by some capitals in the fastest growing metals and engineering industry, the industry as a whole had, in its words, 'been slow to make the fullest possible use of operative labour' during these years.[34]

The other main factor complicating the state's efforts to ensure the assignment of a 'sufficient' number of 'poor white' proletarians to wage-earning places in industry was the emergence of a sizeable settled urban African proletariat in the '30s. We mentioned in previous chapters that the formation of such a class was already evident in the '20s, but by the '30s, particularly after the depression, the numbers had increased enormously. Indeed, by the '30s the presence of a sizeable urban African working class, struggling against, among other things, wage levels determined by the subsistence needs of migrant workers, had begun to pose serious political problems for the dominant classes, some of which will be referred to later. But for the moment, the importance of this factor was that it led to *the beginnings* of an erosion of the previous ready identification by industrial capitalists of semi-skilled with white. Thus, for example, the Wage Board's report on the engineering industry in 1934 referred to a wider realisation that machines 'can be quite efficiently minded or operated by . . . natives' with the result that 'there is a grave danger of a large number of comparatively well paid European operatives) being ousted'.[35]

It was these two factors—semi-skilled places being created at a slightly slower pace than the overall rate of industrial expansion, and *the beginnings* of a movement by Africans into semi-skilled operative places—which created complications, particularly in the early part of the 'fusion' period, for the state in its attempts to ensure the assignment of 'poor whites' to wage-earning places in industry. In particular it meant that the previous approach—which had relied upon piecemeal interventions, mainly through the Wage Board, to confer competitive advantages on the more mechanised capitals in certain industries—could no longer be relied upon to ensure that white industrial employment expanded at a rate at least proportional to the overall expansion of the forces of production and the rate of increase in white unemployment. And at a time when the 'absorption' of the 'poor white' unemployed remained an important political concern for the classes in the power bloc, this indicated a need for the state to seek a new more comprehensive approach, better suited to the new material conditions of production, by which it could serve their still largely common political interests in this regard. The early 'fusion' period was thus a period which saw a restructuring of the apparatuses concerned with the assignment of white agents to wage-earning places in industry. In particular it saw the Wage Board becoming less and less important as an apparatus for the promotion of the 'civilised labour policy'. As the following figures show, the numbers of wage determinations and the numbers of employees covered by such determinations remained almost constant between 1933 and 1936 at a time when overall industrial employment rose by some 60 per cent; and after 1937, as we shall see later, the Wage Board became principally involved in a totally different set of functions.

Table 20[36]   *Wage determinations 1933–1936*

No. of determinations in force at 31st December		Estimated no. of employees covered
1933	19	66,437
1934	20	73,348
1935	19	74,392
1936	19	67,774

At the same time as the Wage Board declined in importance, however, other apparatuses more appropriate to the promotion of white employment under the changed material conditions of production began to assume an increasingly important role in this regard.

Among these were various industrial/training apparatuses, *de facto* if not *de jure*, restricted to whites. Firstly, the 'fusion' period saw a major expansion of all forms of apprenticeship training. Official figures, in fact, show that the numbers undergoing training for eventual assignment to the large number of artisanal places created during the period nearly doubled from 6,103 in 1933 to 11,583 in 1939.[37] But the 'fusion' period also saw the introduction of new forms of training apparatuses intended to reproduce within newly proletarianised 'poor whites' various attributes which it was anticipated would give them competitive advantages over blacks in seeking operative or semi-skilled employment. The particular institutions here were the Special Service and Pioneer Battalions founded in 1933 and 1934 respectively. Jointly run by the Departments of Labour and Defence, they provided no direct industrial training. Rather, their function was officially described as being 'to instil . . . through military training habits of discipline and industry which will stand (recruits) in good stead when applying for and obtaining employment'.[38] However, though they were originally conceived of as a means of placing whites in semi-skilled industrial employment, most of the 9,900 who passed through these institutions between 1933 and 1938 actually ended up, despite the apparent 'good reputation' among 'employers of labour', being employed on the railways or in the state's repressive apparatuses (police and prisons service).[39]

Of much more real significance in terms of the assignment of whites in places as industrial operatives were therefore the other apparatuses involved in this function during the 'fusion' period; in particular, the industrial councils. Indeed, with the decline in the importance of the Wage Board in this regard these became perhaps the most important of the apparatuses concerned with the promotion of the 'civilised labour policy' overall. The assumption of this role by the industrial councils (apparatuses which, as we have seen had developed in the class struggle to isolate and contain the trade union struggles of white wage-earning employees) followed a period of struggle between the state, acting to serve the still largely common political interests of the power bloc with regard to the 'poor white problem', and industrial capital pursuing its economic interests under the above described conditions.

The conflict began in 1933–4 in a subdued enough manner with a propaganda campaign directed by the Department of Labour at industrial capitalists generally, calling on them to accept their 'fair share' of the 'responsibility' for solving the 'poor white problem'. The examples of state departments, then aiming at a 50:50 black: white ratio in permanent employment, and ISCOR, which began production in 1934 with an all white complement,[40] were quoted and, while no specific ratio was set up as a target, each industry and firm was urged to make its own investigations to see how far it could go to match these efforts.[41] The same theme was also taken up in the address to the annual conference of the Federated Chambers of Industries in 1933, by the Minister of Labour (who was also Minister of Commerce and Industries) when he told delegates that he was 'satisfied that there is room to add a large number of Europeans to factory payrolls, and that employers would 'in many instances be distinct gainers if this were done'.[42]

Towards the end of 1934, however, the conflict assumed a more serious dimension. A 'special campaign' conducted by the Department of Labour in the first half of 1934 was regarded by state officials as having produced only a half-hearted response on the part of at least a substantial minority of industrial capitalist employers,[43] and the Department and the Minister began to issue a number of warnings. At the FCI conference, for example, the minister hinted at some form of further state intervention saying that 'the adjustment between civilised and uncivilised will not eventuate if the matter is entirely left in the hands of the employers themselves'.[44] And on other occasions he made even more explicit threats, in particular to withdraw tariff protection.[45] Eventually, when the minister refused to gazette industrial council agreements covering the building and engineering industries on the grounds that they did not contain adequate provisions for the employment of more 'civilised labour', the FCI responded by conducting its own internal investigation which resulted in it producing a number of proposals.

The memorandum which the FCI executive put to the minister in 1934 is a particularly instructive document especially in view of the subsequent mystification surrounding the role of industrial capital in South Africa. In the first place it accepted entirely the

political objectives underlying the 'civilised labour policy' stating
that,

> The executive Council agrees that the encouragement of the
> employment of civilized labour is desirable, even essential, and
> far from cavilling at the operation of the principle, is anxious
> to support it to the fullest extent of its influence.[46]

Indeed, the only qualification which they made to this expressed
desire to see the spread of 'civilised labour' in industry was that they
did not wish to see the exclusion of 'uncivilised labour' from 'the
work which it can fittingly perform such as rough unskilled manual
labour'.[47] The problem as the FCI saw it was that 'good employers'
were being subjected to 'unfair competition' from 'less reputable
employers' (i.e. smaller capitals) which had sprung up during the
expansionary upswing, and instead of the generalised attacks directed
at the industrial capitalist fraction as a whole or at all the capitals
in particular industries, it called for a 'planned approach' under
which 'each industry would be required to employ a definite percentage or ratio of civilised to uncivilised labour based on its own
needs and conditions'.[48] More specifically it suggested that, with
their rapid expansion into most industries and sectors, the apparatuses
best placed to implement such a programme would be the Industrial
Councils, operating under the general supervision of the Department
of Labour. And to this end it suggested that the Industrial Conciliation Act be amended such that a) those not definable as 'employees'
under the Act (i.e. Africans) would no longer be exempted from the
effect of Industrial Council minimum wage agreements, and b) Industrial Councils and the Department of Labour would have greater
powers to enforce the terms of agreements, including the powers to
enforce them in firms which were not represented in the Industrial
Council.[49]

At first however the minister was not prepared to accept this
approach, and in 1935 he announced his intention to proceed with a
Minimum Wages Bill. This bill, if enacted, would have provided for
a national minimum wage of 1*s*. an hour for various categories of
machine operators including surface drill sharpeners on the mines

and it would also have allowed additional occupations to be added at the minister's discretion.[50] Needless to say of course this was a rate which it was considered would enable a greater number of 'civilised labourers' to be placed in these categories. When the bill was published, however, it was, despite the reputed support of some individual large industrial capitalists,[51] opposed by organised mining, industrial and commercial capital on the grounds that it was bureaucratic and did not take account of the differing conditions in different industries.[52] After intensive lobbying by the Chamber of Mines, the FCI and the Associated Chambers of Commerce, a conference was eventually held in November 1935 at which the Minister finally agreed to drop the bill and proceed instead along the lines proposed by the FCI whilst reserving the right to amend the Wage Act to allow the Wage Board to make national minimum wage determinations covering a range of occupations across industries and regions if the industrial council approach did not produce what was regarded as 'satisfactory' results. He also agreed to amend the Industrial Conciliation Act so as to widen the powers of industrial councils along the lines proposed by the FCI.[53]

Thus it was that, on the initiative of industrial capital, the Industrial Councils (and hence the white trade unions) came to play a role in determining the racial allocation of particular places in the industrial division of labour. And, from the point of view of the state in its struggle to find new solutions to the political problems posed by 'poor white' unemployment, they would seem to have acquitted themselves adequately in this regard even before the Industrial Conciliation Act was amended in 1937. The Department of Labour Report for 1935, for example, reported that by the end of that year

approximately 3,100 additional European workers were absorbed into industry . . . as a result of special provisions having been made for them in industrial council agreements.[54]

With this achievement of what was regarded as a fairly high degree of success, and with a decline in overall white unemployment such that from 1936 onwards the 'poor white problem' was broadly speaking regarded by the bourgeoisie if not the white 'labour movement' as under control,[55] this approach of relying upon the activities of the industrial councils remained the central focus of the state's strategy to ensure the assignment of 'poor whites' to wage-earning places in secondary industry throughout the 'fusion' period.

But although these changes in the deployment of particular apparatuses to promote the 'civilised labour policy' in secondary industry were, as indicated above, primarily determined by changes in the material conditions of production and were brought about under these changed conditions in order to make *more effective* interventions to place white agents in separate, distinct and 'superior' places in the division of labour from those occupied by Africans, the shifting of the principal role from apparatuses formally and juridically part of a state department to apparatuses which were in formal and juridical terms (and, it should be emphasised, only in these terms) 'independent' of the state, proved functional to the dominant classes in another direction as well. The '30s were, as indicated earlier, a period which saw a massive increase in the numbers of permanently urbanised African proletarians, completely divorced from any access to any means of subsistence in the 'reserves'. The general level of wages for African workers had however been set in the class struggle at levels based on the subsistence of migrant labourers whose families had access to the means of production in the 'reserves'. Thus, in the euphemistic language of one Government Report,

> The natives who have become urban dwellers and have lost their tribal rights and bonds are in many respects much worse off than tribal natives (migrants—R.D.) . . . The customary rate of wages is largely determined by what tribal natives will take . . . : the reserves reducing the necessity of making the income received adequate to support the family all year round . . . (But) they have neither the home and lands of the tribal native, nor have they the advantages of a system which supplies them with housing, food, fuel and drink . . . for 3 to 6 months a year.[56]

Not surprisingly therefore, the decline in the productive capacity of the 'reserves' and the corresponding creation of a class of permanently urbanised African proletarians, had been accompanied by a number of struggles on the part of the urban African proletariat over, among other things, the wage question. Indeed, such struggles had been a feature of the social formation since the early '20s at least and in fact, as we saw in the last chapter, the first request for an investigation by the Wage Board had come from the ICU following a struggle by the urban proletariat of Bloemfontein in 1925. During most of the '20s, however, the dominant classes had broadly speaking responded to these demands with straightforward resistance seeking to avoid as far as possible making any concession whatsoever. Corresponding to this general stance of the dominant classes the state had been involved in placing various barriers in the way of African workers securing any wage increases at all. The 'loophole' in the Wage Act through which the ICU had obliged the Wage Board, whose intended function was the promotion of the 'civilised labour policy', to conduct an investigation into the wages of African workers, had thus been blocked in 1929 by an amendment to the regulations which required all the supporters of an application to personally sign it (an amendment which effectively prevented most African workers from initiating an investigation).[57]

By the mid '30s however, with the numbers of permanently urbanised African proletarians greatly increased, the general level of struggle by African workers, including among other things the

Table 21[58]   *Selected strike statistics 1933–1939*

	Numbers of blacks involved in strikes	Membership of unregistered trades unions
1933	300	31,100
1934	800	37,400
1935	1,400	29,200
1936	1,600	35,100
1937	4,800	35,200
1938	3,700	37,500
1939	4,800	36,600

struggle over wage demands, had reached a much higher level. As the statistics in Table 21 show, there was a steady rise in the numbers of blacks on strike and also a corresponding rise in the membership of unregistered (i.e. black) trade unions. What is more, in a number of cases these struggles had compelled at least some, mainly industrial, capitalists to grant some minimal concessions.

It is not our intention here to further describe the struggle waged by the urban African dominated classes at this time, nor to describe in any detail the overall response of the dominant classes to this struggle. Lewis has shown[59] that any satisfactory analysis of and explanation for any specific set of state responses to the struggles of the dominated classes has to take account of all the different levels of struggle and also of the nature and character of the organisations leading those struggles. He has also argued that the state's response in the '40s (and to an extent the same holds true of the late '30s as well) was defensive and in many respects ambivalent, reflecting ambivalences and differences among the different fractions in the power bloc. For our purposes, it is sufficient merely to observe that, under the conditions of class struggle of the '30s, industrial capital was finding itself compelled to make a number of piecemeal wage concessions to African workers, and that under these conditions it began to demand some form of state intervention to regularise and spread the minimal wage increases granted across an industry or area both as a means of ensuring that those capitals which had been compelled to grant concessions in the course of struggle were not placed at a competitive disadvantage, and as a possible means of reducing the number of strikes. Thus, for example, after a series of strikes in Durban in 1937 a 'representative meeting of employers' passed the following resolution:

> That this meeting views with concern the growing unrest among native labourers mainly created by the absence of any wage controlled by law. The Government is therefore requested to ... go into the general question of native wages and betterment of labour conditions on a national basis with the minimum of delay.[60]

In order for the state to fulfil this role however it was necessary for there to be some modification to the character of some of its apparatuses. Those set up in terms of the Wage Act and the Industrial Conciliation Act had been quite correctly regarded by Africans as a means of intensifying their exploitation and oppression and it was necessary therefore, if any of these bodies were to fulfil any function related to the struggles of the African dominated classes, that there be certain changes in order that they achieve at least a minimal 'acceptance' among Africans. It was under these circumstances that the position of the liberal bourgeoisie, while not in any sense becoming dominant in its entirety, came to have an influence on actual state policy. Thus, when Rheinallt Jones of the Institute of Race Relations told the 1935 Industrial Legislation Commission that there was a 'profound conviction on the part of Africans that the Industrial Conciliation and Wages Acts were designed to exclude them from employment',[61] his point was well taken and the Commission, while recommending that steps should continue to be taken to ensure that whites remained 'entitled to . . . natural preferential employment at a maximum, earned, differential wage',[62] also recommended that some steps be taken 'to ensure that under these Acts all classes can be looked after'.[63] In particular it recommended that various barriers and forms of racial discrimination, no longer a really necessary part of the overall process of class formation and reproduction, be eliminated.[64]

These two factors: the changing importance of particular apparatuses as a means of promoting the 'civilised labour policy', and the need on the part of industrial capital for some 'orderly' adjustment of African wage levels, were reflected in the Amendments to the Industrial Conciliation and Wages Acts presented to parliament by the new 'liberal' Minister of Labour, J. H. Hofmeyr in 1937. Under the 1937 Wage Act,[65] the Wage Board, largely redundant in its role in connection with the 'civilised labour policy', was transferred into an apparatus concerned with the regulation of African wage levels. The real effective barrier to Africans' initiating a Wage Board investigation (the regulation introduced in 1929) was removed under

the 1937 Act as was the 'civilised minimum' clause which had served
to alienate Africans from the Board.[66] Thereafter as Hirson has
shown[67] the Board began to play an increasingly active part in the
overall struggles of African workers. Its changing role after 1937 is
also clear from the following figures which show a substantial rise in
the numbers and proportion of Africans covered by Wage Board
determinations.

Table 22[68]   *Numbers of employees covered by wage determinations
              (by race)*

	Whites		Africans		Coloureds & Asians	
	no.	% of total	no.	%	no.	%
Determinations in force at 1937 made before 1937	48,063	59·6	23,533	29·2	9,007	11·2
Determinations made during 1937 and 1938	6,135	48·4	4,923	38·8	1,622	12·8
Determinations* made during 1939	48,932	54·8	29,196	32·7	11,087	12·5

*the large increase mainly reflects the renewal of a determination covering the commercial
and distributive trades.

In the case of the Industrial Conciliation Act, on the other
hand, the major changes introduced in 1937 were intended to
allow industrial councils to make more effective interventions to
promote the employment of 'civilised labour'. Industrial councils

were given the powers to make minimum wage agreements applicable to those who were not defined as 'employees' under the Act, and they were also given greater powers of inspection and enforcement.[69] The liberal influence was however not entirely absent even here. Africans still excluded from the definition of 'employee' and thus denied trade union recognition were to be 'indirectly represented' at industrial council meetings by an official of the Native Affairs department.[70] But since the overall thrust of the amended Act was towards allowing the more effective promotion of the 'civilised labour policy', such a 'concession' operated very much at the level of appearances, functioning in essence to mystify and conceal the real purpose of the clause entitling industrial councils to make Wage agreements covering those not definable as 'employees'.

Thus, despite certain liberal embellishments and a change in the role of one previously important apparatus, the 'civilised labour policy' was, far from being moderated, continued and made even more effective during the 'fusion' period. Consequently the overall pattern of class formation, involving the creation of distinct all white wage-earning strata differentiated in a number of ways from the African working class, continued unabated.

So far as wage-earners in secondary industry were concerned, this differentiation continued to operate in the two ways described in the previous chapter: first through the skill and income differentials, and secondly through the operation of the isolation effects produced by the real or imagined relationship of dependence of the white industrial workers on the state. Thus, while a large proportion of the 115,000 odd whites employed in secondary industry in 1939 (an increase of some 68 per cent over the 1933 figure)[71] often performed tasks little different in terms of real content from those performed by at least some blacks (if not in the same plant then at least in some other plant), they were through the 'civilised labour policy' placed in a relationship of real or imagined economic competition with African workers which acted against them realising a community of interests with African workers in struggle. That the isolation effects thus produced remained 'terrifyingly real' throughout the '30s is clear from the writings of contemporary political activists who attempted to transcend them. For example, an article appearing in *Umsebenzi* in 1935 wrote of the effects of the 'civilised labour policy' as follows:

> By ousting the non-European workers out of the more skilled functions in industry (the 'civilised labour policy') is having the psychological effect on the white workers to increase their racial prejudice, to make them think they are superior to Native and Coloured workers. That is how colour bar prejudice and race hatred is inculcated into the white workers, thus causing disunity in the ranks of black and white workers.[72]

Moreover, whenever there were signs that the similarities in terms of the essential relations of production *might* begin to break down these isolation effects, the state was quick to intervene to reinforce them. Thus, for example, in 1937 (the year of the Durban strikes) the Department of Labour and the Railways administration took the initiative to ensure that in the railway workshops in Durban and in certain clothing factories in the Transvaal where white and black were beginning to work together on the same processes, segregation was reimposed.[73]

In the case of employment in state departments, although there were, as the following table (Table 23) shows, comparatively large numbers of whites employed in temporary (mainly manual) places throughout the '30s, there were also during the period a number of important qualitative changes in the nature of white employment which had important effects in terms of the differentiation of white state employees from the black working class. The first indication of this emerges from the figures in the table which show that the numbers of unskilled whites employed in state departments on permanent (regular service) terms increased both as a proportion of the total number of unskilled whites employed by the state departments and in absolute terms. For whilst a number of the unskilled places in 'regular service' remained themselves manual labouring places, their designations as permanent often meant their incorporation into an hierarchical career structure within which they served as the bottom rung of a ladder (at this stage, partly mythical and partly real)

Table 23[75]   *Employment of unskilled and semi-skilled white employees in state departments*

I. *Employment on subsidised relief work schemes*

	1934	1935	1936	1937	1938	1939
1. nos employed on departmental works and by SAR	812	2,727	2,310	1,876	1,569	1,045
2. nos employed on the eradication of weeds, soil erosion, etc.	—	690	481	301	61	45
3. nos employed by provinces, divisional councils, local authorities and 'private employers'	8,684	9,117	5,993	5,432	4,998	4,302
Sub total	9,496	12,534	8,784	7,609	6,628	5,392

II. *Employment in regular services*

	1934	1935	1936	1937	1938	1939
1. Central government depts.		8,326	7,646	7,637	8,195	7,452
2. SAR	18,257	16,963	17,356	18,093	18,961	19,010
3. Provinces		3,205	3,326	3,259	3,680	4,040
Sub total	18,257	28,494	28,328	28,989	30,836	30,502

into the petty bourgeoisie. The 'fusion' period in fact saw a major restructuring of the hierarchies within a number of state departments along these lines.

To take the railways as an example: in October 1934 a new 'career structure' was introduced under which all appointments to graded positions, except for certain artisanal categories, were thenceforth made from the ranks of the permanently employed unskilled white labourers. For this purpose the white labourers were divided into two groups: the first consisting of younger men with certain educational qualifications who were made eligible for promotion to various clerical and supervisory petty bourgeois posts, and the second consisting of older, less educated men for whom promotion was restricted to certain manual labouring and lower supervisory posts.[74] Moreover, whilst promotion remained, during this period at least, a myth for a considerable proportion of the white labourers who remained precisely that throughout, there was nevertheless a considerable increase in the number of promotions. According to figures given by the Minister of Railways, between 1933 and 1938 there were some 11,377 promotions to graded positions which, compared to the 13,888 made over the much longer period 1924–1933, represented an increase of between 75 and 100 per cent.[76]

Thus, in respect of the white unskilled manual labouring employees in state departments in addition to the other factors which differentiated and isolated them from the black working class, the conditions were also created for the emergence among them of petty bourgeois aspirations: a factor which, as we shall see in the next chapter, had critical effects on their political practices.

The state and the economic class struggles of white wage-earning employees 1933–1939

The 'fusion' period did not see any major new forms of state intervention in respect of the economic class struggles of white wage-earning employees. Spokesmen for all the major capitalist fractions told the

1935 Industrial Legislation Commission that they were broadly satisfied with the functioning of the institutions established under the
Industrial Conciliation Act, as indeed did a number of trade union
witnesses. The 1937 Industrial Conciliation Act thus made no significant alterations to the 'industrial relations system' beyond giving
industrial councils their role in the promotion of the 'civilised labour
policy' which we have already examined. In broad terms, therefore,
the 'fusion' period was one of continuity in this respect. Accordingly,
it saw a continuing institutionalisation of these struggles and correspondingly a further decline in white involvement in other more
militant forms of struggle. Some indication of the overall trend is
given in the following statistics which show a sharp fall in the numbers of whites on strike and a substantial rise in the numbers covered
by the various forms of agreement under the machinery of the Industrial Conciliation Act.

As in the Pact period, of course, institutionalisation meant the
bureaucratisation of the organisations of the white 'labour movement'. Towards the end of the period in fact this manifested itself in
a decline in union membership and a degree of apathy on the part of

Table 24[77]   *Statistics relating to industrial conciliation act machinery
and the numbers of whites involved in strikes*

	(1) number of Industrial Council agreements registered	(2) Conciliation Board agreements and awards	(3) numbers of white employees covered by (1) & (2)	numbers of whites involved in strikes
1933	22	6	40,240	1,255
1934	29	7	52,449	1,539
1935	28	7	49,282	1,005
1936	35	8	47,937	640
1937	38	5	71,640	1,077
1938	37	6	86,794	92
1939	43	4	97,147	49

the rank and file members so great that for a time it even threatened the efficient functioning of the system. As the Secretary for Labour put it in his Annual Report for 1938:

> Unfortunately, the multiplicity of boards and committees seems to have had an adverse effect on the effectiveness of organization, particularly in so far as some of the trade unions are concerned . . . During the year . . . the membership of the constituent parties to one industrial council had fallen to such an extent that the minister found himself unable to regard them as sufficiently representative of the industry with the result that the Council's agreement could not be gazetted. Even where membership is maintained at a satisfactory level, so far as numbers are concerned, the Department has found it necessary to watch the position closely. In the case of one industrial council which had negotiated a 'closed shop' agreement, membership of the union was found to be automatic. Trade Union subscriptions were deducted from wages of all employees and a number of these were unable to say whether they were in fact members of the Union. They had never attended meetings or taken part in the affairs of the Union.[78]

Moreover, and this will be of importance when we examine in the next chapter the penetration by the Afrikaner Nationalists into the white 'labour movement', bureaucratisation created the conditions for the emergence of an increasingly visible corruption on the part of increasingly remote bureaucratic union leaderships. As the Secretary for Labour noted again in 1938,

> trade union representatives have not taken firm steps to check a tendency towards extravagance in the payment of allowances to members of statutory boards and committees.[79]

The class positions of the white wage-earning classes 1933–1939

From the standpoint of the political interests of the dominant capitalist classes, the state's policies towards the white wage-earning

classes were, during the 'fusion' period, very largely successful. At
the 'industrial level' the practices of the overwhelming majority of
white wage-earners continued to be tied down to 'tolerable' forms
of economistic and racist trade union struggle, essentially supportive
of the form of state. And at the party political level most white
wage-earners continued for much of the period to express support
for the form of state in the form of electoral support for the coalition
of bourgeois parties or, to a lesser extent, in the form of support for
the social democratic reformist Labour Party. What could, broadly
speaking, be called left wing political practices (support for the Communist party, solidarity with the struggles of the African masses, or
even engagement in militant forms of trade unionism) were, by the
'fusion' period, largely confined to a few clearly recognisable strata
of the white wage-earning classes. Among these were certain categories of relatively low paid manual industrial workers with some
tradition of militant trade union struggle (e.g. garment workers and
leather workers[80]) and certain categories of mainly manual workers
subjected to particular forms of discrimination (e.g. Jewish manual
workers in particular areas[81]).

There was however one major new development which appeared
on the scene towards the end of the period—the penetration into
the 'white labour movement' by various Afrikaner nationalist elements seeking to transform the character of the registered trade
unions. Since this came towards the end of the period and represented
a sufficiently important new development we shall consider it separately in our next section.

Notes to Chapter 6

1 See D. Kaplan, 'An Analysis of the South African State in the "Fusion"
  Period 1932–1939' (*Institute of Commonwealth Studies* seminar paper,
  1976); D. Kaplan thesis (1977), *op. cit.*; R. Davies, D. Kaplan, M. Morris and
  D. O'Meara, 'Class Struggle and a Periodisation of the South African State',
  Review of African Political Economy no. 7 1977.
2 Poulantzas (1973), *op. cit.* p. 317.

3   *Ibid.* pp. 308–321.
4   Cresswell was re-elected as 'coalition-Labour' MP in the 1933 elections although Sampson was not. He continued as an MP until 1938 but spent much of the time abroad, as representative at the International Labour Organisation in 1933 and president of the ILO in 1935 (see M. Cresswell, *op. cit.* Chapters XXIV, XXV, XXVII).
5   *Rand Daily Mail* 10.3.33.
6   See Kaplan (1976), (1977) *op. cit.*
7   *Department of Labour Reports* 1932–1939.
8   *Report of the Native Economic Commission 1930–1932* (UG22, 1932).
9   *Umsebenzi* 7.10.33 reported that there were a number of joint demonstrations by white and black unemployed in Johannesburg at which attempts by Labour Party right wingers ('social fascists') to divide white from black were largely unsuccessful. See also Simons and Simons, *op. cit.* pp. 456–7.
10 Thus, among the speakers were J. Neil-Boss, chairman of the FCI 1930–1, and K. Gundelfinger, associated with the Chambers of Commerce (see Armesorgraad of the Federated Dutch Reformed Church of South Africa: *Report on the National Conference on the Poor White Problem Held at Kimberley 2nd to 5th October 1934* (Cape Town, nd. 1935 (?). While the *Rand Daily Mail* 2.10.34 commented, 'If a real measure of alleviation is achieved the Dutch Reformed Church which has taken the lead, will have earned the sincere gratitude not only of the congregation but the nation as a whole.'
11 Dutch Reformed Church, *op. cit.* p. 22 (my translation).
12 *Report of the Unemployment Investigation Committee* (UG30, 1932).
13 Resolutions from these bodies calling for a more effective solution to the unemployment problem and for a stricter enforcement of residential segregation were quoted in the speech by H. R. Abercrombie to the National Conference on the Poor White Problem, *op. cit.* p. 110.
14 K. Marx, *The Eighteenth Brumaire of Louis Bonaparte (Marx Surveys from Exile: Political Writings* Vol. 2) (London 1973) p. 157.
15 In fact the essential strategy and class interests it was intended to serve cannot be better summed up than in the following remarkable extract from a lecture delivered by one of the leading liberal spokesmen, Professor Edgar Brookes, in 1933:

> Bantu nationalism must . . . reach out towards Bolshevism. How could it be otherwise? If there is a clearly defined proletariat anywhere in the world it is in South Africa. Happier or wiser countries postpone or

altogether avoid a Marxian 'class war' by the creation of common interests, by opening doors of opportunity enabling the ambitious member of the proletariat to escape into the governing class, at the very least by ostentatious professions of a single national unity transcending class distinctions. In South Africa we follow a different course. We try to prevent the multiplication of common interests, we close almost every door of opportunity, and we loudly proclaim the impossibility of union in a single nation. Class becomes associated with something definite and tangible such as colour. The stage is inevitably set for the 'class war'. As a member of the bourgeoisie myself, I hope it is not set for the 'dictatorship of the proletariat'. As a liberal I believe that only swift and far reaching reforms and many more opportunities for self-realisation on the part of the Bantu can create the impossibility of such a dictatorship. I insist . . . that those who are fighting the Battle of the Bantu are the real friends of the white man and the whole South African community.

(E. H. Brookes, *The Colour Problems of South Africa: Being the Phelps-Stokes Lectures, 1933. Delivered at the University of Cape Town* (Lovedale, 1934 (?)) pp. 42–3.)

16 M. Legassick, 'The Rise of Modern South African Liberalism: Its Assumptions and its Social Basis' (University of Sussex seminar paper, 1974).

17 Phrases from Brookes, *loc. cit.*

18 *Industrial South Africa* June 1924.

19 See, for example, Brookes *op. cit.* pp. 28–9.

20 *Ibid.* pp. 123–4. A similar position was also taken in a number of articles in the liberal journal, *Forum* (see, for example, article by E. J. Burford 27.6.38, debate 11.4.38).

21 *Department of Labour Report* for the year ended December 1932 (UG37, 1938) pp. 5–6.

22 *House of Assembly Debates* 1934 column 3452 (description by Minister of Labour).

23 *Department of Labour Report* for the year ended December 1933 (UG43, 1934) p. 6.

24 *House of Assembly Debates* 1934 column 3456 (description by Minister of Labour).

25 *Umsebenzi* 10.3.34 quoting A. L. Barrett.

26 *Ibid.*

27 S. H. Frankel and H. Herzfield, 'An analysis of the Growth of the National

Income of the Union in the Period of Prosperity before the War', *South African Journal of Economics* vol. 12, 1944.

28 *Board of Trade and Industries: Investigation into Manufacturing Industries in the Union of South Africa (first interim Report no 282)* (1945) p. 54 quoting estimates that in the period until 1936, $\frac{2}{3}$ of foreign investment went into mining, and $\frac{2}{3}$ of the rest into commerce, industry and agriculture. The remainder went into land speculation.

29 Kaplan (1976), (1977) *op. cit.*

30 Official statistics quoted in D. Hobart Houghton, *The South African Economy* (Cape Town 1965) p. 118.

31 Depreciated capital stock figure from D. G. Franzen and J. J. D. Williers, 'Capital Accumulation and Economic Growth in South Africa' chapter in R. Goldsmith and C. Saunders ed. *The Measurement of National Wealth* (International Association for Research in Income and Wealth Series VIII, London, 1959) p. 313; Employment figure from Industrial Legislation Commission (UG 62, 1951) *op. cit.* Table 23a.

32 Report reproduced in *Department of Labour Report* 1934 (UG11, 1936), p. 80.

33 *Report of the Industrial Legislation Commission* (UG37, 1935) p. 69.

34 *op. cit.* p. 44.

35 Report 1934 *op. cit.* p. 80.

36 *Department of Labour Reports* 1933–1936.

37 *Ibid.* 1933–1939.

38 *Department of Labour Report* for 1934 *op. cit.* p. 54.

39 See *The Special Service Battalion: A Review of its Activities and Functions* (GP S, 1264, Government Printer, 1938).

40 On ISCOR's employment policies see D. Kaplan, 'The Politics of Industrial Protection . . .' *op. cit.*; M. Morris and D. Kaplan, 'Labour Policy in a State Corporation: a Case Study of the South African Iron and Steel Corporation', *South African Labour Bulletin* vol. 2 no. 6, January 1976 (part 1); vol. 2 no. 8, April 1976 (part 2).

41 See *Department of Labour Reports 1934, op. cit.* p. 18.

42 *Annual Reports of the South African Federated Chamber of Industries: 16th Annual Report 1933* p. 16.

43 See minister's annual address 17th *FCI Report* 1934, p. 14.

44 *Ibid.* p. 14.

45 See ministerial letter quoted in 'Memorandum on the Employment of Unskilled Civilised Labour Prepared by the Executive Council' reproduced

in 17th *FCI Report* p. 56.

46   *Ibid.* p. 57.

47   *Ibid.* p. 63.

48   *Ibid.* p. 58.

49   *Ibid.* p. 60.

50   For descriptions of contents see *Industrial and Commercial South Africa* January 1935, April 1935.

51   According to M. J. van den Berg (Labour, later, Nationalist MP) see *House of Assembly Debates* 26.5.36 columns 4319–4320.

52   *Industrial and Commercial South Africa* March 1935, November 1935, *Department of Labour Report for 1935* (UG4 1937), pp. 59–60.

53   *Ibid.*

54   *Department of Labour Report* for 1935, *op. cit.* p. 16.

55   See *Department of Labour Reports* for 1936 *op. cit.* p. 1; 1937 UG30, 1938) p. 7; 1938 (UG51, 1939) p. 1; 1939 (UG36, 1940) p. 2 for general assessment of a 'satisfactory situation' regarding white employment. See also 1938 *op. cit.* p. 2; 1939 *op. cit.* p. 2 for reports of contrary views from white labour. See also e.g. *House of Assembly Debates* columns 4336, 1936 *et seq.*, for the various positions on this question.

56   *Report of the Inter Departmental Committee on the Labour Resources of the Union* (Government Printer, 1930), p. 12.

57   See the *Native Economic Commission 1930–1932 op. cit.* paragraph 320; *Report of the Industrial Legislation Commission of Enquiry* (UG92, 1951) p. 196 for descriptions of the operation of this clause.

58   Statistics from G. Clack (1962) thesis, *op. cit.* Appendix C, Table 1.

59   D. Lewis, 'The South African State and African Trade Unions 1947–1953' (mimeo, 1976).

60   Quoted *Department of Labour Reports* 1937, *op. cit.* p. 3; see also pp. 3–4 for a report of a similar resolution adopted by the F.C.I. convention in the same year.

61   *Report of the Industrial Legislation Commission 1935, op. cit.* p. 68.

62   *Ibid.* p. 41.

63   *Ibid.* p. 68.

64   See e.g. p. 20, p. 113.

65   Act 44 1937.

66   See e.g. *House of Assembly Debates* 1937 columns 4324 *et seq.*; *Report of the Industrial Legislation Commission of Enquiry 1951, op. cit.* pp. 196–7.

67   B. Hirson, 'The Reorganization of African Trades Unions in Johannesburg

1936–1942' (*Institute of Commonwealth Studies* seminar paper, 1976).

68 Figures from *Department of Labour Reports* for 1938, *op. cit.* pp. 56–58; 1939: *op. cit.* p. 50.

69 See e.g. M. Schaeffer, *The Industrial Conciliation Act no. 36 of 1937* Cape Town 1949); *House of Assembly Debates* 1937 columns 3683 *et seq.*

70 See *House of Assembly Debates* 1937 column 3688.

71 *Figures from Industrial Legislation Commission of Enquiry* 1951, *op. cit.* p. 18 Table 23a.

72 *Umsebenzi* 9.2.35.

73 See *Department of Labour Report* for 1937 *op. cit.* p. 5; *House of Assembly Debates* 1937 columns 204–5, 4521/2 (ministerial answers to parliamentary questions).

74 See *Report of the Committee Appointed to Investigate the Employment of Unskilled European Workers in the Railway Service* (UG29, 1947) pp. 4–5; *House of Assembly Debates* 1937 column 671 *et seq.*

75 *Department of Labour Reports* 1934–1939, *op. cit.*

76 *House of Assembly Debates* 1938 column 464.

77 *Department of Labour Reports* 1933–1939, *op. cit.*

78 *Department of Labour Reports* for 1938, *op. cit.* p. 7, p. 34.

79 *Ibid.* p. 7.

80 The garment workers were involved in a number of strikes in the '30s, notably in 1932 and 1937. The Leather Workers Union which had a Communist president, Willie Kalk, was the first and one of the only registered trade unions in South Africa to open its membership to workers of all races on an equal basis (albeit for only a limited period). See e.g. Simons and Simons, *op. cit.* Chapters 19 and 22.

81 T. Adler provides an interesting account of the support for the Communist Party existing among the members of the Jewish Workers Club in Johannesburg in the '30s. See his 'Class Struggle in Doornfontein: The History of the Jewish Workers Club 1928–1950' (mimeo, 1976).

PART 3

Afrikaner Nationalism, White Wage-Earners and the Apartheid
State 1934–1960

In the previous sections of this study we examined the various forms of state intervention made during the 'segregation' period from 1900 to 1939 to ensure the assignment of white rather than black agents to particular places in the division of labour, and also the emergence in the class struggles of the same period of racially discriminatory 'industrial relations' apparatuses whose role was to isolate and contain the struggles of the white wage-earning classes. In this section we focus on two main issues: firstly on the conditions under which those class forces represented by the Afrikaner Nationalist movement were able to build up a supportive base among certain strata of the white wage-earning classes (the subject of this chapter), and, secondly, on the role of the state in connection with the reproduction of the white wage-earning classes during the early Apartheid period (the subject matter of the next chapter).

The Gesuiwerde Nationalist Party and white wage-earners
1934—1939

The penetration by the Afrikaner Nationalists into the 'white labour movement' has already been the subject of a number of excellent papers by O'Meara[1] and will thus only be discussed here in so far as it reflects upon the particular processes of class formation and class integration which we studied in previous chapters. O'Meara has demonstrated at length that 'Christian National' trade unionism did not arise as an autonomous movement of Afrikaner wage-earners but rather was 'initiatied, inspired, led, financed and maintained'[2] from the outside by certain categories of the petty bourgeoisie organised in and represented by the Gesuiwerde (Purified) Nationalist Party and its associated organisations (Broederbond etc.). The Gesuiwerde Nationalist Party which broke away from the Hertzog Nationalist Party in December 1934 was, he has argued, a party representing, in the southern provinces, an alliance between certain agricultural capitalist interests and certain categories of the petty bourgeoisie, whilst in the northern provinces, where capitalist agriculture had largely remained with the 'fusion' parties, it consisted of 'an almost exclusively petty bourgeois grouping'.[3] More precisely the petty bourgeois grouping represented in the Gesuiwerde Party consisted of a certain stratum of the white traditional petty bourgeoisie (petty commodity producers and small traders) and certain categories of the new petty bourgeoisie associated with various ideological apparatuses (mainly rurally based churchmen, lawyers, teachers etc.).

Essentially the petty bourgeois groupings represented in the Gesuiwerde Party sought to elevate themselves up the 'ladder' into more secure places in the bourgeoisie. Petty commodity producers had seen their position being undermined by the industrial development of the Pact period and in particular by the 'encouragement' given to mechanisation through, *inter alia*, the activities of the Wage Board. And the various (often rurally based) new petty bourgeois categories had seen their role declining with the decline in the white rural population and the growing importance of other ideological apparatuses. The complaint which both advanced against the 'fusion' was that it was an alliance of the 'big' capitalist interests which ignored the aspirations of the 'small man'. In typical petty bourgeois fashion, they therefore adopted a position of 'status quo anti-capitalism'[4] combining a virulent attack on the 'excesses' of existing capitalism itself. Thus, in one typical presentation an MP expressed himself as follows:

> (the) system under which we have worked, a system which allows unlimited profits and unlimited exploitation cannot continue to exist . . . I therefore consider that we should look to an

entirely new system, a comprehensive system which will do away with the possibility of the continuation of exploitation by capitalism. Exploitation by capital is not the exploitation by small capital which makes sound profits—it is exploitation by means of a system which in some cases makes unjustifiable profits by means of unfair methods.[5]

The conscious and deliberate penetration of the 'white labour movement' by this movement of aspirant Afrikaner capitalists, which began in 1934, took place for two main reasons. Firstly, the Afrikaner nationalist petty bourgeoisie needed to secure for themselves a mass base, particularly in the northern provinces where they were extremely weak. And, secondly, they needed to ensure that the savings of Afrikaner wage-earners were made available to finance the activities of the associated 'Afrikaner economic movement'.[6] The then existing state apparatuses and institutions into which the white wage-earning classes were incorporated (predominantly, the Labour Party and the bureaucratised, institutionalised trade unions—what we shall call hereafter the social democratic state apparatuses) were seen as a threat to the realisation of both these objectives. This was because their underlying social democratic ideology though racist, reformist and supportive of the bourgeois state, also included, as a social democratic ideology, elements of class which conflicted with the premises on which Afrikaner Nationalist ideology was constituted. As one MP put it in connection with the trade unions,

. . . class consciousness . . . is systematically encouraged by the trade unions . . . they make an appeal to the class conscious section of the people. It is in direct conflict with the principles of the Afrikaners (read Afrikaner Nationalist ideology).[7]

It was therefore necessary as they saw it to win Afrikaner wage-earners away from these institutions as then constituted and to re-organise them into a 'Christian National' trade union movement based upon an ideology which would stress the alleged 'organic unity' of the Afrikaner volk. This was to be achieved by 'explaining' to the Afrikaner wage-earner that the reasons for his 'cruel exploitation' were not to be located in any characteristics of class relationships but in a 'phenomemon unique to South Africa' ('n einaardige ver-skynsel) viz. that 'the master (baas) was a man of one volk, while the (Afrikaner) worker was a man of another volk':[8] the inescapable implication being of course that his salvation lay in loyal support for his volk and in particular for the endeavours of its aspirant capitalist leaders.

In making their assault on the social democratic apparatuses how-ever it was not sufficient for the Afrikaner Nationalists merely to counterpose a nationalist to a social democratic 'weltanschauung' relying on any inherent predominance of 'nationalist' over 'class con-sciousness' among Afrikaner wage-earners. 'Purified' Afrikaner nationalist ideology was like the ideology of all petty bourgeois movements best described as an 'ideological sub-ensemble' formed through the effects of bourgeois ideology on the aspirations of petty bourgeois agents but also including certain 'borrowings' from the ideology of the working class.[9] As in the case of other petty bour-geois movements too, at different phases and stages of the class struggle different elements in the Afrikaner Nationalist's ideological sub-ensemble were given a greater or lesser degree of prominence. In their struggle for a mass base among the white wage-earning classes in the late '30s and '40s, the Nationalists had necessarily to put for-ward their 'left' face and attempt, under various anti-capitalist slogans, to set themselves up as more effective representatives of certain of the *material* interests of their potential white wage-earning supporters than their social democratic rivals.

In their struggle to outbid their social democratic rivals in this way the Nationalists had from the outset a number of factors operating in their favour. Firstly of course there was the petty bourgeois class determination of a large number of white wage earners, and equally important the petty bourgeois aspirations created among a number of white manual employees (particularly in the state sector) through career structures etc. (factors which made them potentially receptive to a petty bourgeois ideology). Secondly, there was the increasingly bureaucratic and 'unrepresentative' character of a number of registered trade unions arising, as we indicated in the last section, in large part at least from their incorporation into the structures set up under the Industrial Conciliation Act. Thirdly there was the more 'liberal', less overt form which the 'civilised labour policy' had come to assume during the 'fusion' period. And fourthly, there were the rivalries arising between artisan unions and white operative workers in certain industries and areas over questions relating to mechanisation and the assignment of particular productive functions as between the two.[10]

In putting forward its 'left face' then the Nationalist movement was able to capitalise on all of these factors. Bureaucratic union leaderships were accused of not putting forward their members' demands or of blatantly capitulating in negotiations with capital. Certain craft unions were accused of open hostility to the unskilled white wage-earner who was more often than not an Afrikaner. State departments were accused of 'going soft' on the 'civilised labour policy'. And various grievances associated with 'promotion' procedures particularly in the state sector were taken up and manipulated as well.

But although all of these points were made in a general way from a number of platforms throughout the late '30s[11] the Nationalists' major (though still limited) successes in the pre-war period came in two particular concentrations of 'suitable' grievances for them to take up and manipulate.

In the railways, where the first 'Christian National' trade union, the Spoorbond, was set up in 1934, the Nationalists were able to build up a fairly sizeable base among white manual employees as well as among salaried clerical staff by exploiting three main issues. Firstly, they were able to point to the inactivity and bureaucratic character of the existing union (the National Union of Railways and Harbours Staffs). Secondly, by quoting the slight fall in the white: black ratio (e.g. from 1·7:1 in 1934 to 1·2:1 in 1939[12]) they were able to construct a credible though invalid case that the 'civilised labour policy' was being relaxed. And thirdly, and most importantly, they were able to capitalise on the relaxation in 1935 of a regulation relating to bilingualism to allege that the railways administration was favouring English speaking over Afrikaans speaking employees in 'promotion' procedures.[13]

In the other main area where the Nationalists managed to build up a measure of support in the pre-war period—the mining industry —they were particularly favoured by two main factors: firstly by the relatively large influx of newly proletarianised Afrikaners into the industry during the 'fusion' period,[14] and secondly and more importantly by the extreme bureaucratisation of the Mine Workers Union (MWU) the existing union covering non-artisanal underground supervisory employees (the category to which most of these newly proletarianised Afrikaner employees were assigned). After its defeat in 1922 the MWU had been incorporated into an even more rigid bureaucratic 'industrial relations' system (that established under the so-called Brace plan) than most other unions and the effects on the internal character of the union had been correspondingly more acute. By the early 1930s its membership had fallen to an all time low (3,500 in 1934) and it was becoming increasingly apparent by the late '30s that its bureaucratic leadership was failing to represent even the limited sectional economic interests of its petty bourgeois membership. It had, for example, withdrawn a substantial wage claim in return for a modest contribution to a provident fund after the devaluation in 1933; agreed in 1936 to a proposal from the Chamber of Mines to establish a 'voluntary' pension scheme for disabled miners at a cost of £75,000 per annum to offset a proposal in parliament for a statutory scheme costing £270,000; and agreed in the same year to a renegotiation of contract rates which saved the Chamber £1 million per annum.[15] Moreover in addition to the increasingly blatant class collaborationist role played by the MWU leadership was its increasingly visible corruption. The administration of funds was becoming more and more suspect as later commissions confirmed, and it was furthermore resorting to more and more authoritarian methods to bolster up its internal position within the union.

Yet despite making significant gains in these two areas (Spoorbond, for example, had forced NURAHS out of existence by 1935, and the Nationalists claimed to have enrolled 8,000 supporters in the mining industry by 1937[16]) the Nationalists' base within the white wage-earning classes remained until the outbreak of war in 1939 a limited one. The established social democratic apparatuses continued, despite the various factors mentioned above, to function, by and large, fairly effectively organising sufficient concessions within the limits of the system to retain a large measure of support among white wage-earners both for the form of state and for its existing apparatuses and institutions. Trade union bureaucrats supported by state officials and a large number of individual capitalists and capitalist organisations were thus to a large extent able to contain and confine 'Christian Nationalists'. Spoorbond, for example, was restricted through not being recognised by the railways administration until 1942. And in the mining industry the Nationalists were thwarted firstly by a closed shop agreement in 1937 (which forced them to disband their Afrikanerbond van Mynwerkers) and, secondly, by various forms of constitutional manipulation which restricted the influence of their 'Reformers' faction within the MWU in the period after 1937. The Nationalists' real breakthrough in terms of building up a mass base within the white wage-earning classes had to wait until the war and post-war period when certain changes in the material circumstances of the white wage-earning classes and in the role of the social democratic state apparatuses made it possible for them to consolidate and advance their position. It is to these changes during the war and post-war period that we must now turn our attention.

War and the crisis in the social democratic state apparatuses

War came to South Africa in 1939 not of course because of any internal dynamic of South African capitalism but because of South Africa's incorporation, despite the hegemony of national capitalist interests, as a subordinate social formation in the imperialist chain. Nevertheless South Africa's participation in the war on the side of the allies was by no means automatic; rather it depended on an internal struggle between the fractions of the bourgeoisie. In fact, the war question raising as it did important political and ideological questions for the bourgeoisie as well as of course having inescapable implications for the state's economic policies, produced an acute polarisation within the power bloc with major fractions lining up on opposite sides.[17]

Broadly speaking, the major elements within the capitalist agricultural fraction, the leading component of national capital and the source of much of its 'national' ideology, was opposed to the war right from the start arguing that it was a foreign war in which South Africa had no part. When the war motion was carried in parliament in 1939, 36 mainly rural representatives including the then prime minister, Hertzog, split from the United Party, and throughout the war farmers were conspicuously absent from those enlisting in the services. Moreover, the war period was one in which capitalist agriculture suffered a number of losses in terms of the realisation of its economic interests, and these losses (frequently explained by the exigencies of war) reinforced the general tendency towards hostility to the war and war policies on the part of capitalist agriculture. The most important of the losses sustained by capitalist agriculture operated in the sphere of labour. The industrial expansion during the war resulted in a large increase in the numbers of Africans employed in industry, and according to one official estimate, 40 per cent of the increase came from white owned farms.[18] On prices too, capitalist agriculture experienced certain losses during the war. Agricultural control boards, which had been set up under the Marketing Act of 1936 to protect agricultural prices from downward fluctuations, became during the war involved in implementing food rationing policies sometimes, as in the case of the Maize Board, acting to lower rather than to raise prices.[19]

Mining and industrial capital on the other hand both supported the war. In the case of mining capital this was not because it stood to gain in terms of its economic interests from the war. On the contrary the war period was a period of increased costs and higher levels of taxation for mining capital which, coupled with a stable gold price meant a relative loss in these terms. Rather, its position on the war is to be explained by its imperialist ownership structure and its corresponding political and ideological ties with Britain.

Industrial capital, however, did benefit economically from the war. South Africa became, during World War II, an important producer of war materials, and stimulated and encouraged by British imperialism's general interest in expanding South Africa's role as a producer of war materials, industry was able to set up its own particular interests as the general interest of a society at war. State policies emphasised industrial expansion above all else and encouraged by state assistance in such things as financing, marketing, protection and even factory construction, total manufacturing output increased from £69·7 million in 1939 to £132·7 million in 1945: an increase of 90 per cent compared to the 17·6 per cent and 61·2 per cent increases in output by mining and agriculture respectively.[20]

The special circumstance of war thus led to a break in the alliance which had existed since 1924 between industrial and agricultural capital, and created the conditions for the formation of an unstable alliance between mining and industrial capital—unstable because state policies did not directly benefit mining capital. They also created the conditions for industrial capital to assume hegemony. But it was a tenuous hegemony over a divided power bloc locked in continuous struggle throughout the war. The declaration of war did not finally resolve even the war question. Struggles over participation in the war, with demands being put for the negotiation of a separate peace with Nazi Germany, continued to be waged at least until the Nazis began to suffer serious defeats on the Russian front;[21] and struggles over associated political and ideological issues (whether national interests were truly being put before foreign interests etc.) also continued. In addition, of course, there were also struggles over a number of important economic issues e.g. agriculture's loss of African labour to industry.

Under these conditions both sides of the divided power bloc needed the maximum degree of support which they could obtain from other classes in the social formation; particularly from classes which had previously given general support to the form of state. The war question thus reinforced the alliance between capitalist agriculture in the southern provinces and the Afrikaner petty bourgeoisie in revolt, and they were joined by those elements in the agricultural capitalist fraction which had split from the United Party over the war question. At the party political level this took the form of the 're-unification' of the Hertzog Nationalist Party and the Gesuiwerde Nationalist Party under the leadership of Malan. On the other side the capitalist fractions supporting the war turned to and entered into a political alliance with the social democratic and other 'traditionally' supportive fractions within the 'white labour movement'. This alliance operated both at the party political level and at the broader level of political practices. At the party political level it was manifested in the inclusion of the Labour Party in the governing coalition and the inclusion in the Cabinet of its leader, Madeley, as Minister of Labour. And at the broader level of political practices it manifested itself in, on the one hand, the frequent declarations of support both for the allied causes generally and for particular war policies by trade union bureaucrats,[22] and, on the other hand, in the inclusion of 'labour personalities' in war related apparatuses of the state.[23] In addition to the formation of an alliance with 'traditionally supportive factions within the white labour movement', the special circumstances of war also resulted in those capitalist fractions who favoured the war receiving a measure of support (on tactical grounds) from those left tendencies which still had some influence within the white wage-earning classes. With the attack on the Soviet Union in 1941, the Communist Party abandoned its previous opposition to the war and called instead for 'support (for) the Government in the war against fascism', arguing that although

> the Government is a capitalist government which stands for the existing system of exploitation and national oppression . . . the alternative . . . is a Nationalist or OB (Ossewabrandwag—RD) government which would be pro-Nazi, anti-war and an enemy of the USSR.

The Party therefore called for support for the Government in its war policy whilst at the same time calling for certain reforms which would 'improve on that policy'.[24] A similar position was also taken by most other 'left' factions within the 'white labour movement' e.g. by Sachs and his Independent Labour Party in the 1943 elections.[25]

But as well as producing a polarisation within the power bloc and a correspondingly closer relationship between particular capitalist fractions and particular factions in the 'white labour movement', war time economic policies had the effect of eroding in a number of ways the economic position of the white wage-earning classes. In the first place the war period saw certain changes in the racial allocation of particular places in the industrial division of labour.

More particularly, the initial shortages of whites caused by military recruitment and, more fundamental considerations of cost, prompted industrial capital to take the first major steps towards utilising cheap African labour power in hitherto 'white' operative places. The numbers of Africans employed in industry accordingly rose throughout the war years reaching 245,538 by 1945, an increase of 57 per cent over the 156,550 employed in 1939.[26] It should be said at once however that neither the exigencies of war nor the hegemony of industrial capital led to any attempt to modify the racist hierarchical character of the social division of labour. Even in the 'dark days' of war no major fraction of capital seriously proposed anything of the kind. Indeed the van Eck commission, the wartime commission which, reflecting industrial capital's position of hegemony in the power bloc, had formally recommended a policy of encouraging the greater utilisation of cheap African labour power in operative places had been quite specific on this point. It had argued that any such proposals should be limited by the need 'not (to) create a European unemployment problem'[27] and that it was therefore necessary at the same time as Africans were being brought into such places to take steps to reassign whites from the lower strata of industrial and state employment to 'industrial occupations, at adequate wages, in those branches of industry in which Europeans have favourable prospects'.[28] In practice then, as Africans were drawn in —at lower wages and under inferior conditions—to operative places previously filled by whites, steps were taken to reassign previous white incumbents 'upwards' to other places in the division of labour (often to supervisory and artisan places but also, during this particular period, to other operative places). The particular 'model' here, later quoted as such by the Board of Trade and Industry, was the engineering industry which was throughout the war engaged in a continuous process of reclassification and reallocation of work roles, but which emerged at the end of the war with its racist hierarchy intact.[29] Indeed a number of new measures were introduced during the war years for the specific purpose of buttressing and sustaining the racist hierarchical division of labour and/or reinforcing the isolation of white from black wage-earners. To mention just a few: shortages of white males to fill places not immediately subject to reclassification were, even in a number of war industries, met at least initially by recruiting white women rather than Africans; technical training for war related production provided by the Central Organisation of Technical Training (COTT) set up in 1940 was made available to whites and a small number of Coloureds only,[31] the Factories, Machinery and Building Work Act (no. 22) passed in 1941 provided for the making of more effective regulations to impose racial segregation on the factory floor;[32] and two war measures (no. 16 of 1940 and no. 38 of 1941) and an Act (the Soldiers and War Workers Employment Act 40 of 1944) offered various prospects for preferential access to various training programmes or at least guaranteed re-employment in their existing places to returning white soldiers.[33] The much flaunted 'narrowing of the wage gap' which occurred during the war years (from an average of 5:1 in 1939 to an average of 4:1 in 1945[34]) is largely explained by the larger proportion of lower paid white women employed during the war (e.g. 30 per cent in 1940–1 as compared to 27·6 per cent in 1938–9[35]) and the limited successes in the economic class struggle of an increasingly militant and organised African working class.[36] It certainly did not represent any undermining of the racist hierarchical character of the social division of labour.

Despite this the position of some whites occupying places in the lower strata of white state and industrial employment was, given the racist character of the social division of labour, at least potentially threatened by the greater utilisation of African labour power in operative work. Previous 'white preserves' were being closed and if that did not immediately spell unemployment, it did at least represent the loss of a 'fall back' position possibly necessary in the event of a future recession. It was thus a trend resented and opposed by some sections of the white wage-earning classes.

Moreover, in addition to these changes in the racial allocation of particular places, war time economic policies also produced a number of other forms of erosion into the economic position of white wage-earners. Firstly, despite the 'cost of living allowances' payable under certain emergency war measures wage rates did not keep up with the rise in prices with the result that average real wages fell slightly, especially during the early years of the war. This is shown even in the following table, based upon official statistics, which some argued markedly underestimated the rise in prices.[37] The table also shows that the reduction in real wages was particularly marked in the mining industry where mining capital, experiencing its highest production costs per ton since 1922, put up a particularly staunch resistance to demands for 'compensation' for rises in the cost of living.[38]

Table 25[39]   *Index of weekly wage rates of adult male white employees*
(Base 1938 = 1000)

	Goldmining		Engineering		General Manufacturing		Combined Index	
	Nominal	*Real*	*Nominal*	*Real*	*Nominal*	*Real*	*Nominal*	*Real*
1939	999	1,000	1,000	1,001	1,004	1,005	1,002	1,003
1940	1,015	981	1,025	991	1,030	996	1,029	995
1941	1,063	982	1,062	982	1,088	1,005	1,064	984
1942	1,151	981	1,164	993	1,188	1,013	1,143	974
1943	1,193	959	1,335	1,073	1,257	1,010	1,240	997
1944	1,288	1,000	1,352	1,050	1,351	1,049	1,300	1,009
1945	1,344	1,016	1,354	1,024	1,401	1,060	1,334	1,009

Secondly, white wage-earners experienced a loss of certain rights under the industrial relations system. 'Industrial peace' seen to 'be important in peace time' was regarded as 'essential when the country (was) at war'[40] and the state accordingly made a number of interventions to try and ensure that there were no interferences with production through strikes. Although this affected whites to a much lesser extent than Africans (who were subject to a blanket prohibition—under War Measure 145 of 1942—and who received much less by way of compensating concessions) nevertheless white wage-earners too were subject to a more repressive state policy in the war period. The right to strike was to all intents and purposes removed by War Measures 6 and 9 which empowered the Minister of Labour to impose compulsory arbitration on the two parties to an industrial dispute if in his opinion 'that dispute may affect adversely the effective prosecution of the war'.[41] And, when strikes did break out, even those involving white wage-earners were repressed with vigour. For example, in 1940 white women tobacco workers striking over a wage claim were driven back to work by police using batons and tear gas[42] and in 1942 sweetworkers striking for higher wages and a closed shop had a meeting broken up by police using batons.[43] Thirdly, white wage-earners were affected in a number of ways by the actions of the Controller of Industrial Manpower, appointed in 1941 with wide powers 'to take such action as he deems necessary to ensure that the resources of any controlled industry are used in a manner calculated to yield the best result in . . . the prosecution of the War'.[44] Among other things white wage-earners were, under orders issued by the Controller, prevented from leaving particular jobs, compulsorily moved from one job to another, compelled to work a minimum number of hours per week (54 in the engineering industry) or compelled to work compulsory overtime with no overtime pay.[45] In addition the position of skilled artisans in a number of industries was affected by a number of 'dilution orders' relaxing a number of apprenticeship regulations which had previously acted as a barrier to the replacement of skilled artisans in particular processes by operative workers.[46]

It is these two factors——the alliance between the social democratic factions within the 'white labour movement' and those capitalist fractions supporting the war, and the erosion of the economic position of white wage-earners during the war——which we have to understand in order to understand how it was that the Afrikaner Nationalist petty bourgeoisie was able during the war years to consolidate and build up its support within the white wage-earning classes (mainly among new petty bourgeois strata but also among certain strata of the white working class proper). As Poulantzas has argued, and as we have attempted to show in previous chapters of this study at a more concrete level, what we have called social democratic state apparatuses (i.e. reformist 'Labour' parties and bureaucratised, institutionalised trade unions) come into existence in the bourgeois state through the class struggle because of the inability of the bourgeoisie 'to rule through organized physical repression alone'. In addition to its repressive apparatus the bourgeois state also requires 'one or more ideological state apparatuses to inculcate bourgeois ideology' and a 'party of the social democratic type (and for that matter an institutionalised, bureaucratised trade union movement) constitutes such an apparatus . . . in the bourgeois state'.[47] But social democratic state apparatuses are state apparatuses of a specific and distinct kind. In particular if they are to function effectively, they have to maintain a representative base among the working class (or in our case among particular fractions of the new petty bourgeoisie and particular strata of the working class) and they must therefore channel certain demands of the relevant class or fraction through them. They are thus 'bound to a certain policy of compromise with the working class' (or particular strata thereof) albeit to a policy of compromise 'which is in the last analysis that which the bourgeoisie can allow within the normal state forms and its own policy'. And it is for that reason that these apparatuses are not available to the bourgeoisie 'as a mere "tool" for universal use'.[48]

Under the specific circumstances prevailing in the South African social formation during the war, however, the particular political requirements of the hegemonic capitalist fractions resulted in a serious undermining of the conditions necessary for the social democratic apparatuses to fulfil their particular institutional role among the white wage-earning classes, and this produced as a consequence a severe crisis of social democratic ideology reflecting the crisis of bourgeois ideology in the social formation generally. In particular the struggles within the power bloc over the war and related questions and the need on the part of the hegemonic fractions for allies in these struggles produced a situation in which the relative autonomy necessary for the social democratic apparatuses to maintain their representative base within the white wage-earning classes was severely impaired. Instead of channelling certain of the economic demands of their white wage-earning base in the interests of producing among them a general support for the bourgeois state, these apparatuses were required in South Africa during the war to produce support for particular war policies. More specifically, Labour Party politicians and trade union bureaucrats occupying offices ranging from Minister of Labour to representatives on the Advisory Board to the Controller of Industrial Manpower were required to endorse—in the interests of the 'war effort'—specific emergency measures which were imposing economic losses on their memberships. It is true that social democratic apparatuses were required to perform a similar function in other belligerent social formations but in the case of South Africa they were required to perform this role under conditions where the bourgeoisie was divided on the war question and in which bourgeois ideology was not therefore putting forward a united front on the war question. It was this crisis of social democratic ideology, arising from the undermining of the relative autonomy of the social democratic apparatuses at a time when the economic interests of their white wage-earning base were being adversely affected, which created the conditions for the Afrikaner Nationalist movement to consolidate and extend its mass base among the white wage-earning classes during the war years. Still putting forward its 'left' face the Nationalists were able to relentlessly exploit the close identification of the Labour Party and trade union bureaucracies with particular war policies in order to denounce them as traitors 'sitting . . . among the capitalists and imperialists'[49] and to assert that it (the Nationalist movement) was the only true representative of the Afrikaner wage-earner. In parliament Nationalist MPs (particularly Schoeman and Serfontein) conducted a relentless and highly skilful attack on Madeley and the Labour Party accusing them of being 'political acrobats' supporting measures which they would have previously 'violently opposed'.[50] Madeley's acceptance of 'ministerial responsibility' for the relatively low wages paid to some whites employed in government departments,[51] the repression of strikes by whites,[52] the introduction of measures providing for longer working hours[53] and the activities of the Controller of Manpower[54] were all eagerly seized upon and contrasted with the Labour Party's previous position on these questions. When the Minister replied that through the Labour Party's representation in the coalition he was able to introduce 'valuable reforms' (notably a Factories Act in 1941, a Workmen's Compensation Act in 1941 and an Unemployment Benefit Act in 1942) at the same time as assisting in the prosecution of the war,[55] the Nationalists could reply quite correctly that 'in spite of his preaching socialist doctrines (*sic*) for forty years' he (the minister) had introduced nothing which was not 'already on the stocks when the previous government left office'.[56] In addition, certain specific demands and grievances of white wage-earners no longer being channelled through the social democratic apparatuses were taken up and supported and other demands and grievances more suited to the inculcation of Nationalist ideology (e.g. over the actual or alleged effects of the relaxation of racial demarcation of jobs and over actual or alleged discriminations against Afrikaners) were carefully cultivated and manipulated as well.

But although the Nationalists conducted a fairly broad based generalised attack on social democracy along these lines seeking thereby to build up support from Afrikaner wage-earners in a number of industries and areas, their major successes during the war period were once again concentrated among particular strata of the white wage-earning classes in sectors where for various reasons the crisis of social democratic ideology was at its most intense and/or where there was a particular concentration of 'suitable' grievances for them to take up. During the war itself such conditions existed in the railways and in the mining industry—the sectors where, as we saw previously, the movement had been able to make some headway before the war.

In the railways war policies gave the Nationalists further opportunities to manipulate grievances arising among the lower echelons of the petty bourgeois and white labouring employees in connection with promotion procedures. It was not that the number of promotions declined during the war years. On the contrary the overall number increased as indicated by the fact that the number and proportion of whites occupying graded posts rose from 48,084 or 72 per cent in 1939 to 65,998 or 78 per cent in March 1946.[57] Rather what the Nationalists were able to manipulate and exploit were certain grievances arising from two main changes in the processes by which particular agents were selected or not selected for assignment to these places during the war period. Firstly, the sudden loss of staff due to military recruitment during the early part of the war led the administration to further relax the bilingualism requirements and promote to the graded posts a number of unilingual English speaking employees.[58] And secondly, the 'security requirements' of wartime resulted in a relatively large number of Afrikaners suspected of anti-war sympathies, often on the basis of little more than the say so of an informer, being denied promotion. Since this obviously included a number of relatively 'innocent' Afrikaner employees it could be fanned into a general grievance. Indeed when the Nationalist régime came to office in 1948 it appointed a Commission before which some 2,875 railway employees, many even at that stage saying they were 'innocent' of anti-war activities, alleged that they had been denied promotion to places ranging from the junior supervisory and clerical posts to the post of General Manager on these grounds.[59] Through this combination of factors the Nationalists were able to construct a credible case of anti-Afrikaner bias in the railways' promotion policies. For example, in 1941 Spoorbond conducted considerable agitation arguing that there was discrimination against Afrikaners based upon a study of promotions over a two month period which apparently showed that whereas 80 per cent of all railway officials were Afrikaners, 59 per cent of the newly promoted were English speaking.[60] Another 'grievance' which Spoorbond was able to manipulate was in connection with the influx of African workers into certain places formerly filled by whites. Although it was, according to the railways administration only 'with the greatest reluctance that authority was given for the engagement of non European labourers in positions vacated by (white) railworkers',[61] nevertheless there were by 1946 some 3,111 blacks filling these places and Spoorbond was thus able to argue that the position of Afrikaners in the railways was also being threatened from below. Through manipulation of grievances like these—not recognised or taken up by any social democratic rival—the Nationalists were able to set themselves up as the lone champions of the unskilled Afrikaner railway employee in his struggle onto or up the ladder into the petty bourgeoisie. And indeed as early as 1942, the year in which Spoorbond was finally recognised by the railways administration, it had through this approach been able to win the support of 29,000 of the railway's 77,000 white employees.[63]

In the mining industry too the Nationalists were able to build up their support among the lower level supervisory new petty bourgeoisie, firstly, by taking advantage of the blatantly 'corrupt' and 'unconstitutional' practices resorted to by the MWU's bureaucratic leadership in the course of its struggle against them, and secondly and more importantly by exploiting the discontent among the union's membership arising from the total failure of the bureaucracy to represent its interests.

Space does not permit any extended discussion of the complex struggles with the MWU during the war years.[64] Very briefly, the fact that the Nationalists' 'Reformers' ' faction had already established a foothold in the union before the war coupled with the fact that military recruitment had depleted the ranks of the bureaucracy's potential supporters, prompted the union's existing leadership, notorious for 'corrupt' practices before the war, to resort to even more blantantly corrupt practices during the war. In particular, in the elections for the post of General Secretary held in March 1940 it resorted to ill concealed ballot rigging, involving among other things the removal of votes from ballot boxes with false bottoms and the distribution of multiple ballot forms to certain voters. Despite these manoeuvres however the bureaucracy's candidate, Kukkuk, won only by 26 votes and in response to the narrowness of the margin and the soon discovered ballot rigging the 'Reformers' organised a campaign of withholding subscription payments. After some months this campaign began to take its toll on union finances and the leadership was eventually compelled to turn to the Chamber of Mines for a hand-out. When the 'Reformers' threatened to react to this move with a strike the state became compelled to intervene in support of an increasingly vulnerable ally of the hegemonic fraction. At first this involved the appointment of a Commission of Inquiry which, whilst laying the blame for the 'troubles' in the union at the door of the 'puppets' of a 'subversive movement' and essentially endorsing the position of the existing leadership on a number of key questions, attempted to maintain a facade of neutrality by acknowledging the existence of corrupt practices and making some recommendations for modifications in these practices; including recommending the removal from the union and prosecution of Kukkuk (replaced as Acting Secretary by B. B. Broderick). Unfortunately for the union's bureaucratic leadership, however, such modifications were not sufficient to restore its position. During a subsequent court case brought for slander against certain 'Reformers' ' leaders, certain dubious constitutional changes designed to neutralise four 'Reformers' ' candidates who had secured election as officers of the union in 1939, were ruled invalid, which meant, technically, that fresh elections should have been held for these places. Fearing that if elections were actually held under circumstances where the existing bureaucratic leadership had been discredited a number of these posts would fall to 'Reformers' antagonistic to war policies, the state was once again compelled to intervene, only this time more directly through an emergency war measure of 1941 which suspended elections for posts in the MWU until six months after the termination of hostilities. Thus by as early as 1941 the bureaucratic leadership of the MWU had been plainly exposed as corrupt, authoritarian and dependent upon the unconcealed support of the bourgeois state and the Chamber of Mines. But, discredited and weakened though it undoubtedly was by these factors its position of hegemony within the MWU was only finally rendered untenable by its total inability to represent the economic interests of its petty bourgeois membership.

This manifested itself in the bureaucracy's role in struggles over a number of economic issues throughout the war, but the most important was its role in respect of a wage claim during 1943 and 1944. We have already seen that mining capital's economic position deteriorated somewhat during the war due to its being subjected to rising costs and higher taxation on the one hand and a static gold price on the other, and we have also seen that this made mining capital particularly resistant to wage claims during the war years. It had indeed been reluctant to concede even the 'cost of living allowances' provided for under various war measures until compelled to do so under an arbitration award made in terms of another war measure.[65] The result was, as we saw in the table earlier, that the real income of mine employees (African workers, white petty bourgeoisie and white artisans alike) declined during the war years. Eventually under intense pressure from its membership the MWU leadership was compelled in 1943 to submit a claim for a 30 per cent wage increase. Predictably this was refused by mining capital which argued that to have paid it would have cost £1·5 million per annum if confined to members of the MWU and £4·5 million if extended to other white employees, and after an interval the Chamber came up with a counter offer—a grant of £100,000 per annum for five years to be paid to the MWU for various co-operative projects intended to provide members with cheap food, housing and other benefits in return for a guarantee that no further claims would be submitted unless there were 'very material changes' in conditions.[66] The MWU's acceptance of this proposal in 1944 was seen far and wide as a blatant capitulation by them to mining capital. Even the other union bureaucrats making up the Mining Unions Joint Committee (MUJC) were highly critical and in fact at one stage the MWU withdrew from the MUJC because of the 'veiled but somewhat pointed attack' on it by the other unions.[67] Moreover when the MWU leadership embarked on its co-operative projects it did so with such ineptitude and corruption that its members derived few if any of the intended benefits from them.[68] It was this agreement which gave the Nationalists their real opportunity to build up really substantial mass support among the petty bourgeois membership of the MWU. In response to the betrayal of their interests by the MWU leadership a new organisation, called the 'Action Committee', sprung up among the rank and file, led by men who in a subsequent court case at least, claimed that they had never had anything to do with the Mynwerkersbond or the 'Reformers' movement.[69] Its object was to overturn that agreement and it immediately received the support of the Nationalist organisations. Before long it was incorporating previous demands for 'reform' into a broadly based challenge by the rank and file of the MWU against its bureaucratic leadership which was only staved off until the end of the war by the effect of the war measure.

By 1945 then the Nationalists had managed to build up a substantial mass base for themselves among certain key strata of the white wage-earning classes. The Labour Party's gain of 6 seats in the 1943 elections (leaving it with 9 seats as against 3 in the 1938 elections) was largely illusory being to a large extent the product of the electoral pact arrangement with the United Party and the bargaining over constituencies between the leaderships of the two parties. The established social democratic state apparatuses were in deep crisis being unable to hold on to important parts of their constituent base. But despite this and despite the Nationalists' own considerable efforts, they could not extend their influence among a number of other key strata of the white wage-earning classes: notably among artisans and among strongly unionised manual industrial workers. It was after all a particular kind of petty bourgeois ideology which they were seeking to inculcate: one element of which was a demand for a restructuring of the apparatuses of the state which would eliminate trade

union bargaining. As Schoeman put it in a famous speech in 1943:
This system of collective bargaining has outstayed its usefulness entirely . . . Under the new economic system which we
want to bring about it will . . . be redundant . . . The State (will)
accept full responsibility for fixing wages and the regulation of
working conditions (and) the principal function of the present
trade unions will disappear . . . they (trades unions) will be
mainly entrusted with the task of regulating domestic matters
as between the employers and the employees. And for the rest
looking after the spiritual welfare of the workers . . .[70]

It was not therefore an ideology which was likely to draw much support from strata, like the artisans organised into craft unions defending their 'monopoly of skill' or industrial workers with a strong
tradition of successful trade union struggle (such as the garment
workers[71]), whose economic position could clearly be seen to have
benefited materially from trade union struggles. Moreover, in the
case of the former, an additional factor was that the Nationalists
were on record as being opposed to the maintenance of craft barriers.[72] Memberships of artisan craft unions—even in industries
where they were subjected to falling wages or 'dilution orders' (e.g.
engineering)—thus generally remained 'loyal' to the established
social democratic leaderships providing them with their 'hard core'
base. White industrial workers with some experience of trade union
struggle also generally remained loyal to social democratic leaderships, and indeed there were in some cases signs of an incipient movement to the left of orthodox social democracy in crisis by some
white industrial workers. Communist Party members, for example,
had some success in extending their influence in some white industrial
unions during the war years. Danie du Plessis was elected secretary
of the Johannesburg branch of the Building Workers Industrial Union,
Willie Kalk remained secure as General Secretary of the Leather
Workers Union despite a concerted 'Reformers' campaign against him
and Ray Alexander managed to organise a number of hitherto unorganised white as well as black industrial workers into new 'mixed'
(i.e. white/coloured) unions—the most important being the Food,

Canning and Allied Workers Union. In addition there were also some signs of a tentative polarisation towards the black working class on the part of some white industrial workers. A number of hitherto all white industrial unions became 'mixed' and there were even one or two sporadic attempts to admit Africans. For example, both the Garment Workers Union and the Sweet Workers Union took advantage of a loophole in the Industrial Conciliation Act to admit African women who were not then 'pass bearers'.[73] Any such movement to the left however remained very much a minority tendency throughout. The conditions did not really exist in the period for a decisive break on the part of white industrial workers from economistic class practices. White industrial workers after all still remained in a relatively privileged economic position *vis-à-vis* Africans; and the state still continued, albeit less effectively than previously, to guarantee and defend some of their economic interests and thus to engender the isolation effects which acted against them realising any community of interests particularly with the African working class. In addition there was at the time no really viable *mass* revolutionary movement of the principal dominated classes which could have organised non-fundamental classes under its hegemony. All of these factors were reflected both in the fact that the only significant attempt to challenge the hegemony of orthodox social democracy from the left of the 'white labour movement'—that by Solly Sachs and the leadership of the Garment Workers Union in 1943—was itself located within the problematic of white social democratic ideology;[74] and also in the fact that even when white industrial workers showed signs of polarisation towards the African working class they still continued to display a number of reservations and ambivalences. For example, even when 'left' unions, like the Garment Workers Union or the Sweet Workers Union, took steps to admit Africans it was usually on some inferior basis e.g. to a separate ('parallel') branch: a factor which led militants within the African working class to seek quite correctly an independent organisational basis for their struggles.

1945–1948 the crisis deepens

When 'peace' came in 1945 it did nothing to ameliorate any of the factors producing the crisis of social democracy which had enabled the Nationalists to consolidate their position among certain strata of the white wage-earning classes during the war years. In fact just the reverse: the restructuring of South African capitalism after the war produced a whole new series of problems and contradictions both for the hegemonic capitalist fractions in their relationship with the white wage-earning classes and for social democratic politicians and trade union bureaucrats.

In the first place the differences and divisions within the power bloc were in no way reconciled by the defeat of German and Japanese imperialism. On the contrary with 'peace' the differences within the power bloc became even more acute. Serious differences arose between capitalist agriculture and the still hegemonic industrial capitalist fraction over the question of whether or not to reallocate the African reserve army of labour from the towns to meet the 'labour crisis' in agriculture[75] and between capitalist agriculture on the one hand and industrial and mining capital on the other over pricing and agricultural marketing policy.[76] And to compound that the alliance between industrial and mining capital formed specifically for the purposes of prosecuting the war and unsteady at the best of times became, with 'peace', increasingly unstable as differences surfaced over such questions as the migrant labour system and taxation.[77] Finding itself increasingly isolated within the power bloc capitalist agriculture confirmed its alliance with the movement of the Afrikaner petty bourgeoisie in revolt and indeed those elements within the agricultural capitalist fraction which had remained loyal to the United Party during the war deserted to the Nationalists in the years thereafter.[78]

Secondly, as a consequence of certain changes in the pattern of imperialist centre/periphery relations,[79] the post war period saw the beginnings of a process of restructuring of the relations of production in industry, and this coupled with the demobilisation of some

106,000 white and 39,000 black war veterans,[80] produced a number
of new class problems and class struggles over the question of assigning
white war veterans (entitled to various preferential facilities), other
whites and blacks to particular places in the industrial division of
labour.[81] And on top of all that, the post war period saw the climax
of a period of heightened struggle by the African dominated classes,
during which such events as the 1946 African miners strike and the
radicalisation of the African National Congress posing for the dominant (capitalist) classes and for the white trade union movement the
problem of how to respond.[82]

With the continuing acute divisions in the power bloc the politically hegemonic alliance of industrial and mining capital represented
at the party political level by the United Party remained in the post
war years in need of allies and it sought therefore to renew its
alliance with the social democratic faction within the white wage-
earning classes. In return for their support the United Party régime
offered white wage-earners a programme of 'social security'; which
while specifically precluding any 'general redistribution of income'
proposed spending some £40 millions over a ten year period on
unemployment insurance, maternity, pension, sickness and death
benefits.[83] In addition the Labour Party was offered the opportunity
to remain in the governing coalition with its leader Madeley continuing in office as Minister of Labour. For the social democratic 'labour
leadership' however this posed a number of contradictory problems.
On the one hand, they saw their interests lying in the continued
hegemony of those capitalist fractions which would retain the existing 'industrial relations' structure as against those which were allied
to petty bourgeois fractions proposing changes which would eliminate
trade union bargaining.[84] On the other hand, however, they had seen
their position with their base being undermined during the war, in
part through their close identification with the hegemonic capitalist
fractions. Towards the end of the war, in fact, both the Labour Party
and the Trades and Labour Council had seen it as being necessary to
attempt to assert some degree of relative autonomy within the coalition by voicing certain criticisms of the United Party régime's

administration of its own programme and calling for some extensions to it in the form of a 'Workers' Charter'.[85] Ultimately the Labour Party resolved this dilemma by a compromise. In response to a demand from its rank and file membership, it withdrew from the coalition and the cabinet when hostilities were terminated in October 1945. But it nevertheless remained in a relationship of alliance with those fractions of capital represented by the United Party as evidenced by the continuation of the electoral pact between the two parties and Labour's general support for government policies. With respect to the latter the party argued both in parliament and outside that 'the moment' was not right to advance 'our socialist plan of economy' and that the interests of its white wage-earning constituents would best be served by demanding a more effective implementation of the United Party's own 'social security' programme along the lines of its 'Workers' Charter'.[86]

Social democracy then, remained allied to the hegemonic alliance within the power bloc represented at the party political level by the United Party. But what of the effects of the post war restructuring of South African capitalism on the different strata within the white wage-earning classes and what of the position of the hegemonic alliance and the United Party régime with respect to the problems arising therefrom? Essentially, as mentioned earlier, the post war period saw the beginnings of a phase of restructuring of the relations of production in the industrial sector. More specifically the relatively large investments of foreign imperialist capital in manufacturing industry created the conditions for a process of transition in which the relations of monopoly capitalism of the imperialist metropolises were increasingly reproduced within the South African industrial sector. The post-war period thus saw the beginnings of a phase in which the powers of economic ownership in industry were being increasingly concentrated, and in which, therefore, industrial capital began to assume a greater measure of real, as distinct from formal, control over actual labour processes and effect, following the logic of capital accumulation, a greater socialisation of production and a greater separation of mental and supervisory from manual functions.

It was thus, accordingly, a period in which there was being created on the one hand an increased number of manual machine operative places and on the other hand an increased number of specialised supervisory and mental i.e. new petty bourgeois places. Some indication of the increasing mechanisation of production is given by the rise in the average 'depreciated capital stock' per employee (from £191 in 1945 to £199 in 1948 at constant 1938 prices[87]). And some indication of the rapid creation of new petty bourgeois places is given by the repeated references in contemporary Department of Labour Reports and industrial journals to 'acute shortages of . . . technically qualified personnel, clerks and typists' as well as 'capable foremen'.[88]

Industrial capital's position on the question of the assignment of agents of particular race groups to these places remained fundamentally the same as it had been during the war period. It continued to seek to make greater use of cheap African labour power in operative places, but at the same time it continued to envisage that new petty bourgeois places would be filled almost exclusively by whites. Part of the reason for this continuing identification by industrial capital of new petty bourgeois places as 'white' was undoubtedly the political imperative to accommodate some of the demands of the white wage-earning classes. But it was also bound up with industrial capital's own economic interests under the existing conditions of reproduction of white and black labour power. The new petty bourgeois places which were being created—supervisory places, places in the circulation process and technician type places—were like all petty bourgeois places located in the 'camp' of mental labour and agents filling these places were therefore required to possess certain qualifications in terms of 'ideological . . . rituals of knowledge or supposed knowledge from which the working class is excluded'.[89] Given this requirement clearly the cheapest ways of obtaining the necessary labour power were either to import it from abroad or to modify the reproduction process for those strata in the existing stock of labour power whose educational qualifications etc. were closest to those required, or of course both. And given the international division of labour and the existing patterns of reproducing labour power within South Africa, capitalist economic logic therefore implied filling these places in the first instance with 'suitable' whites.

Spokesmen for the interests of industrial capital and government commissions reflecting the hegemony of industrial capital thus presented the ongoing process of restructuring and class formation as a 'complementary' process perfectly compatible with 'the maintenance of white civilization' and which would not therefore 'endanger the position of our white population'.[90] Industrial development, wrote the Board of Trade and Industries following the unquestioned assumption that 'skilled' (i.e. artisan and new petty bourgeois) places would be white,

> is bound under present conditions to result in an increase rather
> than a decrease in the demand for European labour. For not
> only are skilled and unskilled work complementary in character
> but the consequent reduction in unit costs will improve the
> competitive ability of local industries and extend their scope.[91]

The reconciliation of the demand by industrial capital to utilise more cheap African labour in operative places and the 'maintenance of white civilization in South Africa', the Board argued therefore lay in 'the development of the character, industry and enterprise of the European'.[92] If we substitute retraining for new petty bourgeois and artisanal places (principally the former) for the phrase 'development of the character, etc.' in the above quotation, we have the essence of the approach of industrial capital and the United Party regime to the problems of reassigning whites to places in the division of labour after the war. Returning war veterans and whites displaced by the orderly transfer of certain semi-skilled operative tasks to blacks were to be retrained to meet the demand for new petty bourgeois labour power: the exodus of whites from the operative working class into the new petty bourgeoisie which had begun in a limited way during the war was to be accelerated *to meet the requirements of industrial capital* in its phase of transition to monopoly capitalism. The immediate post war years thus saw a major expansion of various forms of training for whites. Overall expenditure on white education increased by some 51 per cent to £19 million over the four years 1944—5 to 1947—8 (see Appendix 2) and the number of whites undergoing apprenticeship training rose from 15,671 in 1944 to 21,513 in 1948 —an increase of 37 per cent.[93] In addition various schemes to train whites for such places by means other than traditional apprentice-ship were expanded or introduced during these years as well. COTT training was continued until 1950 and intensive training with exemp-tion from normal apprenticeship and trade testing were provided in the building industry under the Housing (Emergency Powers) Act of 1945 and in other industries for war veterans under the Soldiers and War Workers Act of 1944. Between 1946 and 1948 in fact some 9,900 whites were allocated to various new petty bourgeois and arti-san places through the operation of such schemes.[94]

However despite the overall commitment on the part of the hege-monic fraction to 'white supremacy' in the division of labour, despite the various extensions in the training of whites for artisan and new petty bourgeois places, and despite the fact that the restructuring of South African capitalism along these lines produced no appreciable increase in overall white unemployment[95] there nevertheless remained as in the war years a number of strata of the white wage-earning classes for whom, given the racist social division of labour in South African capitalism, the reorganisation of the labour process along these lines posed a potential threat. In the first place apprenticeship training was not made equally available to all whites. War veterans were, under the Soldiers and War Workers Act, given preferential access over other whites to a number of training schemes as well as 'a prior claim to employment over other sections'.[96] And, secondly since the needs of capital accumulation remained predominant, press-ing shortages of 'skilled' labour power were in a number of cases met by recruiting immigrants from abroad rather than by extending training facilities for local whites.[97] In 1946, for example, industry recruited 652 'skilled' white immigrants and between 1946 and 1949 the Department of Labour gave advice to nearly 10,000 prospective overseas applicants.[98] The net effect therefore was that whilst the position of war veterans in the division of labour was by and large

secure, for a number of mainly Afrikaner wage-earners occupying the
'lower levels' of white industrial or state employment, the prospects
of an escape from the effects of the reassignment of operative places
to Africans by means of artisan training were in practice far less certain than in the visions presented in commission reports. Indeed,
according to Nationalist sources there were by 1947 as many as
18,000 frustrated would-be trainees unable to obtain access to any of
the various training programmes.[99] Once again therefore there remained as in the war years a number of strata within the white wage-
earning classes for whom the reassignment of operative places to
blacks constituted a potential threat if not by facing them with the
immediate prospect of unemployment then at least by closing down
certain 'white preserves' in the lower echelons of industrial and state
employment which were regarded as possibly necessary 'fall back'
places in the event of a future recession.[100] Indeed with the more
rapid mechanisation of the post-war period the indications are that
the numbers so affected had increased.

Furthermore, in addition to posing certain, at least potential,
problems for whites in the lower echelons of industrial and state
employment, the post war restructuring of South African capitalism
had not produced the kinds of wage increases which white wage-
earners expected or demanded. Real white wages (for adult males)
did rise by an average of about 5 per cent over the three years 1945–
48 (from an index of 1,009 in 1945 to 1,060 in 1948[101]) but after
the relative fall of the war years it was at a rate rather less than many
white wage-earners were demanding. Indeed in some industries,
notably building, real wages in 1948 still remained below the level
which had prevailed in 1939 (an index of 982 compared to 1,001)
and in others, notably mining, real wages though above the 1939
level remained below the levels which had prevailed earlier in the
'30s (e.g. an index of 1061 in 1948 compared to 1075 in 1936[102]).

Thus once again social democracy was in alliance, albeit a looser
alliance, with the hegemonic fraction in a divided power bloc at a
time when the economic demands of important strata of its constituent white wage-earning base were not being met, and in which,

indeed, important strata were at least potentially threatened with displacement by the changes which were taking place in capitalist relations of production. The 'solution' which social democracy offered in respect of the latter—'equal pay for equal work'—implied of course just as much an acceptance of the racist hierarchical division of labour of South African capitalism as did job colour bars: 'equal pay' being intended to preserve particular places as white by removing the lower wage incentive which capital had to employ blacks in these places instead. But whilst the enforcement of 'equal pay' was generally effective as a means of excluding Africans from artisan or technician type places, it was not nearly so effective in preserving the position in the racist hierarchy of those whites at the lower levels of industrial employment under conditions where mechanisation was leading to considerable job fragmentation and redefinition. Witnesses before the 1948–1951 Industrial Legislation Commission, for example, spoke of whites in the baking, furniture, millinery, sheet metal and electrical manufacturing industries being displaced by blacks in spite of various minimum wage determinations operating under the terms of the Wage or Industrial Conciliation Acts.[103]

Indeed, when struggles over the racial allocation of work roles came to a head, as for example in the building industry in 1946, even artisans, the hard core base of social democracy, were prone to demand the straightforward exclusion of African rivals rather than the more nebulous guarantees for their employment at equal pay.[104] Furthermore, with the position of their hard core supporters generally secure, a number of social democratic 'labour leaders' specifically endorsed, from their position of alliance with industrial capital, a number of the measures which acted against certain categories of lower placed white wage-earners escaping the effects of displacement via 'promotion' to artisan or new petty bourgeois places. This included of course supporting all of the measures giving special advantages to war veterans over other whites, and it also included specifically endorsing, in the interests of 'industrial development' 'artisan' immigration.[105] Social democracy in short was under the conditions prevailing in the post war years palpably failing to represent the interests of important strata of its constituent base within the existing structures of South African capitalism and it was, needless to say, incapable of offering any solution to their class problems which in any way transcended those structures.

But there was more. Compounding all the other contradictions arising in the social democratic state apparatuses in the post war years was an acute internal crisis arising from their need to respond to various aspects of the heightened struggle between the dominant and black dominated classes. Smuts' Asiatic Land Tenure and Indian Representation Bill of 1946 split the parliamentary Labour Party right down the middle not because any of its members had any objection to the clauses imposing various forms of segregation on Asians, but because six of the party's MPs and Senators, including the leader Madeley, were opposed to the proposals to give Asians limited representation (by whites) in the Senate, arguing that such a move would create a 'non European bloc' which could potentially eclipse the smaller white parliamentary parties.[106] After a bitter internal dispute the position of the six was eventually voted down at the party's National Executive Council and one resigned to join the Nationalists, three to join the United Party and two into political oblivion; including Madeley who died the next year a broken man complaining of his party's blindness to the 'danger to the white race'.[107] Labour emerged from this conflict with only five parliamentary seats and much of its credibility damaged. However, despite the subsequent capture of the party machine by its 'left wing' (absurdly described by some of the more hysterical of their opponents as 'communists'[108]) and despite, under its new leadership drawing support from 'left' factions in the 'white labour movement' hitherto aloof (e.g. Sachs and the Garment Workers Union which affiliated in 1947[109]) the party still remained a white social democratic party in alliance with the hegemonic fractions in a divided power bloc, whose economic policies were threatening the position of important strata of the party's potential constituent base, and which was itself displaying a number of ambivalences and uncertainties about its response to the struggles of black dominated classes. The party was as such no more capable under its new leadership than it had been under its old of making a decisive move in any direction. It could not give greater support to the demands of its own white wage-earning base against industrial capital (including of course their demand for protection by means of job colour bars) and neither could it make the alternative move of seeking to polarise the 'white labour movement' towards supporting the ongoing struggle of the African working class. The programme adopted by the party under its new leadership remained vague and contradictory. It continued to offer 'equal pay for equal work' as the salvation of the white wage-earner and to display all the familiar ambivalences towards blacks: declaring on the one hand that all people had 'rights regardless of colour', but calling on the other hand for a form of residential and political segregation.[110] Moreover, the new leadership expressed explicit support for the Smuts government's Asiatic Bill as well as for a number of other measures, which led Solly Sachs—as ever a perceptive tactician—to write,

> . . . even from the point of view of expediency support for Smuts is a terrible blunder. It is an axiom in politics that a small politicial party seeking the support of the masses must always have an independent programme.[111]

The change in leadership thus could not and did not solve any of the fundamental problems besetting the party and it could not therefore, arrest the party's continuing decline. Within a year of the split over the Asiatic Bill, the party had lost its majority on the Johannesburg city council and become instead an 'ineffective minority group',[112] and in the same year too even its paper, 'The Illustrated Labour Bulletin', was forced to close.[113]

The effects of the heightened struggle of the African working class also produced an acute crisis within the Trades and Labour Council. Technically the Council had been committed to a policy of calling for Africans to be granted full recognition under the Industrial Conciliation Act in accordance with its policy of opposition to the 'cheap labour bar' and low wage competition. It had, accordingly, allowed a certain number of African unions to join during the war (although in many cases this had been allowed only on the basis of less than full membership so as not to pose any threat to the continued dominance of white unions in the council). On the other hand, however, a considerable element within the 'white labour movement', strongly represented among the leadership of the TLC, saw their position potentially threatened by the increasingly militant struggle being waged by the African working class against a state in which they and their membership occupied a relatively privileged place. When the Smuts government introduced a bill in 1947 proposing to contain the struggle of the African working class by granting limited recognition to segregated, isolated African trade unions under the strict supervision of the Native Affairs Department and subject to various prohibitions (including a blanket prohibition on strikes),[114] many of the ambivalences in the 'white labour movement' surfaced. A substantial element within the existing TLC hierarchy, including the president A. J. Downes of the Typographical Union, were inclined to support the Smuts Bill, though it clearly contradicted stated TLC policy. At the same time too the Nationalists had been conducting considerable agitation against the presence in the Council of 'mixed' and African unions. Eventually at the 1947 Conference these contradictions were brought to a head. A motion from the South African Iron and Steel Trades Association (a right wing though not at the time 'Christian National' dominated union)[115] which proposed to exclude African unions from the council drew support from 34 unions with a membership of 36,373[116] and was only quite narrowly defeated: after which five unions mainly based among new petty bourgeois white wage-earners in the Pretoria area withdrew from the TLC.[117] Moreover, as in the case of 'the Labour Party, the purge of the right wing did little or nothing to solve the TLC's underlying crisis. The Council remained an organisation of bureaucratised institutionalised trade unions, based predominantly on new petty bourgeois and artisan wage-earners, and allied to fractions of capital whose own approach to the struggle of the African working class reflected a number of uncertainties. Not surprisingly then the Council continued to display all of the ambivalences inherent therein. It could not, even after the purge of the right, produce any clear cut position on the question of the struggle of the African working class and it continued to remain divided between those factions which favoured a policy of dominating the African trade union movement 'from within', those factions which essentially supported some form of decisive intervention by the state against the African working class, and a small left wing (mainly Communist Party members) which sought support for the struggles of the African working class. Indeed it was scarcely two years before the council was again subjected to divisions and defections over this question.

Social democracy in the post-war years was in short in multiple crisis: a crisis brought about by its manifest failure to represent the economic interests of important strata of its constituent base, and a crisis of credibility and indecision brought about by its inherent inability, given its bureaucratic character, the class determination of its base and the nature of its alliances, to take any clear cut position on the struggles of the African working class. What is more, to compound all of that the United Party's 'social security' programme—the very foundation of the party's attempt to organise support among white wage-earners—was coming badly unstuck in the face of fierce opposition from various agricultural and petty bourgeois interests to one of the main measures in that programme—the Unemployment Insurance Act of 1946. The distinguishing feature of the 1946 Unemployment Insurance Act which led to it drawing such a hostile response was that whereas previous Unemployment Benefit Acts (passed in 1937 and 1942) had been intended to apply to '(white) skilled and semi-skilled classes of labour . . . in certain well established industries'[118] only, the 1946 Act was intended to apply to all white employees and also, possibly reflecting industrial capital's interest in maintaining a reserve army of labour in the towns,[119] to African workers other than those employed in agriculture and mining or 'tribalised natives doing work for a short period of time'.[120] The 1946 Act provided for the establishment of a centralised fund to be administered by the state and to be financed by compulsory contributions from employers and employees supported by a contribution from state funds. The main opposition to the Act came when it was implemented in 1947. Various agricultural interests complained about what they saw as a system in which unemployed blacks were supported from state funds in the towns instead of being reassigned to labour on the farms[121] (although, in fact, Africans paid more in contributions than they received in benefits which were in any case made extremely difficult for them to obtain[122]). Various municipal departments and private schools also objected to having to pay contributions and so did various categories of new petty bourgeois 'professional' employees like ministers of religion and teachers who saw no prospect of themselves becoming unemployed.[123] Eventually under intense pressure of this sort the Minister of Labour decided in late 1947 to suspend the operation of the Act pending the recommendations of a Commission of Inquiry. The suspension of this Act was a major blow to the United Party's credibility. With another 'social security' measure (a Rent Control Act) moribund as well, it was widely seen, in the words of the *Rand Daily Mail*, as marking the 'end of social security'.[124]

It was thus in the context of an acute crisis for the hegemonic fraction of the bourgeoisie in its relationship with the white wage-earning classes—a crisis grounded in the pursuit of contradictory class interests under specific social conditions and manifesting itself both as a crisis in the social democratic apparatuses of the state and as a policy crisis for the governing party—that the Nationalists were able to extend their mass base among the white wage-earning classes. By offering the prospect of higher wages, job colour bars, racial quotas and the elimination of real or alleged discriminations against Afrikaners, as well as by presenting ideological fairy tales about the 'organic unity' of the Afrikaner volk, the Nationalists were able under these conditions decisively to outbid social democracy as the representative of the economic interests of key strata of the supervisory new petty bourgeoisie and key strata of white industrial working class, particularly, in the latter case, those occupying places vulnerable to job reclassification with little or no experience of trade union struggle. So far as the latter were concerned the Nationalists

could offer an immediately possible reformist solution to the problems of reclassification, whereas any solution coming from the left of
orthodox social democracy had quite rightly to transcend and reject
their immediate demands as put forward. In any case in the post-war
world, bourgeois ideology was at least presenting a united front on
one issue——its opposition to 'communism' and furthermore in the
wake of the 1946 African miners' strike the Communist Party and
other leftist tendencies were being subjected to various forms of
debilitating harassment which undermined both their 'legitimacy'
and their potential effectiveness.[125]

One of the most important arenas of struggle between the
Nationalists and the social democratic allies of the hegemonic fraction continued to be in the Mine Workers Union. When the war
ended the two 'Christian National' groupings, the 'Action Committee'
and the 'Reformers' Movement' merged to form the 'United Mineworkers' Committee' which conducted an intense campaign for elections to be held under a new constitution and for the 1943 agreement
with the Chamber of Mines to be overturned. Taking particular
advantage of the fact that a leading member of the Labour Party,
H. J. Cilliers, was one of those who signed the 1943 agreement and
of an affidavit which connected the United Party directly with the
organisation of constitutional manoeuvring by the 'Broderick
clique',[126] the campaign gathered increasing momentum until eventually it climaxed in two large scale strikes——one in 1946 and one in
1947 involving at their high point some 12,500 out of the total of
16,000 white mining employees.[127] In the face of pressure of this
sort the union's existing bureaucratic leadership and the United Party
government were placed increasingly on the defensive, and eventually
in 1947 the Department of Labour was compelled to accede to the
demand for a commission and a referendum on the constitution,
although it was not until after the 1948 elections that the union
finally fell to the 'United Mineworkers'.

Another important gain for the Nationalists came during the
struggle by white building artisans against the training of African
building workers in 1946. Through their firm support for the

campaign against the training of Africans, the Nationalists had by the end of that year been able to build up a substantial base at least in the Pretoria branch of the Building Workers Union, whilst Danie du Plessis, the Communist Party member who had become secretary of the Johannesburg branch during the war years was forced to resign.[128] In this particular case, however, the Nationalists may have damaged their own prospects somewhat by scabbing during the lengthy strike over wages the next year.[129]

The withdrawal by the Pretoria unions from the SATLC in 1947 was another event which both, in itself, reflected the growing influence of the Nationalists and enabled them to extend their influence further by supporting the formation of a new co-ordinating body (The Co-ordination Council of South African Trades Unions). In addition Nationalists were able to build up at least some sort of a base in unions like the Garment Workers Union and the Leather Workers Union (in the former case mainly outside the Johannesburg area)[130] and their Blankewerkersbeskermingbond was by 1947 claiming to be affiliating 1,238 new members each year.[131]

By the time of the 1948 elections then the Nationalists had already built up a considerable mass base among important strata of the white wage-earning classes, although they had, as previously, manifestly failed to win the support of artisans (other than those in the building industry) or the majorities of white industrial workers in unions with a tradition of militant struggle. In a booklet produced just before the 1948 elections[132] the Nationalists offered potential white wage-earning supporters 'a new economic order'. It was not going to be an economic order which made any inroads into bourgeois property. On the contrary it was to be an order which recognised 'the right to private property and the claims of private initiative', but it was proposed that there be some reorganisation of the state apparatuses in accordance with various petty bourgeois power obsessive notions in the Nationalist ideological sub-ensemble.[133] As the booklet put it 'the system of collective bargaining will be supplemented by a system of state responsibility'. In particular there were to be two new state apparatuses—a Central Economic Council whose task was 'to co-ordinate the diversified economic interests properly' and a Labour Council whose task was to 'act on principle with responsibility to the Government' in such matters as 'the determination of wages and labour conditions of all employees', the regulation of apprenticeship training and in matters concerned with 'the flow of labour and its adjustment to more than one industry'. *White* trade unions were not to be prohibited but the Labour Council would 'exercise effective control over the appointment of officials by, and general activities of, the trade unions or workers' organisations'.

In addition potential white wage-earning supporters were to be offered the 'benefits' of Apartheid which whilst at this stage rather vague and undefined was to mean as far as they were concerned the implementation of some system of job colour bars or racial quotas which would ensure in the words of one MP, that no white wage-earner 'would sink below the economic level of the non-European'.[134] A strong line was also to be taken on the redirection and reallocation of the African reserve army of labour from the towns, which whilst mainly of benefit to capitalist agriculture, would also 'relieve the pressure' on white industrial employees.[135] The Unemployment Insurance Act, unpopular with various white petty bourgeois strata as well as with capitalist agriculture, was to be amended to exclude many categories of Africans and so supposedly reduce the level of contributions from the white petty bourgeoisie.[136] And finally various broad hints were dropped that a Nationalist Party government would support the Mine Workers Union in putting in a claim for a 30 per cent increase in wages.[137]

The United Party's programme offered

the maintenance of white civilization in the Union, . . . the establishment and maintenance of a reasonable standard of living for the country's wage-earners, with due regard to the different levels of civilization of the races in the Union

and, a continuation of the 'policy of social security'.[138] Smuts also promised some support to the mining and railway unions' claims for higher wages, and in respect of the former went so far as to appoint a commission to examine their claims in the midst of the election campaign.[139]

Labour's campaign mainly concentrated on the 'calamity' which would 'overcome the country' if the Nationalists were elected.[140] Party supporters were urged not to let their 'socialist principles' stand in the way of supporting United Party Candidates and the United Party reciprocated by urging its supporters to vote Labour where appropriate.[141]

When the results were announced in June 1948 the Nationalist Party and its ally the Afrikaner Party had secured a small majority of five seats. Most of their new seats were in rural constituencies and reflected the desertion from the United Party by capitalist agriculture. But the Nationalists had also picked up eight seats in the mining areas of the Witwatersrand and five in Pretoria.[142] Labour by contrast had even with the pact with the United Party managed to secure only six seats: four in the Transvaal and two in Natal. In a very real sense then without its allies in the white wage-earning classes, the Nationalist Party would not have secured electoral victory in 1948 and with it the opportunity to begin the struggle to implement some of the class demands of its constituent base.

Notes to Chapter 7

1 D. O'Meara, ' "Christian National" Trade Unionism in South Africa 1934–1948' (paper delivered to conference on Southern African Labour History, University of the Witwatersrand, 1976). See also: 'The Afrikaner Broederbond 1927–1948: Class Vanguard of Afrikaner Nationalism' (Institute of Commonwealth Studies seminar paper, 1976); 'White Trade Unions, Political Power and Afrikaner Nationalism', *South African Labour Bulletin* vol. 1 no. 10, 1975.
2 ' "Christian National" Trade Unionism . . .', *op. cit.* p. 5.
3 *Ibid.* p. 6.
4 On this see Poulantzas (1974), *op. cit.* Part 5.
5 *House of Assembly Debates* 1935, column 4328 (Dr. Carl Bremmer).

6 See O'Meara, ' "Christian National" Trade Unionism . . .' *op. cit.* p. 6.

7 *House of Assembly Debates* 1937, column 5464 (Dr. N. J. van der Merwe).

8 Quotations from speech by A. Hertzog to Ekonomese Volkskongress October 1939 reproduced as Appendix to L. Naude *Dr. A. Hertzog: Die Nasionale Party en die Mynwerkers* (Pretoria 1969) p. 260 (my translation).

9 On this see Poulantzas (1974), *op. cit.* part 5; (1975) *op. cit.* part 3 Chapter 8.

10 For example, in 1935 ironmoulders struck against the replacement of apprentices by semi-skilled whites in railways workshops, and engineering and boilermakers' unions refused to admit unskilled whites in foundries, steel mills and motor assembly plants (see Simons and Simons, *op. cit.* p. 508).

11 One readily accessible forum was the floor of the House of Assembly see e.g. *House of Assembly Debates* 1935, columns 4323 *et seq.* (Labour Vote); 1937, columns 7030 *et seq.* (Labour vote); 658 *et seq.* (Nationalist motion); 1938, columns 2941 *et seq.* (Labour vote); 1939, columns 5575 *et seq.*

12 *Union Statistics for 50 Years* Table G15.

13 These points were all made in debates in parliament by Nationalist MPs quoting Spoorbond material, particularly its paper, Skakel. See, *inter alia, House of Assembly Debates* 1936, columns 6106 *et seq.*; 1938, columns 463 *et seq.*

14 Some indication of this is given by the official statistics which show the numbers of whites employed on the mines rising from 25,000 in 1933 to 36,000 in 1936 (source: Frankel, *Capital Investment in Africa, op. cit.* Table 12).

15 These issues were specifically referred to in the Nasionale Raad van Trustee's official history: see Naude *op. cit.* p. 24; see also *Chamber of Mines Annual Reports* for 1934 and 1936 and 1939: the reports for 1936 and 1939 referring to the 'good', even 'friendly', relations with the white trade unions.

16 Estimate quoted by N. J. van der Merwe *House of Assembly Debates* 1937, column 5343.

17 The characterisation of the power bloc below is largely taken from Davies, Kaplan, Morris and O'Meara, 'Class struggle and a Periodisation of the South African State' *op. cit.*

18 W. Finlay, *South Africa: Capitalist Agriculture and the State* (University of Cape Town honours dissertation, 1976) p. 102 quoting estimate by the 1955 Tomlinson Commission. See also the excellent analysis by M. Morris,

'Apartheid, Agriculture and the State' (South African Labour and Development Research Unit paper, 1977).

19 *Ibid.* Chapter 4.

20 Figures from *Union Statistics for Fifty Years* quoted in Davies, Kaplan, Morris and O'Meara, *op. cit.*

21 The negotiation of a separate peace was, for example, the main theme of the Nationalist Party opposition's 'no confidence' motions in 1940, 1941, 1942 and 1943. In 1944 and 1945 however the theme was the need to guard against the 'communist menace'.

22 The SA Trades and Labour Council pledged support to the war question in 1940 and also approved of the government's assumption of emergency powers (see e.g. *The Times* 26.3.40). They also gave their explicit approval 'in the interests of the war effort' to a number of individual emergency measures.

23 The most important being Ivan Walker who became Controller of Industrial Manpower.

24 *Freedom/Vryheid* (organ of the Central Committee of the Communist Party) no. 9 April 1942, pp. 1–2.

25 On Sach's position see Simons and Simons, *op. cit.* chapter 23 and J. Lewis, 'Solly Sachs and the Garment Workers Union', *South African Labour Bulletin* vol. 3 no. 3, October 1976.

26 Taken from *Report of the Industrial Legislation Commission 1951, op. cit.* Table 23a.

27 *Third Interim Report of the Industrial And Agricultural Requirements Commission* (UG 40, 1941) para 173.

28 *Ibid.* paras 174 and 176.

29 See *Board of Trade and Industries: Investigation into the Manufacturing Industries in the Union of South Africa Report no. 282, 1945* p. 44. See also M. Legassick, 'Legislation, Ideology and Economy in post 1948 South Africa', *Journal of Southern African Studies*, October 1974.

30 See *Dept. of Labour: Summarized Departmental Report for 1941* (printed Annexures to Votes and Proceedings of Parliament 1943) and Simons and Simons, *op. cit.* p. 535.

31 See e.g. statistics in *Report of the Central Organization of Technical Training* (UG 5, 1951) showing whites and coloureds only.

32 See e.g. *Dept. of Labour Report for 1940* (printed Annexures to the Votes and Proceedings of Parliament 1942) and p. 3; *House of Assembly Debates* 1941, columns 4298 *et seq.*

33 See *Dept. of Labour Reports for 1940, op. cit.* p. 1; for 1945 (UG 9, 1947).
34 Ratios (rounded upwards) from statistics given *Report of the Industrial Legislation Commission of Inquiry 1951, op. cit.* Table 37.
35 *Union Statistics for Fifty Years* Table G8.
36 See D. Lewis, *op. cit.*
37 *Inkululeko* 29.4.44 reported that at a meeting with Smuts, one trade union delegation argued that whereas the official index showed a rise in the 'cost of living' of 27% since the beginning of the war, in their estimation it had risen 50%.
38 See *Chamber of Mines Annual Reports 1942* pp. 1–2 also reports for 1940 and 1941.
39 Taken from *Report of the Industrial Legislation Commission 1951, op. cit.* Table 36.
40 *Dept. of Labour Report for 1939, op. cit.* p. 2.
41 See *House of Assembly Debates* 1942, columns 5566 *et seq.*; see also *Dept. of Labour Summarized Report* 1941, *op. cit.*; for 1945 *op. cit.*
42 *House of Assembly Debates* 1943, columns 4455 (issue raised by Nationalist MPs).
43 *House of Assembly Debates* 1943, columns 579–582 (ministerial answer to question).
44 *Dept. of Labour Report* 1940, *op. cit.* p. 4.
45 See *House of Assembly Debates* 1942, columns 5530/1; 5567–70.
46 *Dept. of Labour Summarized Report for 1941, op. cit.*
47 Poulantzas (1974), *op. cit.* p. 151.
48 *Ibid.* pp. 151–2.
49 *House of Assembly Debates* 1941, column 4015 (van Nierop).
50 *House of Assembly Debates* 1942, column 4183 (Schoeman).
51 See e.g. *House of Assembly Debates* 1940, columns 6694/5; 1941, columns 7828 *et seq.*; 1942, column 4184 *et seq.*; 1943, column 4456.
52 See e.g. *House of Assembly Debates* 1943, column 4455 (Schoeman). He was careful to exempt repression of African strikes from his critique, arguing 'obviously I don't approve of native strikes'.
53 See e.g. *House of Assembly Debates* 1942, columns 5530/1; 1941, columns 5036 *et seq.*
54 See e.g. *House of Assembly Debates* 1941, columns 5531/4.
55 See e.g. *House of Assembly Debates* 1940, columns 7020 *et seq.*; 1944, columns 6470 *et seq.*
56 *House of Assembly Debates* 1942, column 5529; 1943, column 4454.

57 Figures from *Report of the Committee Appointed to Investigate the Employment of Unskilled European Workers in the Railway Service 1947, op. cit.* p. 11.

58 See discussion in *House of Assembly Debates* 1942, columns 1907 *et seq.*; 1983 *et seq.*

59 See 1st–6th *Reports of the Commission of Inquiry into Grievances of Railway Servants* (UG 9, 41, 42 of 1950; UG 41, 54 and 58 of 1952).

60 See *House of Assembly Debates* 1942, column 1907 for discussion on Spoorbond campaign.

61 Quoted in *Committee Appointed to Investigate the Employment of Unskilled European Workers in Railway Service 1947, op. cit.* p. 11.

62 *Idem.*

63 O'Meara, ' "Christian National" Trade Unionism . . .' *op. cit.*

64 The following are the sources which I have found most useful in producing the account below—Hepple, *op. cit.*; O'Meara, *op. cit.*; Naude, *op. cit.*; Simons and Simons, *op. cit.*; *House of Assembly Debates*; reports in the *Star* and the *Rand Daily Mail* and official investigating commissions—*Report of the Mineworkers Union Commission of Enquiry 1946* (UG 36, 1946); *Report of the Mineworkers Union Commission of Enquiry 1951* (UG 52, 1951); *Report of the Mineworkers Union Commission of Enquiry 1953* (Government Printer, 1953).

65 See *Transvaal Chamber of Mines Reports 1942* pp. 15–16 (complaints by mining capital against the use of War Measure 9 of 1942 to enforce a 'cost of living allowance').

66 Quoted in Mining Unions Joint Committee minutes 27.11.44 (reproduced in *South African Mining Unions Papers: A Selection of Papers of the Unions in the South African Mining Industry 1919–1960*, microfilms (3 reels) by Microfile Ltd. Johannesburg).

67 MUJC minutes 28.12.44. *ibid.*

68 See particularly *Mineworkers Union Commission of Enquiry 1946* and 1953 *op. cit.*

69 See Report in the *Star* 17.10.46 of submissions by members of the Action Committee for an injunction against Broderick and others.

70 *House of Assembly Debates* 1943, columns 87/8.

71 For an excellent analysis of the reasons for the failure of the Nationalists to capture the Garment Workers Union see O'Meara, ' "Christian National" Trade Unionism . . .' *op. cit.* See also E. S. Sachs, *Rebel Daughters* (London 1957).

72 See, for example, *House of Assembly Debates* 1944, column 5091 *et seq.* (debate on the Apprenticeship Act).
73 See *Report of the Industrial Legislation Commission of Enquiry, op. cit.* pp. 195–6.
74 In 1943 Solly Sachs and the leadership of the Garment Workers Union mounted an unsuccessful campaign against the existing bureaucratic leadership of the Trades and Labour Council, and in the same year formed an 'Independent Labour Party' which put up three candidates in the general election. The ideological basis of this challenge however remained, as indicated above, within the problematic of white social democratic ideology—e.g. the I.L.P. called for a programme of progressive capitalism'. (See Simons and Simons, *op. cit.* pp. 538–9.) The Communist Party was precluded from mounting any such challenge by three main factors: firstly by the narrowness of its base in the white wage-earning classes; secondly, by its commitment to a 'united front' over the war question; thirdly by tactical considerations related to its main arena of activity —the struggles of the African working class. On the last point, the party criticised Sachs' attempts to split the Trades and Labour Council on the Conciliation Act. 'On this point, at least,' a Central Committee member wrote, 'the whole trade union movement has gone on record for a progressive policy . . . A split in the trade union movement would be seized upon joyfully by the reactionaries . . . They will take advantage of the divisions and isolation of the "left" to bring African unions under "official" control (i.e. under the control of the Native Affairs Department––RD)' (H. J. Simons, 'This Question of Labour Unity', *Freedom/Vryheid* no. 12, 1943, p. 5).
75 See Morris, 'Apartheid, Agriculture and the State', *op. cit.*
76 See W. Finlay, *op. cit.*
77 See Davies, Kaplan, Morris and O'Meara, *op. cit.*
78 Finlay, *op. cit.*
79 See Kaplan (1977), *op. cit.* Chapter 9, see also Chapter 8, pp. 334–5 below.
80 Figures given in *Dept. of Labour Report for 1946* (UG 62, 1948) p. 7.
81 This point was also made by M. Legassick, 'Legislation, Ideology and Economy in Post 1948 South Africa', *Journal of Southern African Studies*, vol. 1 no. 1, 1974.
82 See Simons and Simons, *op. cit.* chapter 24 and D. Lewis, *op. cit.*
83 *A Summary of the Social Security Scheme . . . Report no. 2* (Govt. Printer 1944) p. 1.

84 See e.g. *House of Assembly Debates* 1948, columns 3267 *et seq.* (Dr. T. W. B. Osborn leader of Labour Party in succession to Madeley).

85 See *House of Assembly Debates* 1946, column 2295 *et seq.* (Madeley describing the formulation, presentation and contents of the 'Workers' Charter'.

86 *Ibid.*

87 Depreciated capital stock figure from Franzen and Williers, *op. cit.* p. 313; employment figure from 1951 *Industrial Legislation Commission, op. cit.* Table 23a.

88 See *Dept. of Labour Reports* for 1946 (UG 62, 1948) p. 5; for 1947 (UG 38, 1949) p. 5 and for 1948 (UG 50, 1950) p. 5; also article in *South African Industry and Trade* (continuation of *Industrial and Commercial South Africa*) January 1947.

89 Poulantzas (1975), *op. cit.* p. 255.

90 Quotations from *Board of Trade and Industries: Investigation into Manufacturing Industries in the Union of South Africa Report* no. 282, p. 46; F.C.I. Annual Reports 1944, p. 17 (president's address).

91 Board of Trade and Industries, *op. cit.* p. 46.

92 *Idem.*

93 *Dept. of Labour Reports* 1946–1948, *op. cit.*

94 1,269 were registered as electricians under the Electrical Contractors and Wiremens Act of 1939; 6,854 'stage 1' learners were placed in various junior artisan places under the Housing Emergency Powers Act; 626 passed trade tests under the COTT programme (1947 and 1948 only); and 1,151 passed early trade tests under the Soldiers and War Workers Act. (Source *Dept. of Labour Reports* 1946–1948, *op. cit.*).

95 Although the number of registrations rose slightly (from monthly averages of 5,600 in 1945 to 8,162, 8,161 and 7,219 in 1946, 1947 and 1948 respectively) *Dept. of Labour Reports* wrote of white employment prospects in such terms as: 'Anybody capable of performing a day's work could be absorbed, with the exception unfortunately of middle aged and elderly persons without specific qualifications' (1947 *op. cit.* p. 5).

96 *House of Assembly Debates* 1944, column 6470 (Minister of Labour second reading speech). See column 6476 *et seq.* for the position of the Nationalists; basically calling for there to be no discrimination against 'those (whites) who remained here in the fatherland, whether they were against the war or in favour of it'.

97 See *House of Assembly Debates* 1946, column 8157 *et seq.* for discussion of artisan immigration and apprenticeship training.

98   *Dept. of Labour Reports* for 1949 (UG 50, 1951).

99   *House of Assembly Debates* 1947, column 4870.

100 See e.g. discussion in *House of Assembly Debates* 1946, column 8157, *op. cit.* See also Legassick, 'Legislation, Ideology and Economy . . .' *op. cit.*, who makes a similar point using other material.

101 Figures from *Report of the Industrial Legislation Commission of Enquiry 1951 op. cit.* Table 36.

102 *Idem.*

103 *Industrial Legislation Commission of Enquiry 1951, op. cit.* p. 159.

104 For example, a scheme to train Africans for various forms of semi-skilled building work in order to meet the housing crisis after the war was opposed outright by the Building Unions Joint Committee (see statement in the *Star* 24.9.46) which organised pickets at the training centre in Johannesburg. Eventually this opposition forced the government to transfer the scheme to Zwelitsha in the Eastern Cape, but, according to Schoeman in 1951 opposition from the building unions prevented municipalities from employing any of those trained to put up African housing (*House of Assembly Debates* 1951, column 861).

105 See the *Star* 22.8.46 for a report on the Labour Party's position on 'artisan' immigration.

106 On the split in the Labour Party see the *Star* 27.3.46; 2.4.46; 3.4.46; 10.4.46; 13.4.46; 15.4.46; 18.4.46; 25.4.46; *Freedom/Vryheid* June/July 1946; Simons and Simons, *op. cit.* p. 550.

107 Resignation letter quoted in the *Star* 25.7.46.

108 See, for example, *House of Assembly Debates* 1948, column 3273 (exchange between Burnside, ex-Labour MP, and Osborn, leader in succession to Madeley).

109 See *The Garment Worker* March/April 1947 for a long article by Sachs arguing that they had taken this step because 'The immediate major task for all the Trade Union Movement and for all progressives is to find a political home for the thousands of politically homeless European workers and poor people.'

110 For a critical analysis and summary see M. Harmel, 'The South African Labour Party in Decline' (*Freedom/Vryheid* September/October 1947). For an uncritical analysis and reproduction of the programme in full see E. S. Sachs, *The Choice Before South Africa* (London 1953) pp. 50–51.

111 *The Garment Worker* January/February 1947.

112 Harmel, *op. cit.*

113   See *Inkululeko*/Freedom 11.3.46; Simons and Simons, *op. cit.* p. 549.

114   For an excellent analysis of the bill see D. Lewis, *op. cit.*

115   O'Meara, ' "Christian National" Trade Unionism . . .' *op. cit.*

116   Figure quoted *House of Assembly Debates* 1947, column 4881 by Mentz (Nationalist).

117   The South African and Steel Trades Association, The Match Workers Union, The Public Service and Provincial Council Workers Union, the Pretoria Liquor and Catering Trade Employees Union and the Pretoria Retail Meat Trade Employees Union (Walker and Weinbren, *op. cit.* p. 235).

118   *House of Assembly Debates* 1935, column 5193 (Minister of Labour in second reading debate of the original bill).

119   The F.C.I. certainly favoured including urbanised Africans in the scheme. See quotation of statement by F.C.I. president *House of Assembly Debates* 1947, column 4892; see also reference to position of industrialists by Cull (United Party) 1949, column 6743.

120   *House of Assembly Debates* 1946, column 6270 (minister's second reading speech).

121   See *Commission of Inquiry into the Operation of the Unemployment Act 1946* (UG 12, 1949) and parliamentary debates (*House of Assembly Debates* 1947, column 2086 *et seq.*, 4866 *et seq.*).

122   On the Unemployment Act and Africans see speech by Sam Kahn in *House of Assembly Debates* 1949, column 6802 *et seq.*

123   See *Commission of Inquiry* and parliamentary debates *op. cit.*

124   *Rand Daily Mail* article quoted *House of Assembly Debates* 1947, column 4964.

125   After the 1946 African mineworkers' strike the Communist Party's central committee members were placed on trial for 'sedition' and the United Party took up a hostile anti-Communist position generally (see Simons and Simons, *op. cit.* pp. 583 *et seq.*).

126   See *House of Assembly Debates* 1945, columns 6852/3; 1946, column 2485 (on Cilliers and the 1943 agreement); 1947, columns 3328 (Conradie quoting affidavit by Jan Gleisner on United Party involvement in MWU manoeuvrings). See also Naude, *op. cit.* chapters 14 and 15.

127   See reports in the *Star* 16.3.46–23.3.46; 21.1.47–12.3.47.

128   See article by Sachs in *The Garment Worker* September/October 1947 on Nationalists in the union in Pretoria; and Simons and Simons, *op. cit.* p. 561 on Danie du Plessis' resignation.

129   See *The Garment Worker* September/October 1947.

130   Though the Nationalists never captured the union their candidates nevertheless received in the order of 3,500 votes in union elections compared to
12,500 odd for the existing leadership (see Hepple, *op. cit.* p. 50). An
indication that their support probably lay outside Johannesburg is given
by the fact that Hertzog complained that a branch meeting held in Johannesburg in 1948 was not open to members from Germiston (see *House
of Assembly Debates* 1948, column 2818 *et seq.*).

131   *Die Blanke Werker* November 1947.

132   *The Road to a New South Africa* (Nasionale Pers, Cape Town 1948).

133   On power fetishism and petty bourgeois ideology see Poulantzas (1975),
op. cit. pp. 292–3.

134   *House of Assembly Debates* 1946, column 8157. An indication of the
early vagueness in Nationalist circles about the precise means through
which this was to be achieved is given by the fact that some of the witnesses before the 1948–1951 *Industrial Legislation Commission* (see *op.
cit.* pp. 160–163) in favour of 'apartheid' in industry argued for statutory
job colour bars, and some for statutory quotas while the Commission itself
regretted that it was 'not competent to submit specific recommendations
in regard to full protective measures'.

135   See *House of Assembly Debates* 1948, column 2734 (Labour MP Hepple
referring to election speech by Malan which argued that labour bureaux
for Africans would protect white wage-earners). See also the *Star* 29.3.48
for a general outline of Nationalist Policy.

136   See *House of Assembly Debates* 1948, column 2752 *et seq.* for a reference
to the importance of the Unemployment Act in the Nationalists' election
campaign.

137   See reference *House of Assembly Debates* 1948, column 2751.

138   See the *Star* 24.4.48.

139   See the *Star* 4.3.48; 15.5.48; 18.5.48; 24.5.48.

140   See the *Star* 27.4.48; 21.5.48.

141   On Labour supporting the UP see *inter alia* the *Star* 21.5.48; on the UP
supporting Labour see the *Star* 8.5.48.

142   The Nationalists' new seats on the Witwatersrand and Pretoria were Germiston, Kempton Park, Krugersdorp, Maraisburg, Mayfair, North East
Rand, Randfontein and Westdene; Gezina, Koedoespoort, Pretoria Central,
Pretoria West and Wonderboom (Simons and Simons, *op. cit.* p. 673 footnote 23).

8 Capital, State and White Wage-Earners during the Early Apartheid Period (1948 until the early 1960s)

We saw in the last chapter how the crisis in the relationship between the white wage-earning classes and the then hegemonic alliance of industrial and mining capital had enabled the class forces organised in the Nationalist Party to draw sufficient support from the white wage-earning classes to secure victory in the 1948 elections. In this chapter we turn to examine how the political class relationships between capital and the white wage-earning classes were altered (or rather modified) in the post 1948 period and how these modified relationships were reflected in the role of the state in the process of class formation during the period between 1948 and the early 1960s and thus ultimately in the class structure characterising the social formation at the current conjuncture. To begin with we need to advance certain general propositions about the post '48 South African state within which the analysis can be located.

The first point to be made in this regard is that the changes in social relations reflected in the Apartheid state (i.e. distinguishing the Apartheid state from the pre-Apartheid state) were complex, involving changes in relationships between a number of different classes and class fractions—both dominant and dominated.

First and foremost, of course, the change in régime marked a change in the relationship between the dominant and the African principal dominated classes. More particularly it marked the beginning of a new phase in the struggle arising from the creation of a permanently urbanised African proletariat, in which a previously defensive and somewhat ambivalent (albeit often violent and brutal) response from the state was transformed into a concerted offensive

Table 26   Average annual African wage rates in secondary industry and mining showing the fall in living standards during the early apartheid period (Rand)

Secondary industry (including construction)

	at current prices	at constant (1959/60) prices	increase/decrease over previous year at constant (1959/60) prices
1939/40	96	212	
1940/41	102	216	1·9%
1941/42	120	238	10·2%
1942/43	140	258	8·4%
1943/44	162	285	10·5%
1944/45	184	315	10·5%
1945/46	192	322	2·2%
1946/47	200	328	1·9%
1947/48	210	329	0·3%
1948/49	220	324	− 1·5%
1949/50	222	319	− 1·5%

Mining

	at current prices	at constant (1959/60) prices	increase/decrease over previous year at constant (1959/60) prices
1939	96	198	
1945	116	198	
1946	120	194	− 2·0%
1947	122	186	− 4·3%
1948	128	188	1·1%
1949	136	192	2·1%

1950/51	234	317	— 0·6%
1951/52	252	316	— 0·3%
1952/53	266	313	— 0·9%
1953/54	278	320	2·2%
1954/55*	288	323	0·9%
1954/55	292	327	
1955/56	300	328	0·3%
1956/57	308	331	0·9%
1957/58	316	326	— 1·5%
1958/59	330	333	2·1%

1950	150	196	2·1%
1951	160	194	1·0%
1952	170	196	— 1·0%
1953	180	212	8·1%
1954	184	212	0 %
1955	188	210	— 0·9%
1956	192	210	0 %
1957	192	204	— 2·9%
1958	192	194	— 4·9%

*The different figures for 1954/55 reflect certain changes in the coverage of industrial censuses. Statistics for years after 1954/5 are not therefore strictly comparable with those for earlier years.

Sources: W. F. J. Steenkamp, 'Bantu Wages in South Africa' (*South African Journal of Economics*, vol. 30 1962 p. 96); F. Wilson, *Labour in the South African Goldmining Industry* (Cambridge 1972) p. 158; *Union Statistics for 50 Years* Table G4; D. Hobart Houghton, *The South African Economy* (1976 edition) p. 273.

struggle against the organisations and living standards of the popular masses.[1] As a consequence (as Table 26 shows) African wages which had risen slightly during the war years declined sharply during the early Apartheid period (particularly in manufacturing industry), with the result that the capitalist class was able to avert the potentially serious fall in the general rate of profit inherent in the rapid rise in the organic composition of capital during industrial capital's transition to monopoly capitalism, and inaugurate instead a sustained period of expansion and increased profitability for social capital as a whole.[2]

But the change in régime in 1948 also marked, secondly, a change in the balance of class forces in the power bloc i.e. a change in the form of state. This particular aspect of the analysis of the Apartheid state is extremely complicated and many issues are still open to further debate; but it would seem that after 1948 political hegemony passed from the alliance consisting of the major elements of the industrial capitalist fraction and mining capital, which had exercised hegemony since the outbreak of war in 1939, to an alliance consisting of the major elements of the agricultural capitalist fraction and certain smaller, and originally non-monopoly industrial and finance capitals (identifiable in descriptive terms as Afrikaner capital).

However these changes in political relationships within the power bloc had occurred at a particular phase of the imperialist epoch and this substantially affected the terms on which these relationships could be exercised. As distinct from the period prior to World War II, when imperialist domination over dependent and subordinate social formations had mainly been exercised from the 'outside' through the relations of dependence, and when imperialist capital had been as a consequence invested only in certain extractive sectors in peripheral social formations, in the new phase of the imperialist epoch which began after World War II imperialist domination over these social formations came increasingly to be exercised 'internally' through the reproduction of 'the metropolitan mode of production . . . in a specific form, within the dominated and dependent formations themselves'.[3] More particularly in the case of the South African social formation this new phase of the imperialist epoch meant, as we indicated in the last chapter, relatively large new investments of foreign, imperialist capital in industry, and the consequent reproduction within the South African industrial sector of the monopoly capitalist relations of production of the imperialist metropolises. Under the particular circumstances of this new phase of imperialist relations, the newly hegemonic alliance in the South African power bloc could not, unlike the class forces represented by the Pact régime, fundamentally alter the trajectory of capitalist development in the social formation. In particular they could not, except at the cost of a major disruption of capitalist production, have promoted any non-monopoly 'national' path of capitalist industrial development. The fundamental pressures of foreign competition and foreign monopoly capitalist pentration required increasing 'national efficiency'— increasing the organic composition of capital and reproducing monopoly capitalist relations of production on an extended scale. In assuming the role of organiser of the power bloc, and thereby guarantor of the essential conditions for capital accumulation, the Nationalist régime was thus obliged to act as the guarantor of the conditions necessary for the emergence of monopoly capitalist relations of production in industry. The state thus continued throughout the early Apartheid period to act through various apparatuses, such as the Industrial Development Corporation, to facilitate the ongoing process of capital concentration and interpenetration; and, equally important it refrained from making any effective intervention in the form of 'anti-monopoly' or 'anti-trust' legislation which might have impeded the process in any way. Ultimately therefore the role of the state in the early Apartheid period was to create and guarantee the conditions for monopoly capital to assume hegemony some time in the '60s (albeit an hegemony exercised through a governing class drawn from the political representatives of capitalist agriculture and its allies).

On the other hand though capitalist agriculture and its allies were able to utilise their political position in the Apartheid state (as hegemonic fraction in the early Apartheid period, and as governing class and class in charge of the state in the later Apartheid period) to advance and secure a number of important fractional class interests. Firstly they were able to assume the role of organiser of the power bloc's political strategy *vis-à-vis* the popular masses and ensure that it took due account of their specific positions and interests. Secondly they were able to advance and secure a number of important fractional economic interests in a way which ensured that their integration into the emerging dominant relations of monopoly capitalism took place on favourable terms. Various forms of 'official' and 'unofficial' state intervention ensured favourable terms for 'Afrikaner capital' in respect of takeovers, mergers, joint ventures, access to credit etc.; and capitalist agriculture succeeded in the period after 1948 in advancing a number of its specific fractional interests after struggles with other members of the power bloc. Morris has shown, for example, that the labour bureau and 'influx control' systems established during the period were established, in part at least, for the purpose of reallocating part of the African reserve army of labour from the town to meet the demands of capitalist agriculture.[4] And Finlay has shown that capitalist agriculture was also able to secure a number of important gains in respect of pricing and marketing policies.[5]

Having briefly indicated something of the changes in the relationships between the principal dominant and dominated classes and between the different capitalist fractions represented in the Apartheid state, we now need to turn to consider the place in that state of the white petty bourgeoisie and the white wage-earning classes. To begin with it is necessary to emphasise that, despite the representation of petty bourgeois groupings in the governing Nationalist Party, the petty bourgeoisie did not become the politically dominant class. The petty bourgeoisie is not one of the fundamental classes of a capitalist social formation and has for that reason, as Poulantzas has argued, 'no where ever been the politically dominant class'.[6] However as Poulantzas has also argued there have been two ways in which petty bourgeois fractions or categories have 'advanced' themselves in capitalist social formations.

Firstly 'in certain conjunctures and specific régimes (the petty bourgeoisie) has held the place of the governing class, *in the context of the political domination and hegemony of the bourgeoisie*'.

And, secondly, the petty bourgeoisie has on occasions succeeded in dislodging a 'section of the old bourgeoisie and taking its place by way of complex economic and political processes'.[7]

What would seem to have happened during the early Apartheid period at least is that certain categories of the white petty bourgeoisie 'advanced' themselves in both of these ways. Through their position in the Nationalist Party certain categories of the Afrikaner petty bourgeoisie came to assume the role of governing class, though it was a role which they had to share with the political representatives of agrarian capital and its industrial and finance capitalist allies: a factor at least partly underlying the various Cape/Transvaal and later 'verligte/verkrampte' schism in the party. Certain categories also came to occupy the place of the class in charge (or at least partly in charge) of certain apparatuses of the state, some of which were at least to some extent reorganised during the early Apartheid period. In addition through complex struggles within various apparatuses of the state and elsewhere certain categories of the Afrikaner traditional petty bourgeoisie, as well as of course then existing 'Afrikaner capital', were able to secure various economic advantages for themselves which in the case of the petty bourgeoisie concerned enabled some of them to transform themselves into a bourgeoisie. These included such things as technical assistance, 'soft' loans and credit from government agencies, and government contracts from state departments looking unofficially if not officially with more favour on Afrikaner than non-Afrikaner applicants.[8] Also of particular importance in respect of the petty bourgeoisie were a number of measures introduced during the early years of the Apartheid period which restricted competition from the coloured and Asian petty bourgeoisie by preventing the latter from operating in 'white' areas. The following figures showing a substantial rise in the percentage of Afrikaners exercising (juridically defined) ownership in the main sectors of the economy provides some sort of crude index of the not

Table 27[9]   *Afrikaner share in the ownership of main sectors*

	1938/9	1963/4
Mining	3%	10%
Manufacturing	1%	10%
Commerce	8%	31%
Finance	5%	21%

inconsiderable successes which they were able to achieve through these means.

Yet despite these gains, it was certain categories rather than the whole of the white petty bourgeoisie which 'advanced' themselves in these ways. The shared role as the governing class and the class in charge of the state, fell very largely to the petty bourgeois intellectuals who had broken away from the 'fusion' in 1934, and not by and large to the wage-earning new petty bourgeois or white workers whose support had been obtained by the Nationalists during and after the war. 'Christian National' trade unionists were not to any significant extent recruited into the 'heights' of the state, or rather if they were, they were generally the 'Christian National' trade unionists who had come into the 'white labour movement' from the outside (i.e. petty bourgeois intellectuals like Hertzog, Diedrichs, Klopper and Schoeman) rather than the 'leaders' (like Ellis of the MWU or Beetge of the Building Workers Union) who had been generated within it. And, similarly, whilst there were undoubtedly some agents with origins in the white wage-earning classes who were able to take advantage of the various opportunities for members of the Afrikaner petty bourgeoisie to transform themselves into members of the bourgeoisie, the major 'benefits' derived therefrom fell to the small traders and petty commodity producers who already had some access to the means of production, etc.

But if that was the case, what then was the place of the white wage-earning new petty bourgeoisie and white working class in the Apartheid state? Essentially key strata remained an important allied class to the capitalist and incipient capitalist class forces represented in the governing party. Indeed with the power bloc deeply divided over a number of key questions throughout the period, the support of. white wage-earners (electoral and otherwise) was recognised as being crucial if those classes were to retain their own particular place in the state. As Vorster put it in 1956: 'The white worker in South Africa has brought the National Party to the position it occupies today and . . . will keep it in that position in future.'[10]

The Apartheid state, in short, remained fundamentally a capitalist state but one in which certain categories of the white traditional and intellectual petty bourgeoisie were able to 'advance' themselves in various ways and one in which the classes represented in the governing party were critically dependent on the support of their allies within the white wage-earning classes. As such the white wage-earning classes (or at least certain strata thereof) were better placed in the Apartheid state to advance certain of their own economic interests than they had been hitherto, but they were not placed in a position where they could determine the fundamental character either of the class structure or of important state apparatuses. In the Apartheid state as in any other capitalist state such prerogatives rested in the last analysis with capital operating under concrete conditions of class struggle and according to the imperatives of the law of value.

In this chapter we shall argue that these fundamental realities of class power were reflected in the role of the state in the process of reassigning white wage-earners to places in the industrial division of labour which took place during the early Apartheid period. And to begin our analysis we first need to examine the objective requirements of industrial capital in this regard, and the positions taken up as a consequence by the major organisations of and spokesmen for industrial capital during the period.

Essentially, as we indicated previously, the early Apartheid period saw South African industry continuing its transition to monopoly capitalist relations of production. Like the immediate post-war period, therefore the early Apartheid period was one in which more and more labour processes in industry were being reorganised and

socialised to produce an increasing number of manual machine operative places on the one hand, and an increasing number of specialised
supervisory and mental, i.e. new petty bourgeois, places on the other.

Industrial capital's own position on the question of allocating
agents to these places remained in fact throughout the early Apartheid
period fundamentally the same as it had been earlier in the phase of
transition. It sought to maximise the use of cheap African labour
power in the newly created machine operative places[11] but at the
same time it continued, for basically the same reasons as we discussed in the last chapter, to envisage that supervisory and mental
places would be filled by whites reassigned from the operative working class or imported as immigrants. Its contemporary spokesmen
thus continued to describe the ongoing process of restructuring and
class formation as a 'complementary' process in which 'the employment of additional non European labour (in operative places) . . .
creates additional skilled occupations and supervisory posts *for
the European worker*'.[12] And they continued throughout the early
Apartheid period (and beyond) to use terms like 'skilled', 'top strata'
and 'European' interchangeably.[13] Indeed so long as it seemed possible to obtain sufficient quantities of new petty bourgeois labour
power in these ways (the dominant perception among industrial
capitalists at least until the acute shortages of the mid and late '60s[14])
spokesmen tended to reject various liberal proposals for increasing
expenditure to train Africans for these places as, in the words of an
F.C.I. president, 'not . . . a serious possibility'.[15]

What industrial capital continued to seek during the transition
phase of the early Apartheid period when the present class structure
was being formed was not then to eliminate the racist hierarchy in
the social division of labour but rather, as in the period of its own
direct political hegemony, to relocate it at a 'higher' level. And
indeed right throughout the early Apartheid period and beyond its
spokesmen continued to be quite remarkably frank on that point.
In 1959, for example, in a memorandum submitted to the Minister
of Labour, the F.C.I. expressed its 'full agreement with the Minister
and the government that the leading role of the white race should be

maintained' and it went on to suggest that this objective could be and was being achieved through the operation of what it called the 'natural economic process'.[16]

In so far as industrial capital's position on these questions was derived from the fundamental imperatives of capital accumulation, it was not, despite the rhetoric of its spokesmen, *in broad substance*, opposed or thwarted by the Nationalist régime. Industrial capital was not deprived of its African labour force by the Apartheid measures, only, as Morris has shown, of the conveniences and advantages of a 'free selection' from a readily available reserve army of labour.[17] Neither was it prevented (except to a very limited degree as we shall see below) from mechanising its labour processes and transferring operative functions to Africans. In fact, on the contrary, the early Apartheid period saw the African industrial labour force rise rather than fall—by some 78 per cent (from 308,000 in 1948 to 548,000 in 1960[18])—and it also saw the mechanisation of more and more artisan functions with the assignment of more and more of the operative functions thus created to Africans.[19] Indeed, one of the features of the period was a number of ministerial speeches seeking to reassure any industrial capitalists who were inclined to take their 'Grand Apartheid' ideology at face value that it was not the intention of the régime to 'deprive industry of the necessary labour'[20] or to force it to 'freeze the existing labour pattern for ever'.[21]

Moreover, since the ongoing process of labour reorganisation and class formation involved the 'promotion' of white wage-earners the major emphasis of the state's 'white labour' policies continued, under the Nationalist as under the United Party régime, to be placed on harmonising with the process in particular by facilitating the reassignment of whites to new petty bourgeois (so-called 'skilled') places. As Schoeman, the then Minister of Labour put it in 1951,

We have a reservoir of unskilled European labour, and my contention is that we should not create a permanent stratum of unskilled European labour. We should lift them out of it . . . we should take out those unskilled Europeans who are adaptable, who have   necessary aptitude . . . (and) give them training.

That is how we get the movement from the unskilled right up to the skilled. Obviously we will not be able to accommodate all the unskilled labourers in the skilled ranks. I think that should be perfectly obvious to everyone, but I think we can go a long way to accommodate a large number of them.[22]

Industrial capital and the régime were therefore in complete accord about a number of state interventions made during the early Apartheid period to reorganise and restructure industrial training programmes so as to facilitate the reassignment of white agents to the new petty bourgeoisie. The F.C.I., for example, heartily applauded the amendments made to the Apprenticeship Act in 1951 providing for an increase in the number of apprenticeships made available to local whites, in part by reducing the period of indenture and in part by altering the system of training so as to make it more appropriate to conditions under which there was, in the words of an F.C.I. memorandum, a declining (though still present) demand for 'crafts-men' and an increasing demand for 'technical officials' engaged in tasks associated with 'the general direction of production'.[23] It like-wise approved of the Training of Artisans Act, also passed in 1951, which made provision for the establishment of a system of intensive training and trade testing for adults, whom it was acknowledged would 'by the nature of things' be almost exclusively white.[24] Indeed, the latter Act earned for the Minister fulsome praise in one industrial-ists' journal under an editorial headed 'Salute to Schoeman'.[25] And, finally, it also broadly approved of the reorganisation and expansion of technical training in 1955 as well as of the 33 per cent increase between 1947—8 and 1959—60 in expenditure on white education generally.[26]

But if there was broad agreement between the industrial capitalist fraction on the one hand and the governing class and its white wage-earning allies on the other about the general direction of the ongoing process of labour reorganisation and class formation, and about the reassignment of white agents to new petty bourgeois places in par-ticular, they were not in complete unison about all issues arising therefrom. We saw in the last chapter that the process had, at least in some industries and areas, been uneven and that there were therefore a number of cases where the reassignment of whites to new petty bourgeois places proceeded more slowly than the reassignment of blacks to previously 'white' operative places. We also saw that the support of white wage-earning strata whose interests were at least potentially threatened thereby had been crucial to those classes represented by the governing party and that their support had thus been organised by the Nationalists through a programme, heavily influenced by various petty bourgeois ideological notions, promising a 'new economic order' in which these and other class problems would be solved.

In fact, of course, a large number of the idealistic petty bourgeois proposals included in the Nationalist Party's programme were rapidly discarded when the party came to office and confronted the realities of class power and the imperatives of capital accumulation face to face. One example of particular interest to us here was the proposal to replace the existing system of institutionalised trade union bargaining for white wage-earners with a corporatist Labour Council. In the face of fierce opposition from a number of capitalist interests to any tinkering with a system which had served their interests well, these proposals were in fact being repudiated by Nationalist Ministers almost as soon as the party came to office[27] and, of course, the broad essentials of the system set up in 1924 were retained in the 1956 Industrial Conciliation Act.[28]

On the other hand though the dependence of the classes represented by the governing party on the support of their white wage-earning allies meant that their specific demands could not be ignored altogether and it was therefore incumbent on the political representatives of those classes to seek to maintain that support by organising the extraction of certain concessions, including, most important for our purposes, concessions related to the process of labour reorganisation and class formation. In moving to extract concessions of this sort however the régime proceeded extremely warily, reflecting the continued dominance of capitalist interests in the Apartheid state. The commission appointed to make recommendations about this as well as a number of other matters (the 1951 Industrial Legislation Commission) effectively ducked the issue by declaring that after considering various proposals it regarded itself as 'not competent to submit specific recommendations in regard to full protective measures'.[29] It was to be a further three years (after a further investigation by a ministerial committee) before substantial proposals were published and a further two years (i.e. eight years after the régime came to office) before these were incorporated into Section 77 of the Industrial Conciliation Act.[30]

Measures introduced by the régime in the meantime were extremely limited both in scope and effect. The Native Building Workers Act of 1951, though introducing the second statutory job colour bar in South Africa, was not principally intended as a means of making concessions to the demands of white wage-earners and in any case it only applied to one industry. The Act was basically a response to the post-war housing crisis and it was intended to produce a solution to that crisis by providing for the training of African building workers to construct 'sub economic' African housing. The statutory colour bar was intended as a *quid pro quo* to gain the acceptance of white building artisans whose actions had effectively thwarted such training programmes in the past.[31] Indeed, as a response to a 'social problem' with potential implications for the dominant classes as a whole, the job colour bar provisions in this Act were at the time far better received by industrial capital and the parliamentary opposition than their subsequent protestations over job colour bars would suggest. The F.C.I., for example, declared itself at the time in favour of the principles of the Act (though it would have preferred the establishment of an advisory board to allow certain exceptions).[32] And Oppenheimer (then an opposition MP) spoke in the second reading debate of his

> satisfaction that for the very first time in this parliament a Bill
> has been brought forward which touches these very difficult
> and controversial matters of racial relations and yet enjoys a
> wide measure of support on both sides of the house. [33]

In fact, apart from the Building Workers Act the main measures

introduced before 1956 to protect the interests of white wage-earners
in the process of class formation were administrative. They included
a limited reversal of the previous 'free trade' policy in respect of the
importation of 'skilled' labour power from abroad, and the adoption
of a more rigid 'civilised labour' policy in the state sector. The first
was intended to encourage capitalists to rely more on the promotion
of local whites and took the form of a generally less co-operative
response by the Department of Labour to requests from capitalists
to assist in obtaining 'skilled' labour power from abroad. The number of communications concerning immigration handled by the
Department thus fell from an annual average of 1,732 (1946—1949)
to 441, 425 and 928 in 1949, 1950 and 1951 respectively.[34] But
despite the fact that the F.C.I. persistently complained of the 'nega-
tive approach'[35] to immigration policy at least until the acute
shortages of 'skilled labour' led to the 'more active' immigration
policy of the '60s, the real effects were rather slight. There was never
any prohibition on capitalists making their own arrangements to
recruit immigrants nor, in fact, as the above figures show, was there
even a total withdrawal of co-operation by state departments.

The new stricter 'civilised labour' policy in the state sector was
rather more significant, though of course its effects were confined to
employees of central government. It began with the dismissal and
replacement of a number of Africans who had gradually been moved
into places which had been designated 'civilised' by the Pact régime.
According to figures given by the Minister of Labour, between 1948
and 1951 some 1,290 Africans were dismissed and replaced by
whites at an extra cost of £226,310 per annum.[36] However even
state departments were not immune from the overall trends of class
formation and it was not long before the post '48 'civilised labour'
policy settled down to be a process of reclassification and reorganisation of labour processes involving the reassignment of whites from
places as labourers (previously designated 'civilised') to places as
supervisors etc. (although in this case the process may have operated
somewhat more slowly and with rather more concern for the interests
of the lower strata white wage-earners than it did in the case of

'private' industry). For example, the railways administration which began the period by replacing a number of Africans with white 'railworkers' (labourers) was by 1951 reporting an acute 'shortage of applicants for the position of railworker' which was making it necessary for it 'to employ nonEuropeans (on an officially designated temporary basis) . . . on certain work previously undertaken by Europeans'.[37] In fact as the following figures show, the number and proportion of white 'railworkers' declined appreciably between 1950 and 1959 while the number and proportion of blacks increased.

Table 28[38] *Railways employment statistics*

	White graded staff	White 'railworkers'		Blacks	
	no.	no.	%age of total white employees	no.	%age of total employees
1948	80,658	17,407	17·7	89,640	47·8
1950	85,703	17,469	16·9	84,578	45·0
1959	101,595	12,131	10·7	111,827	49·6

When the régime finally did produce its proposals for making more substantial concessions to the demands of white wage-earners in the process of class formation, they were, as we indicated earlier, incorporated into Section 77 of the Industrial Conciliation Bill, first published in 1954 and passed into law in 1956. Section 77 provided for the establishment of an 'industrial tribunal' consisting of various ministerial appointees and representatives of 'interested parties'. On instruction from the minister the tribunal was empowered to investigate complaints about 'unfair inter-racial competition' and if the complaints were considered justified it was to recommend to the minister that he issue a determination imposing some form of legally enforceable 'work reservation'. Several possible forms of determination were provided for in the Act. Determinations could, for example, prescribe racial quotas (i.e. lay down that a minimum percentage of employees of a particular race be employed in a particular industry or firm) or they could reserve particular defined tasks for members of one racial group.[39]

Right from the time of the Bill's publication in 1954 Section 77 was opposed by the F.C.I. and a number of other organisations representing industrial capitalist interests.[40] It was also opposed by the Trades Union Council (the successor to the TLC and the Western Province Federation of Trades Unions), and indeed the SATUC (later TUCSA) was formed at a 'unity conference' called specifically in response to the 1954 bill. However the TUC's opposition to section 77—which was in any case based principally on concerns relating to the possible disruptive effects to capitalist production rather than concerns about the interests of African workers—was far less pronounced than its opposition to the clauses in the bill providing for the dissolution of 'mixed' unions (which it opposed on the grounds that this might result in the emergence of 'breakaway' unions with the potential to undermine the enforcement of 'equal pay for equal work' agreements).[41] Indeed, on one occasion Rutherford, the president of the TUC, attempted (unsuccessfully) to bargain TUC support for, or at least acceptance of, Section 77 in exchange for the removal of the clauses providing for the dissolution of 'mixed' unions.[42]

The principal opposition to Section 77 within 'white politics' came then from industrial capital.[43] This was not of course at the time opposition to the objective of maintaining a racist hierarchy in the social division of labour. On the contrary we have already seen that industry's own position on this question led its spokesmen to give explicit approval to such an objective. Indeed whilst the F.C.I. itself tended to deny that the changes in the labour process were threatening the position of any white wage-earners, some of its parliamentary representatives (notably Helen Suzman) were even prepared to countenance some alternative form of state intervention (namely subsidies) to prevent any white 'marginals' falling below blacks in the hierarchy.[44] Rather what concerned industrial capital about Section 77 was the precise form and precise extent of the interventions proposed by the régime. Statutory job reservation operated directly at the level of relations of production and it was therefore seen as having the potential, if applied to any great extent, to seriously impede the mechanisation of production and thereby the process of capital accumulation. Ministers were portrayed in industrialists' journals as being 'unable to realise' that 'the kinds of jobs in industry and the degrees of required skill are constantly changing'[45] and it was therefore predicted that job reservation would be applied in such a manner that it would 'at the very best greatly retard the industrial progress of the country' and at worst 'very quickly destroy our present industrial achievements'.[46] Another subsidiary concern was that job reservation would impede capital accumulation by undermining the 'incentives' for white wage-earners to retrain for reassignment to new petty bourgeois places. As an F.C.I. memorandum put it

> A tendency is bound to develop . . . that the less responsible
> European worker will make no effort to improve his efficiency
> . . . because of his belief that the Minister will artificially protect
> him by way of a declaration under this Section. Far from serving
> any real purpose, it may in reality undermine the principle that the
> European must maintain his dominant position in the economy.[47]

But of course, despite industrial capital's vigorous opposition to the inclusion of Section 77 in the bill, and despite an initially successful challenge to certain determinations (the latter leading to an amendment giving the minister wider discretionary powers in 1959[48]) statutory job reservation determinations did become operative in a number of industries and sectors. In more recent times capitalists have found it expedient to argue that they acted as a major barrier to capitalist development and as a fundamental determinant of the racist class structure.[49] But of course reality and the ideological expediencies of capitalists need not coincide, and in the case of job reservation determinations their actual effects have in fact been rather more limited.

Table 29[50]   *Statistics relating to section 77 job reservation determi-nations*

year	no. of new determinations made	no. of determinations in force	no. of determinations in force affecting local authorities or non productive sectors	estimated percentage of total employees covered
1957	3	1*	1	
1958	1	2	2	
1959	3	4*	3	
1960	1	5	3	
1961	–	5	3	
1962	4	9	6	
1963	2	11	7	
1964	2	13	7	
1965	1	14	8	5 %
1966	2	16	8	
1967	1†	17	8	
1968	3†	20	9	3·06%
1969	1†	21	9	2·99%
1970	1†	22	9	2·90%
1971	1†	23	9	
1972	–†	23	9	
1973	–†	23	9	
1974	–†	23	9	2·6 %
1975	–†	23	9	2·5 %

*indicates certain determinations invalidated in the courts
†indicates significant relaxations of the provisions of certain determinations in force.

In the first place they have only been applied to a comparatively small (and declining) number of places on the margins of the class structure. As Table 29 shows they have never affected more than an estimated 5 per cent of the total workforce and a large number of those, moreover, have been employees of local authorities or employees in other non-productive sectors.

Secondly, far from being made in any spirit of reckless indifference to their effects on capitalist production, job reservation determinations have in fact only been made after taking the 'utmost care' to 'prevent (any proposed) work reservation from causing any large scale disruption'.[51] Or, as the Minister of Finance put it in 1960: 'Like tariff protection, work reservation could if injudiciously applied be harmful. (He means, of course, to capital accumulation— R.D.) But this Government has not yet applied it like that and will not do so.'[52] The Industrial Tribunal has thus been bound to a procedure of lengthy investigation and consultation with capitalist employers before making recommendations;[53] in other words it has been bound to make its recommendations for the granting of concessions to white wage-earners at the expense of blacks within the latitudes allowable by the requirements of capital accumulation. Indeed when the Tribunal in its early days made one or two recommendations for determinations which might perhaps have had serious consequences for capital accumulation, these rapidly gave way, albeit after fierce struggle, to determinations far more limited in scope. The particular example here is the case of the clothing industry where an original determination (made in 1957) to reserve for whites a number of productive functions 'traditionally' but not at the time filled by whites, gave way to a complex formula taking account of the position of different capitals operating under different conditions in different areas.[54]

Furthermore, exemptions from determinations have been granted, if not as readily as capitalists may have wished in a number of cases where capitalists at the time or subsequently proposed some alternative 'solution' (particularly a 'solution' involving the reassignment of white agents 'upwards'). And exemptions have also been granted when it has become apparent that the process of class formation has reached the stage where insufficient white agents were available to fill the places concerned.[55] The granting of exemptions has been particularly evident in the period after 1967 and it reflects, in the words of the 1972 Reynders Commission the 'clear tendency for whites to move away from secondary industry into white collar jobs'.[56]

Statutory job reservation determinations—the major new concessions made to white wage-earners during the Apartheid period—have, in short, like all previous concessions made available to them operated within the limits dictated by the imperatives of capital accumulation: functioning in this case as 'regulators' of the margins of the class structure during a particular period of transition and restructuring. They have of course been responsible for determining that some agents who would otherwise probably have been rendered marginal to capitalist production,[57] came to occupy certain places at the expense of blacks at the margins of the racial division of labour. But they have not brought about a class structure fundamentally different in its broad composition to that which would otherwise have been brought into existence at that particular stage of capitalist development. In other words, the specific form of racist hierarchical class structure brought about by the restructuring of the relations of production during the early Apartheid period, was determined principally by the requirements of capital accumulation and only secondarily by the demands of white wage-earners.

One effect of this restructuring of relations of production has been to bring about a class structure in which the number of whites occupying places in the productive working class is minimal. As Appendix 1 shows the Apartheid period saw massive decreases in the number of whites still occupying such places matched by substantial increases in the numbers occupying places in the new petty bourgeoisie. For example, between 1946 and 1960 the numbers of whites described in censuses as labourers—probably the only unambiguous white working class category—decreased by 61 per cent while the numbers in the new petty bourgeoisie increased by some 74 per cent. Another effect—partly of the changing place of white wage-earners in the

Table 30[58]   *Real white and African earnings in mining and manufacturing and construction*

(1959/60 prices) Selected Years (Rand)

	Mining			Manufacturing and Construction		
Mining	White	Black	Ratio white:black	White	African	Ratio white:black
1935/6	1,617	144	11·2 : 1	1,074	200	5·4 : 1
1940/1	1,704 + 5·3%	146 + 1·4%	11·7 : 1	1,140 + 6·1%	216 + 8 %	5·3 : 1
1945/6	1,696 − 0·5%	146 —	11·6 : 1	1,337 + 17·3%	322 + 49·1%	4·1 : 1
1950/1	2,018 + 18·9%	145 − 0·6%	13·9 : 1	1,499 + 12·1%	317 − 1·6%	4·7 : 1
1955/6	2,092 + 3·6%	146 + 0·6%	14·3 : 1	1,774 + 18·3%	328 + 3·4%	5·4 : 1
1960/1	2,296 + 9·7%	140 − 4·1%	16·4 : 1	1,907 + 7·5%	365 + 11·3%	5·2 : 1
1970	3,492 + 52·0%	180 + 28·6%	19·4 : 1	2,939 + 54·1%	491 + 34·5%	6·0 : 1

relations of production, and partly of their enhanced capacity to extract concessions in the Apartheid state—has been substantial increases in the incomes of white wage-earners during the period. As Table 30 shows, real white wages which increased relatively slowly during the war and immediate post-war period increased very much faster over the Apartheid period, and, equally important, so too did the gap between average white and average African earnings.

Both these factors—the further concentration of white wage-earners into the new petty bourgeoisie and their improving living standards—have, of course, had important effects on the political practices of the white wage-earning classes. On the one hand they laid the material base for a firmer commitment on the part of white wage-earners to the bourgeois state. One index of this firmer commitment was the disappearance of any 'autonomous' white labour presence (i.e. a specific white labour party) from the political scene, and the growing support of the white wage-earning new petty bourgeoisie for the bourgeois parties, particularly the Nationalist Party. Another similar index has been the rapid disappearance of any vestiges of 'left' or even social democratic politics from any section of the 'white trade union movement'—as manifested, for example, in the rightward shift of TUCSA throughout the '50s and '60s, eventually culminating in its blatant attempt to set itself up as the bourgeoisie's watchdog over the burgeoning African trade union movement in the early 1970s.[59]

On the other hand though, the dependence on concessions so obviously extracted at the expense of the African dominated classes and the overall vulnerability of some strata of the white wage-earning new petty bourgeoisie has produced a tendency for some sections of this class to adopt extreme reactionary class positions. They have from time to time displayed an extreme resistance both to the demands of the masses and to any attempts by the bourgeoisie to defend their own interests by granting limited concessions to black classes, and not only in respect of economic issues directly affecting white wage-earners but over the broad spectrum of economic, political and ideological issues. Generally this resistance has been expressed through the Nationalist Party which has remained dependent on their support and obliged therefore to pay attention to their demands. But on occasions some sections have given support to various far right tendencies. For example Ras Beyers, a member of the far right Republican Party,[60] became prominent in the Mine Workers Union in the late '60s, and Gert Beetge of the Building Workers Union and Co-ordinating Council of Trade Unions joined the Herstigte Nasionale Party in 1971.

Thus, one of the effects of the process of labour reorganisation and class formation during the early Apartheid period was that it produced for the bourgeoisie a class firmly committed to its continued domination. But on the other hand it has also produced a class, certain sections of which are prone to adopt extreme reactionary class positions resisting at least beyond a certain point 'reformist' solutions relating to the black dominated classes. We shall discuss some of the implications of this at greater length in our concluding chapter.

Notes to Chapter 8

1 See D. Lewis, *op. cit.*
2 On this see Kaplan (1977) thesis, *op. cit.* Chapter 9.
3 Poulantzas (1975), p. 45. See also Kaplan thesis (1977), *op. cit.* Chapter 9.
4 'Apartheid, Agriculture and the State' *op. cit.*
5 Finlay, *op. cit.*
6 Poulantzas (1975), *op. cit.* p. 297.
7 *Idem.*
8 Some information on this is given in B. Bunting, *The Rise of the South African Reich* (Harmondsworth 1969) pp. 388 *et seq.*
9 Taken from D. Welsh, 'The Political Economy of Afrikaner Nationalism', chapter in A. Leftwich ed. *South Africa: Economic Growth and Political Change* (London 1974).
10 Quoted in Bunting, *op. cit.* p. 339.
11 See, for example, F.C.I. Memorandum 'The Native in Industry' 8.1.51 for a statement of industry's basic position.

12 'Memorandum submitted to all Members of the Legislature on Protection against inter racial competition and Segregation of Trade Unions' by the Natal Employers Association, National Federation of Building Trade Employers, F.C.I., South African Motor Industry Employers Association, and the Steel and Engineering Industries Federation 21.5.54. This document was one of industry's most important statements of position on this question being reproduced *inter alia* as an Appendix to the F.C.I.'s submission to the *Select Committee on the Industrial Conciliation Bill* (SC 3, 1955).

13 See, for example, memorandum cited above; verbal evidence by F.C.I. representatives to SC 3, 1955 p. 40; F.C.I. president's address *38th F.C.I. Convention Reports 1955* p. 24; F.C.I. president's address *42nd F.C.I. Convention Reports 1959* p. 45.

14 'Skilled' labour shortages arising in the earlier '60s were seen to be 'soluble' by white immigration and indeed industrial capital frequently campaigned for a more active immigration policy. In 1961, for example, F.C.I. president Lulofs made the point in the following terms: 'White South Africans are in danger of losing their title deeds to the country because of the rapidly declining immigration intake.' (*Rand Daily Mail* 9.11.61.)

15 See *41st F.C.I. Convention Report 1958* and *South African Industry and Trade* December 1956 for reports of speeches by R. Bennun, vice president of the F.C.I. and E. R. Savage, then president of the Natal F.C.I., later of the South African F.C.I., both dismissing the possibility of training significant numbers of Africans to fill such places. Quotation from Savage.

16 'Further Memorandum on the Principle of Work Reservation' submitted by the F.C.I. to the Minister of Labour 1959.

17 Morris, 'Apartheid, Agriculture and the State' *op. cit.*

18 1948 figure from *1951 Industrial Legislation Commission* Table 23a, *op. cit.*; 1960 figure (including construction) from Hobart Houghton, *The South African Economy* (Cape Town 1964) p. 224.

19 Thus, for example, A. J. Norval the Chairman of the Board of Trade and Industries which produced Report 282 in 1945 wrote in 1962: a 'number of artisan occupations have been broken down into their constituent elements and work such as machining, certain aspects of welding, press operation and the like is now performed by less skilled workers ... (particularly) Bantu workers who, though unskilled can now undertake semi-skilled work'. (*A Quarter of a Century of Industrial Progress in South Africa* (Cape Town 1962).)

20 Address read by J. F. T. Naude for B. J. Schoeman to *37th F.C.I. Convention 1954* (Report in *The Manufacturer* January 1955).

21 Speech by Minister of Finance to Handelsinstituit 12.9.60, reproduced in Dept. of Labour publication *Work Reservation. . . . Its Background, Motivation and Application to the Benefit of All Racial Groups in South Africa* (Pretoria 1961).

22 *House of Assembly Debates* 1951, columns 5931/3.

23 On the provisions of the 1951 Apprenticeship Act see *House of Assembly Debates* 20.4.1951. On the position of the F.C.I. see *34th Annual Report 1951.* And on the changes in the character of industry's 'skilled labour' requirements see 1954 'Memorandum to Members of the Legislature . . .' *op. cit.*

24 See *House of Assembly Debates* 1951, column 5147.

25 *South African Industry and Trade* May 1951.

26 On industry's position on white education and training see 41st F.C.I. Convention Report 1958; on the sums expended see Appendix 2.

27 Thus as early as August 1948 Schoeman was declaring that 'The Government is wholeheartedly in favour of the continued existence of (non-African —RD) trade unions' (*House of Assembly Debates* 1948, column 2762), although as Opposition MPs pointed out this contrasted with Section 13 of the Party Constitution and a number of speeches in the election campaign.

28 Petty bourgeois influence was not however entirely absent. But it was restricted to more minor matters such as the provisions included in the 1956 Act prohibiting trade unions from engaging in 'political activity' and the provisions for the phased elimination of 'mixed trade unions'. Petty bourgeois influence was of course also evident in the removals from office and the banning of prominent rivals of 'Christian Nationalists' e.g. Sachs and Kalk.

29 *Report of the Industrial Legislation Commission of Enquiry 1951, op. cit.* p. 163.

30 See *House of Assembly Debates* 1954, column 5847 *et seq.*

31 See *House of Assembly Debates* 1951, columns 859 *et seq.*

32 See *35th F.C.I. Convention Report 1951.*

33 *House of Assembly Debates* 1951, columns 1082/3.

34 Figures given in *Department of Labour Reports* for 1949 (UG 50, 1951); 1950 (UG 71, 1951); and 1951 (UG 45, 1953).

35 Phrase used in *38th F.C.I. Report for 1955*, p. 21.

36 *House of Assembly Debates* 1951, column 1396.

37 *Report of the General Manager of South African Railways* for 1951 (UG 60, 1951) p. 131.

38 *Reports of the General Manager of South African Railways* for 1949 (UG 54, 1949); 1950 (UG 59, 1950); 1959 (UG 46, 1959).

39 See Section 77 of Act 28 of 1956 (Butterworths statutes); also M. J. Piercy 'Statutory Job Reservation—Requirement of a Static or of an Expanding Economy' and 'Statutory Work Reservation in the Union of South Africa', *South African Journal of Economics*, vol. 28, 1960, for a convenient descriptive analysis.

40 Among them the Natal Employers Association, the National Federation of Building Trade Employees, the South African Motor Industries Employers Association and the Steel and Engineering Industries Federation all of which signed the 'Memorandum to All Members of the Legislature' along with the F.C.I. in 1954.

41 See their representation to the *Select Committee on the Industrial Concilia-tion Bill* (SC 3, 1955) pp. 149 *et seq.*

42 See discussion in parliament (*House of Assembly Debates* 1956, columns 583 *et seq.*).

43 A letter from F.C.I. Director Burger to 'All Participating Organizations' dated 19.5.59 made it clear that many of the arguments advanced by oppo-sition speakers such as Marais Steyn and Helen Suzman against the 1959 amendment at least originated with the F.C.I. Representations from the Chamber of Mines were rather muted. It did not appear before the Select Committee but it did subscribe to a joint representation of 'employers' organizations' regarding the nomination procedures for 'employers' repre-sentatives' on the Industrial Tribunal (see *Chamber of Mines Annual Reports* for 1956).

44 *House of Assembly Debates* 1954, column 5971 ('. . . it would be cheaper to subsidize such Europeans than to penalize the whole structure of manu-facturing industry by introducing this type of rigid economy in order simply to help a small number of unfortunate European workers who cannot hold their own against competition. Everyone would be quite happy to subsi-dize them.')

45 *South African Industry and Trade* June 1956 (editorial).

46 *Ibid.* August 1954 (editorial).

47 Letter from E. R. Savage, President of F.C.I. to Minister of Labour 3.11.55.

48 See, *inter alia*, Piercy, 'Statutory Work Reservation' *op. cit.* pp. 211–3.

49 Just one among many examples of this came during the 1973/4 African wages campaign during which the then Chairman of British Leyland, Stokes, attempted to argue that 'We are prevented from paying proper wages because

of the South African Government's prohibition on employing Africans in skilled jobs . . . We are constantly trying to get around the laws of job reservation' (reported in the *Guardian* 19.3.73). In this particular case, however, Stokes was later compelled to admit that 'Job reservation does not really apply to us at all. It is not a real problem' (House of Commons Expenditure Committee subCommittee: *Inquiry into Wages and Conditions of African Workers employed by British Firms in South Africa: Minutes of Evidence* Vol. 1, p. 220 (London, 1973/4).

50 Compiled from *Department of Labour Reports* for 1957 (UG 29, 1958); 1958 (UG 40, 1959); 1959 (UG 59, 1960); 1960 (RP 6, 1961); *Institute of Race Relations Annual Surveys of Race Relations* 1961—1975.

51 Department of Labour pamphlet, *Work Reservation . . . its Background* (etc.) *op. cit.* p. 13.

52 Quoted *ibid.* p. 24.

53 *Ibid.* p. 13.

54 The original clothing industry determination sought to reserve the task of machinist, cutter, table hand and supervisor for whites, although several of these places were at the time filled by blacks. One economist estimated at the time that it could not be implemented without closing every clothing factory in the Cape and Natal and three quarters of those in the Transvaal. After massive protests and various court battles it was eventually suspended and replaced by a determination implementing a complex quota system taking account of regional variations. (See *South African Industry and Trade* December 1957 and *House of Assembly Debates* 1960, column 6887/8.)

55 See, *inter alia*, Department of Labour pamphlet, *Work Reservation* etc.

56 Quoted *Survey of Race Relations* 1973 p. 218.

57 By 1957 industrialists were speaking of 'over full' white employment indicating that they would have preferred that some employed whites were consigned to unemployment. For example, L. Lulofs, president of the Transvaal Chambers of Industries spoke as follows: '. . . we are now employing a substantial proportion of unemployables. And it is not sufficiently realised in government circles what effect these 'won't works' are having on morale and discipline in our establishments' (*F.C.I. 40th Convention Reports* 1957, p. 51).

58 Source D. Hobart Houghton, *The South African Economy* (1967 and 1976 editions) the 1970 figure averaged and deflated according to price figures in Table 24 (1976 edition).

59 Thus in 1974 Grobbelaar, the General Secretary of TUCSA, presented his proposals for 'supervised' African trade unionism, as having the 'advantage' of allowing 'a considerable amount of control' whereas alternatives would produce a situation in which 'not only will the Government be brought to its knees but our present way of life will be destroyed' (*Rand Daily Mail* 17.5.74); see also L. Ensor, 'TUCSA's Relationship with African Trade Unions—an attempt at Control—1954–1962', *South African Labour Bulletin*, vol. 3 no. 4, Jan.–Feb. 1977.

60 According to *Rand Daily Mail* 25.11.65.

61 Beetge could not however win over his executive for the HNP. See J. Butler, 'The Significance of Recent Changes within the White Ruling Caste' and F. van Zyl Slabbert, 'Afrikaner Nationalism, White Political Change in South Africa' chapters in L. Thompson and J. Butler ed. *Change in Contemporary South Africa* (California 1975).

9 Conclusions

In the previous sections of this study we argued that the formation and reproduction of a 'privileged' white stratum within the wage-earning classes, integrated into various state apparatuses from which the African working class has been excluded, came about, firstly, because during the formative period between 1900 and the early 1960s the formation and reproduction of such a racist hierarchical division of labour accorded with the requirements of capitalist production and secondly, because under the conditions of class struggle prevailing in the social formation at the time, this particular process of class reproduction and integration served as part of a political solution which created the conditions for the bourgeoisie to maintain its political dominance over the social formation. This is not to say that the interests of all fractions of the bourgeoisie were equally served by all aspects of this particular process of reproduction and integration. On the contrary we saw that by forming particular relationships involving the granting to white wage-earners of certain economic concessions which they would not otherwise have received, particular fractions of the bourgeoisie were able to secure the supportive base which they needed to advance their own position within the power bloc. But we indicated that notwithstanding this the broad essentials of this particular process of class formation and integration accorded to some degree or other during the period in question with the interests of all major fractions of capital.

Since about the mid 1960s and more particularly at the current conjuncture, however, the indications are that the continued reproduction of such a racist hierarchical division of labour has become, at least in its present form, less and less functional to more and more bourgeois interests and, indeed, to the bourgeoisie as a whole.

In the first place it has become increasingly evident that the continued reproduction of a racist hierarchical division of labour within the wage-earning classes has created a number of problems at the level of capital accumulation. These have not arisen, as bourgeois ideology would have it, exclusively from the effects of specific measures, such as statutory job reservation or current white trade union 'pressures'. Rather the problems arising in this regard have to be seen in the context of the general tendency in the capitalist mode of production towards an overproduction of capital,[1] and more specifically in the context of the tendency for capitalist, and in particular monopoly capitalist, relations of production to be reproduced in the South African social formation during the period in question at a rate in excess of the rate of growth of the white population. Under these circumstances *the totality of historical factors* which determined that skilled manual and new petty bourgeois labour power should in the South African social formation be produced predominantly, if not exclusively, from among the ranks of the white population have resulted in acute shortages of certain categories of skilled manual and new petty bourgeois labour power. Moreover whereas such shortages were in the late '60s and early '70s mainly confined to skilled manual and lower level new petty bourgeois places (where their effects could be mitigated under the conditions of 'boom' then prevailing by the process described as 'floating the colour bar'[2]), in more recent times they have appeared at more 'senior' levels and have furthermore become under the current conditions of diminished profitability a much more serious problem for social capital. Some indication of this is given by the fact that they are now being discussed in 'conservative' as well as 'liberal' quarters within the bourgeoisie. In 1976, for example, Erich Leistner of the Africa Institute told a 'businessman's conference' that

> . . . a white monopoly of highly skilled and responsible posts in business administration . . . was no longer tenable. Members of other racial groups would have to move up into such positions

if economic growth rates were not to fall to even lower levels
. . . 500,000 white clerical jobs would be vacant within 15 years
unless other races were trained to fill work gaps vital for industrial expansion.[3]

Whilst in the same year the Managing Director of ISCOR told the
Handelsinstuut that 'the potential for white SA to produce trained
tradesmen and managers for 25 million people was close to ex-
haustion'.[4]

But, secondly and perhaps more importantly, the continued
existence of an overtly racist division of labour, out of step at the
current phase of the imperialist epoch with the prevailing pattern of
social relations in either metropolitan or peripheral social formations,
has created an increasing number of problems for the South African
bourgeoisie in its struggle to maintain its *political* domination over
the social formation. The restriction of blacks to essentially subordinate places in the division of labour has been one factor among
others which has ensured not only that any potential supportive
black petty bourgeois class remains extremely small and insecure, but
moreover that the objective polarisation of key sections at least of
the black petty bourgeoisie is towards the working class rather than
towards the bourgeoisie. Furthermore, as the mass uprisings in
Soweto and elsewhere clearly demonstrated, in the case of some, if
not all, of these sections of the black petty bourgeoisie this objective
polarisation of class determination has now become matched by the
adoption of class positions antagonistic not just to the régime and
specific policies but to the bourgeoisie as a whole and the capitalist
mode of production. As one somewhat bemused bourgeois class
warrior observed in 1976, 'There is a general tendency for young
Africans to be anti-free enterprise'.[5] Indeed, under the current conditions of class struggle a large and increasing number of spokesmen
for bourgeois class interests are coming to regard the absence of a
sizeable 'black middle class' committed to 'free enterprise values' as
one of the most significant long term threats to the 'maintenance of
the free enterprise system' and 'the survival of everything (they) hold
dear'.[6]

To what extent the bourgeoisie can extricate itself from the effects of these particular contradictions of capitalist social relations in the South African social formation is at the time of writing a matter still to be decided in the class struggle. Any attempt to offer an assessment at this stage must of course be placed in the context of a wider assessment of the capacity of the power bloc to restructure and stabilise class relations in the social formation generally and, since this obviously raises a number of complex questions which cannot adequately be discussed here, I intend to be very brief. One factor, however, which it seems to me is of critical importance in this regard is the specific organisation of the power bloc: in particular the fact that the governing class and the class in charge of the state (i.e. the classes directly in charge of the organisation of the bourgeoisie's strategy *vis-à-vis* the popular masses) consist not of the larger mono- poly capitalist fractions but, as we argued in the last chapter, a grouping of smaller more vulnerable agrarian and industrial capitals who, whilst not able to fundamentally alter the trajectory of capital- ist development were nevertheless able to use their political position to advance and secure a number of important fractional interests. This would suggest, among other things, that although as Kaplan has argued[7] a number of factors which precluded the granting of econo- mic concessions or political rights to 'urban blacks' in the late '40s and early '50s have been modified in a way which now makes some form of 'integrative' or 'co-optive' response to the struggles of the black dominated classes likely; there none the less remain a number of critical limitations on the precise scope and terms on which any such response organised by the current power bloc can proceed. In particular the fact that the classes represented by the governing party have a number of vital fractional interests whose continued realisa- tion remains quite critically dependent upon their maintaining their political position, means that even though these classes may now be more willing and able to tolerate the granting of certain economic concessions to blacks or even the incorporation of certain black dominated classes into subordinate places within the state appara- tuses, they cannot afford to tolerate any restructuring of political class relations which might threaten their particular place in the state. They must above all resist any neo-colonial type 'majority rule' solution which could lead to their displacement as governing class and at the current phase of the imperialist epoch this, it seems to me, places severe limitations on the capacity of the power bloc *as currently organised* to stabilise political class relations and fundamentally alter South Africa's current position as a crisis ridden weak link in the imperialist chain.

On the other hand though, as we have argued consistently throughout this study, the white wage-earning classes are not themselves the politically dominant classes, but the allied and supportive classes of the politically dominant capitalist classes. Moreover, they are classes a) whose capacity for 'autonomous' political action has, as a result of their increasing incorporation into new petty bourgeois as distinct from working class places, been diminishing over the past 30 years and .b) for whom there are, as a consequence partly of the historical processes examined in this study, a large number of barriers to their polarisation towards the African working class; and whose existing political allegiances can therefore be expected to remain relatively secure even if they were to lose some of the specific economic concessions made available to them in the past. It is quite likely therefore that whatever the limitations in respect of the capacity of the existing power bloc to restructure fundamental political class relations, some more substantial 'reformist' strategy may emerge in respect of the particular contradictions arising from the continued reproduction of the racist hierarchical division of labour within the wage-earning classes. Such a strategy could be expected to involve, *inter alia*, the withdrawal of certain specific 'privileges' from white wage-earners; some modification to the rigidly racist character of the social division of labour; and some increase in the number of blacks occupying places in the new petty bourgeoisie. Indeed there have been some limited (partly cosmetic and partly real) moves in this direction already. For example expenditure on African education has risen by quite large amounts in recent years; a number of new technical training programmes for blacks have sprung up since about 1974; there have been some moves towards paying the 'rate for the job' to blacks moving into previously 'white' jobs; and a large number of statutory job reservation determinations have been relaxed in recent months (although in a number of cases these have been replaced by 'closed shop' agreements having the same effect in practice).[8] There have also been some signs that the state has become, partly as a result of the current recession but partly also as a result of changing political priorities, much less ready than it once was to intervene to secure concessions for white wage-earners in respect of wage demands. In 1977, for example, state officials and government ministers were prominent in opposing wage increases for white employees in the mining industry and in state departments, and there was even talk in 'government circles' at one stage of taking steps to limit the trade union bargaining power of the white wage-earning classes.[9]

Precisely how much further any such moves may go and precisely what their effect may be on overall class relations can only be matters of speculation at this moment of time. The whole 'industrial relations' legislative framework is at the time of writing (February 1978) currently being reviewed by the Wiehahn Commission and whilst this is fundamentally directed at bringing about some restructuring of the relations between capital and African workers at the industrial level, it is widely believed that the Commission will produce some recommendations affecting white wage-earners (probably a recommendation to end all statutory job colour bars, and possibly also some recommendations to reorganise industrial relations procedures in a way which will weaken the trade union bargaining power of white wage-earners). It is extremely unlikely, however, for the reasons already discussed that any further moves in this direction will lead to a change in the fundamental political polarisation of the white wage-earning classes towards the bourgeoisie. What may happen though, is that they may lead to some heightening of the struggle between capital and the white wage-earning classes at the economic level, and possibly also to an intensification of the resistance on the part of some sections of the white petty bourgeoisie to 'reformist' proposals generally.

But, however that may be, what is clear is that the interests of the popular masses lie in taking advantage of any contradictions which any such process may create to advance their own position and not in simply giving passive support to a bourgeois led process of restructuring the relations of capitalist exploitation—even if one of its eventual outcomes were to be an end to all official and unofficial job colour bars. For although the elimination of all job colour bars is a necessary *part* of the liberation of the masses, it alone is not sufficient. So long as the fundamental relations of capitalist exploitation and class domination are maintained, the removal of job colour bars and racist barriers to 'upward social mobility' can only be an attempt to optimise the conditions for capital accumulation and to co-opt certain elements of the black population in the hope that, as in the case of the equivalent process with the white wage-earning classes, this will strengthen the position of the exploiting classes in their struggle to maintain their domination over the exploited classes. For as Marx put it,

> . . . the circumstance that the Catholic Church in the Middle Ages formed its hierarchy out of the best brains of the people without regard to estate, birth, or wealth, was one of the principal means of fortifying priestly rule and suppressing the laity. The more a ruling class is able to assimilate the most prominent men of a ruled class, the more solid and dangerous is its rule.[10]

Notes to Chapter 9

1 See Marx, *Capital*, Vol. 3, Chapter XV, part III.
2 See e.g. R. First, J. Steele and C. Gurney, *The South African Connection*, Chapter 4; F. A. Johnstone, 'White Prosperity and White Supremacy in South Africa Today', *African Affairs*, vol. 69 no. 2, 1970; and H. Wolpe, 'The Changing Class Structure of South Africa: the African Petit Bourgeoisie' (mimeo 1976) on the incorporation of Africans into the lower levels of the new petty bourgeoisie.
3 Reported in SAIRR *Survey of Race Relations 1976*, p. 291.

4 J. P. Coetzee quoted *ibid.* p. 287.
5 Dr. S. P. du Toit Viljoen, interim council member of the 'Free Market Foundation' (a body supported by ASSOCOM, the F.C.I., Chamber of Mines, the Handelsinstituut, the African Chamber of Commerce and 'organised labour' formed to 'spread the message of free enterprise to young Africans') quoted *Financial Mail* 11.2.77, p. 376.
6 Phrases from interview with Justice Steyn, executive director of Oppenheimer backed Urban Foundation *Financial Mail* 11.3.77, p. 718 and report of a speech by Anton Rupertat establishment of above quoted *Financial Mail* 3.12.76, p. 889. For similar sentiments see also *Financial Mail* 20.8.76, pp. 633–4 (report of a memorandum by Transvaal Chamber of Industries).
7 Thesis (1977), *op. cit.* Chapter 10.
8 In June 1977 three job reservation determinations were scrapped and a fourth relaxed, and in December 1977 all but five determinations were scrapped. As mentioned above, the actual effects in practice have however in many cases been rather limited, 'closed shop' agreements with white trade unions effectively replacing the formal legal job colour bars.
9 See reports in the *Financial Mail* 3.6.77, pp. 79–80 and 6.5.77, pp. 436–7.
10 *Capital*, Vol. III (Chicago, 1909 edition) pp. 705–6.

Appendix 1: Approximate Division of White Population into Class Categories

	1918 Males no. (%age)	1918 Females no. (%age)	1926 Males no. (%age)	1926 Females no. (%age)	1936 Males no. (%age)	1936 Females no. (%age)	1946 Males no. (%age)	1946 Females no. (%age)	1960 Males no. (%age)	1960 Females no. (%age)	1970 Males no. (%age)	1970 Females no. (%age)
A. Bourgeoisie and Traditional Petty Bourgeoisie.												
1. Those in non-agricultural sectors identified as owners, employers, capitalists (*sic*), speculators, brokers, agents, self employed (i.e. neither employer nor employee) or as managers. Also included those identified as top officials in state apparatuses	48,040 (11·73)	10,372 (15·23)	56,995 (11·45)	5,918 (6·51)	54,501 (9·00)	4,692 (3·59)	64,657 (9·36)	5,961 (3·25)	128,039 (15·05)	24,845 (8·48)	159,186 +21,918 (17·52) (see Note 1)	17,087 +2,066 (4·45)
2. Those identified as owners, family workers, employers or managers in agriculture	145,170 (35·45)	3,669 (5·38)	147,329 (29·60)	3,182 (3·50)	167,459 (27·67)	3,321 (2·54)	151,294 (21·88)	7,764 (4·23)	101,513 (11·93)	3,204 (1·10)	86,439 (8·36)	3,431 (0·80)
TOTAL	193,210 (47·18)	14,041 (20·61)	204,324 (41·05)	9,100 (10·01)	221,960 (36·67)	8,013 (6·13)	215,951 (31·24)	13,725 (7·48)	229,552 (26·98)	28,049 (9·58)	267,543 (25·88)	22,584 (5·25)
TOTAL MALE & FEMALE	207,251 (43·39%)		213,424 (36·26%)		229,973 (31·24%)		229,676 (26·25%)		257,601 (22·53%)		290,127 (19·81%)	

| | 1918 | | 1926 | | 1936 | | 1946 | | 1960 | | 1970 | |
| | *Males* | *Females* | *Males* | *Females* | *Males* | *Females* | *Males* | *Females* | *Males* | *Females* | *Males* | *Females* |
	no. *(%age)*	*no.* *(%age)*	*no.* *(%age)*	*no.* *(%age)*	*no.* *(%age)*	*no.* *(%age)*	*no.* *(%age)*	*no.* *(%age)*	*no.* *(%age)*	*no.* *(%age)*	*no.* *(%age)*	*no.* *(%age)*
B. New Petty Bourgeoisie												
1. Those employed in the State Repressive Apparatus (military and police)	15,342 (3·75)	639 (0·95)	8,885 (1·79)	—	12,292 (2·03)	143 (0·11)	26,078 (3·77)	1,882 (1·02)	19,904 (2·35)	174 (0·06)	53,344 (5·16)	897 (0·21)
2. Those employed in ideological apparatuses (mainly education and clergy)	8,011 (1·96)	13,704 (20·11)	10,403 (2·09)	16,077 (17·69)	13,067 (2·16)	16,971 (12·97)	15,121 (2·19)	14,396 (7·84)	21,802 (2·56)	21,978 (7·51)	38,953 (3·77)	34,321 (7·97)
3. Others employed in bureaucratic social category (state employees in local, provincial or central government other than in 1 and 2 above)	7,553 (1·84)	1,153 (1·69)	15,400 (3·09)	2,162 (2·38)	13,729 (2·27)	3,053 (2·33)	17,559 (2·54)	6,764 (3·68)	103,752 (12·19)	43,640 (14·91)	Included in B7 (See Note 2)	
4. Wage-earners involved in the circulation process	24,259 (5·92)	13,768 (20·21)	62,930 (12·64)	27,740 (30·52)	71,550 (11·82)	47,425 (36·26)	81,527 (11·79)	82,094 (44·73)	145,362 (17·09)	154,693 (52·85)		
5. Engineers and Technicians	6,788 (1·66)	310 (0·45)	5,252 (1·05)	54 (0·06)	17,381 (2·87)	238 (0·18)	27,038 (3·91)	728 (0·40)	21,212 (2·49)	1,284 (0·44)	72,657 (7·03)	6,723 (1·57)
6. Clearly identifiable supervisory new petty bourgeoisie (most mining categories and those described as foremen, supervisors, inspectors, overlookers, etc.)	40,248 (9·83)	1,050 (1·54)	30,909 (6·22)	231 (0·25)	36,025 (5·95)	1,900 (1·45)	46,686 (6·75)	2,852 (1·55)	75,044 (8·82)	3,412 (1·17)	97,665 (9·45)	12,199 (2·83)

7. Others based on the description probably involved in mental or supervisory functions	17,233 (4·21)		26,368 (5·30)	23,057 (25·38)	36,569 (6·05)	20,581 (15·74)	38,986 (5·64)	32,850 (17·40)	45,554 (5·35)	28,228 (9·64)	303,422 (29·34)	342,487 (79·56)
TOTAL	119,434 (29·17)	39,995 (58·70)	160,147 (32·18)	69,321 (76·28)	200,613 (33·15)	90,311 (69·04)	252,995 (36·09)	141,566 (77·12)	432,630 (50·85)	253,406 (86·58)	566,061 (54·75)	396,627 (92·14)
TOTAL MALE & FEMALE	159,429 (33·37%)		229,468 (38·99%)		290,924 (39·52%)		394,561 (45·10%)		686,006 (59·99%)		962,688 (65·74%)	

C. *Residual Category*

ensemble of new petty bourgeoisie not readily identifiable from description, craft, unproductive manual workers and productive white working class

1. Those in 'skilled' categories—mainly new petty bourgeoisie and artisans	57,969 (14·15)	2,647 (3·88)	97,478 (19·59)	7,692 (8·46)	116,546 (19·26)	11,222 (8·58)	152,831 (22·10)	8,560 (4·66)	107,318 (12·62)	3,093 (1·06)	200,301 (19·37)	
2. Those described as labourers	21,669 (5·29)	85 (0·12)	16,951 (3·40)	24 (0·03)	44,484 (7·35)	266 (0·20)	29,298 (4·24)	202 (0·11)	10,815 (1·27)	678 (0·23)	11,244 (2·61)	

	1918 Males no. (%age)	1918 Females no. (%age)	1926 Males no. (%age)	1926 Females no. (%age)	1936 Males no. (%age)	1936 Females no. (%age)	1946 Males no. (%age)	1946 Females no. (%age)	1960 Males no. (%age)	1960 Females no. (%age)	1970 Males no. (%age)	1970 Females no. (%age)
3. Those in non-skilled categories not described as labourers—mainly machine operators, those involved in transport in other than supervisory or circulation process positions and various probably manual employees in various services (productive and unproductive)	17,246 (4·21)	11,369 (16·70)	18,784 (3·78)	4,745 (5·22)	21,641 (3·57)	20,997 (16·05)	40,250 (5·83)	19,517 (10·63)	70,522 (8·28)	7,445 (2·55)		
TOTAL	96,884 (23·65)	14,101 (20·70)	133,213 (26·77)	12,461 (13·71)	182,671 (30·18)	32,485 (24·83)	222,379 (32·17)	28,279 (15·40)	188,655 (22·17)	11,216 (3·84)	200,301 (19·37)	11,244 (2·61)
TOTAL MALE & FEMALE	110,985 (23·24%)		145,674 (24·75%)		215,156 (29·24%)		250,658 (28·65%)		199,871 (17·48%)		211,545 (14·45%)	

Total 'Economically Active'	409,528	68,137	497,684	90,882	605,244	130,809	691,325	183,570	850,807	292,671	1,033,905	430,455
Unemployed; those with 'independent means' etc.; and those involved in the reproduction of the above classes (house-wives, scholars, etc.)	37,924	352,660	62,080	441,928	94,721	548,678	135,802	639,061	682,745	1,251,351	847,908	1,461,014
Statistical error (in published statistics)									+ 1,371	+ 1,206		
TOTAL WHITE POPULATION	447,452*	420,797*	559,764*	532,810*	699,965*	679,487*	827,127*	822,631*	1,534,923	1,545,236	1,881,813	1,891,469

(* above 15 years)

Sources: These tables are derived from the most detailed information available in the occupations section of the Population Censuses covering the years in question. The official classification systems have as far as possible been avoided; and instead an attempt has been made to totally rearrange the list of occupations into theoretically generated categories meaningful for an analysis of social classes.

The sources used were the following: 1918 Population Census (UG 1, 1921) Table II; 1926 Population Census (UG 27, 1930) Table 2; 1936 Census Volume VII (UG 11, 1942) Table 1; 1946 Census Vol. V (UG 41, 1954) Table 1; 1960 Census Vol. 8 Table 1; 1970 Population Census: *Occupations* . . . Report no. 02–05–11, 1976, Table 1.

Note 1: The 1960 Census included a breakdown of so-called 'production and transport workers' into Employers, Employees and those described as 'neither employers or employees' i.e. it made it possible to identify certain categories of traditional petty bourgeois classified under these categories. No such breakdown was however made in the 1970 Census. In order to make the two years more comparable I have therefore assumed (unrealistically) that the proportion of employers and those described as 'neither employers nor employees' in these categories remained the same in 1970 as it was in 1960 and attributed an appropriate figure to Category A, reducing Category C accordingly. For that reason no attempt has been made to break down Category C into the three sub categories used for the other years.

Note 2: Unlike earlier Censuses it was not possible to distinguish various categories of mainly clerical employees employed in the state bureaucracy from those employed in commerce etc. Accordingly I have included categories assigned to B_3 and B_4 in the other years in B_7.

Appendix 2: Principal Items of State Expenditure in Connection with the Assignment of White Agents to Places in the Social Division of Labour and/or in Connection with Establishing Ideological Apparatuses of Control Over White Wage-Earners

(Pounds)

A: Expenditure of Major Departments Involved in the Assignment of White Agents to Places in Wage-Earning Classes

	1910–11	1911–12	1912–13	1913–14	1914–15	1915–16	1916–17	1917–18
(1) Dept. of Mines and Industries Labour Division or Dept. of Labour[1]	1,470	1,876	2,202	2,334	4,429	5,868	9,710	3,700*[2]
(2) 'Extra Cost of Employing White Labour in Government Depts.'[3]	—	—	—	—	—	—	—	—
(3) Labour Dept. Expenditure from Loan Funds	—	—	—	—	—	—	—	—
(4) Other	—	—	—	—	—	—	—	—
(5) Provincial Poor Relief Works[8]	18,203	31,727	35,570	36,864	55,404	57,764	56,136	64,160
SUB TOTAL A	19,673	33,603	37,772	39,198	59,833	63,632	65,846	67,860*

B: Expenditure of Departments Involved in the Assignment of White Agents to Places as Landowners and/or with Preventing the Proletarianisation of White Landowners (excluding general subsidisation to farmers)

	1910–11	1911–12	1912–13	1913–14	1914–15	1915–16	1916–17	1917–18
(1) Purchases of land and Advances to White Settlers from Revenue Funds[9]	199,930	79,637	82,515	75,852	53,650	49,602	55,088	146,025
(2) Purchases of Land and Advances to White Settlers from Local Funds[10]	720,363	29,077	102,430	180,408	169,096	40,083	70,869	398,122
(3) Relief of Distress (Revenue)[12]	—	—	—	—	—	—	—	—
(4) Relief of Distress (Loan)	—	—	—	—	—	—	64,563	—
(5) Other	—	—	—	—	—	—	—	—
SUB TOTAL B	920,293	108,714	184,945	256,260	222,746	89,685	190,520	544,147

C: Educational Expenditure

	1910–11	1911–12	1912–13	1913–14	1914–15	1915–16	1916–17	1917–18
(1) Education of Whites (including agricultural education)[14]	1,597,062*	2,148,567*	2,007,343*	2,268,026*	2,458,852*	2,440,407*	2,724,871*	2,865,622*
(2) Higher Education	86,295	107,888	159,252	128,250	113,830	110,288	116,088	133,428
(3) Industrial Schools	4,907	6,370	8,562	12,255	20,168	18,710	23,526	28,639
SUB TOTAL C	1,688,264	2,262,825	2,175,157	2,408,531	2,592,850	2,569,405	2,864,485	3,027,689

	1918–19	1919–20	1920–21	1921–22	1922–23	1923–24	1924–25	1925–26	1926–27	1927–28
A:										
(1)	4,723*	13,271*	30,706	29,058	25,655	26,116	344,126	332,402	252,439	278,546
				(unemployment vote)						
(2)	13,502	19,638	95,623	399,845	421,630	206,190	+	100,441	129,150	121,111
(3)	–	–					–	72,981	56,761	48,600
			distress vote[4]		indus. disputes vote[5]					
(4)	–	–	61,911	–	184,649	–	–	–	–	–
(5)	61,811	71,220	99,369	80,000	80,949	75,512	85,500	84,096	90,486	118,816
SUB TOTAL A	80,036*	104,129*	287,609	508,903	712,883	307,818	429,626	589,920	528,836	567,073
B:										
(1)	165,729	199,930	228,542	244,930	211,238	215,316	232,032	166,011	174,399	182,373
(2)	582,859	720,363	808,344	325,164	171,492	245,741	394,435	531,073	639,051	575,343
(3)	–	–	–	–	–	–	–	20,070	–	–
(4)	–	–	–	–	–	–	371,983	46,373	–	29,937
(5)	–	–	–	–	–	86,432	–	–	–	–
SUB TOTAL B	748,588	920,293	1,036,886	570,094	382,730	547,489	998,450	763,527	813,450	787,653
C:										
(1)	3,313,713	4,166,733	5,401,837	6,057,350	6,035,548	5,906,735	6,236,530	6,243,469	6,358,852	6,720,664
(2)	152,285	198,824	298,221	277,907	307,173	328,102	373,405	550,442	629,631	738,207
(3)	41,481	61,227	98,772	125,412*[15]	142,532*	159,635*	172,444*	197,900*	203,639*	221,387*
SUB TOTAL C	3,507,479	4,426,784	5,798,830	6,460,669	6,485,253	6,394,490	6,782,379	6,991,811	7,192,122	7,680,258

	1939–40	1940–41	1941–42	1942–43	1943–44	1944–45	1945–46	1946–47	1947–48	1948–49	1949–50
A:											
(1)	433,829	417,942	428,860	527,648	608,995	819,785	964,101	950,466	746,797	2,865,928	3,694,093
(2)	ng	ng	ng	ng	ng	4,976	1,636	1,175	2,473	—	ng
(3)	176,074	111,787	35,223	92,224	9,449						—
(4)	Defence 104,000	—	—	—	—	Demob.[7] 96,994	Demob. 2,732,655	Demob. 5,636,767	Demob. 2,461,319	Demob. 636,869	—
(5)	—	54,394[8]	—	17,484	21,799	26,423	23,511	28,323	32,842	ng	ng
SUB TOTAL A	713,903	584,123	464,083	637,356	640,243	948,178	3,721,903	6,616,731	3,243,431	3,502,797	3,694,093
B:											
(1)	327,154	304,942	302,048	424,687	407,816	364,787	419,250	605,718	671,370	579,658	531,061
(2)	1,103,757	639,712	522,389	561,303	635,356	480,025	580,970	655,193	1,010,328	652,472	1,307,981[11]
(3)	—	—	—	—	—	—	—	—	—	—	—
(4)	—	—	—	—	—	—	—	—	—	—	—
(5)	—	—	—	—	—	—	Govt. Villages[13] 69,794	Villages 185,492	Villages 204,832	Villages 175,353	Villages 140,805
SUB TOTAL B	1,430,911	944,654	824,437	985,990	1,043,172	844,812	1,070,014	1,446,403	1,886,530	1,407,483	1,979,847
C:											
(1)	8,242,617	8,374,675	8,406,005	8,988,432	9,331,261	10,850,353	11,499,256	13,256,119	15,460,249	17,250,282	18,047,102
(2)	1,209,375	1,249,449	1,265,873	1,307,506	1,395,670	1,517,501	2,205,147	3,188,280	3,188,010	3,199,497	3,623,985
(3)	191,478	193,369	197,781	225,114	259,079	308,244	403,762	456,207	558,969	602,666	633,126
SUB TOTAL C	9,643,470	9,817,493	9,869,659	10,521,052	10,986,010	12,676,098	14,108,165	16,900,606	19,207,228	21,052,445	22,304,213

A:	1928–9	1929–30	1930–31	1931–32	1932–33	1933–34	1934–35	1935–36	1936–37	1937–38	1938–39
(1)	244,997	232,469	193,441	138,524	201,540	245,891	587,360	950,980	395,314	539,969	464,823
(2)	ng	ng	ng	128,384	ng	148,766	ng	ng	ng	ng	ng
(3)	124,871	215,868	243,948	324,797	751,522	1,109,169	415,981	37,552	515,768	471,789	209,996
(4)	Forestry Dept. 58,501	–	–	–	–	Defence[6] 39,612	Defence 63,066	Defence 17,893	Defence 91,479	Defence 85,506	Defence 98,703
(5)	125,887	105,168	99,799	98,076	118,533	130,533	134,558	146,606	162,622	168,017	178,293
SUB TOTAL A	554,256	553,505	537,188	689,781	1,071,595	1,673,971	1,200,965	1,153,031	1,165,183	1,265,281	951,815
B:											
(1)	159,301	161,093	192,495	162,216	146,518	166,015	181,010	243,321	218,422	254,734	318,975
(2)	618,002	734,866	771,489	500,655	199,271	193,015	386,182	465,720	561,175	1,191,848	1,248,381
(3)	67,433	92,242	5,624	–	–	–	–	–	–	–	–
(4)	425,357	–	–	–	–	–	–	–	–	–	–
(5)	–	–	–	–	–	–	–	–	–	–	–
SUB TOTAL B	1,270,093	988,201	969,608	662,871	345,789	359,030	567,192	709,041	779,597	1,446,582	1,567,356
C:											
(1)	6,639,473	6,912,478	6,710,263	6,612,752	6,416,371	6,461,764	6,884,059	7,172,803	7,444,429	7,705,233	8,121,240
(2)	789,487	854,722	857,630	794,465	717,058	755,866	853,605	903,321	972,155	1,093,216	1,180,779
(3)	227,769*	235,611*	250,911*	232,181*	197,705*	208,269*	244,131*	148,069*	159,091*	178,458*	182,784*
SUB TOTAL C	7,656,729	8,002,811	7,818,804	7,639,398	7,331,134	7,425,899	7,981,795	8,224,193	8,575,675	8,976,907	9,484,803

	1950–51	1951–52	1952–53	1953–54	1954–55	1955–56	1956–57	1957–58	1958–59	1959–60
A:										
(1)	3,709,688	3,771,748	3,939,339	4,498,029	4,450,605	3,178,522	3,144,107	2,583,376	2,690,405	2,872,648
(2)	ng	ng	ng	ng	ng	ng	ng	ng	ng	ng
(3)	–	–	–	–	–	–	–	–	–	–
(4)	ng	ng	ng	ng	ng	ng	ng	ng	ng	ng
(5)	ng	ng	ng	ng	ng	ng	ng	ng	ng	ng
SUB TOTAL A	3,709,688	3,771,748	3,939,339	4,498,029	4,450,605	3,178,522	3,144,107	2,583,376	2,690,405	2,872,648
B:										
(1)	576,378	581,458	547,961	514,288	495,675	570,452	656,555	595,814	611,985	640,771
(2)	1,162,529*	1,215,554*	1,289,872	1,234,690	1,322,077	1,816,197	2,066,142	2,150,988	1,695,375	1,395,345
(3)	–	–	–	–	–	–	–	–	–	–
(4)	–	–	–	–	–	–	–	–	–	–
(5)	Villages 108,509	Villages 121,609	Villages 126,826	Villages 147,315	Villages 157,396	Villages 148,447	Villages 142,098	–	–	–
SUB TOTAL B	1,847,416	1,918,621	1,964,659	1,896,293	1,975,148	2,535,096	2,864,795	2,746,802	2,307,360	2,036,116
C:										
(1)	19,146,472	21,769,194		22,814,000	23,827,000	41,839,000*	42,637,000*	44,661,000*	48,431,000*	51,822,000*
(2)	3,649,607	4,189,720	4,906,586	5,836,128	6,133,722	6,841,772	7,850,803	8,656,774	9,637,797	11,277,404
(3)	599,750	631,621	749,842	785,316	909,713	968,886	1,068,085	1,087,206	811,959	790,145
SUB TOTAL C	23,395,829	26,590,535		29,435,444	30,870,435	49,649,658	51,555,888	54,404,980	58,880,756	63,889,549

Notes to Appendix 2

1 Government labour bureaux and the Department of Labour were also to some extent involved in assigning coloured and Asian proletarians to places in the relations of production. It is impossible to disaggregate the cost of the various departments' activities in connection with whites from those concerned with coloureds and Asians. However for most of the period, activities concerned with coloureds and Asians were very much peripheral to the department's main activities concerned with whites.

2 The figures for 1917–18 and 1919–20 did not, unlike the figures for the years before or since, include administration costs. They are not therefore strictly comparable with figures for earlier or later years.

3 During the later Pact period this calculation was discontinued as it no longer met the ideological requirements of the time.

4 Assigned here instead of to B (3) below because in this particular year the expenditure was in connection with employing whites rather than blacks in certain activities of the Department of Lands.

5 Commissions, conferences etc. in connection with the development of an 'industrial relations' system' etc. (Not the cost of administering Martial Law.)

6 1933–4 to 1939–40, the Defence Department's share of the cost of the Special Service and Pioneer Battalions. After 1940 the battalions' function changed and they became more directly associated with the activities of the repressive apparatus.

7 The cost of the Directorate of Demobilisation whose function was to allocate ex-soldiers to places in the division of labour.

8 Prior to World War II, without doubt, provincial 'poor relief' was mainly concerned with providing 'relief work' for 'poor whites'. However, the provinces also provided rations etc. to certain categories of destitute blacks. Once again it is not possible to disaggregate expenditure on whites from that on blacks. 'Poor relief' handled by the Department of Social Welfare (from 1938–39 onwards) is however excluded (as is the expenditure of the Department as a whole), because that Department was mainly involved with the sick, disabled, etc. and not mainly with providing 'relief works' for the unemployed, etc. The Department of Social Welfare was thus only peripherally involved in class formation.

9 The whole of the Land and Settlements expenditure from Revenue funds.

10 The expenditure of the Department of Lands and Settlements out of land funds, less expenditure on 'loan for public purposes' and land purchased

for African 'locations' etc. (The latter two items usually being less than 10 per cent of the total expenditure.)

11 The large increases in this item from 1949–50 until at least 1951–52 (and probably later) are due in the main to the 'purchase' of certain 'released land' from the Department of Native Affairs i.e. a proportion at least is an 'accounting' rather than a 'real' increase.

12 Emergency expenditure to prevent whites leaving the land; does not include the general subsidisation of agricultural capital.

13 A scheme to assign ex-soldiers to places as landowners.

14 1910–11—1915–16 includes the cost of black education: 1955–56 onwards the total provincial expenditure on education (i.e. coloured and Asians as well).

15 1921–22 onwards includes expenditure on reformatories.

Bibliography

I. Published Primary Sources

1. Official Commissions of Inquiry (Reports and Evidence)

'Cape of Good Hope Labour Commission: Minutes of Evidence and Minutes of Proceedings' (Cape Town, 1893, G 39, 1893).

'Reports of the Transvaal Labour Commission' (London, 1904, cd. 1897, 1904).

'Minutes of Proceedings Transvaal Labour Commission' (London, 1904, cd. 1896, 1904).

'Report of the Transvaal Mining Industry Commission' (Pretoria, 1908 TG 1, 1908).

'Minutes of Evidence: Transvaal Mining Industry Commission' (Pretoria, 1908, TG 2, 1908).

'Report of the Transvaal Indigency Commission' (Pretoria, 1908, TG 13, 1908).

'Evidence to the Transvaal Indigency Commission' (Pretoria, 1908, TG 11, 1908).

'Report of the Transvaal Mining Regulations Commission' (Pretoria, 1910).

'Report of the Commission Appointed to Inquire into the Conditions of Trade and Industries' (Pretoria, 1912, UG 10, 1912).

'Final Report of a Commission Appointed to Inquire into the Grievances of Railways and Harbours Staff' (Pretoria, 1912).

'Report of the Witwatersrand Disturbances Commission' (London, 1913, cd. 7112, 1913).

'Minutes of Evidence to Judicial Commission of Inquiry into Witwatersrand Disturbances June–July 1913' (Pretoria, 1913, UG 56, 1913).

'Reports and Minutes of Evidence to Select Committee of the House of Assembly on European Employment and Labour Conditions' (Cape Town, 1913, SC 9, 1913).

'Minutes of Evidence to Royal Commission on the Natural Resources, Trade and Legislation of Certain Portions of His Majesty's Dominions' (London, 1914, cd. 7706, 1914).

'Report of the Select Committee on the Industrial Disputes and Trades Union Bills' (Cape Town, 1914, SC 10, 1914).

'Report of the Economic Commission' (Pretoria, 1914, UG 12, 1914).

'Report of the Native Grievances Inquiry' (Pretoria, 1914, UG 37, 1914).

'Supplement to the Report of the General Manager of South African Railways for the year ended 31st December 1913, Evidence to Commission of Inquiry into Grievances of Railway Servants' (Pretoria, 1914, UG 46, 1914).

'Report of the Select Committee into the Causes and Circumstances relating to the Recent Rebellion' (Cape Town, 1915, SC 1, 1915).

'Judicial Commission of Inquiry into the Causes and Circumstances relating to the Recent Rebellion in South Africa: Minutes of Evidence' (Pretoria, 1916, UG 42, 1916).

'Report of the Judicial Commission of Inquiry into the Causes and Circumstances relating to the Recent Rebellion in South Africa' (Pretoria, 1916, UG 46, 1916).

'Report of the Special Commissioner Appointed to Inquire into the cost of Living in the Union' (Pretoria, 1916, UG 39, 1916).

'Report of the Select Committee on Drought Distress Relief' (Cape Town, 1916, SC 3, 1916).

'Report of the Commission on Industrial Education' (Pretoria, 1917, UG 9, 1917).

'Report and Minutes of Evidence of the State Mining Commission' (Cape Town, 1917, UG 19, 1917).

'Report of the Railway Commission of Inquiry' (Pretoria, 1917, UG 14, 1917).

'Cost of Living Commission Profits Report' (Pretoria, 1919, UG 1, 1919).

'Report of the Select Committee on the Cost of Living Commission (Profits) Report' (Cape Town, 1919, SC 1, 1919).

'Interim Report of the Low Grades Mines Commission' (Pretoria, 1919, UG 45, 1919).

'Preliminary Report of the Karkamas Commission of Inquiry' (Pretoria, 1919, UG 55, 1919).

'Interim Report of the Cost of Living Commission' (Pretoria, 1920, UG 26, 1920).

'Interim Report of the Unemployment Commission' (Pretoria, 1921, UG 16, 1921).

First—Third 'Reports of the Select Committee on the Subject Matter of the Apprenticeship Bill and the Regulation of Wages Bill (to which was also referred the Juvenile Affairs Bill)' (Cape Town, 1921, SC 9, 1921).

'Report of the Unemployment Commission' (Pretoria, 1922, UG 17, 1922).

'Report of the Martial Law Judicial Commission' (Pretoria, 1922, UG 35, 1922).

'Report of the Mining Industry Board' (Pretoria, 1922, UG 39, 1922).

'Report of the Select Committee on the Industrial Conciliation Bill' (Cape Town, 1923, SC 5, 1923).

'Report of the Mining Regulations Commission' (Cape Town, 1925, UG 47, 1925).

'Report of the Select Committee on the Wage Bill' (Cape Town, 1925, SC 14, 1925).

'Reports of the Economic and Wages Commission' (Pretoria, 1926, UG 14, 1926).

'Report of the Interdepartmental Committee on Labour Resources' (Pretoria, 1930).

'Report of the Unemployment Investigation Committee' (Pretoria, 1932, UG 30, 1932).

'Report of the Natives Economic Commission' (Pretoria, 1932, UG 22, 1932).

'Report of the Industrial Legislation Commission' (Pretoria, 1935, UG 37, 1935).

'Report of the Select Committee on the Industrial Conciliation and Wages Bill' (Cape Town, 1937, SC 5, 1937).

'Department of Social Welfare: Memorandum on Poor Relief' (Pretoria, 1940).

'Third Interim Report of the Agricultural and Industrial Requirements Commission' (Pretoria, 1941, UG 40, 1941).

'Social and Economic Planning Council: Report no. 1 on Re-employment' (Pretoria, 1943, UG 9, 1943).

'Social and Economic Planning Council Report no. 2: Summary of the Social Security Scheme' (Pretoria, 1944).

'Report of the Chairman of the Interdepartmental Committee on Social Security' (Pretoria, 1945).

'Report of the Commission of Inquiry: Karkamas Labour Colony' (Pretoria, 1945, UG 14, 1945).

'Board of Trade and Industries: Investigation into Manufacturing Industries in the Union of South Africa (first interim report no. 282)' (Pretoria, 1945).

'Report of the Mine Workers Union Commission of Enquiry' (Pretoria, 1946, UG 36, 1946).

'Report of the Committee Appointed to Investigate the Employment of Un-skilled Workers in Railway Service' (Pretoria, 1947, UG 29, 1947).

'Reports of the Commission of Inquiry into the Operation of the Unemploy-ment Insurance Act 1946' (Pretoria, 1949, UG 12, 1949).

'Report of the Garment Workers Union Commission of Enquiry 1948/9' (Pre-toria, 1950, UG 16, 1950).

First–sixth 'Reports of the Commission of Inquiry into the Grievances of Rail-way Servants' (Pretoria, 1950: UG 9, 1950; UG 41, 1950; UG 42, 1950; Pretoria, 1952: UG 54, 1952; UG 58, 1952).

'Report of the Mineworkers Union Commission of Enquiry (Pretoria, 1951' UG 52, 1951).

'Report of the Industrial Legislation Commission of Enquiry' (Pretoria, 1951, UG 62, 1951).

'Report of the Mineworkers Union Commission of Enquiry' (Pretoria, 1953).

'Report, Proceedings and Minutes of Evidence to the Select Committee on the Industrial Conciliation Bill' (Cape Town, 1955, SC 3, 1955).

2. Annual Reports and Publications of Government Departments

Department of Mines and Industries:
   'Annual Reports of the Government Mining Engineer' (Pretoria 1901–2—1926).
   'Administrative Report of the Inspector of White Labour for the Year ended 30th June 1909' (Pretoria, 1909, TG 47, 1909).
   'Annual Reports of Labour' (later 'Factories and Labour Division') (Pretoria 1910–1913; 1919–1922).
   'The South African Journal of Industries' (Pretoria, 1918–1925).
Board of Trade and Industries:
   'Commercial and Industrial Gazette' (Pretoria, 1926–1931).
Department of Labour:
   'The Official Labour Gazette' (Pretoria, April–December 1925).
   'The Social and Industrial Review' (Pretoria, January 1926–March 1930).
   'The Labour Gazette' to September 1930.
   'Report to the Hon. the Minister of Labour by the Wage Board upon the Work of the Wage Board for the Three Years ended 28.2.29' (Pretoria, 1929).
   'Report to the Hon. the Minister of Labour by the Wage Board upon the

Work of the Wage Board for the Period 1st March 1929 to 31st December 1931' (duplicated copy ex Dept. of Labour in British Library of Political and Economic Science, London).

'Social and Industrial Review (special editions on Wage Board Determinations)' (Pretoria, 1926–1928).

'Annual Reports of the Department of Labour' (Pretoria, 1932–1941; 1944–1960).

'The Special Service Battalion: A Review of its Activities and Functions' (Pretoria, 1938).

'Work Reservation . . . its background, motivation and application to the benefit of all racial groups in South Africa' (Pretoria, 1961).

Department of Lands:

'Annual Reports' (Pretoria, 1912–1914; 1919–1925; 1948–1952).

South African Railways:

'Annual Reports of the General Manager of South African Railways and Harbours' (Pretoria, 1910–11—1959–60).

'Reports of the Railways and Harbours Board' (Pretoria, 1920–1939).

'Report in Connection with the Poor White Problem by the Labour Superintendent of South African Railways and Harbours' (Pretoria, 1917, An 490, 1917).

Controller and Auditor General:

'Annual Reports on Appropriation Accounts, Finance Accounts and Miscellaneous Accounts' (Pretoria, 1910–11—1959–60).

'Annual Reports on Railway Accounts' (Pretoria, 1918–19—1959–60).

Bureau of Census and Statistics:

'Population Censuses' 1918, 1926, 1936, 1946, 1960, 1970.

'Industrial Censuses' 1915–16—1939–9.

'Union Statistics for Fifty Years, Jubilee Issue 1910–1960'.

3. Parliamentary Debates

House of Commons, London, Hansard (vol. CI, 1902–vol. 192, 1908)—debates concerning labour policy in the Transvaal.

'House of Assembly Debates' (Cape Town, 1910–1915).

'House of Assembly Debates as Reported in the *Cape Times*' (Cape Town, 1915–1925).

'House of Assembly Debates' (Cape Town, 1925–1960).

4. Laws and Statutes

'De Locale Wetten en Volksraad Besluiten de Zuid Afrikaansche Republick' (Pretoria, 1899).

'Transvaal Ordinances' (Pretoria, 1909).

'Industrial Disputes Prevention Bill 1914' (roneoed copy in British Library, London).

'The Industrial Conciliation Act no. 11 of 1924 as amended by Act no. 24 of 1930 and Act no. 7 of 1933' compiled by M. Schaeffer (Juta, Cape Town, 1934).

'The Wage Act of 1925 as amended by Act no. 23 of 1930 together with the regulations and the Wage Determinations Validation Act 1930 and the Wage Determinations Validation Act 1935' compiled by M. Schaeffer (Juta, Cape Town, 1933).

'The Industrial Conciliation Act no. 36 of 1937 together with the Regulations' compiled by M. Schaeffer (Juta, Cape Town 1949).

'Industrial Laws of South Africa' compiled by A. de Kock (Juta, Cape Town, 1973).

Butterworth's 'Statutes of South Africa'.

5. Miscellaneous Government Publications

'Consular Report on Trade, Commerce and the Goldmining Industry of the South African Republic for the Year 1897' (London, 1898, C 9093, 1898).

'Papers Relating to Complaints of British Subjects in the South African Republic' (London, 1899, C 9345, 1899).

'Papers Relating to Certain Legislation of the late South African Republic affecting Natives' (London, 1901, C 714, 1901).

'Papers Relating to the Progress of Administration in the Transvaal' (London, 1903, cd. 1551, 1903).

'Correspondence Relating to Affairs in the Transvaal and Orange River Colonies' (London, 1902–1906, cd. 1894, 1945, 2025, 2183, 2401, 2786, 2788, 2819, 3025).

'Report to the Board of Trade on the Industrial Disputes Act of Canada 1907 by Sir Geo. Askwith, Chief Trade Commissioner' (London, 1913, cd. 6603, 1912–13).

'Interim Report on Joint Standing Industrial Councils' (London, 1917, cd. 8606, 1917).

'Department of Overseas Trade: Report on the Economic Conditions in South Africa by H.M. Senior Trade Commissioner in South Africa' (London, 1923–1933).

'Official Yearbooks' (Pretoria, 1910–1949).

'Minutes of Evidence before the Trade and Industry Subcommittee of the House of Commons into Wages and Conditions of African workers employed by British Firms in South Africa' (4 vols. London, 1973–4).

6. Publications and Journals of other bodies

'Die Blanke Werker' journal of Blanke Werkers se Beskermingsbond (1947).

'The Bolshevik', official organ of the International Socialist League of South Africa (Cape Town, 1919–1921).

'The Call', organ of the League of Soldiers and Sailors (Johannesburg, 1919–1921).

Carnegie Commission: 'Report of the Commission on the Poor White Problem in South Africa' (5 vols., Stellenbosch, 1932).

Dutch Reformed Church Armesorgraad: 'Report of the National Conference on the Poor White Problem' (Cape Town, 1934).

'Forward: the Paper that Supports the Pact' (Johannesburg, 1924–1931).

'Freedom/Vryheid', organ of the Central Committee of the Communist Party 1942–1949.

'The Forum' 1938–1947.

'The Garment Worker', journal of the Garment Workers Union (Johannesburg, 1945–1953).

'Industrial South Africa' 1923–1925 (succeeded by 'Industrial and Commercial South Africa' 1925–1939; succeeded by 'South African Industry and Trade' 1939–1945; succeeded by 'South African Industry and Trade (Industrial Section)' 1945–1960).

Johannesburg Chamber of Trade: 'Open Letter to British Workmen' (London, 31.3.1906).

South African Federated Chambers of Industries: 'Annual Reports' 1924–1961.

Nationalist Party: *The Road to a New South Africa* (Nasionale Pers, Cape Town, 1948).

'South African Labour World' (Johannesburg, 1918–1920).

South African Trades and Labour Council: *The Trade Union Movement in South Africa* (Johannesburg, 1939).

'The South African Worker', organ of the Communist Party of South Africa 1926–1930. (Succeeded by 'Umsebenzi—The South African Worker', 1930–1938; succeeded by 'Inkululeko—Freedom', 1943–1948).

Transvaal Chamber of Mines:

    'Annual Reports' (Johannesburg 1911–1956).

    'Statements Presented to the Economic Commission' (Johannesburg, 1913).

    'Reports of Boards of Reference 1917–1919' (Johannesburg, 1920).

    'The Wage Position on the South African Goldmines' (Johannesburg, 1926).

    'Mining Industry Arbitration Board 1926–1927' (Johannesburg, 1927).

7. Published Writings and Papers of Contemporaries

W. H. Andrews, *Class Struggles in South Africa* (Stewart, Cape Town, 1941).

F. H. P. Cresswell, *The Chinese Question from Within* (London, 1905).

C. Headlam, ed., *The Milner Papers*, 2 vols. (Cassell, London, 1931 and 1932).

C. Kadalie, *My Life and the ICU* (ed. S. Trapido, F. Cass, London, 1973).

S. J. P. Kruger, *The Memoirs of Paul Kruger, Four Times President of the South African Republic, Told by Himself* (T. Fisher Unwin, London, 1902).

L. Phillips, *Some Reminiscences* (Hutchinson, London, 1926).

S. van der Poel, ed., *Selections from the Smuts Papers*, 6 vols. (Cambridge University Press, 1966–1973).

8. Newspapers

Transvaal Leader Johannesburg.

Cape Times Cape Town.

Rand Daily Mail Johannesburg.

Star Johannesburg.

The Times London.

Financial Mail Johannesburg.

Guardian London.

II. Unpublished Primary Sources

1. Government Papers

'Colonial Office Correspondence' and 'Colonial Office Confidential Print', Public
Record Office, London: Files no. CO 529, 1902/3; CO 417, 1903; CO 389,
1903; CO 879/113, 1913; CO 879/115, 1914; CO 551/149, 1922; CO 551/
150, 1922; CO 551/151, 1922.

2. Papers of Other Organisations and Individuals

South African Federated Chambers of Industries: photostat copies of selected
memoranda and correspondence 1950–1959 made available to me by Dave
Kaplan and Mike Morris, to whom I am grateful.
South African Mining Unions Papers: 'A Selection of Papers of the Unions in the
South African Mining Industry 1919–1960' (microfilms by Microfile Ltd.,
Johannesburg).
South African Railways Chief Engineer: 'Address on Employment of Unskilled
Whites to White Expansion Society 1910' (duplicated copy ex Duncan Papers,
made available by Martin Legassick to whom my thanks are due).
Transvaal Chamber of Mines: microfilm copy of 'Chinese Labour South African
Mines File 12 1902' kindly made available by Peter Richardson.
Photostat copies of selected correspondence from the Cresswell, Duncan and
Merriman Papers, again made available by Martin Legassick.

III. Select Bibliography of Theoretical Literature

H. Alavi, 'The State in Post Colonial Societies—Pakistan and Bangladesh' (*New
Left Review*, no. 74, July/August 1972).
L. Althusser, *For Marx* (Allen Lane, London, 1969).
L. Althusser, *Lenin and Philosophy and Other Essays* (New Left Books, London,
1971).
L. Althusser and E. Balibar, *Reading Capital* (New Left Books, London, 1970).
E. Altvater, 'Reproduction Conditions of the Capitalist Relation and the Bour-
geois State' (*Bulletin of the Conference of Socialist Economists*, no. 13,
1976).

C. H. Anderson, *The Political Economy of Social Class* (Prentice Hall, Englewood Cliffs, 1974).

C. Bettleheim and P. Sweezy, *On the Transition to Socialism* (Monthly Review Press, New York, 1971).

H. Braverman, *Labor and Monopoly Capital* (Monthly Review Press, New York, 1974).

Brighton Labour Process Group, 'The Production Process of Capital and the Capitalist Labour Process' (paper delivered to Conference of Socialist Economists, July 1976).

P. Bullock, 'Defining Productive Labour for Capital' (*Bulletin of the Conference of Socialist Economists*, Autumn 1974).

G. Carchedi, 'On the Economic Identification of the New Middle Class' (*Economy and Society*, vol. 4 no. 1, 1975).

G. Carchedi, 'Reproduction of Social Classes at the Level of Production Relations' (*Economy and Society*, vol. 4 no. 4, 1975).

G. Carchedi, 'The Economic Identification of State Employees' (*Social Praxis*, vol. 3 (1—2), 1976).

M. Dobb, *Political Economy and Capitalism* (Routledge, London, 1940).

F. Engels, *The Condition of the Working Class in England* (including 1892 Preface on the 'labour aristocracy') (Blackwell, Oxford, 1958).

A. Giddens, *The Class Structure of Advanced Societies* (Cambridge University Press, 1973).

A. Gorz, 'Technical Intelligence and the Capitalist Division of Labour' (*Telos*, no. 12, 1972).

I. Gough, 'Marx's Theory of Productive and Unproductive Labour' (*New Left Review*, no. 76, 1972).

I. Gough, 'State Expenditure and Capital' (*New Left Review*, no. 92, 1976).

A. Gramsci, *Selections from the Prison Notebooks* (Lawrence and Wishart, London, 1973).

B. Hindess and P. Hirst, *Pre-Capitalist Modes of Production* (Routledge, London, 1975).

J. Hirsch, 'The State Apparatus and Social Reproduction: Elements of a Theory of the Bourgeois State' (mimeo, 1977).

P. Hirst, 'Economic Classes and Politics' (paper delivered to British Sociology Association Conference, 1977).

E. Hobsbawn, *Labouring Men: Studies in the History of Labour* (Weidenfeld, London, 1968).

P. Howell, 'Once Again on Productive and Unproductive Labour' (*Revolutionary Communist*, no. 3–4, 1976).

E. Laclau, 'Feudalism and Capitalism in Latin America' (*New Left Review*, no. 67, 1970).

E. Laclau, 'The Specificity of the Political' (*Economy and Society*, vol. 4 no. 1, 1975).

V. I. Lenin, *British Labour and British Imperialism: A Compilation of Writings by Lenin on Britain* (Lawrence and Wishart, London, 1969).

V. I. Lenin, *Imperialism and the Split in Socialism* (collected works, vol. xix, Moscow, 1964).

V. I. Lenin, *Imperialism the Highest Stage of Capitalism* (collected works, vol. xix, Moscow, 1964).

E. Mandel, *Marxist Economic Theory* (2 vols, Merlin Press, London, 1968).

E. Mandel, *Late Capitalism* (New Left Books, London, 1975).

K. Marx, *Capital: A Critical Analysis of Capitalist Production* vol. I and III (Lawrence and Wishart, London, 1974).

K. Marx, *The Grundrisse* (Penguin, Harmondsworth, 1973).

K. Marx, *The Eighteenth Brumaire of Louis Bonaparte* reprinted in *Marx Surveys from Exile: Political Writings, vol. 2* (Allen Lane, London, 1973).

K. Marx, *Theories of Surplus Value* vol. 1–3 (Lawrence and Wishart, London, 1969–1972).

K. Marx, *Theories of Surplus Value* (selection edited by K. Kautsky, Lawrence and Wishart, London, 1951).

R. Miliband, 'Poulantzas and the Capitalist State' (*New Left Review*, no. 82, 1973).

M. Nicolaus, 'Proletariat and Middle Class in Marx: Hegelian Choreography and the Capitalist Dialectic' (*Studies on the Left*, vol. 7, 1976).

S. Piciotto and J. Holloway, 'Capital, the State and European Integration' (mimeo, 1976).

S. Piciotto and J. Holloway, 'Towards a Materialist Theory of the State' (mimeo, 1977).

N. Poulantzas, *Political Power and Social Classes* (New Left Books, London, 1973).

N. Poulantzas, *Fascism and Dictatorship* (New Left Books, London, 1974).

N. Poulantzas, *Classes in Contemporary Capitalism* (New Left Books, London, 1975).

N. Poulantzas, *The Crisis of the Dictatorships: Portugal, Greece and Spain* (New Left Books, London, 1976).

N. Poulantzas, 'On Social Classes' (*New Left Review*, no. 78, 1972).

N. Poulantzas, 'The Capitalist State: A Reply to Miliband and Laclau' (*New Left Review*, no. 95, 1976).

A. Sohn Rethal, 'The Dual Economics of Transition' (*Bulletin of the Conference of Socialist Economists*, Autumn 1972).

IV. Select Bibliography of Secondary Sources on South Africa and Comparative Material

T. Adler, 'Class Struggle in Doornfontein: The History of the Jewish Workers Club 1928–1950' (mimeo, 1976).

A. Aiken, *The Cost of Living in Johannesburg* (British and South African Association, London, 1907).

G. Arrighi and J. Saul, *Essays on the Political Economy of Africa* (Monthly Review Press, New York, 1973).

H. A. F. Barker, 'The Clothing Industry in South Africa' (*South African Journal of Economics*—hereafter SAJE—vol. 29, 1961).

M. A. Bieneveld and D. Innes, 'Capital Accumulation and South Africa' (*Review of African Political Economy*—hereafter RAPE—no. 7, 1977).

J. Bisset, *James William Jagger and the South African Railways 1921–1924* (University of Cape Town Honours dissertation, 1973).

B. Bozzoli, *The Roots of Hegemony: Ideologies, Interests and the Ligitimation of South African Capitalism 1890–1940* (University of Sussex D.Phil. thesis 1975).

E. Brookes, *The Colour Problem in South Africa* (Lovedale Press, Lovedale, 1932).

C. Bundy, 'The Rise and Decline of an African Peasantry' (*African Affairs*, vol. 71, no. 258, 1972).

B. Bunting, *The Rise of the South African Reich* (Penguin, Harmondsworth, 1964).

G. Clack, *The Changing Structure of Industrial Relations in South Africa with special reference to Racial Factors and Social Movements* (London University Ph.D. thesis, 1962).

V. S. Clark, *The Labour Movement in Australasia: A Study in Social Democracy* (Constable, London, 1906).

D. G. Clarke, 'Foreign Migrant Labour in South Africa: Studies on Accumulation in the Labour Reserves, Demand Determinants and Supply Relationships'

(World Employment Programme Working Paper, International Labour Organisation, Geneva, 1977).

R. K. Cope, *Comrade Bill: the Life and Times of W. H. Andrews Workers' Leader* (Stewart, Cape Town, 1940?).

M. Cresswell, *An Epoch of the Political History of South Africa in the Life of Frederick Hugh Page Cresswell* (Balkema, Cape Town, 1956).

F. J. C. Cronje, 'The Textile Industry in the Union of South Africa' (SAJE, vol. 20, 1952).

R. Davies, 'The White Working Class in South Africa' (*New Left Review*, no. 82, 1973).

R. Davies, 'The Class Character of South Africa's Industrial Conciliation Legislation' (*South African Labour Bulletin*—hereafter SALB—vol. 2 no. 6, January 1976).

R. Davies, 'Mining Capital, the State and Unskilled White Workers in South Africa 1901—1913' (*Journal of Southern African Studies*—hereafter JSAS —vol. 3 no. 1, 1976).

R. Davies and D. Lewis, 'Industrial Relations Legislation: One of Capital's Defences' (RAPE, no. 7, 1977).

R. Davies, D. Kaplan, M. Morris and D. O'Meara, 'Class Struggle and a Periodisation of the South African State' (RAPE, no. 7, 1977).

D. J. N. Denoon, 'The Transvaal Labour Crisis 1901—1906' (*Journal of African History*, vol. 8, 1967).

D. J. N. Denoon, ' "Capitalist Influence" and the Transvaal Government during the Crown Colony Period' (*Historical Journal*, vol. xi no. 2, 1968).

D. J. N. Denoon, *A Grand Illusion: the Failure of Imperial Policy in the Transvaal Crown Colony during the period of Reconstruction 1900–1905* (Longman, London, 1973).

G. V. Doxey, *The Industrial Colour Bar in South Africa* (Oxford University Press, Cape Town, 1961).

L. Ensor, 'TUCSA's Relationship with African Trades Unions—An Attempt at Control—1954–1962' (SALB, vol. 3 no. 4, Jan.–Feb. 1977).

W. Finlay, *South Africa: Capitalist Agriculture and the State* (University of Cape Town Honours thesis, 1976).

R. First, J. Steele and C. Gurney, *The South African Connection* (Penguin, Harmondsworth, 1973).

S. H. Frankel, *Capital Investment in Africa: Its Course and Effects* (Oxford University Press, London, 1938).

S. H. Frankel and H. Herzfield, 'An Analysis of the Growth of the National

Income of the Union in the Period of Prosperity before the War' (SAJE vol. 11, 1943).

M. Fransman, 'A discussion of some issues related to the South African Social Formation' (University of Sussex seminar paper, 1975).

M. Fransman, 'Theoretical Questions in the Understanding of South Africa' (*Marxistisk Anthropologi*, vol. 2, 1976).

M. Fransman and R. Davies, 'The South African Social Formation in the early period circa 1880–1930: Some views on the Question of Hegemony' (University of Sussex seminar paper, 1975, reproduced in T. Adler, ed., *Perspectives on South Africa*, African Studies Institute, University of the Witwatersrand, 1977).

M. Fransman and D. Kaplan, 'Some Thoughts on the Value of Labour Power and "Archaic" Surplus Value in the Analysis of South Africa' (mimeo, 1976).

E. Gitsham and J. F. Trembath, *A First Account of Labour Organization in South Africa* (Durban, 1926).

R. Goldsmith and C. Saunders, ed., *The Measurement of National Wealth* (*Income and Wealth Series VIII*, Bowes and Bowes, London, 1959).

T. Gregory, *Ernest Oppenheimer and the Economic Development of Southern Africa* (Oxford University Press, Cape Town, 1962).

W. K. Hancock, *Smuts—The Fields of Force 1919–1950* (Cambridge 1968).

D. Hemson, 'Dock Workers, Labour Circulation and Class Struggles in Durban 1940–1959' (Institute of Commonwealth Studies—hereafter ICS—seminar paper, 1976).

A. Hepple, *Trade Unions in Travail—The Story of the Broederbond Nationalist Plan to Control South African Trade Unions* (Unity Publications, Johannesburg, 1954).

N. Herd, *1922 The Revolt on the Rand* (Blue Crane, Johannesburg, 1966).

B. Hirson, 'The Reorganization of African Trades Unions in Johannesburg 1936–1942' (ICS seminar paper, 1976).

D. Hobart Houghton, *The South African Economy* (Oxford University Press, Cape Town, 1964 and 1976 editions).

D. Hobart Houghton and J. Dagut, *Source Material of the South African Economy 1860–1970* (3 vols, Oxford University Press, Cape Town, 1970–1973).

R. Horwitz, *The Political Economy of South Africa* (Weidenfeld, London, 1967).

D. Humphris and D. Thomas, *Benoni: Son of My Sorrow* (Benoni, 1968).

W. H. Hutt, *The Economics of the Colour Bar* (Deutsch, London, 1964).

'Indicus', *Labour and Other Questions in South Africa Being Mainly Considera-*

tions on the Rational and Profitable Use of the Coloured Races Living There* (1903 reprinted New York, 1969).

D. Innes, 'Accumulation and Expansion in the South African Gold Mining Industry 1945–1960' (University of Sussex seminar paper, 1976).

D. Innes, 'The Mining Industry in the Context of South Africa's Economic Development' (ICS seminar paper, 1976).

A. H. Jeeves, 'The Administration and Control of Migratory Labour in the South African Goldmines: Capitalism and the State in the Era of Milner' (JSAS, vol. 2, no. 1, October 1975).

F. A. Johnstone, 'Class Conflict and Colour Bars in the South African Gold-mining Industry 1910–1926' (ICS seminar paper, 1970).

F. A. Johnstone, 'White Prosperity and White Supremacy in South Africa Today' (*African Affairs*, vol. 69, 1970).

F. A. Johnstone, *Class and Race Relations in the South African Gold Mining Industry* (Oxford University D.Phil. Thesis, 1972).

F. A. Johnstone, *Class, Race and Gold: A Study of Class Relations and Racial Discrimination in South Africa* (Routledge, London, 1976).

E. Kahn, 'The Right to Strike in South Africa—An Historical Analysis' (SAJE, vol. 11, 1943).

B. S. Kantor and H. F. Kenny, *The Poverty of Neo-Marxism: the Case of South Africa* (JSAS, vol. 3, no. 1, Oct. 1976).

D. E. Kaplan, 'Capitalist Development in South Africa: Class Conflict and the State' (University of Sussex IDS Internal Working Paper no. 20, 1974, reprinted in Adler, *op. cit.*).

D. E. Kaplan, 'An Analysis of the South African State in the "Fusion" Period 1932–1939' (ICS seminar paper, 1976).

D. E. Kaplan, 'The Politics of Industrial Protection in South Africa' (JSAS, vol. 3 no. 1, 1976).

D. E. Kaplan, *Class Conflict, Capital Accumulation and the State: An Historical Analysis of the State in Twentieth Century South Africa* (University of Sussex, D.Phil. thesis, 1977).

E. Katz, 'White Workers Grievances and the Industrial Colour Bar' (SAJE, vol. 42, 1974).

A. Leftwich, ed., *South Africa: Economic Growth and Political Change* (London, 1974).

M. Legassick, 'The Making of South African "Native Policy" 1903–1923: The Origins of "Segregation" ' (ICS seminar paper, 1973).

M. Legassick, 'The Rise of Modern South African Liberalism: Its Assumptions and its Social Base' (University of Sussex seminar paper, 1974).

M. Legassick, 'South Africa: Capital Accumulation and Violence' (*Economy and Society*, vol. 3 no. 3, 1974).

M. Legassick, 'Legislation, Ideology and Economy in Post 1948 South Africa' (JSAS, vol. 1, no. 1, 1974).

M. Legassick, 'The Analysis of Racism in South Africa: the Case of the Mining Industry' (IDEP/UN seminar paper, Dar es Salaam, 1975).

M. Legassick and D. Hemson, *Foreign Investment and the Reproduction of Racial Capitalism in South Africa* (Anti-Apartheid Movement, booklet, 1976).

A. Lerumo, *Fifty Fighting Years* (Inkululeko Publications, London, 1971).

D. Lewis, 'The South African State and African Trade Unions 1947–1953' (mimeo, 1976).

J. Lewis, 'Solly Sachs and the Garment Workers Union' (SALB, vol. 3 no. 3, October 1976).

W. M. MacMillan, *The South African Agrarian Problem and its Historical Development* (C.N.A., Witwatersrand, 1919).

J. S. Marais, *The Fall of Kruger's Republic* (Oxford University Press, London, 1961).

A. A. Mawby, 'Capital, Government and Politics in the Transvaal 1900–1907: A Revision and a Reversion' (*Historical Journal*, vol. 17, 1974).

J. X. Merriman, *Selections from the Correspondence of J. X. Merriman* ed. P. Lewsen (3 vols, Cape Town, 1960, 1963, 1966).

F. Meyer, 'The Development of the Iron and Steel Industry in South Africa' (SAJE, vol. 20, 1952).

F. Molteno, 'The Historical Significance of the Bantustan Strategy' (paper presented to Congress of the Association for Sociology in Southern Africa, Swaziland, 1977).

M. Morris, 'Capitalism and Apartheid: A Critique of Some Current Conceptions of Cheap Labour Power' (paper delivered to Oxford conference, 1974, reprinted in Adler, *op. cit.*).

M. Morris, 'Periodisation, Class Struggle and the State' (paper presented to Nordic Political Science Conference, 1975).

M. Morris, 'The Development of Capitalism in South African Agriculture: Class Struggle in the Countryside' (*Economy and Society*, vol. 3 no. 3, 1976).

M. Morris, 'Apartheid, Agriculture and the State' (South African Labour and Development Research Unit Paper, Cape Town, 1977).

M. Morris and D. Kaplan, 'Labour Policy in a State Corporation: a Case Study of the South African Iron and Steel Industry' (2 parts: SALB, vol. 2 no. 6; vol. 2 no. 7, 1976).

L. Naude, *Dr. A. Hertzog, Die Nasionale Party en die Mynwerkers* (Nasionale Raad van Trustees, Pretoria, 1969).

A. J. Norval, *A Quarter of a Century of Industrial Progress in South Africa* (Juta, Cape Town, 1962).

D. O'Meara, 'The 1946 African Miners Strike and the Political Economy of South Africa' (*Journal of Commonwealth and Comparative Politics*, July 1975).

D. O'Meara, 'White Trade Unions, Political Power and Afrikaner Nationalism' (SALB, vol. 1 no. 10, 1975).

D. O'Meara, 'The Afrikaner Broderbond: Class Vanguard of Afrikaner Nationalism' (ICS seminar paper, 1975).

D. O'Meara, ' "Christian National" Trade Unionism in South Africa 1934–1948' (paper delivered to University of Witwatersrand Conference on Labour History, 1976).

G. F. D. Palmer, 'Some Aspects of the Development of Secondary Industry in South Africa since the Depression of 1929–1932' (SAJE, vol. 22, 1954).

A. Paton, *Hofmeyr* (Oxford University Press, Cape Town, 1964).

M. J. Piercy, 'Statutory Job Reservation—Requirement of a Static or of an Expanding Economy' (SAJE, vol. 28, 1960).

M. J. Piercy, 'Statutory Work Reservation in the Union of South Africa' (SAJE, vol. 28, 1960).

D. E. Pursell, 'Bantu Real Wages and Employment Opportunities' (SAJE, vol. 36, 1968).

D. E. Pursell, 'The Impact of South African Wage Board Policy on Skilled/ Unskilled Wage Differentials' (*Eastern African Economic Review*, vol. 1, 1969).

D. E. Pursell, 'South African Labour Policy: "New Deal" for Non Whites?' (*Industrial Relations*, vol. 1, 1971).

M. T. Rankin, *Arbitration and Conciliation in Australasia* (G. Allen and Unwin, London, 1916).

J. W. Reedman, 'Report of the Industrial Legislation Commission—Review Article' (SAJE, vol. 4, 1936).

P. Richardson, 'Coolies and Randlords: The North Randfontein Chinese "Strike" of 1905' (JSAS, vol. 2 no. 2, 1976).

G. Routh, 'Industrial Relations in South Africa' (SAJE, vol. 20, 1952).

E. S. Sachs, *Rebel Daughters* (McGibbon, London, 1957).

E. S. Sachs, *The Choice Before South Africa* (London, 1953).

H. J. and R. E. Simons, *Class and Colour in South Africa 1850–1950* (Penguin, Harmondsworth, 1969).

H. Simson, 'Fascism in South Africa' (*African Review*, vol. 3 no. 3, 1973).

H. Simson, 'The Myth of the White Working Class in South Africa' (*African Review*, vol. 4 no. 2, 1974).

H. Simson, 'The Theory of Fascism and a Critique of Fascism in South Africa' (mimeo, 1975).

J. Slovo (with B. Davidson and A. Wilkinson), *Southern Africa: The New Politics of Revolution* (Penguin, Harmondsworth, 1976).

South African Institute of Race Relations, *Handbook on Race Relations* (Johannesburg, 1949).

South African Institute of Race Relations, *Annual Surveys of Race Relations in South Africa* (Johannesburg, 1950–1976).

A. Spandau, 'South African Wage Board Policy: An Alternative Interpretation' (SAJE, vol. 40, 1972).

The Steel and Engineering Industries Federation of South Africa *Organization and Structure of the Metal and Engineering Industries in the Republic of South Africa* (Johannesburg, nd).

W. F. J. Steenkamp, 'Bantu Wages in South Africa' (SAJE, vol. 30, 1962).

W. F. Thomas, ed., *Labour Perspectives on South Africa* (D. Phillip, Cape Town, 1974).

L. M. Thompson, *The Unification of South Africa 1902–1910* (Oxford University Press, 1960).

L. M. Thompson and J. Butler, ed., *Change in Contemporary South Africa* (University of California Press, 1975).

S. Trapido, 'South Africa in a Comparative Analysis of Industrialisation' (*Journal of Development Studies*, vol. 7, 1970–1).

S. T. van der Horst, *Native Labour in South Africa* (1942 reprinted F. Cass, London, 1971).

S. T. van der Horst, 'Some Effects of Industrial Legislation on the Market for Native Labour in South Africa' (SAJE, vol. 3, 1935).

C. van Onselen, 'Randlords and Rotgut, 1886–1903: an essay on the role of alcohol in the development of European Imperialism and Southern African Capitalism' (*History Workshop Journal*, 2, Autumn 1976).

I. L. Walker and B. Weinbren, *2000 Casualties—A History of Trade Unions and the Labour Movement in the Union of South Africa* (SATUC, Johannesburg, 1961).

M. Williams, 'An Analysis of South African Capitalism: Neo-Ricardianism or Marxism' (*Bulletin of the Conference of Socialist Economists*, February 1975).

F. Wilson, *Labour in the South African Goldmining Industry* (Cambridge University Press, 1969).

M. Wilson and L. Thompson, *The Oxford History of South Africa* 2 vols (Oxford University Press, London, 1968 and 1970).

H. Wolpe, 'Capitalism and Cheap Labour Power: From Segregation to Apartheid' (*Economy and Society*, vol. 1 no. 4, 1974).

H. Wolpe, 'The Theory of Internal Colonialism—the South African Case' (*Bulletin of the Conference of Socialist Economists*, Autumn, 1974).

H. Wolpe, 'Draft Notes on (a) Articulation of Modes of Production and the Value of Labour Power (b) Periodisation and the State' (University of Sussex, seminar paper, 1975).

H. Wolpe, 'The White Working Class in South Africa: Some Theoretical Problems' (IDEP/UN seminar paper, Dar es Salaam, 1975).

H. Wolpe, 'The Changing Class Structure of South Africa: the African Petit Bourgeoisie' (mimeo, 1976).

Index

If you would like to receive regular news on Harvester Press publications, please just send your name and address to our Publicity Department, The Harvester Press Ltd., 16 Ship Street, Brighton, Sussex. We will then be pleased to send you our new announcements and catalogues and special notices of publications in your fields of interest.